Chinese as a

Heritage Language:

Fostering Rooted

World Citizenry

Chinese as a Heritage Language: Fostering Rooted World Citizenry

edited by
AGNES WEIYUN HE
YUN XIAO

series editor
RICHARD SCHMIDT

NATIONAL FOREIGN LANGUAGE RESOURCE CENTER
University of Hawai'i at Mānoa

Manufactured in the United States of America

The contents of this monograph were developed under a grant from the U.S. Department of Education (CFDA 84.229, P229A020002). However, the contents do not necessarily represent the policy of the Department of Education, and one should not assume endorsement by the Federal Government.

ISBN 978–0–8248–3286–5

 The paper used in this publication meets the minimum requirements of the American National Standard for Information Sciences–Permanence of Paper for Printed Library Materials.   ANSI Z39.48–1984

book design by Deborah Masterson

distributed by
University of Hawai'i Press
Order Department
2840 Kolowalu Street
Honolulu, HI 96822–1888
www.uhpress.hawaii.edu

About the
National Foreign Language Resource Center

THE NATIONAL FOREIGN LANGUAGE RESOURCE CENTER, located in the College of Languages, Linguistics, & Literature at the University of Hawai'i at Mānoa, has conducted research, developed materials, and trained language professionals since 1990 under a series of grants from the U.S. Department of Education (Language Resource Centers Program). A national advisory board sets the general direction of the resource center. With the goal of improving foreign language instruction in the United States, the center publishes research reports and teaching materials that focus primarily on the languages of Asia and the Pacific. The center also sponsors summer intensive teacher training institutes and other professional development opportunities. For additional information about center programs, contact us.

Richard Schmidt, Director
National Foreign Language Resource Center
University of Hawai'i
1859 East-West Road #106
Honolulu, HI 96822–2322

email: nflrc@hawaii.edu
nflrc.hawaii.edu

Contents

The
Learning

Foreword

Scott McGinnis
Defense Language Institute, Washington, DC

The development of the field of Chinese as a Heritage Language (CHL) has been nothing short of astounding. Consider the following statistics. At the 1997 annual meeting of the Chinese Language Teachers Association (CLTA), not a single paper was devoted to any aspect of CHL education. Nine years later, at the 2006 annual meeting, two multi-paper panels and a half dozen individual papers were dedicated to some aspect—pedagogical, acquisitional, or textual material—of the teaching and learning of CHL. The situation with regard to publications is no less dramatic. Only a decade ago, the "critical mass" of experiential and empirical knowledge in print regarding Chinese as a heritage language consisted of a single monograph of a dozen articles focusing only on Chinese community schools, and a single article in the annual volume of the American Association of University Supervisors, Coordinators and Directors of Foreign Language Programs. What you have in your hands is a resounding confirmation that both quantitatively and qualitatively, CHL now constitutes a distinct and scholarly rigorous sector of the broader field of Chinese language pedagogy.

In assembling what is truly a cross-generational international representation of teachers and researchers, both Chinese-specific and not, Agnes Weiyun He and Yun Xiao are to be commended—both for the sheer challenge of doing so in so short a period of time, and for the tremendously high quality of these authors and their work. It is a credit to Agnes and Yun's own energy and expertise that so many terribly busy language professionals have worked so hard and so fast with them to help bring this volume together. For there is indeed a sense of urgency in making this sort of knowledge widely available to all interested parties—not just teachers of CHL, but language program administrators, parents of CHL children—and yes, the students themselves. In all instructional settings of the Chinese language education field—K–12, community school, and colleges and universities—many of us know far too well that not just regionally, but increasingly nationally and internationally, CHL learners now play (or at least should play) a very significant role in the ways in which we train teachers, design curricula, and assess students. With the establishment of the Advanced Placement (AP) Chinese Language & Culture Course and Exam this academic year, and with so many CHL learners taking that course and exam, the stakes have never been higher.

Equally important, the models developed in and lessons learned from the studies presented here may provide useful intellectual fodder for researchers and teachers of other heritage languages. After decades of Chinese language scholarship and pedagogy that has had to focus on derivative approaches based upon more commonly taught languages such as French, German, and Spanish, it will be at once refreshing and remarkable for a less commonly taught language to help lead the way. As someone who has been fortunate enough to be part of this emerging CHL field, I commend this volume to researchers, teachers and learners of all languages, more *and* less commonly taught.

Preliminaries

Chinese as a Heritage Language: An Introduction

Agnes Weiyun He
State University of New York at Stony Brook

This volume is motivated by matters of the heart. It arises from a deep concern with the socio-cultural, cognitive-linguistic, and educational-institutional trajectories along which Chinese as a Heritage Language (hereafter CHL) may be learned, acquired, maintained, and developed and the impact of such trajectories on individuals, families, schools, and communities. It is a continuation of age-old stories of language maintenance and language development written through the experiences of recent Chinese immigrants in English speaking countries. This volume is also informed by inquiries of the mind. It is guided by bodies of disciplinary knowledge, including but not limited to, developmental psychology, functional linguistics, linguistic and cultural anthropology, discourse analysis, orthography analysis, reading research, second language acquisition, and bilingualism. It aims to lay a foundation for ideas, theories, models, master scripts to be discussed, critiqued, debated, and developed for CHL; to stimulate research and dialog both within and beyond Chinese language education; and to provide teachers and administrators with research results that can be imported and interpreted for the advancement of CHL teaching and learning.

Although research bearing the label heritage language has had a relatively short history and consequently holds a relatively small body of literature, the notion of "heritage language" has existed for a long time under various names such as "home language," "mother tongue," "circumstantial bilingualism," or "community language." Despite social and psychological pressures to assimilate to mainstream American ways of life, minority language communities have been deeply committed to maintaining languages of the home countries by, for example, establishing weekend community-based language schools. The earliest research on heritage language could be dated to about half a century ago, when Fishman (1964) established language maintenance and language shift as a field of inquiry. The significance of Fishman's proposal was, however, not realized until very recently when heritage languages began to be recognized as valuable national and personal resources (Brecht & Ingold, 2002; Brinton & Kagan, 2008; Campell & Rosenthal, 2000; Creese & Martin, 2006; Kondo-Brown, 2002, 2006; Krashen, Tse, & McQuillan, 1998; Li & Duff, this volume; Lynch, 2003; Peyton, Ranard, & McGinnis, 2001; Roca & Colombi, 2003; Tao, 2006; Wiley & Valdes, 2000).

He, A. W. (2008). Chinese as a heritage language: An introduction. In A. W. He, & Y. Xiao (Eds.), *Chinese as a heritage language: Fostering rooted world citizenry* (pp. 1–12). Honolulu: University of Hawai'i, National Foreign Language Resource Center.

As a resource and recourse to manage, maintain, and create hybrid identities and synergetic cultures, CHL has been taught and learned as long as the Chinese American experience itself (Chang, 2003; Chao, 1997). As early as the nineteenth century, Cantonese classes were offered to children of early immigrants residing in Chinatowns in a number of larger U.S. cities such as San Francisco and New York. Today, according to a 2005 Asia Society report (Asia Society, 2005), approximately 150,000 students are taking Chinese (primarily Mandarin) in community-based language schools nationwide. A vastly increasing number of students of Chinese descent are taking Chinese within the U.S. educational system from kindergarten to college. Some private and public schools, such as Portland Public Schools in Oregon, are experimenting with K–8 Chinese/English bi-lingual education. Also, funded by the National Security Education Program, the University of Oregon has established a K–16 Chinese flagship program, which aims to collaborate with the K–12 Chinese immersion and bilingual programs in proximity to create superior-level Chinese proficiency professionals of business, sciences, law, and so forth out of our future college graduates. Needless to say, there is also the little documented, informal, everyday learning of Chinese at home.

In this chapter, I first provide a working definition of "Chinese as a heritage language," consider some of the fundamental questions associated with CHL development, and then explore CHL along the following three dimensions:

1. **The CHL learner.** This dimension includes the linguistic, socio-cultural, cognitive characteristics of the heritage learner, their motivations, and attitudes.

2. **The CHL learner language.** This dimension includes the development of reading, writing, grammar, vocabulary, accent, interactional strategies, and literacy.

3. **CHL learning.** This dimension includes the various resources that bear on the learning of CHL—institutional infrastructure and policies, Chinese language programs, classroom discourse, and pedagogical approaches.

These three dimensions correspond to the three main sections of the book—Parts II, III, and IV—which bear the same headings. Hence the overall purpose of this introduction chapter is twofold: to discuss the major issues associated with CHL and to foreshadow the contents of the sections and chapters in the book.

Chinese as a heritage language

Following Valdés (2001, p. 38), the heritage language (HL) learner in this book is defined broadly as a language student who is raised in a home where a non-English target language is spoken and who speaks or at least understands the language and is to some degree bilingual in HL and in English. More specifically, these learners see HL "with a particular family relevance" (Fishman, 2001, p. 169). Furthermore, the HL learner brings with himself/herself a set of ambiguities and complications which are typically absent in the second or foreign language leaner or mother tongue learner and which can be sources of both challenges and opportunities. As heritage culture itself is ever changing as the immigrants' life unfolds in the new country, the HL learner also exhibits varying expertise and allegiance (Rampton, 1995), varying degrees of investment (Norton, 2000; Pierce, 1995) along a bicultural, biliteracy continuum (Hornberger, 2004).

In addition to sharing general commonalities with other HLs, CHL has its own specificities. Learning CHL can have very different entailments to different learners, depending upon their backgrounds and objectives. "Chinese" is an umbrella term that subsumes numerous dialects which are grouped under Wu, Xiang, Gan, Min, Cantonese, Hakka, and Mandarin. Many of the dialects are mutually incomprehensible. "Mandarin" is a term referring to the majority dialect family of China. Its pronunciation and grammar are associated with the speech of Beijing and its surrounding countryside, regions which for centuries have enjoyed political and cultural significance. Also known as 普通话 *putonghua* in mainland China, 国语 *guoyu* in Taiwan, and 华语 *huayu* in Singapore, Mandarin serves as the standard dialect and is thus the most commonly taught variety in Chinese language classrooms. Yet, even Mandarin Chinese is not a monolithic entity—Mandarin used in mainland China, Taiwan, and Singapore, for example, varies in terms of lexis, phonetics, and discourse norms. In terms of writing, although there is one unifying writing system, there are two variant forms: the simplified script, which is officially used in mainland China and Singapore, and the traditional script, which is mainly used in other Chinese-speaking regions (Chen, 1999; Norman, 1988, Wiley, de Clerk, Li, Liu, Teng & Yang, this volume). One or both forms may be taught in CHL classrooms. Hence CHL learning, roughly speaking, can be any one of the following possibilities:

> Mandarin is the learner's home dialect or is comprehensible to home dialect.
> - classroom script same as home script (i.e., both use traditional and/or simplified scripts)
> - classroom script different from home script (i.e., traditional in class, simplified at home, or vice versa)
> - no home literacy in Chinese

> Mandarin is unintelligible to home dialect.
> - classroom script same as home script (i.e., both use traditional and/or simplified scripts)
> - classroom script different from home script (i.e., traditional in class, simplified at home, or vice versa)
> - no home literacy in Chinese

This scenario runs counter to our intuition that to learn one's heritage language is to (re)establish similarities with members of one's heritage culture and/or to (re)establish differences from members of mainstream American culture. As argued elsewhere (He, 2006), to learn CHL appears not merely to inherit one's heritage language and maintain one's heritage cultural identity but also to transform the heritage language (in terms of changes in dialect, script, accent, discourse norms, etc.) and re-create one's identity. This leads to several fundamental questions we need to consider in CHL research.

First, what does it mean to know Chinese as a heritage language? This volume considers language practice as a set of indexicals participating in a network of semiotic systems and treats language acquisition and socialization as an integrated process (Dai & Zhang; He; Kelleher; Li & Wu; all this volume). Linguistic meanings and meaning makings are therefore necessarily embedded in cultural systems of understanding. An account of linguistic behavior must then draw on accounts of culture. Accordingly, to know a heritage language means not merely to command the lexcio-grammatical forms in both speech and writing, but also to understand or embrace a set of norms, preferences, and expectations relating linguistic structures to context.

Second, how does Chinese heritage culture relate to Chinese heritage language? Heritage language learner's acquisition of linguistic forms requires a developmental process of delineating and organizing contextual dimensions in culturally sensible ways. Learners are socialized to associate grammatical forms with the social identities of interlocutors and the types of social events. Learner's use and understanding of grammatical forms are thus linked to complex yet orderly and recurrent dispositions, preferences, beliefs and bodies of knowledge that organize how information is linguistically packaged and how speech acts are performed within and across socially recognized situations (Dai & Zhang; Li & Wu; all this volume).

Unlike foreign or second language learning, HL learning is often motivated by neither strictly instrumental nor integrative goals; learner motivations are derived not merely from pragmatic or utilitarian concerns but also from the intrinsic cultural, affective, and aesthetic values of the language (Hendryx; Wiley et al.; Lu & Li; all this volume). Unlike mother tongue acquisition in a monolingual environment, HL is in constant competition with English (the mainstream language). Hence the question arises as to how HL learners position themselves vis-à-vis mainstream culture/language? This volume examines the construction of multiple yet compatible/ congruent identities, blended and blurred identities in multilingual, multicultural, immigrant contexts.

Thirdly, what constitutes evidence of CHL learning? In this volume, we investigate not only frequency in output as evidence of learning (Jia; Jia & Bayley; Koda, Lü, & Zhang; Ming & Tao; all this volume), but also culturally meaningful practices across settings and situations (Li & Wu; Xiao; all this volume). In other words, we consider heritage language acquisition as increasing competence in both the formal and functional potential of language. Over developmental time, CHL learners acquire repertoires of language forms associated with contextual dimensions.

The last but not the least question to consider is the route via which HL is acquired and socialized. Collectively, all contributors to this volume show that the transmission of HL is not merely horizontal (i.e., formal education in the classroom) but also, and perhaps more importantly, vertical (i.e., across generations at homes and in the communities). Language attitudes (Wiley et al., this volume), learner motivation (Lu & Li, this volume), learner history and disposition (Dai & Zhang, this volume), linguistic and ethno-linguistic backgrounds (Hendryx, this volume), morphological awareness (Koda et al., this volume), lexico-grammatical competence (Jia; Jia & Bayley; Ming & Tao; all this volume), classroom discourse (Li & Wu, this volume), institutional infrastructure and learner investment (Kelleher, this volume), and the kinds of literacy activities in the classroom and in households (Xiao, this volume) all play important roles in heritage language acquisition and heritage cultural development.

With these fundamental considerations in mind and in keeping with the major issues outlined in a comprehensive and complementary overview by Li and Duff in the same section of this volume (Part I), I will next provide an overview of the book, which is organized along three dimensions: the CHL learner, the CHL learner language, and CHL learning. For each of the thematic topics, I will begin with a discussion with reference to existing literature if available, followed by a summary of the relevant chapters in the section.

The CHL learner

There is a long tradition of conceptualizing language as an integral part of the development of the self, the mind, and society. Philosophers like Wittgenstein (1973) argue that language is not a metaphysical present, nor a coherent system, but a context-specific tool for achieving our purposes. Identity is structured in the everyday flow of language, and stabilized in the pragmatic narratives of our day-to-day, fluid social life. For heritage language learners, the language study is thus constitutive of identity, which is accomplished in the everyday social conversations.

Consistent with this line of thought, many researchers have focused on heritage language as intricately woven with learner identity formation or transformation. Tse (1997) attempts to explain the relationships among ethnic identity, attitudes and motivation, and HL development. Based on a study of American-born Asian-American adults, Tse concluded that language acquisition is facilitated when an individual has positive attitudes toward the language and feels positively about her ethnic group. In a further study, Tse (2000) examines published narratives of Americans of Asian descent to discover whether feelings of ethnic ambivalence/evasion extend to the heritage language, and if so, how they affect language beliefs and behaviors. The results suggest that for many, the HL is closely associated with the ethnic group so that attitudes toward the ethnic group and its language speakers also extend to the narrators' own language ability and their interest (or lack of interest) in maintaining and developing their HL.

A more general identity-based approach is presented by He (2006), which looks at how the HL learning takes place as the learner moves across time and space. Learner identity (trans)formation is considered by He as the primary motivation for HL learning and the learner is situated in his/her ongoing, evolving assessment and adjustment of him/herself vis-à-vis other persons in interactions across varying settings and during different developmental stages. It is posited that HL development is contingent upon the degree to which the learner is able to construct continuity and coherence of identity in multiple communicative and social worlds. Conceptualizing HL development as a socialization process with multiple agencies, multiple directions, and multiple goals, He further puts forth 10 hypotheses to describe and predict the key variables responsible for HL development.

Similarly, Li Wei (1994) posits that HL proficiency correlates positively with a well-developed sense of ethnic identity and network with the ethnic group, such that group members have a greater understanding and knowledge of their groups' cultural values, ethics, and manners. The same is echoed in Beckstead and Toribio (2003), Chinen and Tucker (2006), Cho (2000), Duisberg (2001), Kaufman (2005), Kim (2001), Kondo-Brown (2005), Lee (2002), and Pacini-Ketchabaw, Bernhard, and Freire, (2001), all of whom suggest that in addition to internal factors such as attitudes, motivation, and social identity, ethnic identity is also a key factor in HL development.

Other researchers have examined how HL use socializes cultural values and speech roles. Lo (2004) demonstrates how expressions of epistemic stance relate to moral evaluations by looking at cases in which teachers at a Korean heritage language school claim to read their students' minds with a high degree of certainty. Lo argues that Korean HL learners are socialized to portray their access to the thoughts and sensations of individuals whom they deem morally worthy as more distant and uncertain, and of individuals whom they deem morally suspect as self-evident. He (2000) details the discourse processes via which CHL learners are socialized to values of respect for authority and group conformity through modalized and moralized teachers' directives in weekend Chinese language schools, where teachers do not merely impart knowledge/facts but also function as moral guides to the students.

Part II of this volume is dedicated to CHL students and their motivations for learning CHL. The CHL learner traits are explored through the lens of the cultural, situational, and affective contingencies, the various learner profiles, language attitudes toward different dialects, learner motivation, and the symbiotic CHL development and learner identity formation.

Enya Dai and Lihua Zhang draw on post-structural theories to examine how CHL learners' linguistic, social and cultural dispositions are inculcated, structured, sustained, and transposed in both local and global contexts. They describe CHL learners' bilingual and bicultural environments, the multiple agents they interact with in various speech situations and speech events, and the CHL learners' motivation to learn CHL vis-à-vis specific interactional, pragmatic, situational, as well as socio-cultural contingencies.

To furnish empirical evidence that CHL learners are far from a monolithic group and to understand the tremendous range of linguistic knowledge and abilities when they begin studying Chinese at the college or university level, Jason Hendryx portrays various CHL learner profiles based on observations from several years of classroom interactions, interviews with CHL learners, and a survey of a recent Chinese heritage language class. Hendryx suggests that accessing that knowledge and building onto it in an efficient and meaningful manner will enable CHL instructors to reexamine their own understandings of their students' existing knowledge and develop appropriate methods to best engage that knowledge.

Taking into account the enormous linguistic/dialectal diversity within "Chinese" as well as diversity within "the Chinese speaker," Terrence Wiley, Gerda de Klerk, Mengying Li, Na Liu, Yun Teng, and Ping Yang report findings from a recent large-scale survey of Chinese immigrants and international students regarding their attitudes toward the maintenance of "Chinese" as a heritage (HL) and/or community language (CL) along with language attitudes toward language diversity among Chinese. Their survey results generally support the relevance and importance of current attempts in the United States to promote Mandarin as a heritage or community language. Among respondents in their survey Mandarin is used often, is highly regarded, and is seen as a resource to be preserved despite high levels of multilingualism and multi-dialectism.

Any account of the language learner will be inadequate without an explicit reference to learners' motivation. Xuehong Lu and Guofang Li present a comparative analysis of the effect of different motivational factors (integrative, instrumental, and situational) on heritage and non-heritage college students' Chinese learning in mixed classrooms. Their results indicate that both integrative and instrumental motivations are important to students' self-confidence in their language proficiency, but integrative motivation is more important to students' overall tests scores. Further, CHL students are more influenced by instrumental motivation than non-heritage students but less influenced by situational factors (such as teacher effect, effect of mixed-classes).

Part II of the book ends with an identity-based model for CHL development presented by Agnes He (a rewrite of He, 2006). Based on the characteristics of the CHL learner and drawing insights from language socialization, second language acquisition, and conversation analysis, He posits that CHL development takes place in a three-dimensional framework with intersecting planes of time, space, and identity. Temporally, CHL development recontextualizes the past, transforms the present and precontextualizes the future. As such, it fosters rooted world citizenry with appreciation of and competence in Chinese language and culture. Spatially, it transforms local, independent communities into global, interdependent communities. A learner's CHL development depends on the degree to which s/he is able to develop hybrid, situated identities and stances.

The CHL learner language

Research that focuses on the developmental language of the heritage language learner—pronunciation, grammar, lexicon, listening, reading, writing, narrative skills, register, and so forth—is just emerging. Almost in all cases, research is carried out in comparison with either monolingual speakers or foreign language learners.

Godson (2004) investigates whether the age at which English becomes dominant for heritage speakers of Western Armenian in the United States affects their vowel production in Western Armenian. Participating in the study were 10 Western-Armenian bilinguals who learned English before age 8, 10 bilinguals who did not learn English until adulthood, and one Western Armenian monolingual. Vowel production was measured using recordings from oral reading of a list of sentences. Results showed that English affects the Western Armenian vowel system but only for those vowels that are already close to English. This bifurcation of vowel behavior indicates that a single across-the-board principle that governs the influence of a dominant language on a minority language is too general. Other forces such as universal tendencies, normal diachronic change, and sociolinguistic pressures must be considered.

Using both proficiency tests and self-assessment measures, Kondo-Brown (2005) investigated (a) whether Japanese heritage language learners (JHL) would demonstrate language behaviors distinctively different from those of traditional Japanese as a foreign language learners (JFL), and (b) which domains of language use and skills would specifically identify such differentiation. Her findings suggest that there were striking similarities between the JFL learner group and JHL students with at least one Japanese-speaking grandparent but without a Japanese-speaking parent and JHL students of Japanese descent without either a Japanese-speaking parent or grandparent. In contrast, JHL students with at least one Japanese-speaking parent proved to be substantially different from other groups in (a) grammatical knowledge, (b) listening and reading skills, (c) self-assessed use/choice of Japanese, and (d) self-ratings of a number of can-do tasks that represented a wide range of abilities.

Several researchers from Roca and Colombi (2003) address the areas of register and genre in Spanish heritage language use. Their work indicated that Spanish HL learners need to make adjustments in their speech as they move from the informal oral settings to formal settings or to written communication such as oral presentations in academic settings and writing assignments. While the way they speak Spanish among friends and family is completely appropriate for that setting, what they lack is the ability to modify their speech for other settings, audiences, and purposes.

In addition to phonology, grammar, reading, writing, register, and genre, broader features of narration and interaction of HL learners have also been researched. Kaufman (2005) investigates narratives produced by speakers of Hebrew as a heritage language. Compared to monolingual norms, the HL narrative data showed considerable fragmentation in all aspects of the language. The HL learners are lacking in communicative fluency, grammatical accuracy, and lexical specificity as evidenced in their use of developmental forms characterized by present-tense temporal anchoring, frequent pauses, false starts, repairs, lexical substitution, simplification, redundancy, and circumlocution.

In the case of CHL, we are yet to see some detailed consideration, description, and documentation of the kinds of knowledge and abilities that CHL learners already have at different developmental stages. It is commonly said that CHL learners know a lot already. But we are yet to have a good grasp of what CHL students already command in the specific domains of phonology (do they have Mandarin pronunciation, or other dialectal variation and accommodation, etc.), morphology (do they already understand character formations, the notion of Chinese words, phrases, phrase structures, etc.), syntax (is grammar conscious to CHL learners or does it need to be made conscious to CHL learners), pragmatics (to what extent are CHL learners aware of different speech styles, genres, speech acts, speech events, and so forth and their social distributions and functions). With Chinese as foreign/second language, we could safely assume that everything needs to be taught; CHL learner proficiency levels are much harder to define.

Part III of this volume fills in this gap through an exposition of the role of morphological awareness in CHL learning, an examination of CHL literacy development, an evaluation of the learner's home literacy practices, a careful description of a CHL written corpus, an investigation of CHL learners' reading ability and grammaticality judgment ability, and an assessment of the CHL learners' use of perfective aspect marker.

Addressing both the universality of language learning and the specificity of Chinese character learning, Keiko Koda, Chan Lu, and Yanhui Zhang explore how the quality and quantity of print input shape morphological awareness and subsequent character knowledge development among school-age CHL learners. The ability to analyze a word's morphological structure helps CHL learners in inferring the meanings of unfamiliar characters and accessing stored character information. The study findings demonstrate that properties of input such as print exposure and experience have powerful impacts on the formation of morphological awareness, which, in turn, influences the learning and retention of morphologically complex characters.

Based on theories of cross-language transfer, reading universals, and meta-linguistic awareness, Keiko Koda, Yanhui Zhang and Chin-Lung Yang address CHL literacy development among school-age students. These children typically use Chinese at home, receive primary literacy instruction English at school, and pursue ancillary literacy in Chinese in a weekend school. As such, their primary literacy tends to build on underdeveloped oral proficiency, and secondary literacy reflects heavily restricted print input and experience. Despite these inadequacies, however, their study shows that many children are able to offset the limited linguistic support with additional meta-linguistic and cognitive resources and succeed in their primary literacy, and some even in heritage language literacy.

Continuing with the theme of literacy development, Yun Xiao reports a survey that involved 127 CHL learners in three American universities. Conceptualizing CHL learning as a process and practice that extends across situations and settings, her study reveals substantial correlation between CHL learners' home literacy environment and their HL literacy development, namely, the higher the instructional level, the richer the CHL home literacy environment. Compared with the mainstream dominant language, however, the CHL home literacy environment is bleak. The findings of the study suggest that interventions in HL learners' homes, communities, and mainstream schools are needed to prevent CHL attrition.

Tao Ming and Hongyin Tao report on the construction of a CHL corpus and discuss its significance for CHL learning and teaching. Based on a corpus that comprises about 1,000 samples of written essays and narratives, with a total of about 200,000 characters, Ming and Tao devised a coding system with ten major categories and thirty-six subcategories for HL errors. Grounded in corpus linguistics, their study provides a well-designed analysis of CHL written discourse, which bodes the potentials of an accurate, the first-of-its-kind empirical description of CHL learner language, casting in doubt existing descriptions about HL learner language that are based on intuition and speculation.

To gain insight into the factors accounting for CHL maintenance or attrition, Gisela Jia reports findings from a study on first generation Chinese immigrants in New York City, in terms of their speaking, reading, and writing skills for each 2-year interval of their residence in the US. A grammaticality judgment task in Mandarin is also used to measure participants' sensitivity to Mandarin grammar. The findings show that, in certain contexts, at the same time the exposure to English and the English skills grew steadily over the years, heritage language skills continuously declined. Her study also uncovered several major predictors of participants' current CHL proficiency, including age of immigration, social economic status, and self-reported Chinese cultural identity.

In the area of syntactic development, Li Jia, and Robert Bayley examine the acquisition and reacquisition of the perfective aspect marker *-le* by U.S.- and China-born learners. Variable rule analysis of over 500 tokens of the learners' grammatical or ungrammatical use of *-le* indicates that learners are more likely to use *-le* in sentence final than in post-verbal position, that learners are more likely to use *-le* in obligatory than in optional contexts, that China-born HL learners favor more grammatical use than U.S.-born HL learners, and that learners who regularly interact in Mandarin at home are more likely to use *-le* appropriately than those who frequently or exclusively interact in English at home. Their study shows the contributing factors in HL learning, such as the learner arrival age, birthplace, frequency of HL use at home, and linguistic constraints of the morpho-syntactic marker *-le*.

CHL learning

As mentioned previously, heritage language education in general has been understudied so far, and Chinese as heritage language, with its heterogeneity and complexity in its speakers, dialects, and their associated social, cultural, historical ramifications, has received even less scholarly attention. Many Chinese language programs are still primarily designed for foreign language learners. As a result, it has been challenging for CHL students to find legitimate and suitable placement in these programs. Many Chinese language classes are conducted either in the same manner as CFL classes or as Chinese a native language classes where it is assumed that the students need little explicit instruction in terms of grammar and pronunciation. The tacit but important aspect of language ideology enacted through interaction between teachers and CHL students is yet to be explored. In Part IV of this volume, we consider some crucial contextual variables for CHL learning including classroom discourse and institutional infrastructures and policies.

Li Wei and Chao-Jung Wu examine the conflicts between the ideologies and practices of code-switching by the teachers in the CHL schools context in the UK. The authors suggest that a truly bilingual classroom should encourage rather than discourage code-switching and that code-switching can be used effectively as a pedagogical tool in bilingual classrooms. At the same time, they caution that the teachers' use of code-switching can have the effect of giving English more pedagogical as well as social importance, and indirectly helping to maintaining the English dominance and enhancing English as a language of authority and knowledge.

Ann Kelleher presents findings from a case study concerning the pedagogic policies around the teaching of university-level Mandarin. She shows that CHL learners resist the simple categorization that is imposed by institutional structures and enacted through the placement process. Because current institutional policies neither meet the students' language needs nor are in accord with their evolving sense of ethnic identity, some CHL students re-place and re-position themselves within the program, seeking to resolve tensions they face as they are caught at the intersection of institutional values, program structure and their own linguistic and cultural resources.

To conclude this volume, Yun Xiao summarizes the characteristics of the CHL learner language, examines its associated contextual and individual factors, and sketches the CHL developmental path. In her account, CHL-specific features presented in this volume and elsewhere such as high variability, increasing attrition, frequent use of code-switching, insufficient HL input, multi-level social contact, high pressure for social acceptance, immigrant family background, and learner identities and motivations are shown to be intertwined and to collectively contribute to the trajectory of CHL investment and maintenance.

Contributions and significance

The studies collected in this volume represent a rich, if not yet focused or systematic, body of work on CHL learners as a heterogeneous population that encompasses learners from a wide range of backgrounds at various levels of language proficiency. Collectively, we present a multi-faceted, multi-layered, picture of the CHL learner and build comparisons and contrasts between CHL development in different sites including home, school, and community. We show that CHL competencies, choices, and ideologies change over the learner's lifespan, reflecting changing motivations, social networks, institutional opportunities, instructional design and other variables. The CHL learner is engaged in multiple speech events in multiple settings for multiple purposes. The learning of CHL takes place through the learner's interactions with multiple participants including language instructors, parents, grandparents, siblings, and peers, each of whom positions the learner in unique speech and social roles and each of whose reactions and responses to the learner helps to shape the path of his/her language development.

This volume works toward building a theoretically warranted and empirically sound foundation for CHL as a field of inquiry. As we draw insights from various existing disciplines, CHL learning also compels us to reconsider dichotomous concepts such as native language versus target language, native speech community versus target speech community, instrumental versus integrative motivations, basic interpersonal communication skills vs. cognitive academic language proficiency. It further challenges us to re-evaluate our unit of analysis from single snapshots of one-on-one, unidirectional processes of learning to trajectories of growth and change over space and time for the CHL learner as well as other participants.

As the Chinese saying goes, 千里之行始于足下, a 1,000-mile journey begins with a first step. We hereby take our first firm step and with this volume we invite our colleagues to join our journey.

References

Asia Society. (2005). *Expanding Chinese language capacity in the United States.* Retrieved November 6, 2007, from http://www.internationaled.org/publications/ChineseLanguage5.pdf

Beckstead, K., & Toribio, A. (2003). Minority Perspectives on Language: Mexican and Mexican-American adolescents' attitudes toward Spanish and English. In A. Roca & C. Colombi (Eds.), *Mi lengua: Spanish as a heritage language in the United States* (pp. 154–170). Washington, DC: Georgetown University Press.

Brecht, R. D., & Ingold, C. W. (2002). Tapping a national resource: Heritage language in the United States. *ERIC Digests* No. ED 464 515. Retrieved July 4, 2007, from www.ericdigests.org/2003–1/tapping.htm

Brinton, D., & Kagan, O. (Eds.). (2008). *Heritage language acquisition: A new field emerging.* New York: Routlege/Taylor & Francis.

Campbell, R. N., & Rosenthal, J. W. (2000). Heritage languages. In J. W. Rosenthal (Ed.), *Handbook of undergraduate second language education* (pp. 165–184). Mahwah, NJ: Lawrence Erlbaum Associates.

Chang, I. (2003). *The Chinese in America.* Penguin Books.

Chao, T. H. (1997). Chinese heritage community language schools in the United States. *ERIC Clearinghouse on Languages and Linguistics Digest, 1997.* Retrieved October 2, 2005, from http://www.cal.org/resources/digest/chao0001.html

Chen, P. (1999). *Modern Chinese: History and sociolinguistics.* New York: Cambridge University Press.

Chinen, K., & Tucker, G. R. (2005). Heritage language development: Understanding the role of ethnic identity and Saturday school participation. *Heritage Language Journal, 3*(1). Retrieved July 4, 2007, from www.heritagelanguages.org

Cho, G. (2000). The role of heritage language in social interactions and relationships: Reflections from a language minority group. *Bilingual Research Journal, 24*(4), 369–384.

Creese, A., & Martin, P. (Eds.). (2006). Interaction in complementary school contexts. Special Issue, *Language and Education, 20*(1).

Duisberg, S. (2001). *High school heritage learners of Spanish: An investigation of language attitudes.* Unpublished doctoral dissertation, University of Arizona.

Fishman, J. A. (1964). Language maintenance and language shift as a field of inquiry. *Linguistics, 9,* 32–70.

Fishman, J. A. (2001). Heritage languages in America: Preserving a national resource. In J. Kreeft Peyton, D. A. Ranard, & S. McGinnis (Eds.), *Heritage Languages in America. Preserving a National Resource* (pp. 81–89). McHenry, IL: CAL.

Godson, L. (2004). Vowel production in the speech of Western Armenian heritage speakers. *Heritage Language Journal, 2*(1), Retrieved on November 7, 2007, from http://www.heritagelanguages.org/

He, A. W. (2000). Grammatical and sequential organization of teachers' directives. *Linguistics and Education, 11*(2), 119–140.

He, A. W. (2006). Toward an identity-based model for the development of Chinese as a heritage language. *The Heritage Language Journal, Special Issue: Chinese Heritage Language Teaching.* Retrieved July 4, 2007, from http://www.heritagelanguages.org/

Hornberger, N. (2004). The continua of biliteracy and the bilingual educator: Educational linguistics in practice. *International Journal of Bilingual Education and Bilingualism, 7*(2&3), 155–171.

Kaufman, D. (2005). Acquisition, attrition, and revitalization of Hebrew in immigrant children. In D. Ravid & H. Bat-Zeev Shyldkrot (Eds.), *Perspectives on language and language development* (pp. 407–418). Dordrecht, The Netherlands: Kluwer Academic Publishers.

Kim, H.-S. H. (2001). Issues of heritage learners in Korean language classes. In J. Ree (Ed.), *Korean language in America 8: Papers from the Eighth Annual Conference and Professional Development Workshop* (pp. 37–50). Honolulu, HI: American Association of Teachers of Korean.

Kondo-Brown, K. (2002). Heritage language development. In B. J. Guzzetti, (Ed.), *Literacy in America: An encyclopedia of history, theory, and practice* (pp. 219–223). Santa Barbara, CA: ABC-CLIO.

Kondo-Brown, K. (2005). Differences in language skills: Heritage language learner subgroups and foreign language learners? *The Modern Language Journal, 89,* 563–581.

Kondo-Brown, K. (Ed.) (2006). *Heritage language development: Focus on East Asian immigrants.* Philadelphia, PA: John Benjamins Publishing.

Krashen, S. D., Tse, L., & McQuillan, J. (Eds.). (1998). *Heritage language development.* Culver City, CA: Language Education Associates.

Lee, J. S. (2002). The Korean language in America: The role of cultural identity in heritage language learning. *Language, Culture and Curriculum, 15*(2), 117–133.

Li, W. (1994). *Three generations, two languages, one family.* Clevedon, England: Multilingual Matters.

Lo, A. (2004). Evidentiality and morality in a Korean heritage language school. *Pragmatics, 14*(2/3), 235–256.

Lynch, A. (2003). The relationship between second and heritage language acquisition: Notes on research and theory building. *Heritage Language Journal, (1)*. Retrieved October 2, 2005, from www.heritagelanguages.org/article.asp?parentid=3615

Norman, J. (1988). *Chinese.* Cambridge, England: Cambridge University Press.

Norton, B. (2000). *Identity and language learning: Gender, ethnicity, and educational change.* Essex, England: Longman.

Pacini-Ketchabaw, V., Bernhard, J. K., & Freire, M. (2001). Struggling to preserve home language: The experiences of Latino students and families in the Canadian school system. *Bilingual Research Journal, 25*(1/2), retrieved November 6, 2007 from http://brj.asu.edu/v2512/articles/art7.html

Peirce, B. N. (1995). Social identity, investment, and language learning. *TESOL Quarterly, 29*(1), 9–30.

Peyton, J. K., Ranard, D. A., & McGinnis, S. (Eds.). (2001). *Heritage languages in America: Preserving a national resource.* McHenry, IL: The Center for Applied Linguistics and Delta Systems.

Rampton, B. (1995). *Crossing language and ethnicity among adolescents.* New York, NY: Longman.

Roca, A., & Colombi, M. C. (Eds.). (2003). *Mi lengua: Spanish as a heritage language in the United States.* Washington, DC: Georgetown University Press.

Tao, H. (Ed.). (2006). Special Issue, *The Heritage Language Journal.* Retrieved July 4, 2007, from http://www.heritagelanguages.org/

Tse, L. (1997). *Ethnic identity development and the role of the heritage language.* Unpublished doctoral dissertation from the University of Southern California.

Tse, L. (2000). The effects of ethnic identity formation on bilingual maintenance and development: An analysis of Asian American narratives. *International Journal of Bilingual Education and Bilingualism, 3*(3), 185–200.

Valdés, G. (2001). Heritage language students: Profiles and possibilities. In J. K. Peyton, D. A. Ranard, & S. McGinnis (Eds.), *Heritage languages in America. Preserving a national resource* (pp. 37–80). McHenry, IL: Center for Applied Linguistics.

Wiley, T., & Valdés, G. (Eds.). (2000). Heritage language instruction in the US [Special Issue] *Bilingual Research Journal, 24*(4).

Wittgenstein, L. (1973). *Philosophical investigations.* (G. E. M. Anscombe, Trans.). Englewood Cliffs, NJ: Prentice Hall.

2

Issues in Chinese Heritage Language Education and Research at the Postsecondary Level

Duanduan Li
Patricia A. Duff
The University of British Columbia

NFLRC
monographs

This chapter provides an overview of some of the most important current issues and challenges for research and educational practice in the teaching, learning, and assessment of Chinese as a heritage language (CHL) at the postsecondary level. We review existing research and identify areas in which further theoretical and practical attention is needed with regard to political, social-psychological, linguistic, and curricular dimensions of CHL. The shift in recent research to ecologically valid qualitative investigations of the lived experiences of CHL and other language learners, in terms of their shifting (or multiple, hybrid) identities, trajectories, and literacies, is highlighted. Salient practical concerns are also discussed, such as identifying heritage and non-heritage students' diverse needs and planning curriculum accordingly; accommodating different student populations in single-track versus dual-track programs; developing effective and engaging instructional resources and assessment procedures and instruments; and providing advocacy for the legitimacy of CHL learners while at the same time attending to non-CHL students' needs equally well. Finally, we argue that understanding CHL students' heterogeneity and their potential will help us to better serve linguistically diverse learners in language courses and maximize the social, academic, economic, and cultural benefits of HL maintenance and development in Canada, the United States, and other diaspora contexts.[1]

The cultural and linguistic diversity of modern society and of our educational institutions is rapidly increasing. Faced with the pressures and promises of globalization and global citizenship, educational communities and society at large are becoming more aware of, and responsive to, the diverse linguistic backgrounds, needs, aspirations, and potential of their student population, whether they are international, immigrant, domestic-born, or Aboriginal (Native) students. Heritage language (HL) teaching, previously the domain of non-credit community weekend schools or bilingual classes in elementary schools primarily, is now beginning to gain attention in such credit programs as "Spanish for Spanish," "Russian for

[1]   The authors acknowledge, with thanks, funding from the Social Sciences and Humanities Research Council of Canada, which has supported the preparation of this chapter.

Li, D., & Duff, P. (2008). Issues in Chinese heritage language education and research at the postsecondary level. In A. W. He, & Y. Xiao (Eds.), *Chinese as a heritage language: Fostering rooted world citizenry* (pp. 13–33). Honolulu: University of Hawai'i, National Foreign Language Resource Center.

Russians," and "Chinese for Chinese" in university foreign language (FL) departments, a clear manifestation of institutional responses to these demographic changes (Duff, 2002, 2005, 2008b; Kagan, Akishina, & Robin, 2003; McGinnis, 1996; Valdés, 1997). However, accommodating students with a very different profile from more traditional, essentially monocultural, English-L1 backgrounds raises a number of practical, conceptual or theoretical, and academic issues and thus opportunities for careful reflection and further research. This chapter identifies critical issues and challenges in Chinese as a HL and suggests a set of research priorities and questions—political, sociological, psychological, linguistic, and curricular—for further exploration.[2]

Making the case for HL education: Demographic, social-psychological, and academic factors

Canadian 2001 census data, the most recent available, lists Chinese (several dialects combined) as Canada's third most common mother tongue, the most widely spoken after the official languages of English and French (Statistics Canada, 2004). Almost 872,400 people reported Chinese as their mother tongue, up 136,400 or 18.5% from 1996 (2004). In the US, Chinese (including both Mandarin and Cantonese) is, for the first time, the second most common FL spoken by those living on U.S. soil, following Spanish. Today an estimated 2 million Americans regularly speak Chinese at home (U.S. Census Bureau, 2000).[3]

Drawing from research and practice in linguistics, psychology, and language education, HL education research has emerged as both a valid and distinct field within applied linguistics (Brecht & Ingold, 1998; Brinton, Kagan, & Bauckus, 2008; Campbell & Peyton, 1998; Hinton, 1999; Kono & McGinnis, 2001). Considerable recent research has focused on issues associated with the teaching and learning of HL learners, especially with Hispanic learners of Spanish, in school and university language courses (e.g., Brinton, Kagan, & Bauckus, 2008; Valdés, 2005; Hornberger, 2005; Wiley & Valdés, 2000), while other languages (e.g., Russian, Chinese, Japanese, Korean) are just catching up.

Existing research argues convincingly that developing HL speakers' linguistic and cultural knowledge to advanced levels is valuable not only for the students themselves and their families and communities, but also for individuals' sense of personal identity and connectedness to their past and to their extended families, and for society more broadly (Fishman, 1991; Hornberger, 2003a, 2005). A strong foundation in one's HL is associated with enhanced language and literacy achievement in English or the dominant societal language, and in other languages such as French in French immersion contexts with minority-language students (e.g., from Italian backgrounds in which Italian has been actively maintained; Swain & Lapkin, 1991). Research on HL learners has shown that minority-language students who maintain their own culture, literacy, and ethnic identity, in addition to enjoying pride in their heritage and close relations within their family and community social networks, will benefit from greater social mobility and personal empowerment, and will more likely succeed in mainstream school and society (e.g., Cho & Krashen, 1998; Cummins, 1993, 2004; Krashen, Tse, & McQuillen, 1998; Kondo-Brown, 2002, 2003; Write & Taylor, 1995). Their countries also benefit from nurturing highly competent bilingual and multilingual

---

[2]   Some of the observations made in this chapter are based on the first author's 11 years of Chinese teaching and administration experience at university programs in the US and Canada, each with a substantial population of HL students.

[3]   To call Chinese and Spanish "foreign" languages when they play such an integral role in the lives of so many Canadians and Americans is, of course, a persistent misnomer, especially in the United States.

citizens who can pursue careers requiring these skills; for example, in national defence, international business, diplomacy, social work, medicine, and academia, both at home and abroad. Preserving or cultivating the language/literacy skills and cultural knowledge or "capital" of HL learners while they become fully proficient in English through additive bilingualism or multilingualism is therefore an important educational priority in an increasingly global marketplace and diversified society (Brecht & Ingold, 1998; Cummins, 2004; Krashen, 1998; Tavares, 2000).

Chinese as a HL at the postsecondary level: Contexts, constraints, and challenges

At many universities and colleges, HL learners are becoming an increasingly important constituency in the Chinese language classrooms (Lu & Li, this volume; McGinnis, 2005). Whereas there has been a relatively long history of debate and research about the advantages of K–12 bilingual, immersion, and HL education for children in Canada and the United States, almost no attention has been paid to issues in the postsecondary education sector where the number of HL learners in some fields, such as Chinese, is expanding exponentially in some cases. Considering the size, vitality, and growth of this learner population (He, this volume; Wang, 2005), research on teaching Chinese as a HL (CHL) in higher education has not yet received due attention. The linguistic histories, profiles, and needs of CHL students, their diverse language learning and socialization processes and outcomes, and the benefits and challenges of fully developing their HL proficiency must be examined more closely using a variety of methods (as exemplified in this volume), across the quantitative and qualitative spectrum (He, 2006; Li, 2005).

Furthermore, existing research on other heritage languages (K–16) does not address issues particular to Chinese. Chinese teaching and learning are beset with some intriguing, complicating factors, apart from the sheer numbers of students. Unlike many other languages associated historically with a somewhat more homogeneous population, geographical area, or nation-state, and with a shared standard variety (e.g., Korean or Japanese; Sohn, 2004), Chinese itself is far from monolithic. It is spoken and written differently in Mainland China, Taiwan, Singapore and elsewhere, and these differences have historical, political, cultural, and social undertones and ramifications for both HL and non-HL education.

Yet, despite the desire among many Chinese students to reconnect with their HL language(s) in colleges and universities in North America and around the world, Chinese courses are still designed primarily for learners in FL courses—with no significant prior familiarity with, or connection to, the language and culture. For example, only 7 out of 19 Canadian universities or colleges included in a national postsecondary Chinese program database indicate that they offer Chinese HL courses on an annual basis, and then typically just one or two, mostly Mandarin courses designed for Cantonese speakers (Canadian Teaching Chinese as a Second Language [TCSL] National Database, 2007). HL students are treated either the same as non-HL students and then placed in classes they are overqualified for (and consequently often bored with), or simply dismissed as "native speakers" who do not need any instruction, or are discussed derisively by administrators, teachers, and classmates as people seeking inflated grades, "an easy A."

Therefore, issues commonly grappled with by administrators and instructors include defining or categorizing HL learners, understanding their identities and motivations for learning, designing curriculum to meet their special needs as compared with non-HL students (who have their own pressing needs), developing effective and appropriate placement or assessment instruments and procedures, developing or adapting suitable and challenging teaching materials, and matching instructional approaches with different learner types. In what follows, we explore these issues in turn.

Who is a legitimate HL learner? The constitution of legitimacy in HL programs

Deciding who can be included under the "HL learner" label raises a number of issues related to the reification of identity and ethnicity, inclusion and exclusion, access and denial. As Leung, Harris, and Rampton (1997) write, citing cultural theorist Hall (1988),

> Members of minority groups are not simple inheritors of fixed identities, ethnicities, cultures, and languages but are instead engaged in a continual collective and individual process of making, remaking, and negotiating these elements, thereby constantly constructing dynamic new ethnicities. (p. 547)

On the basis of their research in multilingual urban Britain and its implications for heritage and dominant-language learning (Standard English in their case), Leung et al. suggest that we consider the dimensions of *language expertise* (actual linguistic or communicative competence in students' repertoire of languages, including the HL[s]), *language affiliation* (degree of personal or emotional commitment or connection to the home, community, or other languages and cultures), and *language inheritance* (the connection to one's ostensibly "inherited" language—the language of the home). These overlapping but often contested aspects of experience, identification, and investment in a (heritage) language are pertinent to our attempts to classify HL learners. Which of the following could be classified as a "legitimate" CHL learner? A 3rd-generation Chinese-Canadian student who has never been exposed to the HL, but has a particular (ethnic) inheritance? A Caucasian, non-ethnically Chinese, native-English-speaking student who received elementary schooling in Taiwan when her parents were doing business overseas, and therefore has some (possibly limited) degree of expertise in and affiliation with that language but not through inheritance? A Cantonese speaker who can write college essays in Chinese without being able to understand basic Mandarin? That is, someone who has expertise in L1 Cantonese but not Mandarin, affiliates with the former and not the latter, and has "inherited" the former but not the latter. Or a fluent Mandarin-speaking student (ethnically Chinese or not) who can't read even the simplest Chinese characters—someone who may or may not have any kind of "inheritance" of the language, has expertise in one modality but not in another, and may be strongly affiliated with Mandarin but more invested or experienced in orality than literacy? What does it mean to try to create a shared language learning experience for these very diverse learners whose only commonality may have been their own unique, albeit partial, prior experience with a variety or modality of Chinese?

According to Wiley (2001),

> The labels and definitions that we apply to heritage language learners are important, because they help to shape the status of the learners and the languages they are learning. Deciding on what types of learners should be included under the heritage language label raises a number of issues related to identity and inclusion and exclusion. (p. 35)

In other words, our labels and classroom discourse practices may position learners in ways that they might not otherwise position themselves.

Generally speaking, in the HL literature there are two perspectives commonly found in definitions of HL learners: (a) a perspective reflecting an ethnic, historical, or sociopolitical investment in the language; and (b) a perspective based on actual linguistic competence as well as familial affiliation. The former might define a HL learner as follows: A heritage student is an individual who has a personal interest or involvement in *an ancestral language* (Fishman, 2001; Wiley, 2001). This first definition represents an ethnic orientation, harking back to one's roots but is also sociopolitical in the sense that students may feel a certain entitlement to reclaim aspects of that history in the present. The latter definition, on the other hand, based more closely on linguistic competence, defines the learner in terms of knowledge: "A heritage student is a student who is raised in a home where a non-English language is spoken, who speaks or merely understands the HL, and who is to some degree bilingual in English and the HL" (Valdés, 2001, p. 38).

Of course, both of these perspectives privilege an ethnic or linguistic inheritance (i.e., heritage), which the Caucasian student referred to earlier—whose expertise and affiliation may be comparable to some CHL learners'—is categorically denied or excluded from. Thus, for the purpose of developing HL learning programs, proficiency-based definitions of HL learner are important. Carreira (2004) notes that because our labels are so foundational to our program characteristics we need to consider them carefully:

> In the realm of education, the labels and definitions that teachers and administrators apply to HL learners undergird decisions about course and program design, materials selection, placement and assessment of students, and teacher training. They are also crucial to the task of tracking national and regional trends in language education. (p. 2)

For this reason, many college or university Chinese language programs with HL tracks place 3rd- or 4th-generation Chinese descendants who have had little or no HL exposure in regular FL classes, but include in HL tracks non-Chinese students who have had considerable exposure of the target language by living, studying, or working in Chinese-speaking communities. Some programs have even replaced the term *HL students* with *students with [some Chinese-language] background*, precisely because many students who have had previous exposure to the target language are not necessarily "heritage" language speakers based on ethnicity.

However, even within a proficiency-defined "HL" group, learners generally have a very uneven grasp of the HL, falling along a continuum of having very little HL knowledge to being highly proficient. Some may have impressive receptive or conversational skills and tacit cultural knowledge, but their literacy, grammar, and vocabulary typically remain underdeveloped. In addition, they may speak a non-standard dialect and have a limited range of sociolinguistic and pragmatic competence as well, that is, the ability to speak or write to people with appropriate levels of formality and politeness, across a range of genres and for different audiences, and for a wide range of purposes (Sohn, 2004). Furthermore, immigrant students who have received elementary or even secondary education in their native (Chinese-speaking) country are joining the increasing population of HL learners.

To cope with this current situation, newer definitions have emerged, such as the following, which appeared on the Slavic Language Program website at UCLA in 2004: "By 'heritage speaker' we mean those who grew up with Russian in this country [USA] without a native Russian's *full* educational or cultural background."[4] The question then is: At what level is native language education regarded as "full"—elementary, junior high or senior high school? Program directors and instructors commonly question the legitimacy of these newly arrived heritage students, dismissing them as "native speakers" who do not need any instruction.

---

4   In 2007, the website lists only "Russian for Russians" or "Russian for Native Speakers," with no reference to "heritage speakers" (http://www.humnet.ucla.edu/russian/RussianForRussians.htm).

To investigate the legitimacy of Russian heritage students with a native-country educational background, Kagan and Dillon (2004) compared the Russian language use of native speakers in Russia with Russian HL students at the University of California, Los Angeles. They divided the HL students into 3 groups: (a) students who graduated from high school in Russia; (b) students who attended junior high schools in Russia; and (c) students who were born in the United States to Russian-speaking families, or those who had elementary school education in Russia prior to immigrating. The results showed, not surprisingly, that students from Group 1 were the closest in grammatical accuracy and breadth of vocabulary to educated native speakers or Russian, while both Groups 2 and 3 displayed significant gaps in using the language. The study also supported "the premise that heritage speakers [the latter groups] cannot be considered native speakers and thus are legitimate students in a Russian language program" (Kagan & Dillon, 2004, p. 3). Therefore, at UCLA, the cut-off for a HL speaker of Russian (in 2004) was 8th grade of native-country education.

To some extent, the academic or educational issues connected with definitions of eligible students may become conflated with economic and sociopolitical ones: the larger the (legitimate) student population in a department, the more funding it receives for language instructors and other personnel, and the greater overall viability of that program and range of offerings. Thus, universities must indicate clearly which students can be considered legitimate for a variety of programmatic reasons.

For CHL learners, a comparable situation exists. The "traditional" HL learner with only receptive oral language skills is now being joined by recent immigrants from China, Taiwan, and Hong Kong, many of whom have received elementary or even high school education in their native language (Cantonese or Mandarin). They nevertheless may seek opportunities at university to complete their primary (or "heritage") language education. For example, Li (2005) conducted a survey of 975 Chinese HL students at a Canadian university (with 695 questionnaires returned and analyzed), regarding their ethno-linguistic backgrounds, their attitudes to and motivations for studying Chinese, and their perceptions of the status of different Chinese dialects and writing systems. Figure 1 reveals that the majority of new, foreign-born CHL learners had received considerable native language education before immigration: 48% had done elementary school in Chinese; 37% had done both junior high and elementary school in Chinese; and 8% had done some senior high school coursework in their native language. Note that only 7% fit the traditional profile of a HL student who might have had some preschool exposure to Chinese.

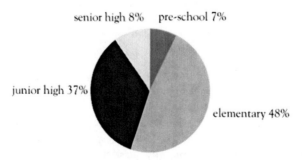

Figure 1. Native language education of CHL students born outside of Canada (Li, 2005)

Despite such trends in HL programs to enroll students with many years of prior formal schooling in the HL, no research has been conducted to determine which level of Chinese native language education should constitute a "full educational and cultural background" (Kagan & Dillon, 2004), and which students should continue to receive HL education to ensure complete bilingualism and biliteracy.

Hornberger and Wang (2008) emphasize that there is no single profile of HL students, as they cover a very heterogeneous population. A narrow definition such as "those whose home language is the HL" might exclude some language groups and individuals (see Weger-Guntharp, 2006). Thus, regardless of institutional classifications and tracking, researchers and teachers should be made aware of the diversity and multifaceted identities brought into the classroom setting by language learners and should not make unwarranted assumptions about affiliation or expertise on the basis of ethnolinguistic "inheritance" alone. Hornberger and Wang offer an inclusive "ecological perspective" which acknowledges both ethnic/sociopolitical and linguistic definitions and accepts anyone who self-identifies as a HL learner of a particular language, even through multiracial marriages or multinational adoptive families.

The validation of HL learners' affiliation, motivation, and linguistic rights

As the preceding section has shown, deciding whether to offer HL courses in academic programs and determining who can enrol in these courses is a struggle for legitimacy for both programs and HL students in the educational system. Skepticism about students' genuine motivation—whether they are seeking "easy credit" or an "easy A" versus a real opportunity to develop in Chinese may disallow some university HL students from taking HL courses. However, very little empirical research has investigated what exactly motivates students to seek enrolment in HL courses.

Since the 1970s, initially within Canadian bilingual contexts, social-psychological research on the role of motivation in language learning has attempted to determine the motives students have for studying particular topics, such as additional languages—whether to obtain employment or some other practical benefit (an instrumental orientation), or to get to know people from other cultures better and to become a potentially valued member of the target-language group (an integrative orientation)—and their eventual language learning outcomes (e.g., Gardner, 1985). Some research has also tried to determine the strength of correlations between one or the other type of motivation and proficiency. But, regardless of the type of motivation, it is well understood that

> greater personal motivation—be it "instrumental" or "integrative"—produces a greater likelihood of attaining high levels of L2 proficiency. The same is likely true in HLA [acquisition], though the question of motivation in HL classrooms has gone unexplored to date. (Lynch, 2003, p. 3)

As Dörnyei and Skehan (2003) report, learners' attitudes and motivation remain the strongest and most consistent predictors of second language success. Motivation, they explain, accounts for "*why* people decide to do something, *how long* they are willing to sustain the activity, and *how hard* they are going to pursue it" (p. 614). Whereas some earlier conceptions of motivation portrayed it as a rather static trait—rather than a fluctuating and fluid one—and mainly examined conscious, self-reported motives as opposed to subconscious desires, current views are much more dynamic, multifaceted and interdisciplinary. In poststructural and phenomenological work, motivation (or investment as it has been reconceptualized by Norton, 2000) is seen to be a co-construction within discursive, social and political (power) structures that cannot easily be compartmentalized into one "type" or another originating uniquely from or residing within the individual learner. Rather, motivation is also an artifact of social and institutional interactions and experiences. Thinking, for example, of *why, how long,* and *how hard* people try to learn an HL according to Dörnyei and Skehan's formulation, over a HL learner's lifetime these will change many times over—with different reasons or goals for studying at different ages, different lengths of time and intensity of study, and varying degrees of effort expended. From one context to the next (practicing with a relative, with a peer, or with a teacher), on more engaging versus less engaging tasks, and performing in low-stakes versus high-stakes situations, motivation is apt to vary considerably. Yet, few longitudinal studies have been able to capture, in qualitative ways, the waxing and waning of HL learners' psychological or affective orientations and stances in the way that immigrant English as a second-language learners and European language learners have been studied by themselves and others (e.g., Pavlenko & Lantolf, 2000).

A few cross-sectional studies on HL learner motivation have yielded mixed results about students' reasons for affiliating with the HL. Most of the research reported that HL students show strong integrative orientation (e.g., for Korean HL, Han, 2003; Kim, 1992; for Russian HL, Andrews, 2001; Geisherik, 2004; Kagan & Dillon 2001; and for Chinese HL, Wen, 1997), whereas some found HL students are motivated by strong instrumental orientation (e.g., for German HL, Noels & Clement, 1989). While acknowledging the difficulties of differentiating between types of motivation in HL contexts, Li (2005) found that her large sample of university CHL learners were strongly motivated by *both* integrative orientation and instrumental orientation. Furthermore, the instrumental orientation was more geared to future career opportunities than to imminent academic achievement (e.g., credits or grades). CHL learners wanted to know more about their cultural roots and identities but also wanted to participate in the burgeoning Chinese economy. Traditional dichotomies of motivation (integrative vs. instrumental) just as those related to "native" and "non-native" speakers or "native" versus "target" languages/cultures become blurred and blended among CHL learners. The theoretical literature on language learners' identities and agency (Norton, 2000), their discursive positioning by themselves and by others (Duff, 2002), and the language socialization they experience (Duff & Hornberger, 2008; Li, 2000) have received a great deal of attention in recent years, but with only minimal reference to HL populations (e.g., He, 2006). Learners' identities and trajectories in diasporic Chinese communities, like their own affiliation with the language and motivation for studying it, are dynamic, contingent, multidirectional, and hybrid. Chinese HL children may first acquire a dialect of Chinese (their first language), begin to lose that HL after age 5 when English supplants it, go on to learn another language (e.g., French, Spanish), until they come to university and discover the internal desire (unlike the externally imposed pressures of their childhood) to re-claim their HL language and identity, perhaps by learning the standard variety, Mandarin, though they may later show some tendency toward a Taiwanese-accented or Beijing-accented variety. Thus, the motivation of most CHL learners, at least from Li's (2005) study, is not simply to obtain "easy credits," as is often suspected; rather, they are aiming at a "better investment" (Norton, 2000) in legitimate transformational education and opportunities for their future (Cummins, 2005; He, this volume) in which their desires, hopes, and diverse past experiences and identities can be harmonized somewhat.

Issues in assessment and placement

Once HL students are deemed to be legitimate and are accepted into a program, ideally because they are motivated to learn, a major challenge for instructors is to find valid, reliable assessment instruments to place them into appropriate classes, and to monitor and determine their progress and achievement. There is a pressing need for more appropriate instruments to measure HL proficiency and use. Issues such as non-HL students being intimidated by HL students in mixed classes, or low-proficiency HL students being intimidated by higher-proficiency HL learners in HL classes, or criticism of the "easy credit" seekers all speak to the necessity and importance of having effective placement procedures. Locally developed or adapted placement instruments used by different programs mainly include student background questionnaires, oral interviews, proficiency tests, or some combination of the above.

Among these procedures, oral interviews and background questionnaires seem to be the most widely used because there is no existing standardized placement test specifically designed for HL students. The single most reliable indicator of HL proficiency seems to be the amount of schooling received in the target language, which can be obtained from questionnaires or interviews. However, there are considerable individual differences in linguistic skills in the target HL even among students from the same class, not to mention CHL learners from very different educational systems in China, Taiwan, or Hong Kong. Due to the limited number of courses that can be offered in most 4-year university programs, how can all CHL (and non-CHL) students be accommodated satisfactorily and brought up to comparable criterion levels of proficiency in such a short time—from those with very little exposure to the language to those who have completed elementary or junior high school native language education? In addition, is Cantonese oral proficiency counted as an advantage or a disadvantage in learning Mandarin? For students who are ethnically Chinese but have had no prior exposure to the ethnic language and culture, is it more appropriate to place them in HL or non-HL courses (an issue discussed in a previous section)?

Placement decisions are made by teachers on the basis of students' individual characteristics as well as organizational constraints (e.g., number and type of courses offered, class size, available materials). We urgently need more research investigating how effective and appropriate such placement procedures are for identifying CHL students' proficiency across their diverse backgrounds, and their strengths and weaknesses. This information can be used for diagnostic purposes and will thus inform pedagogical decisions.

Secondly, how to assess these students' progress in our programs remains another issue. Learners enter our programs with varying degrees of prior knowledge and exposure to the HL, depending on their age of arrival, the place and length of their native-language education, and the level of HL maintenance after their immigration. The monitoring and measurement of students' progress must be also addressed. How do we set criteria for their evaluation and assessment based on our instructional objectives and expected outcomes? And what instruments should be selected for different programs or classes?

Thirdly, in order to accommodate and build upon the diversity of skills which HL learners bring to the classroom situation, the assessment instruments should ideally elicit and measure not only their language proficiency in the standard language required for effective performance in classroom contexts but also their interpersonal language skills in different but related language varieties or dialects. These varieties have value in their own right as part of the learner's linguistic repertoire, and they may also serve to bridge the acquisition of standard forms. In sum, much research and development must take place in the area of CHL assessment for placement/diagnostic purposes, for establishing students' linguistic repertoires, and then measuring their progress against language program criteria. On a related note, more research is needed on standardized tests such as the HSK (Mandarin) Chinese Proficiency Test to determine its reliability and validity with our populations of learners (both HL and non-HL) in North America since it was originally designed for non-HL learners, but many HL learners are also taking it for proficiency assessment purposes.

Meeting the learners' needs through CHL curriculum design

Responding to the complexity of HL learners' needs is one of the challenges that postsecondary educators face when designing HL programs and planning instruction that has traditionally been geared mostly to "foreign" language learners. What these HL learners already know, what they need to learn, and how to teach them are not clear in our current language curriculum design guidelines or textbooks. As a result, when teachers attempt to apply a standard FL curriculum and related teaching methodologies to the teaching of a HL, it can lead to frustration or even failure for students (HL and non-HL) and teachers.

Because language indexes social identity, social acts, affective, epistemic or political stances (Ochs, 1996) and because language/literacy choice is closely bound up with national, ethnolinguistic, and personal identities, CHL learning (like all learning) is closely intertwined with learners' identity (re-)construction, attitudes, and literacy development (He, 2004; Tse, 1998). Their place of birth, length of residence in Canada or the US, age of immigration, and family socio-economic, educational, and political backgrounds all play an important role in the language development and identity formation of HL students. Self-identification by minority groups is closely related to their language environment and social context. Every time language learners speak, they are exchanging information or negotiating meaning with their interlocutors; they are also constantly engaged in identity construction and negotiation (Norton, 1997). According to Norton, "[i]dentity relates to desire—the desire for recognition, the desire for affiliation, and the desire for security and safety" (p. 410). It also relates to people's understandings of "their relationship to the world, how that relationship is constructed across time and space, and how people understand their possibilities for the future" (p. 410). CHL learners, like all students, have social-psychological needs as well as linguistic and educational needs which are interconnected and vary enormously from group to group, and from individual to individual. The significance of Chinese as a HL in the global context and the complexity of intersections between varieties of Chinese and identity choices and identity positioning make it necessary to develop a more informed pedagogy that takes into account CHL learners' special needs and unique profiles.

For example, programs may offer a perceived standard form of a language (e.g., Mandarin) that does not meet the needs of the community concerned (e.g., in a local community that has traditionally been mainly Cantonese). The standard variety may be (almost) incomprehensible to the "HL" community, or may have a damaging effect on relations within the community. On the other hand, CHL learners may need to expand the domains or repertoire of their language use from that of the family (e.g., Taiwanese, Cantonese) and community to those of the academic institution and, later, work. In this way, education doesn't simply teach them more of what they may already have a good foundation in but increases their verbal repertoires, or the total range of linguistic competencies developed through linguistic resources available to them. In addition, HL students typically need to increase, even for their home languages, their sociolinguistic sophistication, and need to upgrade their HL proficiency from that of a child in an intimate or informal family situation to an age-appropriate academic level and register (see Sridhar, 1996; Valdés & Geoffrion-Vinci, 1998). To date, there has been too little research on the effect of mismatches between the expectations and requirements of students and programs, or children and parents or of gaps between vernacular knowledge and more formal academic registers.

According to Campbell (2000), HL speakers typically have the following attributes:

- native pronunciation and fluency
- command of a wide range of syntactic structures ("80% to 90%" of the grammatical rules)
- extensive vocabulary
- familiarity with implicit cultural norms essential for effective language use

At the same time, they also have these typical gaps or discrepancies in their HL knowledge:

- lack of formal or sophisticated registers in the language
- poor literacy
- non-standard variety

However, with CHL learners, these characteristics are not necessarily applicable. Dialect speakers (such as Cantonese) may not necessarily possess "native pronunciation" when they learn Mandarin. What's worse, they may not even understand Mandarin. As a result, some Chinese language programs (e.g., UCLA) have adopted a 3-track system, further dividing the HL track into a Cantonese-speaker track and a Mandarin-speaker track. But so far, to our knowledge, no research has compared the learning processes between Cantonese- and Mandarin-speaking learners in CHL programs.

Unlike learning certain other HLs in which students' background competence in speaking and listening facilitates reading and writing, several studies (Ke, 1998; Shen, 2003; Xiao, 2006) have found that a home background in Chinese had little or no effect on learning Chinese writing, vocabulary, or reading comprehension. The reason is that the logographic nature of Chinese writing does not help CHL speakers tap into their existing oral skills and phonology, whereas heritage speakers of languages with alphabetic orthographies are able to do so.

Another complication with Chinese language curriculum is that the preferred orthography (e.g., simplified vs. traditional characters, or even the romanization system) differs from region to region and thus geopolitics intersect with HL education in both unpredictable and predictable ways. Certainly, this factor affects the attitudes of learners from different Chinese regions or sub-cultures towards the oral and written varieties of CHL they aspire to learn. The question of which writing system should be taught in Chinese courses has been debated at length. Some programs insist that the simplified character system used in Mainland China is favoured by the majority of Chinese people, and therefore should be used. Opponents of this position argue that the traditional character system used in Hong Kong, Taiwan, and Chinese diaspora communities in North America preserves the best of Chinese writing since it is the original form. The debate has stirred up heated responses from supporters on both sides as it is deeply associated with political ideology, social affiliation, and cultural identity in Mainland China, Hong Kong, and Taiwan. Some people even link simplified characters with communism and traditional characters with anticommunism or "non-communism." Li (2006) illustrates how CHL learners' preferences regarding choice of writing system are closely related to their own social, cultural, and political identities as well as their language ideologies. There is, however, some sign of growing tolerance, acceptance, and accommodation among HL learners on each side with respect to learning both systems. Figure 2 reveals that, as one might expect, 76.6% of Mainland Chinese HL students surveyed by Li indicated a preference for simplified characters, in contrast to just over 7% from Kong Kong, and 2% from Taiwan making the same choice. Conversely, the majority of students from Hong Kong and Taiwan (approximately 70%) opted for the original characters. Diaspora students from other locations were more balanced in aligning with one or another script, but in general also preferred the original characters. But a proportion of students across all groups (ranging from nearly 10% to 27%) thought both systems should be taught, and not just one or the other.

As Cummins (2006) points out,

> Behind language/cultural labels such as "Chinese" or "Spanish" there exists considerable diversity and complexity of historically-generated patterns of power relationships. These relationships and identity affiliations express themselves in ways of linguistic expression (e.g., speaking/accent, choice of writing system). This diversity needs to be recognized in the design of HL programs—these programs are helping students to become a particular kind of person rather than just attempting to transmit a language.

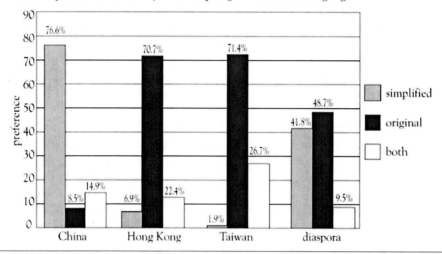

Figure 2. CHL students' preference for script systems (Li, 2006)

However, practical limitations often make it necessary to group students with vastly different goals, not to mention abilities, in the same CHL class. It has been documented that tension between home and classroom-privileged Chinese dialects and in the choice of writing systems can make certain groups of students perceive their language abilities as devalued and wasteful (Weger-Guntharp, 2006). Thus, some CHL programs strive to be linguistically hybrid or inclusive, incorporating several varieties of Chinese. Some switch from simplified to original, or vice versa, when students reach higher levels and have mastered the first system. Others make an effort to incorporate both systems in their curriculum and encourage students to make their own choices or to learn both systems simultaneously.

Educators should tailor their programs with these considerations in mind, according to both class-internal and external considerations. External considerations encompass issues related to the sociolinguistics of CHL: the conditions that regulate the use of Chinese (in its many varieties) by individuals and groups in local communities, the country, and around the world. Class-internal considerations relate to the levels of proficiency, and goals and attitudes of students in particular CHL classes. Course sequences should be designed to build on the skills that students bring, develop additional skills, use their HL in new contexts/domains, and increase their pride in their heritage. CHL speakers are legitimate students in our language classes if the curriculum recognizes them as having a unique starting point and particular needs and sets challenging but reasonable and appropriate goals.

Separate tracks for CHL learners at postsecondary institutions

The markedly different language and cultural backgrounds between HL learners and non-HL learners, even acknowledging the great variation within each group, supports the development of a separate-track (heritage and non-heritage) system. It is now widely believed that if local conditions and student demographics allow it, a separate track specifically designed for CHL learners' backgrounds and needs is ideal in helping them learn their HL. As mentioned before, some universities even further divide HL tracks into sub-tracks according to students' oral and written varieties of the HL. However, due to limited resources, some Chinese programs can only offer separate tracks for HL and non-HL learners at the elementary and/or intermediate levels (McGinnis, 1996) but many small-scale programs cannot afford to open separate tracks, so HL students are mixed with non-HL students throughout. In these latter programs, if no effort is made to recognize and tap into HL learners' reservoirs of knowledge and the identities that they bring to the classroom, they will most likely find the language learning experience profoundly disappointing and invalidating. On the other hand, if the non-HL learners only feel intimidated by HL students, without being given the opportunity of interacting with "native speakers" and benefiting from their rich linguistic and cultural resources, their learning experience will also be unsatisfactory.

Therefore, curriculum research is needed to investigate the following three questions:

1. What are the advantages (or disadvantages) of separate tracks of HL and non-HL learners?

2. What is the most appropriate level for HL and non-HL tracks to be combined?

3. Are there any advantages (or disadvantages) for both HL and non-HL students in mixed classes, and if so, how can programs make the most of the advantages to counteract the disadvantages?

Teaching high-level registers in postsecondary HL programs

Until very recently, and especially in the United States prior to September 11, 2001, less emphasis was placed on maintaining and developing students' existing HL competencies to advanced levels than developing foreign language competencies to less advanced levels. That is now changing though, with major HL policies and funding initiatives in the US connected with identified "critical languages" (e.g., Arabic, Mandarin, Korean) for reasons of "homeland security" (McGinnis, 2004). Unfortunately, the political tenor of such initiatives is that speakers of these languages are potentially dangerous.

Recent years have seen an unprecedented interest among applied linguists and educators to become advocates for HL education and research in higher education (e.g., Brecht & Ingold, 1998; Campbell & Peyton, 1998; Hinton, 1999), in part to provide a counter-discourse to such national sentiments and suspicions. Scholars have increasingly emphasized that respect for linguistic human rights (Phillipson, Ranut, & Skutnabb-Kangas, 1995) and the achievement of high linguistic proficiency of HL speakers will preserve invaluable national resources and thereby contribute to individuals' and societies' well-being (Brecht & Ingold, 1998). HL educators have been interested in developing curriculum models to deal with the discrepancy between HL learners' highly developed competence in informal, non-prestigious (vernacular) language varieties, acquired primarily at home and often restricted to the domain of immediate personal use, on the one hand, and their lack of competence in formal, prestigious language varieties and registers, which are more valuable for academic learning and professional development (e.g., Campbell, 2000; Fairclough, 2001; Valdés, 1995).

Therefore, the acquisition of sophisticated, academic, and other registers is an appropriate goal for advanced postsecondary HL programs. Future research should investigate (a) what higher-level registers, genres, and language varieties should be included in curricula for advanced level CHL learners—modern Chinese language (Mandarin), classical Chinese, modern literature or classical literature, business or professional/academic language proficiency; and (b) the effect of formal instruction on the acquisition of multiple registers in postsecondary CHL.

In curriculum design, programs need to better align standards with students' proficiency levels and needs; value students' heritage, backgrounds, learning styles, and abilities; and promote a balanced worldview and positive intergroup or intercultural relationships. Ideally, the resulting curriculum will be cognitively appropriate for university-level students; linguistically challenging, so as to engage them; culturally relevant; and academically sound, well articulated across levels, and meaningfully assessed.

Appropriate teaching materials and teacher education

This final section is linked to all of the others issues: students' backgrounds and identities, their motivation, assessment, and the curriculum. The lack of relevant instructional materials for HL students is one of the most frequently raised issues by teachers and students. There are very few textbooks written specifically for CHL learners. So far, only two textbooks have been published for beginners: *Oh, China* by Princeton University Press (Chou, 1999), and a *Primer for Advanced Beginners of Chinese* by Columbia University Press (Li et al., 2003). Published course materials for intermediate and advanced level CHL students are non-existent. Indeed, for many years, most university programs have used the same textbooks for foreign-language and HL learners, only at an accelerated speed for the latter. However, this universalizing approach to teaching two distinct kinds of learners has proved ineffective over the years. The foreign language textbooks produced in North America are ill-suited for HL learners, with their coverage of basic grammar, survival vocabulary, and everyday routines such as greetings.

There is clearly a need for teaching materials designed to meet the unique (and also diverse) needs of heritage students. Such materials need to start at an appropriate linguistic and cognitive level, move quickly but steadily through material, using a systematic, language awareness approach to grammar instruction. They also need to focus on literacy and higher-level register development, and contain relevant (advanced level) cultural, sociocultural, and sociolinguistic information. Only with such instructional materials can we challenge heritage speakers sufficiently, foster their retention in language programs, and promote their attainment of professional-level proficiency. Innovative ways of using media and technology (television, computer, online resources) to enhance language instruction and broaden access should also be explored (e.g., as the online journal *Language Learning and Technology* demonstrates, typically for European languages). HL learners who engage in reading and writing contextualized, vernacular content that expresses their own ethnic identity and heritage will be more highly motivated and competent to succeed academically and in their broader participation in society.

Similarly, to motivate students the emphasis in teacher education and professional development must shift so that educators realize that (a) they need to examine their beliefs and attitudes toward HL speakers and their oral/written language varieties; (b) they must understand the linguistic needs as well as social-psychological orientations of HL students in order to maximize the effectiveness and suitability of their instruction; (c) they must develop curriculum and instructional approaches, materials, and assessment tools that respond meaningfully to that complexity as well as to the needs and profiles of non-HL students.

In this way, we will maximize the supply of qualified CHL educators who embrace the opportunities and responsibilities for being proactive in nurturing HL development or fostering language and literacy socialization within mainstream classrooms. CHL education should therefore start where the students are and move forward with them; it must be relevant. Without appropriate articulation of the curriculum, old material will continually be recycled at a basic level without the accumulation of new knowledge and students' language proficiency will plateau early. Students must be made aware of the linguistic strengths they possess and can build upon. We should also help them develop a sense of pride in their heritage through language and culture study, and expand their ability to use HL in new contexts and at higher levels in both speech and writing.

Future directions in CHL research

Throughout this chapter, we have tried to identify salient current issues in CHL education, drawing on existing research and identifying apparent gaps in the literature. Valdés (1995) pointed out that Spanish HL instruction, regrettably, "has developed multiple practices and pedagogies that are not directly based on coherent theories about the kinds of language learning with which they are concerned" (p. 308). She urged that "it is time for teachers and applied linguists working in this area to examine their research and practice and to begin to frame the agenda that will guide them in the years to come" (p. 321). The same plea could be made for CHL, which has a shorter research history in applied linguistics than Spanish, fewer developed materials and trained teachers, and a more complex set of issues connected with literacy.

To summarize, HL students' identities must be seen as dynamic, multiple, situated, and diverse. Students often feel a great deal of ambivalence about their dual or multiple identities and about how they have been positioned, sometimes unfavourably and sometimes in contradictory ways (Duff, 2002), by their families, communities, peers, and mainstream schools, with respect to their heritage and their language and academic abilities—as "model minority students" or as "linguistically deficient" or as possessing inadequate literacy skills in L1 and L2, as Generation 1.5 students, for example. Using longitudinal qualitative (and/or quantitative) multiple-case studies (e.g., Duff, 2008a), the personal trajectories, investments, and abilities of students with respect to their HL and the other languages and literacies they know could be documented and tracked over time. Our own work in progress, funded by a 3-year Social Sciences and Humanities Research Council of Canada grant, is tracking 20 CHL university students from four different HL backgrounds in a large multiple-case study of students' evolving CHL language practices, identities, literacies, and ideologies over time.

Researchers must also investigate in a more fine-grained way the highly situated and contingent nature of motivation itself across learning contexts, geographical and transnational space and communities, and as learners mature (e.g., He, 2006, this volume). In addition, appropriate research-based materials, curriculum, and assessment tools and procedures must be developed in accordance with widely divergent levels of students and types of programs.

A broader set of research questions relevant to HL education to be explored include the following two from Hornberger (2003b):

1.   What global, societal, and local factors encourage and promote intergenerational transfer, maintenance, revitalization, and development of HLs?

2.   What educational approaches—policies, programs, and practices—best serve HL learners attain the highest levels of proficiency possible and the intergenerational transfer of their languages?

To these questions we can add the following: How are oral and written language development related, especially for those who already have highly developed oral skills but underdeveloped written language (and possibly equally underdeveloped writing in English) and vice versa? What are the upper limits possible for HL versus non-HL students in four-year university programs in terms of the attainment of accuracy, fluency, and complexity in language and literacy?

A third set of questions might examine ethnographically the discourse communities of HL students, both locally and globally, the mediating tools such as pop culture, the Internet, or other technologies and new media that connect them to the languages and cultures they affiliate with, and mediate their socialization into new modes of language use, possibly involving hybrid texts and semiotic systems (e.g., Lam, 2004). Lastly, whereas considerable study-abroad research has been conducted on students learning European languages, little has been done on Chinese HL learners and their socialization within target-culture contexts where they may be mistaken for native speakers but then criticized for their incomplete mastery of Chinese. Thus, many opportunities exist for researchers, program administrators, and teacher educators in CHL.

Conclusion

Examining Chinese as a HL language at the postsecondary level is a relatively new endeavor. Rigorous research is needed to help develop more effective curriculum, pedagogical approaches, instructional materials, and assessment practices to better harness and build on the knowledge of these students and communities. Encouraging HL learning can expand worldviews and possibilities which confer personal, professional and economic benefits that will continue long after the students leave university. Researchers should look into the complex ecology of CHL, not only in Canada and the United States but in the various other diaspora contexts worldwide in which Chinese is being taught and learned. The role of policy in fostering CHL in postsecondary programs and the ongoing struggle for curricular and administrative legitimacy of CHL learning and teaching must also be addressed in an ongoing manner. Sociolinguistic and educational issues connected with language, literacy, and identity among contemporary CHL learners as global, multilingual, potentially transnational citizens should also be investigated. Understanding their linguistic heterogeneity and potential will help us to better accommodate linguistically diverse learners in language courses and maximize the social, academic, economic, and cultural benefits of HL maintenance and will help us improve our educational offerings for non-HL students as well.

References

Andrews, D. (2001). Teaching the Russian heritage learner: Socio- and psycholinguistic perspectives. *The Slavic and East European Journal, 45,* 519–530.

Brecht, R. D., & Ingold, C. W. (1998). *Tapping a national resource: Heritage languages in the United States.* Washington, DC: ERIC Clearinghouse on Languages and Linguistics (ERIC Digest No. EDO– FL–98–12).

Brinton, D., Kagan, O., & Bauckus, S. (Eds.). (2008.) *Heritage language acquisition: A new field emerging.* New York: Routlege/Taylor & Francis.

Campbell, R. (2000). Heritage language. In J. W. Rosenthal (Ed.), *Handbook of undergraduate second language education* (pp. 165–184). Mahwah, NJ: Lawrence Erlbaum.

Campbell, R., & Peyton, J. (1998, Fall). Heritage language students: A valuable language resource. *ERIC Review, 6*(1), 38–39.

Canadian Teaching Chinese as a Second Language (TCSL) National Database. (2007). Retrieved June 17, 2007, from http://www.canadiantcslassociation.ca/data_index.htm

Carreira, M. (2004). Seeking explanatory adequacy: A dual approach to understanding the term "heritage language learner." *Heritage Language Journal, 2*(1), 1–25.

Cho, G., & Krashen, S. (1998). The negative consequences of heritage language loss and why we should care. In S. D. Krashen, L. Tse, & J. McQuillan (Eds.), *Heritage language development* (pp. 31–39). Culver City, CA: Language Education Associates.

Chou, C. (1999). *Oh, China!* Princeton, NJ: Princeton University Press.

Cummins, J. (1993). The research basis for heritage language promotion. In M. Danesi, K. McLeod, & S. Morris (Eds.), *Heritage language and education: The Canadian experience* (pp. 1–21). Ontario, Canada: Mosaic Press.

Cummins, J. (2004). Multiliteracies pedagogy and the role of identity texts. In K. Leithwood, P. McAdie, N. Bascia, & A. Rodrigue (Eds.), *Teaching for deep understanding: Towards the Ontario curriculum that we need* (pp. 68–74). Toronto: OISE/UT and ETFO.

Cummins, J. (2005). Proposal for action: Strategies for recognizing heritage language competence as a learning resource within the mainstream classroom. *The Modern Language Journal, 89,* 585–592.

Cummins, J. (2006, June). Discussant comments on P. Duff & D. Li (Organizers), Colloquium on "Heritage Languages, Identity, and Education." Annual conference of the American Association for Applied Linguistics, Montreal, Quebec.

Dörnyei, Z., & Skehan, P. (2003). Individual differences in second language learning. In C. Doughty & M. H. Long (Eds.), *Handbook of second language acquisition* (pp. 589–630). Malden, MA: Blackwell.

Duff, P. (2002). The discursive co-construction of knowledge, identity, and difference: An ethnography of communication in the high school mainstream. *Applied Linguistics, 23,* 289–322.

Duff, P. (2005). Thinking globally about new literacies: Multilingual socialization at work. In J. Anderson, M. Kendrick, T. Rodgers, & S. Smythe (Eds.), *Portraits of literacy across families, communities and schools* (pp. 341–362). Mahwah, NJ: Lawrence Erlbaum.

Duff, P. (2008a). *Case study research in applied linguistics.* Mahwah, NJ: Lawrence Erlbaum/Taylor & Francis.

Duff, P. (2008b). Heritage language education in Canada. In D. Brinton, O. Kagan, & S. Bauckus (Eds.), *Heritage language education: A new field emerging* (pp. 71–90). New York: Routlege/Taylor & Francis.

Duff, P., & Hornberger, N. H. (Eds.). (2008). *Language socialization. Encyclopedia of language and education*, *Vol. 8*. New York: Springer.

Fairclough, M. (2001). *Language and power* (2nd ed.). London: Longman.

Fishman, J. (1991). *Reversing language shift*. Clevedon, England: Multilingual Matters.

Fishman, J. (2001). 300-plus years of heritage language education in the United States. In J. Peyton, D. Ranard, & S. McGinnis (Eds.), *Heritage languages in America: Preserving a national resource* (pp. 81–89). McHenry, IL: Delta Systems.

Gardner, R. C. (1985). *Social psychology and second language learning: The role of attitudes and motivation*. London: Edward Arnold.

Geisherik, A. (2004). The role of motivation among heritage and non-heritage learners of Russian. *Canadian Slavonic Papers*, *46*(1/2), 9–22.

Hall, S. (1988). New ethnicities. In A. Rattansi & J. Donald (Eds.), *"Race," culture and difference* (pp. 252–259). London: Sage/Open University.

Han, S. (2003). *Culture or capital: What motivates heritage language achievement among Korean-American youth?* Master's monograph, Stanford University. Retrieved March 30, 2007, from http://suse-ice.stanford.edu/monographs/Han.pdf

He, A. (2004). Identity construction in Chinese heritage language classes. [Special issue on Relationality: Discursive constructions of Asian Pacific American identities.] *Pragmatics*, *14*(2/3), 199–216.

He, A. (2006). Toward an identity theory of the development of Chinese as a heritage language. *Heritage Language Journal*, *4*(1), 1–28.

Hinton, L. (1999). Involuntary language loss among immigrants: Asian-American linguistic autobiographies. *CAL Digest*. Washington, DC: Centre for Applied Linguistics. Retrieved March 30, 2007, from http://www.cal.org/resources/digest/involuntary.html

Hornberger, N. H. (Ed.). (2003a). *Continua of biliteracy: An ecological framework for educational policy, research, and practice in multilingual settings*. Clevedon, England: Multilingual Matters.

Hornberger, N. H. (2003b). *Biliteracy and heritage languages*. Los Angeles: UCLA Center for World Languages. Retrieved March 30, 2007, from http://www.international.ucla.edu/languages/article.asp?parentid=3908

Hornberger, N. H. (Ed.). (2005). Heritage/community language education: U.S. and Australian perspectives. *International Journal of Bilingual Education and Bilingualism*, *8*(2&3), 101–108.

Hornberger, N. H., & Wang, S. (2008). Who are our heritage language learners? Identity and biliteracy in heritage language education in the United States. In D. Brinton, O. Kagan, & S. Bauckus (Eds.), *Heritage language acquisition: A new field emerging* (pp. 3–35). New York: Routlege/Taylor & Francis.

Kagan, O., Akishina, T., & Robin, R. (2003). *Russian for Russians: Textbook for heritage speakers*. Bloomington, IN: Slavica Publishers.

Kagan, O., & Dillon, K. (2004). Heritage speakers' potential for high-level language proficiency. In H. Byrnes & H. Maxim (Eds.), *Advanced foreign language learning: A challenge to college programs* (pp. 99–112). Boston: Heinle & Heinle.

Ke, C. (1998). Effects of language background on the learning of Chinese characters among foreign languages students. *Foreign Language Annals, 31*(1), 91–100.

Kim, Y. (1992). *The role of attitudes and motivation in learning a heritage language: A study of Korean language maintenance in Toronto*. Dissertation Abstracts. University of Toronto, Canada. Retrieved March 30, 2007, from http://wwwlib.umi.com/dissertations/preview/NN78824

Kondo-Brown, K. (2002). Family and school factors influencing academic performance of bilingual Shin Nisei students in Hawai'i. In E. Tamura, V. Chattergy, & R. Endo (Eds.), *Asian and Pacific Islander American education: Social, cultural, and historical contexts* (pp. 149–174). South El Monte, CA: Pacific Asia Press.

Kondo-Brown, K. (2003). Heritage language instruction for post-secondary students from immigrant backgrounds. *Heritage Language Journal, 1*, 1–25.

Kono, N., & McGinnis, S. (2001). Heritage languages and higher education: Challenges, issues, and needs. In J. Peyton, D. Ranard, & S. McGinnis (Eds.), *Heritage languages in America* (pp. 197–206). Washington, DC: Center for Applied Linguistics.

Krashen, S. (1998). Heritage language development: Some practical arguments. In S. D. Krashen, L. Tse, & J. McQuillan (Eds.), *Heritage language development* (pp. 3–13). Culver City, CA: Language Education Associates.

Krashen, S., Tse, L., & McQuillan, J. (Eds.). (1998). *Heritage language development*. Culver City, CA: Language Education Associates.

Lam, W. S. E. (2004). Second language socialization in a bilingual chatroom: Global and local considerations. *Language Learning and Technology, 8*(3), 44–65.

Leung, C., Harris, R., & Rampton, B. (1997). The idealized native speaker, reified ethnicities, and classroom realities. *TESOL Quarterly, 31*, 543–560.

Li, D. (2000). The pragmatics of making requests in the L2 workplace: A case study of language socialization. *The Canadian Modern Language Review, 57*, 58–87.

Li, D. (2005, August). *Attitudes, motivations and identities in learning Chinese as a heritage language*. Paper presented at the 14th World Congress of Applied Linguistics, Madison, WI.

Li, D. (2006, June). *Heritage language learning and identity: The case of Chinese*. Paper presented at the Joint AAAL and ACLA/CAAL Conference, Montreal, Quebec.

Li, D., Liu, I., Liu, L., Wang, H., Wang, Z., & Xie, Y. (2003). *A primer for advanced beginners of Chinese*. New York: Columbia University Press.

Lynch, A. (2003). The relationship between second and heritage language acquisition: Notes on research and theory building. *Heritage Language Journal, 2*(1), 26–43.

McGinnis, S. (1996). Teaching Chinese to the Chinese: The development of an assessment and instructional model. In J. Liskin-Gasparro (Ed.), *Patterns and policies: The changing demographics of foreign language instruction* (pp. 107–121). Boston: Heinle & Heinle.

McGinnis, S. (2004, May). *Heritage language initiatives and research in the US*. Paper presented at the International Symposium on Language, Diversity, and Education, Centre for Intercultural Language Studies, University of British Columbia.

McGinnis, S. (2005). More than a silver bullet: The role of Chinese as a heritage language in the United States. *Modern Language Journal, 89*, 592–594.

Noels, K., & Clement, R. (1989). Orientations to learning German: The effects of language heritage on second-language acquisition. *Canadian Modern Language Review, 45*, 245–257.

Norton, B. (1997). Language, identity, and the ownership of English. *TESOL Quarterly, 31*, 409–429.

Norton, B. (2000). *Identity and language learning: Gender, ethnicity and educational change*. Harlow, England: Pearson Education.

Ochs, E. (1996a). Constructing social identity: A language socialization perspective. *Research on Language and Social Interaction, 26*, 287–306.

Pavlenko, A., & Lantolf, J. P. (2000). Second language learning as participation and the (re)construction of selves. In J. P. Lantolf (Ed.), *Sociocultural theory and second language learning* (pp. 155–178). New York: Oxford University Press.

Phillipson, R., Rannut, M., & Skutnabb-Kangas, T. (1995). Introduction. In R. Phillipson & T. Skutnabb-Kangas (Eds.), *Linguistic human rights* (pp. 1–22). New York: Mouton de Gruyter.

Shen, H. (2003). A comparison of written Chinese achievement among heritage learners in homogeneous and heterogeneous groups. *Foreign Language Annals, 36*(2), 258–266.

Sohn, S. (2004). Placement of Korean heritage speakers: Challenges and strategies. Unpublished invited lecture, Centre for Korean Research, University of British Columbia.

Sridhar, K. (1996). Societal multilingualism. In S. L. McKay & N. H. Hornberger (Eds.), *Sociolinguistics and language teaching* (pp. 47–70). New York: Cambridge University Press.

Statistics Canada (2004). 2001 *Census: Population by mother tongue, provinces and territories.* Retrieved January 9, 2004, from http://www.statcan.ca/english/Pgdb/demo18c.htm

Swain, M., & Lapkin, S. (1991). Heritage language children in an English-French bilingual program. *The Canadian Modern Language Review, 47*(4), 634–641.

Tavares, A. (2000). From heritage to international languages: Globalism and Western Canadian trends in heritage language education. *Canadian Ethnic Studies, 32*(1), 156–172.

Tse, L. (1998). Ethnic identity formation and its implications for heritage language development. In S. Krashen, L. Tse, & J. McQuillan (Eds.), *Heritage language development* (pp. 15–29). Culver City, CA: Language Education Associates.

U.S. Census Bureau (2000). *U.S. census 2000*. Retrieved March 30, 2007, from http://www.census.gov/main/www/cen2000.html

Valdés, G. (1995). The teaching of minority languages as academic subjects: Pedagogical and theoretical challenges. *Modern Language Journal, 79*, 299–328.

Valdés, G. (1997). The teaching of Spanish to bilingual Spanish-speaking students: Outstanding issues and unanswered questions. In M. Colombi & F. Alarcón (Eds.), *La enseñanza del español a hispanohablantes. Praxis y teoría* (pp. 8–44). Boston: Houghton Mifflin.

Valdés, G. (2005). Bilingualism, heritage language learners, and SLA research: Opportunities lost or seized? *The Modern Language Journal, 89*, 410–426.

Valdés, G., & Geoffrion-Vinci, M. (1998). Chicano Spanish: The problem of the "underdeveloped" code in bilingual repertoires. *Modern Language Journal, 82*, 473–501.

Wang, S. (2005). *Expanding Chinese language capacity in the United States*. Report of the Asia Society. Retrieved March 30, 2007, from http://www.askasia.org/chinese/publications.htm

Weger-Guntharp, H. (2006). Voices from the margin: Developing a profile of Chinese heritage language learners in the FL classroom. *Heritage Language Journal, 4*(1), 29–46.

Wen, X. (1997). Motivation and language learning with students of Chinese. *Foreign Language Annals, 30*(2), 235–251.

Wiley, T. (2001). On defining heritage languages and their speakers. In J. Peyton, D. Ranard, & S. McGinnis (Eds.), *Heritage languages in America* (pp. 29–36). Washington, DC: Center for Applied Linguistics.

Wiley, T., & Valdés, G. (2000). Heritage language instruction in the United States: A time for renewal, Editors' introduction. *Bilingual Research Journal, 24*(4), iii–vii.

Write, S., & Taylor, D. (1995). Identity and the language of the classroom: Investigating the impact of heritage versus second language instruction on personal and collective self-esteem. *Journal of Educational Psychology, 87*, 241–52.

Xiao, Y. (2006). Heritage learners in the Chinese language classroom: Home background. *Heritage Language Journal, 4*(1), 47–57.

The Learner

3

NFLRC
monographs

What Are the CHL Learners Inheriting? *Habitus* of the CHL Learners

Jin-huei Enya Dai
Monterey Institute of International Studies, California

Lihua Zhang
University of California, Berkeley

We employ the notion of habitus *(Bourdieu, 1991) to examine what the CHL learners inherit in the context of both local and global fields in order to find explanations for CHL learners' unique experiences. We investigate CHL learners' habitus from three dimensions—linguistic, cultural, and social habitus—which we define as their bilingual and bicultural environments, the people they interact with, their desire and intimacy for CHL and for learning Mandarin Chinese. Data from 80 CHL learners' questionnaires, some interviews, and a number of CHL learners' oral accounts are examined. We unravel various dimensions of CHL learners' experiences to tease out the characteristics of their habitus, such as heritage language intimacy, diverse cultural identities, and varying modes in social interactions. We also explore CHL learners' desire and intimacy for their heritage languages in relation to a semiotic time and space. Capturing their memories of using heritage languages creates CHL learners' intimacy toward the language, which brings a semiotic space where they are situated.*

Chinese HL learner language

A. 中文我只是在家里说的, 跟别人说不好意思。
"I only speak Chinese at home; it's embarrassing to speak it with others."

B. He failed in his Chinese class at X university because of his accent.

C. 售货员觉得我很奇怪。我说得这么好，可是连一个中文字都看不懂。我觉得很丢脸。
"The salesperson felt that I was weird. [He wondered] how come I could speak fluently, but could not even read a word. I felt very embarrassed."

D. 我来上中文课是因为我想学一些很有意思的话。
"I take Chinese class because I want to learn some meaningful words."

Student A in the example, a Mandarin Chinese heritage learner, was asked to speak Mandarin in a group discussion. He felt embarrassed because he considered Mandarin Chinese his *language of intimacy* used only at home. A. W. He, a speaker at the National Colloquium on

Dai, J. E., & Zhang, L. (2008). What are the CHL learners inheriting? Habitus of the CHL learners. In A. W. He, & Y. Xiao (Eds.), *Chinese as a heritage language: Fostering rooted world citizenry* (pp. 37–51). Honolulu: University of Hawai'i, National Foreign Language Resource Center.

U.S. Language Educational Policy (2005), presented Student B as an example of professional language misevaluation. Student B was a successful Chinese-American professional who frequented Taiwan but failed in the Chinese language program at a prestigious U.S. university because of his variant pronunciation, which deviated from standard Chinese. Student C, a very fluent Mandarin Chinese speaker, mentioned an embarrassing incident she encountered when attempting to make a purchase in Beijing. The salesperson saw her as just another Chinese person and found it strange that she was not able to read Chinese. Student D, an intelligent CHL learner in his discipline, was asked why he took Chinese in the first year heritage-track class and he answered that he wanted to learn "很有意思的话" (meaningful words). His limited Chinese vocabulary prevented him from using a more precise expression, but his response reflects his desire to "learn some meaningful words in Chinese."

These four students' experiences reveal some canonical dimensions of internal and external conflicts in CHL study: *linguistic habitus, CHL illiteracy and expectation clash, linguistic gap,* and *Mandarin as language of intimacy.* This article demonstrates what CHL learners inherit from their upbringings and experiences and what they bring to the classroom from the perspective of Bourdieu's *habitus.*

Theoretical background

Bourdieu (1991, p. 12) employs the notion of *habitus* in a specific and unique way. He defines it as "a set of *dispositions* which incline agents to act and react in certain ways…The dispositions which constitute the habitus are inculcated, structured, durable, generative and transposable." We apply Bourdieu's notion and recognize habitus, a set of dispositions, in our CHL learners according to Bourdieu's five features of dispositions. As Bourdieu states, the acquisition of dispositions goes through "a gradual process of *inculcation* in which early childhood experiences are particularly important" (p. 12). This habitus has been gradually *inculcated* or inscribed in our CHL learners since their early childhood through "a myriad of mundane processes of training and learning" (p. 12). The dispositions they have acquired are *structured* on the basis of their social upbringings in a heritage home and in the Chinese community as well as in American society. Therefore, "the similarities and differences that characterize the social conditions of existence of individuals are reflected in the *habitus*" (p. 12). Per Bourdieu (pp. 12–13), *structured* dispositions are *durable.* Such dispositions are ingrained in one's body, carried throughout one's life, and operate both pre-consciously and non-reflectively. *Structured* dispositions are also *generative* and *transposable*: They generate a multiplicity of practices and perceptions in other fields. We also explore practices and perceptions generated by our CHL learners' dispositions.

Bourdieu's notion of *habitus* also provides us with knowledge of the function of *habitus.* It *orients* individuals' actions and prompts individuals to act and respond in their daily life in certain ways without thought or planning. This is because the habitus already provides a sense of proper behavior for any given set of circumstances. Bourdieu refers to such sense as "*le sens pratique*" [practical sense], or as "a state of the body" or "a state of being" (1991, p. 13). Since dispositions are ingrained in the body, certain ways of acting and responding are just as natural as bodily movements themselves. In Bourdieu's theory, the body becomes "a site of incorporated history" and reacts to natural patterns of social and cultural behaviors as a result of individuals' upbringings.

Bourdieu (1991, p. 14) further maintains that individuals act and react in specific social contexts, and what determines their practices and perceptions is not the habitus, but "the *relation between* the habitus and the specific social contexts or 'fields.'" We employ the notion of the *relation between the habitus and the fields* to situate CHL in a local field, a global field, and a heritage language classroom. We relate the CHL learners' habitus to the fields of language, culture, and social interaction and utilize *linguistic habitus*, *cultural habitus*, and *social habitus* to differentiate the ambivalent threshold of what CHL learners are inheriting. Bourdieu (p. 17) states, "the linguistic habitus is a sub-set of the dispositions which comprise the habitus: it is the sub-set of the dispositions acquired in the course of learning to speak in particular contexts (the family, the peer group, the school, etc.)." In the CHL field, linguistic habitus also relates to a certain distinguished "articulatory style" (Pierre Guiraud, cited in Bourdieu, p. 17) that CHL learners have acquired at home (e.g., zh/ch/sh vs. z/c/s). This is a manifestation of the socially structured character of the linguistic habitus.

Cultural habitus, as we utilize it, refers to a set of dispositions that an individual embodies in a particular cultural system. The cultural habitus orients the individual to act and react in certain ways while coping with the world and with one another. In the CHL field, CHL learners inherit from their social upbringing a set of durable structured dispositions regarding core values, customs, life styles, and demeanors. The cultural habitus provides CHL learners with the medium to survive. Social habitus refers to a set of dispositions that one acquires oriented by an internal cultural habitus through socialization with family, school, friendship groups, institutions, and the mass media. The social habitus automatically disposes one to interact in ways that conform to the norms, values, and culture expected by others in society. In the CHL field, CHL learners' social dispositions are created through the orientation of their internal cultural habitus to specific social contexts and guide CHL learners to cope with different social agents in certain ways. While cultural habitus is somewhat inward in orientation, social habitus is more of an outward orientation.

Habitus inscribed in the body provides people with a sense of how to articulate, behave, and respond in daily life. The body becomes a site of personal history and "a repository of ingrained dispositions" (Bourdieu, 1991, p. 13) and makes people's ways of speaking, walking, feeling and thinking durable and natural. When habitus relates to specific social contexts, practices and perceptions are generated.

Research method

What are CHL learners inheriting? We investigate by asking, Who and what are the CHL learners? What environments have they been exposed to? What are they inheriting linguistically, culturally and socially from their background?

We conducted the study in the San Francisco Bay area in California, which is home to the largest Asian populations in America,[1] of which approximately one third are ethnic Chinese, primarily immigrants from China, Taiwan, and the Canton region. The Chinese languages spoken in the Bay area are primarily Cantonese and secondarily Mandarin Chinese. The linguistic and cultural landscape has shaped and is reflected in the participants' backgrounds.

This study draws research data primarily from 80 written questionnaires, but some from oral interviews and CHL learners' own stories. The questionnaire contained four parts: general information, family background, Chinese language background, and cultural aspects. The questionnaire is reproduced in the Appendix.

Participants in this study were 80 HL college students of Chinese (36 males, 44 females). While the majority of the participants were 18 to 23 years old, one was 26 and another 27.

---

[1]   Survey of Asians in the Bay Area (2004), available at http://www.kff.org/newsmedia/pomr121204pkg.cfm

Among them were 8 freshmen, 18 sophomores, 28 juniors, 22 seniors, 2 graduate students, and 2 recent alumni. Of the participants, 57 were born in the US, and 23 immigrated to the US with their parents at ages ranging from 8 months to 11 years old.

After the Human Subjects Protection Review Board approved the project, a consent form was distributed to the students who had shown an initial interest. This was followed by a written questionnaire that students completed in their free time. Participation in the survey was entirely voluntary.

After the consent forms were received, a total of 125 questionnaires were distributed to the students. One hundred and seventeen (117) questionnaires were returned, 80 of which were selected for the study using the criterion that they were all college CHL learners, namely, they were taking a college Chinese class at the time of the survey or had previously taken one. Among the 80 participants, 59 of them were enrolled in a Chinese class, 19 had previously taken college Chinese classes, and 2 had learned Chinese through summer study-abroad programs.

Data analysis and discussion

This section analyzes the questionnaire data, some interviews, and a number of CHL learners' oral accounts to determine what the CHL learners inherit from three key dimensions of habitus: linguistic, cultural, and social. For each, the findings are presented and followed by a discussion.

Linguistic habitus

Linguistic habitus refers to "a sub-set of the dispositions acquired in the course of learning to speak in particular contexts (the family, the peer group, the school, etc.)" (Bourdieu, 1991, p. 17). Certain linguistic practices and perceptions take place when linguistic habitus interact with such social contexts as language learning and use, language identity, and linguistic competence.

Data analysis

The questionnaire data provides information in two particular contexts. The first context is participant's learning of their first/native (L1) and second (L2) languages. For L1, among 79 responses,[2] 28 reported Mandarin, 28 Cantonese, 12 English, 8 other Chinese dialects (4 Taisanese, 2 Shanghainese, 1 Hakka, and 1 Fukienese), 2 Cantonese and another dialect or English, and 1 Vietnamese. Sixty-seven participants reported their L2. The 12 participants whose L1 is English all reported Mandarin or Cantonese as their L2.

Table 1.   Language choice and use frequency

frequency / audience	always my dialect (%)	mostly my dialect (%)	equal (%)	mostly English (%)	always English (%)	number of respondents
grandparents	80.3	11.3	0	0	8.5	71
mother	23.1	28.2	21.8	19.2	7.7	78
father	22.1	24.7	20.8	16.9	15.6	77
siblings	1.5	6.2	13.8	26.2	52.3	65
friends	1.3	2.5	7.6	32.9	55.7	79

---

[2]   One participant did not respond.

The survey reveals that participants use more Chinese than English when speaking to their grandparents and parents but more English than Chinese when speaking to their siblings and friends. Among the participants, 52.6% had lived with grandparents. With the exception of five participants whose grandparents were still living with them at the time of the survey, the duration of living with grandparents ranged from 3 months to 13 years. Even participants who did not live with grandparents communicated with them in Chinese since the grandparents usually could not speak English. The frequency of speaking Chinese versus English to grandparents/parents as compared to siblings and friends is tabularized in Table 1.

The second particular context is participants' Chinese language education background, be it formal in the classroom or informal parental instruction at home. All but two participants (74.4%) reported having a formal/informal Chinese language education in their childhood or adolescence. The formal/informal break-down is as follows: formal, 50%; informal, 7.7%; and formal and informal combined, 16.7%. In a formal setting, 73% of the participants attended Chinese schools, while 27% learned Chinese in high school, college, or in China/Taiwan. Learning time varies widely, from a summer or a few months to 12 years. In an informal setting, learning time also varies and learning materials differ substantially. The participants learned with children's books, newspapers, and story books, as well as with children's poems, songs, and comic books, Chinese pre-school/elementary school textbooks, and lesson materials prepared by their parents.

Discussion

The linguistic habitus that endures in CHL learners has several characteristics. Firstly, the acquisition and maintenance of CHL occurs in a vertical and reciprocal *intimate* relation between grandparents/parents and their CHL learner grandchildren/children. Secondly, as CHL learners acquired English, the relation between their linguistic habitus and a pertinent social context resulted in their reserving their heritage language for communicating with their grandparents/parents and using English with others. Thirdly, CHL learners' linguistic habitus in using their heritage language reflects regional variations. Lastly, CHL learners' linguistic habitus reveals an unbalanced nature and distinct disparity in their four skills. In short, it reveals their heritage language illiteracy.

The findings demonstrate that parents and grandparents, in particular, both provided CHL learners with their earliest L1 acquisition experiences in daily life and contributed to the maintenance of the language. This key group provided the space in which CHL learners could use, or had to use, their L1. It was in the context of these experiences that the CHL learners acquired linguistic dispositions. Beyond these experiences, their linguistic habitus was further nurtured and cultivated by additional formal and informal CHL learning experiences.

However, the questionnaire data also reveal that the participants often switched to English when interacting with their siblings and Chinese friends. This linguistic practice demonstrates a particular characteristic of CHL learners' linguistic habitus and is explainable by Bourdieu's (1991, p. 12) concept of *structured dispositions*: "The dispositions produced...are also *structured* in the sense that they unavoidably reflect the social conditions within which they were acquired." In their childhood, the CHL learners acquired certain dispositions while learning Chinese. When they began school, they felt that their linguistic disposition those acquired by other schoolmates, or for that matter, when they were lea They also came to realize that Chinese was a language spoken in the family people with similar backgrounds. Tse (1998, p. 52) points out that "...langu important role as one of the most salient ethnic group identifiers... and as a marker used for those social comparisons." Thus, developing the mainstream

English, becomes CHL learners' *desire*, and/or the parents' desire, to construct a new identity with the dominant society (Lemke, 2002). They may continue to use the heritage language, but only minimally in a limited environment, that is, in the home. The case with Student A (中文我只是在家里说的, 跟别人说不好意思。"I only speak Chinese at home. It's embarrassing to speak it with others.") reflects the CHL learner's perception of the heritage language as well as its *intimate* nature or, put another way, heritage "language shyness" (Krashen, 1998, p. 41). The development of this *intimacy* is found within a familiar space, the home. Moreover, the participants' inclination to speak less Chinese with their siblings further reflects the vertical and reciprocal *intimacy* of the heritage language: a language that is vertically transmitted to CHL learners by grandparents and parents and is used principally reciprocally between parents/grandparents and CHL learners.

Another structured disposition in CHL learners shows the regional conditions within which heritage language is acquired. Chinese language has many dialects with even standard Mandarin having accents that vary from region to region. CHL learners acquire certain dispositions while learning to speak their heritage language that is often colored with regional variations. These regional dispositions stay with CHL learners as "a stigmatized variety" (Valdés 2000, p. 386). They are lasting because, according to Bourdieu (1991, p. 13), "they are ingrained in the body in such a way that they endure through the life history of the individual, operating in a way that is pre-conscious and hence not readily amenable to conscious reflection and modification." This characteristic of CHL learners' linguistic habitus is reflected in Student B who failed in his Chinese class. His life-long linguistic habitus, his regional articulatory style, was transposed to his Chinese language class where it persisted.

Finally, heritage language illiteracy is another typical characteristic of CHL learners' linguistic habitus. In the third incident illustrated in the beginning, Student C attempted to make a purchase in Beijing. She remarked, 售货员觉得我很奇怪。我说得这么好，可是连一个中文字都看不懂。我觉得很丢脸。"The salesperson felt that I was weird. [He wondered] how come I could speak fluently, but could not even read a word. I felt very embarrassed." This illiteracy attests to CHL learners' typical imbalanced bilingual capability. However, it was this CHL learner's experience in that social context that awakened her appreciation of her heritage language and encouraged her to learn to write Chinese. We return to this scenario when we discuss social habitus below.

Cultural habitus

The notion of *cultural habitus* refers to a set of dispositions that an individual embodies in a particular cultural system. The cultural habitus has the individual acting and reacting in certain ways when coping with the world and with one another. Cultural practices and perceptions are produced when the cultural habitus relates to particular social contexts such as customs, behavior, etiquette, beliefs and values, life style, and cultural identity.

Data analysis

The data is drawn from the participants' answers to two questions. The first question is whether they consider themselves to represent Chinese culture, American culture, both Chinese and American cultures, or neither. The second question is why they identify with a particular culture.

Three participants did not provide answers to the first question. The other participants' answers vary: While 72.7% of them identified with both Chinese and American cultures, 13% identified with only Chinese culture, 7.8% with only American culture, and 3.9% with neither culture. The fifth group, comprising 2.6%, wrote in detail that they were both Chinese and American as well as neither Chinese nor American.

Among the participants, five did not respond to the second question, but others provided a variety of answers from differing perspectives. In Table 3 the answers are organized according to the five groups, Group 1 Chinese culture, Group 2 American culture, Group 3 both Chinese and American cultures (Both), Group 4 neither Chinese nor American culture (Neither), and Group 5 both cultures and neither culture (Both & Neither).

Table 2.   Reasons for cultural identity

groups	reasons	questionnaire participant
Chinese culture	Chinese ethnic and heritage inheritance	QP3
	Chinese ethnic appearance, personality, habits	QP1, QP5, QP15, QP17, QP24
	Chinese language and entertainment	QP15, QP30, QP44
	Chinese life style	QP15, QP30
	Chinese mindset	QP2, QP12, QP37, QP44
American culture	lack of knowledge of Chinese tradition and customs	QP9, QP43
	lack of speaking competence in a Chinese language	QP48
	substantial difference between self and other Chinese in China	QP52
	way of life, liberal, act American	QP48, QP78, QP79
both Chinese and American cultures	Chinese working etiquette, a focus on academics, language ability, but interested in American cultural things	QP4, QP14, QP22, QP31, QP40
	Chinese customs, culture, values, traits, language, but American liberal mind, action, neighborhood, individual	QP6, QP7, QP8, QP16, QP26, QP27, QP34, QP35, QP36, QP38, QP54, QP55, QP60, QP63, QP69
	knowledge/mix of/experience Chinese and American cultures	QP11, QP39, QP42, QP49, QP64, QP77, QP80
	American education, culture, language, but maintain/identify with Chinese culture	QP13, QP18, QP28, QP29, QP33, QP50, QP68
	celebrate cultural Chinese *and* American events; do things that fit into both cultures	QP21, QP47
	being bilingual, bicultural, and being seen by others as so	QP32, QP45, QP74, QP75
	other • language • live in Chinese family, but live in US • ABC, but socialize with Chinese people • be Chinese American • respect culture while being ignorant of most	QP46 QP56 QP57 QP71 QP76
neither culture	less Chinese than Chinese, less American than Americans	QP58, QP61
both and neither	prefer the more powerful term "Asian American culture"	QP10
	thinking shaped by Chinese and American cultures, but not inherently Chinese or American	QP23

These groups provide a general guide. Some of them can be collapsed and some answers can be placed in more than one group.

Discussion

When CHL learners grew up in a Chinese home integrated in American society, certain cultural traditions and practices evolved into a kind of cultural structure and permeated their bodies and minds. The cultural embodiment became a cultural habitus that automatically guides CHL learners to perform in certain ways. The following discussion centers on two characteristics of CHL learners' cultural habitus: First, CHL learners perceive their own cultural identities very differently. Second, the practices and perceptions generated by CHL learners' cultural habitus may be either complementary or adversarial.

Data from the previous section give us some idea of the diversity of the CHL learners' perceptions of their cultural identity. On the basis of their Chinese ethnic background, Group 1 CHL learners identified themselves as "I am Chinese by blood and the Chinese culture is my heritage" (QP3), "I have a Chinese way of thought—often times I give up what I like in order to do what (is) beneficial or practical" (QP12), and "I look Chinese and my personality is kind of quiet. I do what my parents tell me to do and don't have a fiercely independent spirit." (QP24).

Group 2 CHL learners do not reject Chinese culture completely, but rather feel *more* knowledgeable about American tradition, customs and way of life than about Chinese ones, or they act *more* like Americans than like Chinese. For example, QP43 states, "I consider myself more American than Chinese; I know more about American culture, tradition, and way of life than I know about Chinese," and QP48 states, "I don't speak Chinese language fluently, I am much more liberal than many Asians, and I act mostly American."

Although Group 4 CHL learners identified themselves with "neither" culture, they did not deny their Chinese culture. Rather, they felt they were not as Chinese as Chinese residing in China or Taiwan. But neither were they as American as the Americans born in the US to a non-Chinese family. As QP 58 claims, "I don't believe I represent either the Chinese or American culture because I am still trying to figure out which I am. I feel like I am Chinese because I speak Chinese at home and I have Chinese physical features. Yet, I feel no national ties for China. I feel like I am an American because I am an American citizen. But at the same time, I don't feel American because I was not born in America," and QP61 states that "I am less Chinese than the Chinese, and less American than the Americans."

Group 5 tried to find a better term for the cultural identity they represent. For QP10, the culture he wished to identify is "Chinese-American" that "*incorporate(s)* [italics added] parts from both, but it's much greater than the sum of the two." He explains, "the Chinese-American identity is an identity that is created out of certain historical events. It's in part retaliation against the assumption that Chinese people are foreigners, as well as a contrast to "traditional Chinese cultural values." As QP10 suggests, a Chinese-American cultural habitus may also include historical dispositions.

The majority, those in Group 3, considered themselves to embody both cultures. Their reflections show that the two cultures complement each other in ways of life and thought. Their way of life is Chinese, influenced and nurtured by parents/grandparents and the Chinese community, and yet their way of thought is American, shaped and instilled by American institutions and environments outside the home. Having this kind of cultural habitus embodied in them, they act and respond in certain ways exercising their cultural knowledge according to time and space. For example, QP29 explains,

> I feel that I keep both cultures with me depending on my environment, whether it is a family gathering for holidays or hanging out with friends at school. I still enjoy eating

Chinese food and prefer home cooked Chinese meals over other types of food. I also enjoy cooking Chinese food. However, I use English 95 percent of the time that I speak, which I clearly adopted from living in America."

Similarly, QP73 reports,

I'm diversified. I have an appreciation for what represents each culture, such as the music, life style, and way of thinking. Although I may be more American, I still see myself as a blend of both since there is a large part, the Chinese culture plays in my life.

QP 69 explains in detail,

I consider myself Chinese because 1) I am ethnically Chinese, 2) I can speak at least one dialect of Chinese, 3) I hold fairly conservative values especially associated with Chinese people/culture, 4) I love learning about Chinese language and culture, and 5) I feel most comfortable when I am around Chinese people or in "Chinese" places (temples, Chinatowns, etc.). Although I don't like admitting it, I cannot deny that I am American because 1) my ability to speak Cantonese isn't that good and English is actually the language I speak best, 2) I value certain "American" values like freedom, and 3) I am more in tune with American sensibilities.

These participants' self-reflections on their cultural practices and perceptions are the second characteristic of CHL learners' cultural habitus. In Bourdieu's theory, the habitus orients one's thoughts and actions, and is transposed to and generates practices and perceptions in other fields. Other examples from our findings are that participants described themselves as having Chinese values, customs, working etiquette, language ability, and a focus on academics on the one hand; and on the other, having an interest in American cultural things, a liberal mind, and individualism. In these cases, values from two very different cultures interlock and create an individual who appreciates both cultures and is able to propel her/himself forward in both of them.

However, the practices and perceptions generated by CHL learners' cultural habitus may not be complementary, but adversarial, in certain social contexts. In the CHL field, for example, Chinese people are concerned about maintaining Chinese language and culture and strongly encourage and push their children to learn it. Yet, a great number of young CHL learners resent going to a weekend Chinese school because it reduces their play time. Since CHL learners are influenced by both Chinese and American cultures, CHL learners' cultural practices and perceptions may cause conflicts with parents who usually have a Chinese cultural habitus. A number of the survey participants reported such conflicts in choosing an academic major, planning their future, evaluating their study habits, and purchasing a car.

Finally, not all practices and perceptions generated by the Chinese cultural habitus are celebrated in every cultural environment. For example, Chinese believe teachers are authority figures who should be respected and obeyed. This cultural habitus is inscribed in Chinese children's behavior and often guides their actions. Students with a Chinese family background are generally seen as being quiet and obedient. For example, when a teacher makes a mistake, these students tend not to directly address it in class. This practice places the student at a disadvantage in an American classroom which often consists of a dialogic interaction between teachers and students. This point will be addressed again later from a social perspective.

Social habitus

Social habitus as used here refers to a set of dispositions that one acquires, oriented by an internal cultural habitus, through socialization with family, school, friendship groups, institutions and the mass media. The social habitus automatically disposes one to interact in ways that conform to the norms, values, and culture expected by others. Particular social practices and perceptions are produced when the social habitus interacts with certain social contexts.

Data analysis

The relevant data are the participants' responses to a question about their ethnic friendship. Three of the 80 participants did not answer the question. Among the other 77 respondents, 46.8% reported that most of their friends are ethnic Chinese, 39% reported they have an equal number of ethnic and non-ethnic Chinese friends, and 14.3% reported most of their friends are non-ethnic Chinese. The results indicate that CHL learners relate socially more to ethnic Chinese than to non-ethnic Chinese. The subsequent discussion also draws on participants' reflections on their cultural identity and interview data.

Discussion

Inculcated with a kind of internal cultural disposition, CHL learners have developed a particular social habitus in a social space comprised of a multiplicity of relational social fields. As social agents in a specific social context, the educational field, CHL learners reproduce social practices and perceptions that have been almost pre-determined by their relations with fellow learners and other social agents in the same field. CHL learners' social habitus also has several characteristics. "Like attracts like" is one. The second is the varying degree of using culturally oriented interactive modes. The third is the complicating and paradoxical coexistence of social practices and perceptions.

The survey results show that CHL learners tend to have more friends with a similar cultural habitus, a Chinese cultural habitus, than they have with people with a dissimilar cultural habitus. Thus, the shared cultural factors provide a vital basis for CHL learners' social inclinations. A similar understanding about norms, values and culture among social agents warrants corresponding behaviors.

In interacting with other social agents in a multicultural social space, some CHL learners are very aware of the nuances of the different interactive behavioral patterns between themselves and others. QP11 writes that s/he is "more reserved than Americans." In an interview, a CHL learner contrasts the typical "reserved" Chinese person with the typical "outgoing" American. CHL learners also learn to employ a context-appropriate mode of interacting with others in a multicultural social context. The same CHL learner mentioned above, when asked by the interviewer if he considers himself "reserved" or "outgoing," answered that "[it] depends on the situation. I have to see whom I am interacting with. You got to use an appropriate mode to interact with them." He adds, "I am careful with what I am saying to certain people, too." QP29 also writes, "I feel that I keep both cultures with me depending on my environment, whether it be a family gathering for holidays or hanging out with friends at school."

However, not all CHL learners have reached the same level of understanding on how to employ interactive strategies in different social contexts. We can see this from QP26's comment: "My parents raised me with Chinese values, but I truly do act like an American in the way I speak and interact with other people." Although this CHL learner identifies with both Chinese and American cultures, her dominant interactive mode is American. It is the built-in American cultural habitus that is embedded in her social behavior and shapes her particular social habitus, which in turn determines her natural social actions. The following interview segment with another CHL learner witnesses again the American interactive mode driven by the internal American cultural habitus:

CHL learner:	…高中学了三年的西班牙文，我刚开始的时候讲得很棒！
	"…(I) learned Spanish for three years. My spoken Spanish was great in the beginning!"
Interviewer:	所以你对语言应该有天份？
	"So, then you are talented at languages?"
CHL learner:	对对对。
	" Yes, you are right."

This CHL learner is conversant in Chinese and initiates the topic about his accomplishment in speaking Spanish; he then immediately accepts the interviewer's compliment with a confirmation. This direct mode in discussing one's achievements is characteristic of many CHL learners' social habitus, in contrast to the indirectness that is typical of people who have a Chinese cultural and social habitus.

The third characteristic of CHL learners' social habitus is the complicating and paradoxical coexistence of its dispositions that comes from CHL learners' cultural habitus. In the field of academia, both typical Chinese and American interactive modes paradoxically co-exist. The teacher and classmates are the principal social agents with whom CHL learners interact in a classroom and who may or may not be familiar with the characteristics of CHL learners. With their particular social habitus, CHL learners choose to use one mode or the other or switch from one to another. The paradoxical coexistence of different interactive modes is, for example, seen in QP27's perception of his/her own interactive behavior, "Many of my characteristics are Americanized. …I'm outgoing, I like to raise my hand in class. Yet at the same time, I've adopted many Chinese traits such as being modest…" In a CHL classroom, CHL learners generally relate to the teacher because the teacher is almost always a Chinese person whose characteristics are somewhat familiar. Yet, they do not really know the teacher due to the special social space that they share with the teacher—that of an academic setting in an American institution of higher education. They may feel the teacher knows them based on a common understanding of Chinese culture, but they may also feel the teacher does not really know them because they were born and/or grew up in America. They may keep quiet even when the teacher makes a mistake, and yet they may speak out about the homework load, the amount of class activities, and onerous exams.

Moreover, as discussed in the section on cultural habitus, students with a Chinese family background are generally seen as being quiet. They avoid directly addressing issues and confrontation in an academic setting because of Chinese people's beliefs and values about teachers. This social practice places a student at a disadvantage, for teachers and students are expected to interact in an American classroom. A lack of this dialogic interaction leads to a misunderstanding and misevaluation of these students' achievements.

Finally, the paradoxical coexistence of CHL learners' Chinese and American social dispositions combined with their linguistic and cultural habitus may run counter to the expectations of those with different dispositions and habitus. In such cases, when a CHL learner interacts with others with different expectations, a clash occurs. What CHL individuals often encounter is, for example, described by QP31, "Those in America see me as Chinese, while those in China see me as an American." In America, it is the physical appearance and cultural habitus that separates a Chinese from a non-Chinese, but in China, it can be a linguistic habitus that turns a Chinese into a non-Chinese and hinders social interaction. As one CHL learner said,

> When shopping, it was difficult to get my points across due to a lack of vocabulary, so I would have to resort to English, which of course the person on the other end may not have a particularly good command of, making communication difficult occasionally.

In this situation, the CHL learner's limited vocabulary runs counter to the expectation of her interlocutor in the shopping context, so the interaction is difficult and unpleasant. In another example, the third scenario of Student C's interaction with a salesperson, it was the linguistic habitus of her CHL illiteracy that was responsible for the breakdown of the communication. Both the salesperson's reaction (售货员觉得我很奇怪。 "The salesperson felt that I was weird.") and the expectation that Student C should have been able to respond to the written signs since she could speak well were barriers that prevented her from being a social agent— she became faceless and lost her social identity in that context.

In addition to CHL learners' linguistic habitus, conversations on topics unexpected by CHL learners with their culturally oriented social habitus produce negative effects. A CHL learner interviewee's remark on her encounter with her uncle illustrates this,

> "Um, (…) sometimes they are much more straightforward, but sometimes…, because when I went back to Taiwan, the first thing my uncle said to me is "you gained weight." You never get such thing in America, so I know he is being nice, tries to help me, to get back to a more healthy stage, but I felt really bad when he said that."

In this scenario, expectations clash about discussing one's weight, which is taboo to appraise so straightforwardly in America, but not so among Chinese people. Such a clash of expectations creates a tension that is often difficult to articulate, at least for this CHL learner in this scenario. As a final example, alien interactive patterns may result in clashing expectations. Another CHL learner in his interview describes how being unfamiliar with interactive patterns in Mandarin Chinese led to a misunderstanding over the name of a hotel between a taxi driver and himself in Beijing. When asked how he felt in that incident, he said "scared" and described his fear using a "Fog of War" metaphor.

Conclusion

This study investigates what CHL learners inherit from three dimensions of *habitus*: linguistic, cultural, and social. The characteristics of each dimension are

Linguistic habitus

- The acquisition and maintenance of CHL occurs in a vertical and reciprocal *intimate* relation between grandparents/parents and their CHL learner descendants.
- As CHL learners acquire English, the relation between their linguistic habitus and their social context restricts their use of the heritage language for communication with their grandparents/parents, while using English with everyone else.
- CHL learners' articulatory style reflects regional variations.
- Heritage language illiteracy attests to their asymmetrical bilingual capabilities.

Cultural habitus

- CHL learners have diverse perception attitudes toward their own cultural identities.

- The practices and perceptions that CHL learners' cultural habitus generates may be either complementary or adversarial.

Social habitus

- "Like attracts like."
- CHL learners use varying (i.e., Chinese and American) culturally oriented modes in social interactions.
- Chinese and American social dispositions paradoxically coexist.

References

Bourdieu, P. (1991). *Language and symbolic power* [Translation of *Ce que parlerv veut dire*, G. Raymond & M. Adamson, Trans., J. B. Thompson, Ed.]. Cambridge, MA: Harvard University Press.

He, A. W. (2005). *Language of the heart*. Paper presented at the Chinese heritage language panel, ACTFL, Baltimore, MD.

Kramsch, C. (1993). *Context and Culture in Language Teaching*. Oxford, England: Oxford University Press.

Krashen, S. D. (1998). Language shyness and heritage language development. In S. Krashen, L. Tse, & J. Mcquillan (Eds.), *Heritage language development* (pp. 41–49). Culver City, CA: Language Education Associates.

Lemke, J. L. (2002). Language development and identity: Multiple timescales in the social ecology of learning. In C. Kramsch (Ed.), *Language acquisition and language socialization* (pp. 68–87). New York: Continuuum.

Tse, L. (1998). Affecting affect: The impact of heritage language programs on student attitudes. In S. Krashen, L. Tse, & J. Mcquillan (Eds.), *Heritage language development* (pp. 51–72). Culver City, CA: Language Education Associates.

Valdés, G. (2000). The teaching of heritage languages: An introduction for Slavic-teaching professionals. In O. Kagan & B. Rifkin (Eds.), *The learning and teaching of Slavic languages* (pp. 375–403). Bloomington, IN: Slavica Publishers.

Appendix: Student questionnaire

Part I: General info

1. school _____

2. your major _____

3. year of study _____

4. intended future profession _____

5. the highest level of your Chinese course _____

6. your age _____

Part II: Family background

1. Where were you born? _____

2. If you were not born in the US, how old were you when you came to the US? _____

3. You were born and raised in a home in which was spoken? Please check below.

   ☐ Mandarin   ☐ Cantonese   ☐ other (specify) _____

4. Where were your parents born?

   father _____ mother _____

5. If they were not born in the US, how old were they when they came to the US?

   father _____ mother _____

6. Have you ever lived with your grandparents? ☐ yes ☐ no

   If "yes," at what age and for how long? _____

7. How many siblings do you have?

   elder brother(s) _____ elder sister(s) _____ younger brother(s) _____ younger sister(s) _____

Part III. Chinese language background

1. What is your first/native language/dialect? Please check below.

   ☐ Mandarin   ☐ Cantonese   ☐ Taiwanese   ☐ other (specify) _____

2. What is your second language/dialect? _____

3. Please indicate languages you have also learned other than #1 and #2.

   kindergarten _____ elementary school _____

   high school _____ college _____

4. Circle/highlight how often you use Chinese and English when you speak to the following people[3]:

father	always English	mostly English	equal	mostly Chinese	always Chinese	na
mother	always English	mostly English	equal	mostly Chinese	always Chinese	na
siblings	always English	mostly English	equal	mostly Chinese	always Chinese	na
grandparents	always English	mostly English	equal	mostly Chinese	always Chinese	na
Chinese friends	Always English	mostly English	equal	mostly Chinese	always Chinese	na

5. If you were born in a Chinese-speaking country and your first language was Chinese, did you receive any formal education in that country?   ☐ yes   ☐ no ☐ na

If "yes," the highest grade you completed: _____

6. Did your parents teach you how to read and write in Chinese?   ☐ yes   ☐ no

   6–1. If "Yes," since what age? _____

   6–2. For how long? _____

   6–3. What kind of things did you read? _____

7. Have you taken any formal Chinese classes before college/university?   ☐ yes ☐ no

   7–1. If "yes," where? _____

   7–2. For how long?_____

   7–3. What dialect(s) have you learned? (Mandarin, Cantonese, etc.) _____

Part IV: Cultural aspects

1. Do you consider yourself representing

   ☐ Chinese culture

   ☐ American culture

   ☐ both Chinese and American cultures

   ☐ neither Chinese nor American cultures

2. What makes you think you represent the selected culture(s)?

_____

_____

_____

---

[3]   This question is adapted from the "Students' Proficiency and Need-Analysis Questionnaire by UCSD Heritage Language Program" (UCSD, 2007).

4

The Chinese Heritage Language Learners' Existing Linguistic Knowledge and Abilities

Jason D. Hendryx
University of Washington

Chinese heritage language (hereafter CHL) learners have a tremendous range of linguistic knowledge and abilities when they begin studying Chinese at the college or university level. Accessing that knowledge and building onto it in an efficient and meaningful manner is a primary concern of all CHL instructors. This chapter presents CHL learner profiles based on observations from several years of classroom interactions, interviews with CHL learners, and a survey of a recent Chinese heritage language class. It is hoped that this, along with suggestions for describing CHL learner knowledge as sprouting instead of gap-filled or skewed, will enable CHL instructors to reexamine their own understandings of their students' existing knowledge and develop appropriate methods to best engage that knowledge.

In this chapter the importance of CHL learners' existing linguistic knowledge and abilities as a starting point for instruction will be shown; a new, more constructive and approachable metaphor for viewing these students' knowledge will be presented; and suggestions for best accessing this knowledge will be provided.

Attempting to better understand and access the existing linguistic knowledge and ability of CHL students as they enter the college foreign language classroom is a primary concern of all Chinese language instructors. Achieving maximum alignment between what these learners already know and what they are about to learn can serve to validate these learners' existing knowledge, provide the proper curriculum and motivation to help them improve upon their current abilities, and remove or greatly reduce much of the potential redundancy some of these CHL learners may experience during language instruction (Liu, 2006). Furthermore, a solid understanding of existing learner knowledge and abilities can also help lead to establishing the rapport, structure, engagement, and interaction needed for teaching effectiveness (Wulff, 2005). By knowing where CHL learners are in terms of their own Chinese language development, and effectively engaging learners at those levels, instructors can simultaneously support existing language while promoting new language growth.

To be sure, CHL learners operate in rather unique learning spaces. This is because of the many different types and periods of contact they have had with the language before entering the

Hendryx, J. (2008). The Chinese heritage language learners' existing linguistic knowledge and abilities. In A. W. He, & Y. Xiao (Eds.), *Chinese as a heritage language: Fostering rooted world citizenry* (pp. 53–66). Honolulu: University of Hawai'i, National Foreign Language Resource Center.

college classroom. Therefore, to reach those spaces where heritage learners function most effectively, methods of instruction need to be adapted accordingly.

Imagine, if you will, a stream with banks on either side. There are several large stones in the stream that form a path across it. On one side of the stream are native speakers of Chinese, on the other side there are native speakers of different languages. CHL learners are those who are standing on one of the stones in the stream attempting to cross to the Chinese speaking side; some standing closer to the far bank where Chinese is the native language than others. So how can we best reach out to these learners and support their language development?

Beginning with what the learner knows has always been a fundamental educational concept. Everson (1996), in an article on exploiting background knowledge for developing Chinese reading materials, cites theorist David Ausubel (Ausubel, Novak, & Hanesian, 1978) who stated that, "The most important single factor influencing learning is what the learner already knows. Ascertain this and teach him accordingly" (p. 94). More recently, Zull (2002), in an examination into the biology of brain functions and what that means for teaching and learning states,

> We must let our students use the neuronal networks they already have. We cannot create new ones out of thin air or by putting them on a blackboard. And we cannot excise old ones. The only recourse we have is to begin with what the learner brings. (p.105)

Gambhir (2001) adds to these understandings nicely and situates them in the context of heritage language learners by remarking,

> Heritage language learners not only speak many different languages, but they also represent many dialects and nationalities. They may be immigrants or children of immigrants. They may come from well-established families or from families struggling to enter the social and economic mainstream. It is common to find a wide range of language levels, educational backgrounds, and cognitive abilities in a class of heritage language learners. Heterogeneity is generally the norm in these classes. As a result, the advice most often heard in regard to teaching heritage language students is to "start where the student is and move forward"… (p. 237)

Of course the marked heterogeneity in linguistic knowledge and abilities of the students in these classes can potentially make that a very difficult proposition. To address this issue, some Chinese language programs have started offering multiple heritage language tracks that separate CHL learners with speaking and writing skills from those with just speaking skills (see Duff & Li, 2004).

Based on these observations it would seem prudent to suggest that CHL instructors can help bring a sense of order to their classes by becoming more familiar with what their students bring with them linguistically to the classroom. Instead of seeing themselves as transmitters of knowledge, perhaps it would be more appropriate if instructors envisioned themselves as being guides to offer assistance when needed. Also, maintaining a certain amount of flexibility in their instructional methodologies and being willing to envision alternative approaches in how they go about accessing and building on student knowledge would be advisable (Schinke-Llano, 1995). It is only with instructional imagination and a willingness to operate outside more traditional approaches that Chinese language instructors who work with CHL students will be able to respond to critics who claim they employ "…outmoded, impractical methods" (Mair, 2006, p. 9).

As mentioned previously, one way to respond to critics and better serve heritage learners is to better understand the existing linguistic knowledge and abilities of the heritage learners who come to class. To that end, several types of CHL learners commonly found in Chinese language classes will be presented here. Each learner type was constructed from a collage of actual learners encountered in CHL classrooms over a 3-year period. In many ways, this approach to data collection was guided by Mercado's (2000) observation of how teachers have been attempting to identify heritage language learners' linguistic knowledge and abilities. He states,

> Because the knowledge students have about their heritage language is variable and may differ considerably from norms of standard usage…teachers are examining how students' oral and written productions conceal (or reveal) what students know and what they have yet to learn. (p. 227)

It should be remembered that while the CHL learners about to be presented are representative of actual learners found in the Chinese language classroom, there are certainly many types of CHL learner that will not be identified in this chapter. The importance of presenting learner types here is not so much in attempting to capture and describe every possible kind of CHL learner that may be found in the classroom and his or her knowledge and abilities with the language, but in providing general profiles for CHL instructors to reflect on and then relate to their own CHL learners, what they might know about the language, and how to best gain access to that knowledge.

Overview of CHL learner types

Chinese Heritage Language (CHL) learners come to Chinese language classes at the college and university level in North America with a tremendous range of existing linguistic knowledge and abilities related to the Chinese language. Students in these classes may have been born in North America, are the children or grandchildren of immigrants, or are immigrants themselves. They or their families will have come from places like China, Indonesia, Hong Kong, Singapore, Taiwan, or Vietnam, to name just a few. These learners may speak one or multiple dialects of Chinese at home or in their communities, and they may even consider Chinese to be just one of their heritage languages.

At one end of the linguistic knowledge and ability spectrum of these students are those who have very little command of Chinese, knowing only a few rudimentary words or phrases. These students may be able to recognize the Chinese character that represents their family name, but they cannot pronounce or write that character if asked. These students "…are likely to have some fuzzy notions and intuitions about the language" (Gambhir, 2001, p. 214). This is not to say that these students do not possess a great deal of cultural background knowledge that would aid them in mastering the language more quickly and completely. For example, if they were studying a chapter on Chinese holidays or customs, the CHL learner may be able to connect the content of the chapter with real life events she or he had experienced.

Moving a little farther along the spectrum, there are students who have a smattering of speaking and listening skills. Gambhir (2001) identifies these students in the following way:

> Often, they can get a general sense of what is being said, but they have limited speaking competence, indicating that their parents and others often spoke to them at home in the native language but that they responded in English. Typically they have little or no ability to read and write the language. (p. 214)

This group of students in turn can often be confused with students found further along the spectrum. These more advanced students, while still possessing only marginal reading and writing abilities if any at all, have fairly developed speaking and listening skills. However, because they have such mastery over the "conventions for short answers," it is often difficult to determine with any accuracy how much they really know about the language (Moag, 1995, p. 177).

The next group of students on the spectrum are those who are fluent or nearly fluent in a dialect of Chinese but have little knowledge of spoken Mandarin. The most common dialects one encounters in the Chinese heritage classroom is some form of Cantonese or Taiwanese (McGinnis, 1996). While Taiwanese speakers usually have some command of spoken Mandarin, Cantonese speakers typically do not. These learners are usually able to read and write in Chinese fairly well but lack even the most basic Mandarin speaking and listening skills.

At the far end of the spectrum are the students who have a solid command of speaking, listening, reading, and writing skills. These students typically have spent more time with the language in a formal or semi-formal setting before beginning studying it at college or university. This means that they either left their native country at an older age, return to a region where their heritage language is spoken on a regular basis, or have spent considerable time and effort in after-school Chinese language programs or with Chinese language tutors. These students can produce very detailed, highly personalized, standardized language.

Individual learner profiles

The following learner profiles are composites of many learners encountered across several years of 1st-year Chinese language instruction at the university level. The profiles were constructed from informal observations of CHL learners in four classes (two summer classes and two year-long classes) of approximately 20 students each from 2000 to 2002 at a large public university. These observations focused on students' uses of linguistic features that fell well outside of what had been taught or covered in the classroom. When several students were observed engaging in similar uses of language that had not yet been covered or introduced in class, these language events were collapsed into a single profile. Additional data for these profiles were drawn from interviews with three CHL learners conducted for a separate study on language use in 2005, and a survey of a CHL class collected in the summer of 2006 ($N=16$). Further data concerning these students were gathered through informal conversions that occurred on campus over the years as students would mention in passing their future plans and aspirations. All student names are fictional.

Nancy. Nancy was born in Hong Kong and then moved to America with her parents when she was 4 years old. She heard Cantonese spoken in her home her entire life, however she was never formally taught any Chinese at any time before she entered college. At 18, she felt it was important to better understand her own culture so she decided to start taking Mandarin Chinese at college (Cantonese not being offered at the college she was attending).

While she was fairly functional in Cantonese, she only knew a few phrases of Mandarin. At different periods during her childhood, her parents gave her Chinese character books to practice writing Chinese. She also watched a lot of Chinese television programs when she was a teenager. When she entered college she could write from memory approximately 100 Chinese characters, including her name. One time in class at college she asked if *qing* (to invite) meant *qin* (to kiss) because they sounded the same to her and seemed to have a similar origin. While *qing* was vocabulary covered in the class up to that point, *qin* had not yet been discussed. Although Nancy had a noticeable Southern Chinese accent when she spoke Mandarin, her speech was very clear and intelligible.

Nancy had to work two jobs to help pay for her own tuition and had little time to work with her classmates on class projects outside of class. She finished 2 years of Chinese language instruction at college. After graduation she went to work for the U.S. government. She no longer uses the Chinese she learned in college, but she hopes to brush up on her Chinese language skills in order to pass a language proficiency test that would entitle her to a small raise in salary.

Mark. Mark was born in Taiwan and came to America with his parents when he was 6 years old. After coming to America he attended after-school Chinese classes sponsored by a local church for several years (see also Wong, 1988). One time in Chinese class at the university during a skit, he corrected his classmate on the tone of *bao* (to explode) for *luntai bao le* (a flat tire). How to say a flat tire had not been introduced at any point during the Chinese classes up to that point.

Mark took 2 years of Chinese at college. After graduation he went into business. He only uses Chinese now with family, friends, and acquaintances from church.

Steve. Steve was born in Indonesia to Chinese parents. He came to America with his parents when he was 8 years old. In addition to English and Chinese, he also speaks Indonesian. He has advanced Chinese speaking and listening skills and can read many characters but has a difficult time writing. One time in class he heard the Chinese word *men* (stuffy) and immediately asked if that was the same word for *men* (boring). Steve had a very interesting pronunciation of Mandarin that was altogether different from other Chinese heritage learners who came from Hong Kong, China, and Taiwan.

Steve only studied Chinese for 1 year. After graduation he returned to Indonesia and started a business. He only uses his Chinese now occasionally with his friends and sometimes with a few of his employees.

Lucy. Lucy was born in mainland China. She came to America with her parents when she was 5 years old. She attended Chinese language programs offered on weekends up through high school and developed fairly functional speaking and writing skills. In high school she took Chinese as part of an after-school program for 2 years. Her parents would also often quiz her on character recognition and writing. She returns to China every summer for at least 1 month. One day in class at college she showed her classmates one of her tattoos. She knew the Chinese name for the tattoo she showed to the class (i.e., a bird), although that was vocabulary that had never been covered.

Lucy was very precise and accurate in her Chinese language production. She took Chinese for 2 years at the university. She then entered medical school. She is now studying to be a doctor.

Henry. Henry was born in America. Both his parents grew up in Taiwan. He heard Mandarin and Taiwanese spoken at home his entire life. While he had only marginal skills with Taiwanese, his spoken Mandarin was very advanced. He knew several uses of the grammatical function word *le* before starting Chinese language instruction at the university. However, he had almost no reading or writing abilities. As a child his parents sent him to a Chinese school that offered classes on weekends for a brief period but he did not like it because of the rigid style of instruction so he stopped attending, claiming it was boring (Liu, 2006). Henry took 3 years of Chinese instruction at college. He retained a noticeable Taiwanese accent throughout his studies. He often said *zanglang* instead of *zhanglang* for cockroaches. He justified his pronunciation and the understanding he assigned to the word because he knew *zang* meant dirty and it seemed only logical to him that dirty should be applied to cockroaches. Dirty and cockroaches had never been introduced in class when he first started using the terms.

After graduation Henry went to work for a large engineering firm. He has returned to Taiwan several times since graduation, and speaks Chinese with relatives and friends. He does not use his Chinese for his current job and is saddened by how quickly the advances he made with the language while in college were so quickly lost after he finished school.

Tom. Tom was born in America. His parents are from Hong Kong. As a child he learned to speak Cantonese from his parents. When he was a little older, his parents hired a tutor to teach him Mandarin. He also attended an after-hour Chinese language program during high school. In college, Tom had solid language skills. Once in class, he asked about *Leishen* (the God of thunder) and where more information about this Chinese deity could be found.

Tom took 2 years of Chinese at the university. He then focused his attention on meeting the requirements for entering law school. Tom is now in law school and plans to be a lawyer.

Looking across these learner types we find proficient speakers (i.e., Steve, Mark, Henry, Tom, Lucy), those that have some command of reading and writing (i.e., Nancy), but only a few with what could be considered a complete package of language skills (i.e., Lucy, Tom) when they came to the college language classroom (see Table 1). These learner types do, however, all share similar motivations for studying Chinese.

Table 1.   Learner profiles

name	Nancy	Mark	Steve	Lucy	Henry	Tom
born	Hong Kong	Taiwan	Indonesia	China	USA	USA
home language	Cantonese	Mandarin	Mandarin	Mandarin	Mandarin/ Taiwanese	Cantonese
listening	fair	good	good	good	good	good
speaking	fair	superior	good	superior	superior	good
reading	fair	good	fair	good	fair	good
writing	poor	fair	poor	good	poor	good
career	government	business	business	medicine	engineering	law
language observed	verbal usage	verbal usage	vocabulary	vocabulary	vocabulary/ grammar	cultural marker

Motivation

The primary motivation for all these learners to take Chinese at the college level was to learn more about Chinese language and culture and be able to communicate with relatives and friends more easily. This would mean in Gardner and Lambert's (1972) model that they had a primarily *integrative motivation* for studying Chinese, meaning they wanted to improve on their ability to participate in Chinese culture. They lacked any sense of what Gardner and Lambert have called *instrumental motivation*, or desiring to enhance their language skills to realize professional goals. All of them, including Nancy, thought Chinese classes would be a "snap course" and not take too much time away from their studies in business, science, medicine, engineering, and law (Moag, 1995, Walton, 1996, Wen, 1999).

A future study worth conducting would be to investigate how Chinese instructors might address the initial integrative motivation that students bring with them to the classroom and then try and infuse it with instrumental motivation. Perhaps exposing students to potential careers that rely on strong Chinese language skills and offering classes that teach the fundamentals of translation and interpretation would be good places to start.

Learning about CHL learners

All CHL learners have a unique story to tell. And they will share these stories if someone has the time and patience to listen. Instructors can easily acquire student artifacts if they show even the remotest interest. The Chinese textbooks CHL learners used previously, the calligraphy they have created, and essays they might have written in Chinese are all there for the asking.

Instructors must be cautious with how the information they gather is used however. Because of the serious penalties that some colleges and universities have in place for heritage learners found to possess language skills that are considered too advanced for the language courses they might be taking (i.e., loss of all language related credits and grades), some heritage learners may try and conceal parts of what they might know about the language. Also, some students may provide instructors with long lists of information that they covered when they were young but have long since forgotten. Therefore, while gathering information about one's CHL learners is an important and necessary step, the information that is collected must be used wisely, in a manner that serves to both reacquaint and expand on learner knowledge.

Institutional and instructional hurdles

The instructional challenge of dealing with a group of learners who have greatly differing knowledge and abilities as CHL learners usually do can be in a large part be linked to how schools have traditionally functioned.

> Schools...typically...process students in batches, treating them as if each were the prototypical normal student for whom they constructed the curriculum. Being part of such a batch naturally constrains the student to behave, as best he can, as though he were prototypical...(Becker, 1972, p. 88)

Unfortunately, or fortunately depending on your view, CHL instructors will probably never be in a position to describe and predict with absolute accuracy what a "normal" CHL learner's language knowledge and abilities will be like when they enter a university or college level program despite claims of assessment tools to the contrary. But such descriptions and predictions are not necessary for CHL instructors to be successful. If CHL instructors educate themselves as to how to best access the various kinds of knowledge that their students do come to the classroom with they can have great success (Mercado, 2000). In fact, all instructors, regardless of the subject they teach, have no way of knowing exactly what knowledge of the subject their students have when they begin their courses.

Recent developments such as advance placement exams and proficiency guidelines for Chinese would seem to offer some assistance to CHL instructors in not only determining what their students know when they come to the classroom but also what their students should strive to achieve with the language. However, I would argue that such exams and guidelines do not in fact take any pressure off actual classroom practice, as they are primarily concerned with access (who gets into what class) and impact (what does an assessment tool suggest a student can do with the language). These tools totally ignore the opportunities and responsibilities that CHL instructors must provide and foster in their classrooms if their students are to be truly successful with the language. Therefore, these developments can be seen largely as instructional measures that only capture what a CHL learner knows before and after learning Chinese at the college level.

One way to truly help CHL students succeed in the classroom will be to create a powerful new metaphor for framing the CHL learner's existing knowledge. Such a metaphor is needed to replace existing metaphors that may be preventing language teachers from envisioning more productive instructional models. It has recently been stated that heritage learners' knowledge of language is like "Swiss cheese" (Sweley, 2006, p. 22). Perhaps this is because the learners' linguistic knowledge has been interpreted as having many holes in it, or areas that are missing or underdeveloped. This description is certainly a very vivid one (I myself have described CHL learners' knowledge this way in an informal talk with Chinese language teaching assistants in 2001), and works well for certain understandings of language learning and instruction (i.e., noticing the gap; Cross, 2002).

Such an interpretation can also find purchase with previously forwarded views of heritage learners being seen as operating with skewed bilingualism, passive bilingualism, and semi-native language skills. This orientation also operates well if the learner is seen as having experienced atrophied acquisition, and is functioning with significant gaps in basic knowledge (Moag, 1995) However, in the final analysis such a framing of learners' knowledge is still affixing a deficit model onto the language learners and what they know.

There are many reasons for interpreting the heritage learners' language as deficient and incomplete from an instructional standpoint. The first and most important of these reasons I believe is that instructors need to distance themselves from their own relative ignorance in knowing how to best approach and instruct students with broadly differing abilities effectively as a group. As a result, it could be suggested that instructors have projected their own instructional deficiencies onto the heritage learner.

Another important reason for handicapping what the heritage learner knows is to create access to assessable outcomes. Instructors "… wish to demonstrate to themselves and others that their work produces results" (Becker, 1972, p. 89). Of course, this is difficult to achieve if the learner comes to the classroom with an existing knowledge of the language that sometimes operates in support, and sometimes operates against, the curriculum being used in very legitimate ways (i.e., knowledge of exceptions to certain rules). This means that some abilities with the language that CHL learners use will be acceptable to the instructor, while other language abilities may not. However, these language abilities deemed unacceptable by the instructor, may be accepted, and even understood as the norm, outside the classroom (i.e., many types of colloquial or localized speech).

The final justification for limiting the amount and type of knowledge accredited to the heritage learner can probably be linked to issues of power.

> Teachers assume that the student is as inferior in knowledge as he usually is in age…They assume that what they know, they student needs to know. They may want to take his opinions into account, but they do not propose to let him decide which portions of the curriculum he will learn. They insist on having the upper hand in the relationship, searching for ways to augment and solidify control when it is disputed… (Becker, 1972, p. 89)

More recently, McGinnis (1999) urged Chinese teachers to not see the types of students they now find in their language classrooms as a challenge to their authority. However, this can be difficult, especially when instructors can never be completely sure what a heritage learner might say or respond to in the classroom. Many might think it a prudent course to maintain more traditional teacher and learner roles. Indeed, as Shulman (2000, p. 133) noted, "As long as you are the one doing the talking, 85 percent of the time you know what is going to be said. When you start inviting students to speak, the complexity rises and the unpredictability increases." However, this is exactly what is needed for student achievement and it brings us, "face to face with one of the teacher's greatest challenges—the necessity of giving control to the learners" (Zull, 2002, p. 178).

This is not to say that CHL instructors are doing anything but an outstanding job in their classrooms or that heritage learners come to these classrooms with nothing to learn. Heritage languages are very complex constructs that span across social, cultural, political, religious, linguistic, and historical domains. Parents of heritage learners oftentimes pressure their children and their children's teachers to embrace linguistic realities that they associate with their own linguistic identities. However, these linguistic realities may have already disappeared or evolved. Governments too, in their quest to see heritage languages as national "resources," only identify with styles and types of language that best serve their own needs and interests. I would argue that neither of these outside forces truly reach all the way down to the heritage learner and foster genuine support. Instead, these outside pressures make it very tempting for heritage language instructors to disregard and pull up the knowledge and abilities that heritage learners bring with them and replace that knowledge with what parents and governments would find more recognizable. For whatever reason, by framing the heritage learner's knowledge as inherently flawed (i.e., filled with holes and gaps, not being what parents and governments place value on), instructors do themselves and their heritage learners a great disservice.

To avoid placing the CHL learner within such a deficit frame and based on the learner profiles presented earlier, I suggest that instead of "Swiss cheese" we envision CHL learners' linguistic knowledge as complete, functional (for the learner at least), living systems that are at various stages of development. It could be argued that CHL learners in many instances lack the ability to make fine distinctions with the language. I would instead view such instances as revealing that learners have simply not yet developed the performance aspect of those skills with the language or are drawing on different sets of more readily available skills that have functioned for them in some capacity in similar types of situations in the past.

Therefore, instead of Swiss cheese, I would suggest first an adapted interpretation of Morgan's (1998) "iceberg analogy," with what is visible being the heritage learner's performance and what is under the surface being the heritage learner's competence as a nice place to start. That being said, an even more powerful orientation can be drawn on. This is to see CHL learners' linguistic knowledge and abilities as sprouts or seedlings. There are compelling knowledge-based, instructional, pedagogical, philosophical, and even brain-based reasons for making such a comparison that cannot be ignored.

The first of these is that the knowledge the heritage learner does have is well-rooted, as Gambhir (2001) states,

> Heritage language learners have acquired some of the aspects of a communicative system that are often difficult to impart in the formal setting of a classroom. Well-rooted in the home language and culture, most heritage language learners have the potential to achieve native proficiency. (p. 213)

These roots extend out into various locations as Gambhir (2001) further remarks,

> Many heritage language speakers bring…a firsthand knowledge of the language and its social uses. Linguistically, these learners bring with them knowledge of the phonology, lexicon, and syntax that varies in interesting ways from the way the language is spoken in the home country. On the communicative level, they often have a native-like, though limited, appreciation for intonation and for linguistic collocations that defy a straightforward connection between word and meaning. They are often quick to understand humor and sarcasm. (p. 213)

It would seem then that it is possible, even advantageous, to see our heritage learners as seedlings, with well-rooted, developmentally varied elements of linguistic knowledge.

What does this mean in terms of an instructional approach? Hammerly (1982) offers us some insights in this regard: "Good language teachers, like good farmers, have always been interested in the development of a better plant with better yield" (p. 640). Accepting Hammerly's view that good language teachers are interested in developing a better plant, meaning creating more effective teaching strategies that do more for their learners, instructors can envision their students as requiring proper tending, rather than as having holes or gaps in their knowledge that need to be filled. Additional support for embracing such an instructional approach can be found in Brown (2000), who presents an entire ecological language acquisition system (pp. 294–296), Fox's (1983) "growing theory" for teaching, and Liu's (2003) "seed germination" method.

Of course, instructionally here we are not necessarily talking about immediately imposing purely native-like language outcomes on CHL learners. It would seem there is now a critical mass of Chinese language materials (e.g., newspapers, television programs, Internet pages) generated in North America, about North America, that could be drawn on for instructional purposes that would more accurately address the needs and identities of our heritage learners (Zhou & Cai, 2002). Indeed, the Chinese idiom, *ju hua wei zhi* (a tangerine becomes a trifoliate orange), while fitting into the seedling theme presented here, also can be used to describe the linguistic situation of Chinese heritage learners. They are not entirely native speakers because of environmental factors (i.e., where they live). Therefore, they are something else.

CHL learners have access to a different kind of language environment and lifestyle (see Kagan, 2005, p. 219). This is not to say that North America has its own Chinese dialect, but CHL learners in North America have different needs and goals with Chinese language than their Chinese counterparts living elsewhere and those differences should be recognized during instruction.

To make this distinction more clear let us turn to Chinese restaurants in North America. Chinese food in these restaurants is in most cases very much different from the actual food one would find in China. The availability and prices of vegetables, spices, and equipment in North America gives the food a different composition and taste than Chinese food made in China. However, this food is still without a doubt Chinese food. Put back in terms of CHL instruction, I have had several conversations with native Chinese language instructors in North America who remark that their children, CHL learners themselves, have good Chinese language skills, but not good enough skills so as to function flawlessly in China or Taiwan. So in terms of instruction we should remember that we cannot impose native speaker standards on CHL learners from the outset or we are only setting them up to fail.

The next part of seeing Chinese heritage learners as seedlings involves pedagogy. Shulman (2000) provides an excellent account of how he understands pedagogy that fits in very nicely with a seedling or sprout interpretation.

> Understanding begins with what is already inside the learner's head. All students come to us with prior ideas, and our first pedagogical challenge is to bring what is inside, out…In a simple, yet deep sense, that is the essence of pedagogy: putting the inside out, working on it together while it is out, then putting the inside back in. Why is that so complicated? One reason is that it is not easy to discover how to put the inside out. You are not sure you have got it all, and of course you never do; it comes out in different representations and different forms, and you must always make inferences about it. You then want to help students take this reformed, transformed stuff and make it internally their own again in ways that will not leave those ideas inert. (p. 133)

Of course, finding out what the student knows and determining how much to pull out is the tricky part. In this regard we can turn to Mencius (372–289 BCE), the second most important philosopher in the Confucian tradition, who remarked,

> There are few in the world who can resist the urge to help their seedlings grow. There are some who leave the seedlings unattended, thinking that nothing they can do will be of any use. They are the people who do not even bother to weed. There are others who help the seedlings grow. They are the people who pull at them. Not only do they fail to help them but they do the plants positive harm. (Lau, 2003, p. 33)

Zull (2002), too, noticed a tangle of would-be weeds, not in the fields, but in the neural networks of our students' minds:

> These networks are a true tangle, some with branches hanging off one side or the other, some drooping bedraggled on the ground, some sticking bare and brave into the sky, some with weak connections to others, some with strong connections to others. We see this in our experience with students as we come to know about their needs, their misunderstandings, their partial ideas, and their talents and skills. Our inclination is to straighten out the tangle. We want to correct what we find to be in error, trim up the loose ends, prune out the useless branches, and construct new ones that will be of more value. It's simple! We will just explain what is right and what is wrong, and that will be that! We cling tightly to this illusion…But we know that this doesn't work. It's not possible to get in and fix things. (pp. 104–105)

So instead of attempting to "pull up" their students' Chinese language, what can CHL instructors do to best access their students' knowledge?

Some suggestions include emphasizing what students do know and making materials as interesting and entertaining as possible (Moag, 1995; Zull, 2002). This would help bring alternative understandings, possibilities, and emotions to what may have previously been very rigid and dominating language contexts. Other suggestions include beginning with what is concrete or established, provide specific examples, expect and respect student confusion and developing theories, and treasure the knowledge that students do bring with them as a precious resource to tell you where to begin (Zull). From the learner profiles presented in this chapter, this would mean being proactive in creating instructional spaces that include and promote more varied language that would then become part of the curriculum as the learners themselves gradually exercise more control over their learning. It is also possible for learners in heritage classrooms to effectively learn from one another, especially if instructors promote an environment that allows for Vygotsky's Zone of Proximal Development to be employed (Schinke-Llano, 1995). Finally, instructors must recognize that heritage learners have both heritage and non-heritage needs that should be addressed if instruction is to be truly effective (Lee, 2005).

Conclusion

The existing linguistic knowledge and abilities of CHL learners when they begin Chinese classes at college or university vary tremendously. While this chapter touched on some general CHL learner types, and offered an alternative way for instructors to interpret the knowledge these learners have, there is certainly much more that can and should be added to the conversation. Future advances in this area should strive to develop richer and more detailed interpretational models that guide how CHL learners' existing knowledge should be framed for instructional purposes.

Acknowledgments

I would like to thank Professors Agnes Weiyun He, Yun Xiao, Zev Handel, and De Zhang for providing valuable suggestions and comments on earlier versions of this chapter.

References

Ausubel, D. P., Novak, J. D., & Hanesian, H. (1978). *Educational psychology: A cognitive view* (2nd ed.). New York: Holt, Rinehart, and Winston.

Becker, H. S. (1972). School is a lousy place to learn anything in. *The American Behavioral Scientist, 16*(1), 85–105.

Brown, H. D. (2000). *Principles of language learning and teaching* (4th ed.). New York: Longman.

Cross, J. (2002). "'Noticing" in SLA: Is it a valid concept. *TESL-EJ, 6*(3), 1–9.

Duff, P. A., & Li D.-d. (2004). Issues in Mandarin language instruction: Theory, research, and practice. *System, 32*, 443–456.

Everson, M. E. (1996). Exploiting background knowledge in the development of Chinese pedagogical reading material. In S. McGinnis (Ed.), *Chinese pedagogy: An emerging field* (pp. 93–105) (Chinese Language Teachers Association Monograph No. 2). Columbus, OH: Foreign Language Publications.

Fox, D. (1983). Personal theories of teaching. *Studies in Higher Education, 8*(2), 151–163.

Gambhir, S. (2001). Truly less commonly taught languages and heritage language learners in the United States. In J. K. Peyton, D. A. Ranard, & S. McGinnis (Eds.), *Heritage languages in America: Preserving a national resource* (pp. 207–228). McHenry, IL: CAL.

Gardner, R., & Lambert, W. (1972). *Attitudes and motivation in second language learning.* Rowley, MA: Newbury.

Hammerly, H. (1986). *Synthesis in language teaching: An introduction to linguistics.* Blaine, WA: Second Language Publications.

Kagan, O. (2005). In support of a proficiency-based definition of heritage language learners: The case of Russian. *The International Journal of Bilingual Education and Bilingualism, 8*(2&3), 213–220.

Lau, D. C. (Trans.). (2003). *Mencius.* New York: Penguin Books.

Lee, J. S. (2005). Through the learners' eyes: Reconceptualizing the heritage and non-heritage learner of the less commonly taught languages. *Foreign Language Annals, 38*(4), 554–567.

Liu, G. (2003, July). Seed-germination teaching and learning theory net-distribution tissue methods. *The China Papers,* 104–107.

Liu, R. (2006). *Maintaining Chinese as a heritage language in the United States.* Unpublished paper presented at the Second Language Research Forum (SLRF), Seattle, WA.

Mair, V. (2006, May 24). On learning Mandarin in America. *Language Log.* Retrieved June 27, 2006, from http://itre.cis.upenn.edu/~myl/languagelog/archives/003184.html

McGinnis, S. (1996). Teaching Chinese to the Chinese: The development of an assessment and instructional model. In J. E. Liskin-Gasparro (Ed.), *Patterns and policies: The changing demographics of foreign language Instruction* (pp. 107–121). Boston: Heinle & Heinle.

McGinnis, S. (1999). Student goals and approaches. In M. Chu (Ed.), *Mapping the course of the Chinese language field* (pp. 151–167; Chinese Language Teachers Association No. 3). Kalamazoo, MI: Chinese Language Teachers Association.

Mercado, C. I. (2000). Monitoring the progress of heritage learners: Assessment trends and current practices. In J. B. Webb & B. L. Miller (Eds.), *Teaching heritage language learners: Voices from the classroom* (pp. 209–230). Yonkers, NY: The American Council for the Teaching of Foreign Languages.

Moag, R. F. (1995). Semi-native speakers: How to hold them and mold them. In V. Gambhir (Ed.), *The teaching and acquisition of South Asian languages* (pp. 168–181). Philadelphia: University of Pennsylvania Press.

Morgan, C. (1998). Cross-cultural encounters. In M. Byram, & M. Fleming (Eds.), *Language learning in intercultural perspectives: Approaches through drama and ethnography* (pp. 224–305). New York: Cambridge University Press.

Schinke-Llano, L. (1995). Reenvisioning the second language classroom: A Vygotskian perspective. In F. R. Eckman, D. Highland, P. W. Lee, J. Mileham, & R. R. Weber (Eds.), *Second language acquisition theory and pedagogy* (pp. 21–28). Mahwah, NJ: Lawrence Erlbaum.

Shulman, L. S. (2000). Teacher development: Roles of domain expertise and pedagogical knowledge. *Journal of Applied Developmental Psychology, 21*(1), 129–135.

Sweley, M. H. (2006, April). Heritage language learning: Where we stand today. *The Language Educator, 1*(3), 20–25.

Walton, A. R. (1996). Reinventing language fields: The Chinese case. In S. McGinnis (Ed.), *Chinese pedagogy: An emerging field* (pp. 29–79) (Chinese Language Teachers Association Monograph No. 2). Columbus, OH: Foreign Language Publications.

Wen, X. h. (1999). Chinese language learning motivation: A comparative study of different ethnic groups. In M. Chu (Ed.), *Mapping the course of the Chinese language field* (pp. 121–150) (Chinese Language Teachers Association No.3). Kalamazoo, MI: Chinese Language Teachers Association.

Wong, S.-L. C.(1988). The language situation of Chinese Americans. In S. L. McKay, S.-L. C. Wong (Eds.), *Language diversity problem or resource: A social and educational perspective on language minorities in the United States* (pp. 193–228). New York: Newbury House.

Wulff, D. H. (2005). Using the alignment model of teaching effectiveness. In D. H. Wulff, W. H. Jacobson, K. Freisem, D. H. Hatch, M. Lawrence, & L. R. Lenz (Eds.), *Aligning for learning: Strategies for teaching effectiveness* (pp. 3–15. Bolton, MA: Anker.

Zhou, M., & Cai, G. (2002). Chinese language media in the United States: Immigration and assimilation in American life. *Qualitative Sociology, 25*(3), 419–441.

Zull, J. E. (2002). *The art of changing the brain: Enriching the practice of teaching by exploring the biology of learning.* Sterling, VA: Stylus.

5

Attitudes Toward Mandarin, Heritage Languages, and Dialect Diversity Among Chinese Immigrants and International Students in the United States

Terrence G. Wiley
Gerda de Klerk
Mengying Li
Na Liu
Yun Teng
Ping Yang
Arizona State University

Chinese as a heritage (HL) and/or community language (CL) is receiving increased attention in the United States. "Chinese" is an ambiguous label because it is associated with ethnicity, and/or national origin. Studying Chinese as an HL/CL is further complicated by the diversity of Chinese language varieties and minority ethnic languages, as well as by competing written standards. Our study analyzes the attitudes of Chinese immigrants and international students toward the maintenance of Mandarin and other varieties of Chinese as HLs and/or CLs, along with attitudes toward language diversity among Chinese. To address these issues, we surveyed 766 participants from Mainland China, Taiwan, and Hong Kong. Our major findings showed a considerable degree of tolerance toward language diversity generally, and HLs and CLs specifically. We present additional findings on patterns of language use, preferences for Chinese scripts, and attitudes toward the promotion of Mandarin and other varieties of Chinese. Sub-group differences among those of Chinese-origin are analyzed in terms of place of origin (Hong Kong, the Chinese Mainland, and Taiwan) and language background based on the major variety of Chinese spoken as a mother tongue [1]

This chapter reports findings from a recent survey of Chinese immigrants and international students in the US regarding their attitudes toward the maintenance of "Chinese" as a heritage (HL) and/or community language (CL), as well as their attitudes toward language

---

[1] This research project was conducted in affiliation with the UCLA Center for African Studies and the UCLA National Heritage Language Resource Center. A portion of the work reported herein was supported under the Language Resource Centers, U.S. Department of Education. The findings and opinions expressed in this report do not reflect the positions or policies of the Department of Education, and you should not assume endorsement by the Federal Government.

Wiley, T. G., de Klerk, G., Li, M., Liu, N., Teng, Y., & Yang, P. (2008). Attitudes toward Mandarin, heritage languages, and dialect diversity among Chinese immigrants and international students in the United States. In A. W. He, & Y. Xiao (Eds.), *Chinese as a heritage language: Fostering rooted world citizenry* (pp. 67–87). Honolulu: University of Hawai'i, National Foreign Language Resource Center.

diversity among Chinese. Currently, there is considerable interest in China and Chinese in the United States because of China's growing economic prosperity and international status. There is also increasing interest in promoting "Chinese" or Mandarin as a foreign language (FL) in the United States along with increased attention to expanding instruction in Mandarin as an HL/CL (McGinnis, 2005). Much of the focus on "Chinese" as an HL/CL in the United States is primarily a focus on Mandarin, which is the official language in mainland Chinese and Taiwan, as well as an official language of Singapore.

When we analyze extant language data related to "Chinese" in the United States, however, the label is problematic. Chinese can be used to refer to language, ethnicity, and/or national origin. People who are of Chinese origin may be speakers of any language, and some people who are ethnically Chinese do not speak Mandarin or any other Chinese language varieties. According to the 2000 U.S. census (Table 1), there are slightly over 2,000,000 speakers of language varieties that fall under the Chinese label. Among those who speak "Chinese," approximately 93% are ethnically of Chinese origin.

Table 1.   Chinese ethnicity and language distributions in the U.S. population (2000)

race/ethnicity	Chinese language speakers	%
Chinese ethnicity alone	1,864,435	93.2
all other races	136,518	6.8
total Chinese language speakers	**2,000,953**	100.0

language	speakers indicating race as Chinese alone	%
Chinese language speakers	1,864,435	82.7
English only speakers	321,000	14.2
speakers of other languages	69,396	3.1
total speakers indicating race as Chinese alone	**2,254,831**	100.0

source: Compiled by M. Castro (Language Policy Research Unit of the Southwest Center for Educational Equity and Language Diversity, ASU) based on the 2000 1% PUMS (U.S. Census Bureau, 2003). Chinese language: Chinese, Min; Cantonese, Toishan; Mandarin; Formosan, Fukien, Hokkien, Min Nan, Taiwanese.

note: Some of the linguistic categories identified above are confounded.

There is also ambiguity in using the "Chinese" label in reference to language as it includes language varieties other than Mandarin. Unfortunately, even the U.S. census in some cases confounds Chinese language varieties that are not mutually intelligible. Moreover, even though the use of "Chinese" to mean Mandarin is common, not all "Chinese" programs in the United States teach Mandarin. Some offer instruction in Cantonese in communities where there are large numbers of immigrants from Hong Kong and the Canton province of Mainland China. In Taiwan, there have been increased efforts to promote the local variety of *Min*, or *Taiwanese*, which is widely spoken on the island, as well as *Hakka*; thus, for some immigrants from Taiwan there is interest in these languages as heritage languages as well. Lastly, even among programs that teach only Mandarin, not all use the same character form of the Chinese writing system. Thus, when we think of Chinese as a heritage or community language in the United States there is much heterogeneity to consider.

Our study aims to elaborate on existing language profiles of speakers of Chinese in the US in order better to inform HL/CL initiatives geared to communities of Chinese speakers regarding the language varieties, attitudes, and expectations that may be found among their clientele.

With increased mobility that accompanies globalization, the US has, over the last few decades, become the temporary or permanent home to large numbers of young, highly educated people of Chinese origin. This population is of interest to HL scholars because many of them may return to their country of origin, many of them may stay in the US, and a substantial sector may move between the two countries. Regardless of which outcome, it may be desirable and necessary for this population to maintain their home language for themselves, as well as for their children, in order to facilitate mobility between the cultures of two economic and political superpowers.

Ethnic and language diversity in China

Currently, there are 56 officially recognized ethnic groups in mainland China, of which Han is the largest group (Teng & Weng, 2001). Even though non-Han groups constitute only about 8% percent of the total population among these, there are at least 61 indigenous languages, which belong to five language families. Thus, when considering Chinese ethnicities and heritage languages in the United States, it is also necessary to consider how minority status and language minority status are constructed in China.

Although Mandarin is China's major language and the world's leading mother tongue, according to a recent survey conducted in mainland China, only 53% of that country's population speaks "standard" Mandarin (National Language Committee, 2005); however, many are multilingual. Based on this Chinese mainland survey, 86% of those surveyed indicated that they speak dialects. Speakers of officially designated ethnic minority languages account for only 5% of all speakers in China; thus, the overwhelming majority of mainland Chinese, including the ethnic Han majority, speaks either other Chinese languages or regional varieties of Mandarin. The proportion of standard Mandarin speakers increase based largely on their educational backgrounds. Only 10% of those people without formal schooling are speakers of standard Mandarin, increasing to 56% for those with junior high school education, and 87% for those with junior college education and above. Ability in standard Mandarin also correlates with age. Approximately 70% of those ranging in ages between 15 and 29 years speak standard Mandarin. This declines to only 31% for those between 60 and 69. Speaking standard Mandarin also correlates with urbanization. Some 66% of urban dwellers speak standard Mandarin compared to only 45% for those in rural areas.

There are seven major varieties of Chinese, of which Mandarin is the major variety that is recognized as the *Putonghua*, or common language. Customarily, Chinese refer to the six additional major language varieties other than Mandarin as "dialects," or *Fangyan*, which are categorized based on geographical and linguistic-structural characteristics (Li, 1994). Despite the mutual unintelligibility among *Fangyan*, Chinese have generally been reluctant to call them different languages (Taylor & Taylor, 1995). Nevertheless *Fangyan* tend to function as markers of social group boundaries that identify different origins and social backgrounds among Chinese (Li). Seven *Fangyan* are recognized by custom, although linguists typically make finer distinctions among these by using phonological and grammatical criteria. Norman (1988), for example, identifies 12 major, largely geographicallly distributed Chinese dialects, which roughly correspond to a north-south distribution (see Norman, pp. 182–183). Sociolinguists have more recently identified additional varieties of Mandarin, (see Yan, 2006). The seven traditional *Fangyan* are *Beifang Hua* (Northern or Mandarin), which is the native language for over 70% of the Chinese mainland population, *Wu, Xiang, Yue, Min, Hakka (Kejia),* and *Gan* (Ramsey, 1987).

The *Yue* dialect, which includes Cantonese, is found mostly in Guangdong province, the southernmost province of China. Large numbers can also be found among overseas Chinese diaspora. *Kejia* (Hakka) has many users who came from small agricultural areas and are now scattered throughout southeastern China and Taiwan. Varieties of *Min* are spoken in Fujian (the mainland province on the western side of the Taiwan Strait), as well as in Taiwan and Hainan Islands. *Min* is often further distinguished by northern and southern varies. *Wu* varieties are spoken in the lower Changjiang (the Yangtze River) region, which includes the heavily populated metropolitan area of Shanghai. *Xiang* varieties are mainly spoken in south central region. *Gan* varieties are spoken chiefly in the southeastern inland provinces. (Ramsey, 1987; see also Li, 1994). More recently, the National Language Committee of China (2005) has identified additional regional varieties as *Hui, Gin, Pinhua, Guanhua,* and others.

Subvarieties can also be identified within each of the seven major *Fangyan*. Mandarin, for example, has four major regional varieties: Northern, Northwestern, Southwestern, and Eastern (Yan, 2006). *Cantonese* is a subvariety or "dialect" of the *Yue* group (Li, 1994). *Taiwanese* belongs to the *Min* group (Ramsey, 1987). The *Min*-speaking region of China also includes the southeastern province of *Fujian*. Taiwanese Min is of particular interest in this study, because a substantial number of U.S. immigrants and international students are from Taiwan, where the Taiwanese variety of Min is the majority home language of the island despite the influx of mainlanders "who fled to Taiwan following the Nationalist [*Kuomintang*] defeat at the hands of the Communists in 1950" (Ramsey, 1987, p. 107). Following several decades of official Mandarin policies, most Taiwanese are bilingual and fluent in Mandarin.

As is common with spoken varieties of major languages, regional differences in pronunciation of Mandarin are common. Those accents which diverge from Beijing's tend to be marked for their regional "accents." Over the past 60 years there have been various efforts to minimize differences in regional pronunciation and to facilitate standard pronunciation. Toward these ends, *Pinyin* was developed as a phonetic spelling system based on Roman alphabetic characters to help both nonnative Mandarin speakers and those who are speakers of other Chinese dialects learn a standardized Mandarin pronunciation (Li, 1994).

The significance of the written standard

As Ramsey (1987) notes "the speakers of all [Chinese] dialects look toward a common model. … It is also true that when most Chinese think of a language that unites them as a people, the 'common language' they have in mind is still fundamentally their written language" (p. 17). Chinese characters can be adapted to other *Fangyan*, and other languages such as Korean and Japanese. Nevertheless, as Li (1994) observes "only Mandarin has a corresponding written form, which is shared by all literate Chinese whatever *Fangyan* they may speak" (p. 41). Traditionally, from a Chinese perspective, the written standard overrides the different oral varieties as a standard" (Ramsey, p. 18). Nonetheless, there has been controversy regarding the written language.

Historically, as Li observes, there have been two major written forms of Chinese: *Wenyan*, which was the script of literary classics and formal documents of ancient China, and the colloquial *Baihua* based on spoken Mandarin. "Normally the Chinese learn to read and write in *Baihua*. *Wenyan* is now studied as an example of the Chinese cultural heritage" (Li, p. 42). In the early Twentieth Century there was a major effort to promote *Baihua* as a means of making literacy more accessible to the common people. The differences between Wenyan and Baihua were largely related to sentence structure, grammar, and semantics. Beyond the efforts to promote *Baihua*, there have also been a number of efforts to make literacy more attainable through the simplification of the written character system. There was even some debate regarding using an alphabetic system such as *Pinyin* to facilitate that purpose. Thus, efforts to promote "both phonetic writing and character simplification thus began simultaneously" (Ramsey, p. 143). Ultimately, simplification of traditional characters won out over Romanization (Dayle, 1983; Hsia, 1956; Ramsey, 1987). Efforts to refine the simplified character system continue in the People's Republic of China (PRC).

Despite the progress of the PRC in promoting literacy through the use of simplified characters, as Ramsey (1987) observes, in Taiwan, the literacy rate has been high despite the use of traditional characters, thus casting doubt on the assumption that simplified characters are more conducive to learning. Given the sheer numbers on the Chinese mainland, it is clear that simplified characters will continue to be the primary medium for the promotion of literacy. However, because traditional characters are still used as the primary medium of literacy in Taiwan and Hong Kong, and they are still considered important for academic use, we included several questions related to their utility and efficacy in our surveys.

A brief historical sketch of Chinese immigration the US

According to Chang (2003), Chinese immigrated to the US in three major waves: the first coincided with the 1849-era California gold rush; the second included migration of the anti-Communist elites after the 1949 Communist revolution; the third was comprised largely of Chinese of those from more well off socioeconomic backgrounds who entered the US during the last two decades of the 20th century.

The initial wave of immigration had included mostly poor peasants from Guangdong Province (Canton), China. Most of them spoke Cantonese, of the *Yue* dialect group (Wong & Lopez, 2000). It was common for the second-generation to use Chinese mother tongues during the 1920s (Li, 1982). Nevertheless, language shift to English occurred, since this generation tended to integrate to the mainstream society, especially those with higher education. Some families forbade their children to speak English at home (Chang, 2003); however, many children could not see the need to maintain their Chinese because assumed they would remain in the United States and had never been to China.

The second wave of immigration began during the mid–20th century and decreased in the 1970s. In China, the war with Japanese (1937–1945) was followed by the civil war (1945-1949), which resulted in the Communist Party establishing the People's Republic of China. As a result of the civil war, many bureaucrats, businessmen, and intellectuals fled the country. Some went first to Hong Kong, others to Taiwan, but for most of them, America was their final destination (Chang, 2003).

This second wave of Chinese immigrants consisted of more highly educated and wealthy Chinese immigrants than the first wave of laborers, and they tended to settle down around universities or research centers rather than in Chinatowns. Most could speak English; however, some who came as political refugees did not speak English and many among this group ended up in Chinatowns doing the manual labor work (Chang, 2003). The immigrants from mainland China and Taiwan spoke mostly Mandarin and those from Hong Kong spoke Cantonese; most of the literate among this group of immigrants used traditional Chinese characters.

The growing international Chinese student population in the US

After the normalization of Sino-American diplomatic relationships in 1979, increasing numbers of Chinese students and scholars were allowed into the US. By the end of the 1980s, more than 80,000 young PRC students had gone to study in the United States. This was the largest immigrant wave of Chinese scholars in American history (Chang, 2003). By the end of 20th century, Chinese immigrants constituted the largest group of foreign students in the United States. Most were from professional backgrounds, particularly science and engineering, and they spoke Mandarin as well as other dialects and used simplified Chinese characters. By 2006, 62,582 students from Mainland China were enrolled in U.S. higher education institutions: 27,876 from Taiwan; and 7,849 from Hong Kong (Institute of International Education, 2006).

Chinese HL/CL instruction in the US[2]

We propose that in order to inform Chinese HL/CL instruction in the US, it is necessary to understand the notion of heritage language among Chinese first among their home region settings and secondly within the United States. As stated earlier, instruction efforts may be ignoring the subtleties of language varieties, usage, and attitudes that exist in the home region. Our survey relies on informants who are of immigrant stock as well as those who are international students. One limitation of our study is that since we did not ask questions about citizenship or intention to stay in the US, we cannot disaggregate which of our respondents are, or will be, in the US permanently. However, the demographics of the most recent wave of Chinese migration to the US show a relatively young population and the trends in globalization point toward more mobility of individuals between the US and China. Both these factors suggest a new HL interest group emerging, namely young people who may want to maintain their heritage language for themselves as well as their children in order to facilitate communication with people in their home country while they are in the US, or when they visit or return to China.

According to McGinnis (2005), there is considerably more Chinese heritage language instruction going on at the community level, than in the public schools or universities, and that these can learn from community efforts. A complicating factor in designing and aligning instruction for HL/CL learners, however, occurs when the target standard variety does not correspond with a prestige variety. Regional and social differences among language varieties are also important because awareness of them is used as markers of social boundaries. Consequently, many HL/CLs may be socially stigmatized resulting in differential treatment or outright discrimination (Baugh, 2000; Lippi-Green, 1997). Among Chinese, regional Fangyan are often thought of being associated with localism, lower educational attainment, and poverty. Thus, dialect speakers may also face additional challenges when attempting to learn Mandarin as an HL (Wiley, in press). Within China, however some Fangyan have high status within their local regions. This issue has received some attention in the popular press regarding the use of Shanghai dialect. (Chao, 1997).

In terms of written characters, the simplified version has taken predominantly the lead (95%) in mainland China (National Language Committee, 2005). Again, however, in Taiwan and Hong Kong, the traditional characters are still the primary ones used. Therefore, choice of

---

[2]   Over the past decade, the HL has gained recognition. Although there is some disagreement (see Wiley, 2001) over the elasticity of the label with some preferring the "community" language (cf. Horvath & Vaughan, 1991), the HL label is widely used in the United States in reference to both immigrant and indigenous languages. Foreign language programs are increasingly focusing on HL learners in an effort to respond interest among HL immigrant students. While many community-related HL efforts are attempting to maintain and revitalize threatened languages (Fishman, 1991, 1999, 2001; Hinton & Hale, 2001), promoting other languages is seen as addressing a perceived national "crisis" in terms of the lack of critical language resources needed for economic, diplomatic, and national security purposes (Brecht & Ingold, May, 2002; see Wiley, in press for a critique).

scripts, simplified or the more complex traditional characters has been an issue for Chinese instruction in the United States. Community-based programs receive some materials from outside the United States. Thus, those programs that serve more immigrants from Taiwan tend to focus on teaching traditional characters and those from the mainland tend to teach simplified characters, while a number of university programs now teach both. Thus, one prediction for our survey is that those from the mainland would tend to support teaching simplified characters; whereas those from Taiwan would support the teaching of traditional characters .

Research questions

Given that language diversity among Chinese people is often masked under the umbrella term "Chinese," we were interested in a profile of language proficiency and use among our respondents. Since dialects can serve as social boundary markers, we wanted to investigate if whether a person is a dialect speaker or a speaker of standard Mandarin makes a difference to their attitudes about a range of language matters in their home country and in the US.

This study seeks to answer the following six questions:

1. What is the distribution of varieties of Chinese and Chinese dialects among respondents?

2. What are the contexts in which respondents use different languages and dialects?

3. Are there differences in respondents' attitudes to script preference according to their experience of a particular script?

4. Does whether a person is a dialect speaker or a speaker of standard Mandarin make a difference to her/his attitudes about dialect speakers in Mainland China, Taiwan, and Hong Kong?

5. Does whether a person is a dialect speaker or a speaker of standard Mandarin make a difference to her/his attitudes about maintenance of minority language in Mainland China, Taiwan, and Hong Kong and about language diversity in these regions?

6. Does whether a person is a dialect speaker or a speaker of standard Mandarin make a difference to her/his attitudes about maintenance of heritage language in the US and about language diversity in the US?

Survey methods

Data were collected using an online survey that was sent out to approximately 130 managers of listservs of Chinese students and professionals in the US, between May and October, 2006. We were unable to track on how many of these listservs the survey was posted, and where responses came from. A link to the survey was posted on the Arizona State University China Initiatives website homepage. The survey was also made available as a paper survey if respondents preferred not to complete it online. Sixty respondents (all more senior) to the Taiwanese survey chose the paper version. We received 766 fully completed surveys.

The survey was comprised of 70 questions; the majority of these were Likert scale type point-and-click questions; a few required typing in a one word answer, and all open ended questions that asked for explication of some of the shorter responses were optional. Respondents had to choose one of the three surveys, depending on whether they were from Mainland China, Taiwan, or Hong Kong. The questions in all three surveys were the same, however, the surveys aimed at people from Taiwan and Hong Kong included questions about Taiwanese

(Min), Hakka, and Cantonese (Yue) that were not in the survey for people from Mainland China. The survey questions were in English, but there were translations of some key terms into Mandarin. Respondents could answer the open-ended questions in Mandarin if they chose to do so because the survey software supported Chinese script. The Taiwanese and Hong Kong surveys used traditional characters for key word translations; the Mainland survey used simplified characters.

Results

The demographic breakdown for survey respondents can be found in Table 2. The goal of this survey was not to collect generalizable information as random sampling was not feasible, but to provide a reference point for current attitudes among Chinese immigrants and international students residing in the US as well as for further research on this issue. Because the survey was voluntary, it can be assumed that the sample is biased in favor of those persons who already take an interest in, or care about their heritage language and about English fluency. Not surprisingly the survey respondents fit the profile of the third wave of immigrants described earlier.

Table 2. Characteristics of survey respondents

from		years in US	
Mainland China (n=479)	62.5%	0–3	37.0%
Taiwan (n=234)	30.5%	4–10	30.8%
Hong Kong (n=53)	6.9%	11+	32.1%
gender		**occupation**	
male	43.8%	student	47.5%
female	52.6%	business	11.9%
		medical	3.8%
age		government	2.0%
18–20	6.9%	education	15.1%
21–30	41.9%	other	19.7%
31–40	25.7%		
41–50	16.7%		
51–60	6.9%		
60+	2.4%		

Given the extent of multilingualism among Chinese, as expected, only a minority of respondents grew up in monolingual environments. Less than a third (27.9%) of respondents came from Mandarin-only households, and 3.8% from Cantonese only households. Table 3 shows language use for the three regions.

Table 3. Language use while growing up

language spoken by region	n	%
Mainland China (n=476)		
Mandarin only	166	34.9
mostly Mandarin and another dialect	133	27.9
mostly another Chinese dialect and some Mandarin	89	18.7
dialects only	77	16.2
some Chinese and another language	11	2.3

Taiwan (n=231)		
Mandarin only	45	19.5
mostly Mandarin and another dialect	102	44.2
mostly another Chinese dialect and some Mandarin	49	21.2
dialects only	14	6.1
some Chinese and another language	21	9.1
Hong Kong (n=53)		
Mandarin only	1	1.9
mostly Mandarin and another dialect	2	3.8
Cantonese only	29	54.7
Cantonese and Mandarin mostly	6	11.3
mostly Cantonese and another dialect	10	18.9
mostly another dialect and some Cantonese	1	1.9
some Chinese and another language	4	7.5

Current language use among respondents indicates an even higher level of multilingualism. None of the respondents was monolingual, and in many cases respondents spoke more than two languages. Given that the respondents were residing in the US, it is not surprising that nearly all of the respondents spoke English, with the majority indicating that they spoke it well or very well. Table 4 shows the percentages of various levels of fluency at which respondents answered the question: "Right now, which of these languages do you speak, and how well do you speak them?" This was a multiple choice question with only the languages noted here given as possible answers.

Table 4.   Current language use among respondents

region	fluency	language (%)				
		Mandarin	English	Cantonese	Taiwanese	Hakka
Mainland China	not at all	.4	0.0	78.3	*	*
	not well	.6	13.0	10.8	*	*
	well	7.7	62.2	2.7	*	*
	very well	91.3	24.8	8.1	*	*
Taiwan	not at all	0.0	1.3	*	11.5	87.8
	not well	3.9	8.4	*	30.0	6.4
	well	16.3	48.5	*	28.6	3.2
	very well	79.8	41.9	*	30.0	2.6
Hong Kong	not at all	4.1	0.0	0.0	*	*
	not well	30.6	0.0	0.0	*	*
	well	46.9	35.3	13.7	*	*
	very well	18.4	64.7	86.3	*	*

* There is no answer possible in region-specific survey.

When, after this question, respondents were asked if they spoke "any other" dialect of Chinese, 352 respondents answered *no*, 365 answered *yes*, and 49 did not answer this question. This question apparently was interpreted differently by different respondents: Some respondents from Taiwan and Hong Kong, who initially indicated Taiwanese or Cantonese as one of their current languages, answered *no* to the dialect question; others answered *yes*, and then listed Taiwanese or Cantonese as the dialect they spoke. In many cases, these labels were not used, rather, "Min" was used to refer to Taiwanese, and "Yue" to refer to Cantonese. When comparing responses in the aggregate, we recoded all those who indicated Taiwanese at a higher fluency than other languages as Min Fanyang speakers, and those who indicated Cantonese at a higher level of fluency than other languages as Yue Fanyang speakers. Where respondents indicated the same level of fluency for Taiwanese and Hakka, they were coded as Hakka Fangyan speakers (even though they may more accurately be described as Min-Hakka bilinguals or bidialectal speakers). Once we had coded Taiwanese and Cantonese as Min and Yue, respectively, the percentage of dialect speakers (in contrast to standard Mandarin speakers) in the sample rose to 76.3%. It is important to note then that the categories used in this analysis do obscure some complex multilingual configurations. In order to be able to analyze the data quantitatively, we needed to retain subgroups of our sample of 766 that would still be large enough to yield useful results. Within a vastly larger sample it will be possible to refine dialect configurations into more complex categories.

Respondents who answered *yes* to speaking a dialect were asked in an open-ended question to identify this dialect. We reviewed all these responses and coded the dialects to correspond with the customary classification system, discussed earlier in this chapter (although finer distinctions are often made by sociolinguists). Table 5 shows the classification by the traditional seven Fangyan, with Mandarin disaggregated into standard and dialect varieties, and Table 6 shows the same Fangyan with all sub-varieties of Mandarin noted.

Table 5.   Respondent backgrounds by standard Mandarin, Mandarin dialects, and other Fangyan

language and dialect categories	n speakers	% speakers
standard Mandarin	170	23.7
Mandarin dialects	127	17.7
Wu	81	11.3
Xiang	22	3.1
Min	205	28.6
Yue	73	10.2
Gan	9	1.3
Hakka	31	4.3

Table 6.   Respondent backgrounds by Mandarin with sub-varieties, and other Fangyan

language and dialect categories	n speakers	% speakers
standard Mandarin	170	23.7
northern Mandarin	42	5.8
northwestern Mandarin	12	1.7
southwestern Mandarin	58	8.1
eastern Mandarin	15	2.1
Wu	81	11.3
Xiang	22	3.1
Min	205	28.6
Yue	73	10.2
Gan	9	1.3
Hakka	31	4.3

As can be expected among those from multilingual societies, the language use patterns of the respondents varied systematically depending on their context. In general, the more local and private the space, the more dialects were used. And the more formal and public the context, the more Mandarin was used. This does not hold for communication with children, where Mandarin was by far the primary language of communication for respondents from Mainland China and Taiwan. For respondents from Hong Kong, Cantonese was widely used in all local and private spaces. Tables 7, 8, and 9 show the patterns in the three different regions.

Table 7. Contexts in which respondents from mainland China use specific languages

communicating	n	mostly dialect	dialect and Mandarin fairly equally	mostly Mandarin	dialect or Mandarin depending on context
with family and close relatives in the home country	472	43.9	8.9	47.2	*
at work in the home country	427	1.6	4.7	88.5	5.2
with friends in home country	472	5.7	14.2	68.2	11.9
with own children	181	6.1	2.8	91.2	*
when in the hometown	473	49.0	12.9	38.1	*

* This option was not given as a possible answer to the question.

Table 8. Contexts in which respondents from Taiwan use specific languages

communicating	n	mostly dialect	dialect and Mandarin fairly equally	mostly Mandarin	dialect or Mandarin depending on context
with family and close relatives in the home country	229	19.7	30.1	50.2	*
at work in the home country	176	4.0	11.4	76.7	8.0
with friends in home country	214	4.7	16.8	69.2	9.3
with own children	93	7.5	10.8	81.7	*
when in the hometown	209	27.3	23.4	49.3	*

* This option was not given as a possible answer to the question.

Table 9. Contexts in which respondents From Hong Kong use specific languages

communicating	n	mostly Cantonese	Cantonese and Mandarin fairly equally	mostly Mandarin	mostly English	mostly Cantonese and English	Cantonese and another dialect	mostly Mandarin and English	Mandarin and another dialect
with family and close relatives in the home country	52	86.5	1.9	3.8	*	*	7.7	*	*
at work in the home country	38	44.7	0	0	0	55.3	0	0	0
with friends in home country	52	57.7	0	0	3.8	36.5	0	1.9	0
with own children	10	60.0	10.0	10.0	*	*	20.0	*	0
when in the hometown	50	84.0	2.0	6.0	*	*	6.0	*	2.0

* This option was not given as a possible answer to the question.

Preferences for Chinese scripts

Because respondents from Hong Kong and Taiwan have learned traditional Chinese characters in their schooling system, and respondents from Mainland China have typically simplified Chinese characters, we wanted to probe the extent to which respondents from each area were loyal to the scripts they had likely studied in school and open to studying an alternative. When Taiwan and Hong Kong respondents were asked to respond to the statement "Residents of Taiwan/Hong Kong should also learn simplified characters," the majority of Taiwan respondents and all Hong Kong respondents disagreed. When asked the inverse—"Residents of Taiwan/Hong Kong should only learn traditional Chinese characters"—the majority of Taiwan respondents agreed, and over 90% of Hong Hong respondents agreed. Among Taiwan respondents, differences were split more equally with over 40% support found for the minority opinion. See Tables 10, 11, and 12 for detailed results.

Table 10. Taiwan respondents' opinions of type of Chinese characters

opinion	In Taiwan people should *also* learn simplified characters. % respondents	In Taiwan people should *only* learn traditional characters. (current practice) % respondents
strongly disagree	25.5	2.6
disagree	33.3	41.3
agree	37.7	32.6
strongly agree	3.5	23.5

Table 11. Hong Kong respondents' opinions of type of Chinese characters

opinion	In Hong Kong people should *also* learn simplified characters. % respondents	In Hong Kong people should *only* learn traditional characters. (current practice) % respondents
strongly disagree	69.8	1.9
disagree	30.2	5.7
agree	0.0	24.5
strongly agree	69.8	1.9

Table 12. Mainland China respondents' opinions of type of Chinese characters

opinion	In Mainland China people should *also* learn traditional characters. % respondents	In Mainland China people should *only* learn simplified characters. (current practice) % respondents
strongly disagree	4.9	7.9
disagree	28.1	40.0
agree	55.7	38.2
strongly agree	11.3	13.9

Attitudes toward dialects

Although this was primarily a descriptive study, one hypothesis we expected to confirm was that "dialect speakers" would be more tolerant toward dialect speakers than those who only spoke standard Mandarin. Similarly, we also expected dialect speakers to have more favorable opinions regarding language diversity in their home country and the US than standard Mandarin speakers would have. We were also interested in seeing if any differences would emerge between dialect speakers and standard Mandarin speakers regarding heritage language maintenance in both their home countries and the US.

In Tables 13 to 17, we present the results of language/dialect groups and their opinions regarding dialects in the home country. The results in these tables are descriptive of the sample, and great caution should be exercised not to generalize from these results. Significance tests run on these cross tabulations were ambiguous. Despite the large sample size, in many cases some of the cells had very low frequencies, which meant that since a minimum frequency threshold was not reached, using a chi-square test of significance to draw conclusions would not be appropriate. When other tests of significance for nominal and ordinal cross tabulations were run, we found relatively weak associations between the variables, but the tests were significant at the 0.05 level. It may be that because of the large sample size there is enough power for these tests to be significant, but that in the light of the weak associations, as well as the nonrandom nature of the sample, significance cannot be used to generalize. The sample sizes reported in the tables (the total found in the last column and bottom row) for each of these cross tabulations differ, since we took out missing data on a question by question basis, and not for the dataset as a whole. It is important to note that the sample sizes for the Xiang, Gan, and Hakka subsets were very low, and much lower than for the other subsets, and any patterns that may emerge from these three subsets should be interpreted extra cautiously.

The overarching pattern emerging from these analyses is that the majority of respondents have a positive predisposition toward dialects and dialect speakers. When asked if dialects should be respected, the majority in each language/dialect group agreed, including Mandarin only (i.e., non-dialect) speakers (see Table 13). However, in this group we do find the largest proportion (11.2%)—compared to the other seven dialect groups—that disagreed with this proposition. The groups with the highest proportion of respondents that agreed were Mandarin dialect, Min, Hakka, and Yue. In the analyses to follow, Mandarin dialect speakers are all those who indicated a regional variety of Mandarin rather than just indicating "Mandarin" or "standard Mandarin" (see Table 6).

Given that these dialects can also be used to mark social boundaries between speakers from different regions, we also probed respondent attitudes in this regard. When asked whether respondents' considered speakers of some dialects as somewhat arrogant with those who do not speak their dialect (see Table 14), there was a fairly even split in opinion on this matter, with Hakka and Xiang speakers the groups with the highest proportion of disagreement with the statement. As noted earlier, these two groups are very small. The majority opinion in all of the dialect/language groups was that speakers of some dialects are *not* ashamed of speaking their dialects (see Table 15). In this case, the biggest proportions "not ashamed" responses were found among Hakka, Xiang, and Min speakers. Out of all eight categories of language/dialect speakers, the vast majority of respondents disagreed with the statement that Chinese people who use dialects are backward (see Table 16). The groups which had the largest proportion of respondents who disagreed were Wu, Mandarin dialect, and Xiang. Along the same line, within all groups the vast majority of respondents disagreed with the statement that Chinese people who use dialects are less educated (see Table 17). The groups which had the largest proportion of respondents who disagreed that dialects speakers are less educated, were Xiang and Min.

Table 13. Response to statement, "Residents of my home country should respect dialects."

language/dialect group	- disagree -		- - agree - -		total (100%)
	n	%	n	%	
Mandarin only	19	11.2	151	88.8	170
Mandarin dialects	3	2.4	123	97.6	126
Wu	7	8.8	73	91.3	80
Xiang	2	9.0	119	90.5	21
Min	5	2.5	197	97.5	21
Yue	4	5.5	69	94.5	73
Gan	1	11.1	8	88.9	9
Hakka	1	3.2	30	96.8	31
total	42	5.9	670	94.1	712

Table 14. Response to question, "Do you think speakers of some dialects are a bit arrogant with those who don't speak their dialect?"

language/dialect group	- - - no - - -		- - - yes - - -		total (100%)
	n	%	n	%	
Mandarin only	96	58.2	69	41.8	165
Mandarin dialects	49	38.9	77	61.1	126
Wu	45	57.7	33	42.3	78
Xiang	13	61.9	8	38.1	21
Min	117	59.1	81	40.9	198
Yue	43	60.6	28	39.4	71
Gan	2	22.2	7	77.8	9
Hakka	19	61.3	12	38.7	31
total	384	54.9	315	45.1	699

Table 15. Response to question, "Do you think speakers of some dialects are somewhat ashamed of speaking their dialects?

language/dialect group	- - - no - - -		- - - yes - - -		total (100%)
	n	%	n	%	
Mandarin only	128	77.6	37	22.4	165
Mandarin dialects	100	79.4	26	20.6	126
Wu	66	84.6	12	15.4	78
Xiang	18	90.0	2	10.0	21
Min	179	89.5	21	10.5	198
Yue	54	77.1	16	22.9	71
Gan	7	77.8	2	22.2	9
Hakka	28	90.3	3	9.7	31
total	580	83.0	119	17.0	699

Table 16. Response to statement, "Chinese people using dialects are backward."

| language/dialect group | - disagree - | | - - agree - - | | total (100%) |
	n	%	n	%	
Mandarin only	150	88.2	20	11.8	170
Mandarin dialects	116	92.1	10	7.9	126
Wu	73	92.4	6	7.6	79
Xiang	19	90.5	2	9.5	21
Min	177	88.9	22	11.1	199
Yue	59	80.8	14	19.2	73
Gan	8	88.9	1	11.1	9
Hakka	27	87.1	41	2.9	31
total	629	88.8	79	11.2	708

Table 17. Response to statement, "Chinese people using dialects are less educated."

| language/dialect group | - disagree - | | - - agree - - | | total (100%) |
	n	%	n	%	
Mandarin only	132	78.1	37	21.9	169
Mandarin dialects	97	77.0	29	23.0	126
Wu	67	84.8	12	15.2	79
Xiang	20	95.2	1	4.8	21
Min	184	91.1	18	8.9	202
Yue	55	76.4	17	23.6	72
Gan	7	77.8	2	22.2	9
Hakka	22	71.0	9	29.0	31
total	584	82.4	125	17.6	709

Language maintenance and diversity in the home country

One of the primary points of interest in this survey was in probing attitudes toward Mandarin as a heritage language as well as regarding heritage dialects, given that there has been little discussion in the US regarding the maintenance of dialects with the possible exception of Cantonese. Thus, we examined the attitudes of respondents regarding language maintenance and diversity in their home country or region, as well as the US. Given the central position of Mandarin as a standard language, we here report centrally the responses as they relate to Mandarin. Tables 18 to 21 show details regarding language diversity in the home region, while Tables 22 to 27 show details pertaining to the US.

The majority of respondents felt that children in China should receive basic schooling only through Mandarin (see Table 18). However, once these responses were disaggregated by dialect groups, a 55.2% majority of Min speakers and a 76.4% majority of Yue speakers disagreed with the proposition.

When the data were disaggregated by region, a similar pattern emerged: a 76% majority of Mainland China respondents agreed with Mandarin only for basic schooling, while a 51.7% majority of Taiwan respondents and a 92.3% majority of Hong Kong respondents disagreed (see Table 19).

Table 18. Response to statement, "Residents of my home country should receive basic schooling only through Mandarin."

language/dialect group	- disagree - n	%	- - agree - - n	%	total (100%)
Mandarin only	3	1.8	31	18.2	170
Mandarin dialects	80	47.1	56	32.9	126
Wu	3	2.4	29	23.0	80
Xiang	66	52.4	28	22.2	21
Min	2	2.5	13	16.3	203
Yue	36	45.0	29	36.3	72
Gan	0		6	28.6	9
Hakka	9	42.9	6	28.6	31
total	28	13.8	84	41.4	712

Table 19. Response to statement, "Residents of my home country should receive basic schooling only through Mandarin."

region	strongly disagree n	%	- - disagree - - n	%	- - - agree - - - n	%	strongly agree n	%	total (100%)
Mainland	12	2.5	101	21.4	223	47.2	136	28.8	472
Taiwan	30	12.9	90	38.8	69	29.7	43	18.5	232
Hong Kong	25	48.1	23	44.2	2	3.8	2	3.8	52
Total	67	8.9	214	28.3	294	38.9	181	23.9	756

When the question about medium of instruction was posed differently, and provided respondents with a bilingual option that would include Mandarin, the pattern of responses changed (see Table 20). Support for bilingual education was 45.5% among Mainland respondents, which means that many respondents who supported Mandarin-only instruction initially shifted to support for bilingual education once that option was offered in a way that left the position of Mandarin still strong. When Taiwan respondents could choose an option that included oral Taiwanese with Mandarin, only 41.6% disagreed. Among Hong Kong respondents, only 22.6% of respondents disagreed when presented with a Mandarin/Cantonese bilingual schooling scenario.

Table 20. Support for bilingual education

language combination in region	strongly disagree	disagree	agree	strongly agree
"In Mainland China children should receive basic schooling through Mandarin and their regional dialects."				
Mainland China n=479	8.1	46.4	37.8	7.7
"In Taiwan children should receive basic schooling through Mandarin and oral Taiwanese."				
Taiwan n=234	7.8	33.8	44.2	14.3
"In Hong Kong children should receive basic schooling through Mandarin and Cantonese."				
Hong Kong n=53	11.3	11.3	37.7	39.6

While respondents may not have been overwhelmingly supportive of using minority languages as mediums of instruction, when they were asked if minority language speakers should maintain their ethnic language, the response was overwhelmingly positive (see Table 21).

Even in the groups with lowest levels of agreements these were still very high, with Wu at 91.1%, Xiang at 90.5%, and Yue at 90.4%.

Table 21. Response to statement, "Residents of my home country who are minority language speakers should maintain their ethnic language."

language/dialect group	- disagree -		- - agree - -		total (100%)
	n	%	n	%	
Mandarin only	4	2.4	164	97.6	168
Mandarin dialects	3	2.4	123	97.6	126
Wu	7	8.9	72	91.1	79
Xiang	2	9.5	19	90.5	21
Min	6	3.0	194	97.0	200
Yue	7	9.6	66	90.4	73
Gan	0		9	100.0	9
Hakka	0		31	100.0	31
total	29	4.1	678	95.9	707

Language maintenance and diversity in the US

In the US, there has been considerable interest in HL and CL maintenance. The preponderance of "Chinese" instruction has been carried out through community-based efforts. Moreover, heritage language learners are beginning to receive more attention. Thus, a related area of interest was the extent to which respondents were supportive of heritage language maintenance, generally, as well as formal language instruction and whether it should be available in public schools or only through community efforts. Table 21 addresses the first issue. The overwhelming majority of respondents agreed on the importance of children of Chinese origin living in the US to learn or maintain Mandarin. Among Xiang and Hakka speakers there was nobody who felt this was not important.

Table 22. Response to question, "How important do you feel it is for children of Chinese origin living in the US to learn/maintain Mandarin?"

language/dialect group	not important		slightly important		important		very important		total (100%)
	n	%	n	%	n	%	n	%	
Mandarin only	3	1.8	13	7.7	44	26.2	108	64.3	168
Mandarin dialects	1	.8	8	6.4	51	40.8	65	52.0	125
Wu	1	1.3	6	7.6	26	32.9	46	58.2	79
Xiang	0		3	14.3	4	19.0	14	66.7	21
Min	7	3.5	21	10.4	65	32.3	108	53.7	201
Yue	2	2.8	5	6.9	28	38.9	37	51.4	72
Gan	1	11.1	0		2	22.2	6	66.7	9
Hakka	0		0		8	25.8	23	74.2	31
total	15	2.1	56	7.9	228	32.3	407	57.6	706

As for perceptions regarding private or public support for Mandarin instruction for children, respondents seemed overwhelmingly to support both types of instruction. The question about private instruction (in the absence of public support) was posed as a statement where respondents had to indicate where they agreed or not with this notion, and 92.1% did (see

Table 23). Regarding public schooling, we probed peoples' attitudes as to whether they thought a strong form of bilingual instruction would be a good idea, and then followed up by asking how they would behave if such an option was available. Of the respondents, 80.7% said they would send their children to such a school.

Table 23. Response to statement, "There should be private instruction (tutors/weekend schools) in Mandarin for Chinese origin children if not available in public schools."

language/dialect group	- disagree - n	%	- - agree - - n	%	total (100%)
Mandarin only	13	7.7	156	92.3	169
Mandarin dialects	8	6.4	117	93.6	125
Wu	7	9.1	70	90.9	77
Xiang	1	4.8	20	95.2	21
Min	18	8.9	184	91.1	202
Yue	8	11.1	64	88.9	72
Gan	1	11.1	8	88.9	9
Hakka	0		31	100.0	31
total	56	7.9	650	92.1	706

Table 24. Response to question, "Would you send your children to a two-way immersion English/Mandarin school?"

language/dialect group	not at all n	%	unlikely n	%	- - likely - - n	%	definitely n	%	total (100%)
Mandarin only	8	4.8	20	12.0	74	44.6	64	38.6	166
Mandarin dialects	3	2.4	14	11.3	67	54.0	40	32.3	124
Wu	4	5.3	11	14.5	37	48.7	24	31.6	76
Xiang	0		2	9.5	9	42.9	10	47.6	21
Min	14	7.0	33	16.5	88	44.0	65	32.5	200
Yue	4	5.7	16	22.9	32	45.7	18	25.7	70
Gan	0		1	11.1	3	33.3	5	55.6	9
Hakka	2	6.5	2	6.5	13	41.9	14	45.2	31
total	35	5.0	99	14.2	323	46.3	240	34.4	697

When it comes to languages other than Mandarin in the US, respondents attached some importance to Chinese origin children learning Spanish, though about one fourth felt it was not important (see Table 25).

There was not much support for Chinese origin children to learn any languages other than Chinese, English, or Spanish (see Table 26). The overwhelming support for children (in general) retaining their parents' language (see Table 27) may indicate that respondents' positive attitude to bi- and multilingualism may have more to do with maintaining heritage than with the desirability of multilingualism per se, or Mandarin as an instrumentalist language.

Table 25. Response to question, "How important is it for children of Chinese origin living in the US to learn Spanish?"

language/dialect group	not important n	%	slightly important n	%	important n	%	very important n	%	total (100%)
Mandarin only	44	26.3	78	46.7	36	21.6	9	5.4	167
Mandarin dialects	37	29.8	52	41.9	29	23.4	6	4.8	124
Wu	21	26.9	26	33.3	24	30.8	7	9.0	78
Xiang	10	47.6	7	33.3	4	19.0	0		21
Min	24	11.9	80	39.6	77	38.1	21	10.4	202
Yue	13	18.3	35	49.3	22	31.0	1	1.4	71
Gan	2	22.2	4	44.4	3	33.3	0		9
Hakka	2	6.5	17	54.8	10	32.3	2	6.5	31
total	153	21.8	299	42.5	205	29.2	46	6.5	703

Table 26. Response to question, "How important is it for children of Chinese origin living in the US to Learn languages other than Chinese, English, or Spanish?"

language/dialect group	not important n	%	slightly important n	%	important n	%	very important n	%	total (100%)
Mandarin only	59	34.9	67	39.6	33	19.5	10	5.9	169
Mandarin dialects	50	40.3	45	36.3	26	21.0	3	2.4	124
Wu	19	24.4	35	44.9	19	24.4	5	6.4	78
Xiang	12	57.1	8	38.1	1	4.8	0		21
Min	45	22.4	77	38.3	58	28.9	21	10.4	201
Yue	19	26.8	33	46.5	15	21.1	4	5.6	71
Gan	5	55.6	3	33.3	1	11.1	0		9
Hakka	4	12.9	16	51.6	7	22.6	4	12.9	31
total	213	30.3	284	40.3	160	22.7	47	6.7	704

Table 27. Response to question, "How important is it for children to retain/learn their parents' languages, assuming they are already learning English?"

language/dialect group	not important n	%	slightly important n	%	important n	%	very important n	%	total (100%)
Mandarin only	3	1.8	13	7.7	70	41.4	83	49.1	169
Mandarin dialects	1	.8	6	4.8	58	46.4	60	48.0	125
Wu	3	3.9	10	13.2	26	34.2	37	48.7	76
Xiang	2	9.5	5	23.8	5	23.8	9	42.9	21
Min	3	1.5	17	8.4	83	41.1	99	49.0	202
Yue	2	2.8	5	7.0	23	32.4	41	57.7	71
Gan	0		1	11.1	3	33.3	5	55.6	9
Hakka	0	0		9	29.0	22	71.0		31
total	14	2.0	57	8.1	277	39.3	356	50.6	704

Conclusions

The results from our survey generally support the relevance and importance of current attempts in the US to promote Mandarin as a heritage or community language. Among respondents in our survey Mandarin is used often, is highly regarded, and is seen as a resource to be preserved despite high levels of multilingualism and multidialectism among our respondents. The majority of these participants have favorable attitudes toward linguistic diversity and language maintenance generally, which includes Mandarin, and in many cases too another Chinese heritage language variety.

Even though it is not possible to know how many of the respondents are residing permanently, or will end up residing permanently in the US, there is enthusiastic support all round for Chinese origin children in the US to have the opportunity for Mandarin language learning and maintenance as part of their American K–12 education. For most respondents there seems to be no conflict between learning English and having a bilingual education for their children.

Some differences are noteworthy regarding those from Hong Kong and Taiwan. Those from Hong Kong indicated lesser proficiency in Mandarin. The respondents from Taiwan were more likely to be multidialectal speakers of Mandarin and Taiwanese or Mandarin and Hakka. Those from Taiwan and particularly Hong Kong were less likely to support instruction in simplified characters. This reluctance may be associated with the age of the respondents; those from both areas tended to be older than those from the Mainland.

Within our sample, there is not much difference between how standard Mandarin speakers and dialect speakers look at linguistic diversity. However, because of the limitations of the sample—nonrandom, very small numbers in some of the subsets—a better investigation of potential differences can only be made utilizing a sample design that would ensure generalizability.

Despite the overall tolerance for language diversity and support for heritage language maintenance for Mandarin and the major dialects, the absence of formal instruction for most of the major dialects in the US, with the possible exception of Cantonese, makes it unlikely that these varieties will be maintained over time. This topic goes beyond the scope of our current survey but is the focal point of our ongoing research.

References

Baugh, J. (2000). *Beyond Ebonics: Linguistic pride and racial prejudice.* New York: Oxford University Press.

Brecht, R. D., & Ingold, C. W. (May, 2002). *Tapping a national resource: Heritage languages in the United States.* ERIC Digest. EDO–FL–02–02

Chang, I. (2003). *The Chinese in America.* New York: the Penguin Group.

Chao, T. H. (1997, June). Chinese heritage community language schools in the United States. *ERIC Digest,* No. EDO-FL–97–10.

Dayle, B. (1983). The implementation of language planning in China. In J. Corbarribias & J. Fishman (Eds.), *Progress in language planning: International perspectives* (pp. 291–308). Berlin: Mouton Publishers.

Fishman, J. A. (1991). *Reversing language shift.* Clevedon, England: Multilingual Matters.

Fishman, J. A. (1999). *Handbook of language and ethnic identity.* Oxford, England: Oxford University Press.

Fishman, J. A. (Ed.). (2001). *Can threatened languages be saved?* Clevedon, England: Multilingual Matters.

Hinton, L., & Hale, K. (2001). *The green book of language revitalization*. London: Academic Press.

Horvath, B. M., & Vaughan, P. (1991). *Community languages: A handbook*. Clevedon, England: Multilingual Matters.

Hsia, T.-T. (1956). *China's language reforms*. New Haven, CT: Far Eastern Publications, Yale University.

Institute of International Education. (2006). *New enrollment of foreign students in the U.S. climbs in 2005/06*. Retrieved January 10, 2007, from http://opendoors.iienetwork.org/?p=89251

Li, W. (1994). *Three generations, two languages, one family: Language choice and language shift in a Chinese community in Britain*. Clevedon, England: Multilingual Matters.

Li, W. L. (1982). The language shift of Chinese-Americans. *International Journal of the Sociology of Language, 38,* 109–124.

Lippi-Green, R. (1997). *English with an accent: Standard language ideology and language attitudes: Language, ideology, and discrimination in the United States*. New York: Routledge.

McGinnis, S. (2005). More than a silver bullet: The role of Chinese as a heritage language in the United States. *The Modern Language Journal, 89,* 592–594.

National Language Committee. (2006). *Chinese language usage survey*. Retrieved February 16, 2006, from http://www.moe.edu.cn/edoas/website18/info14493.htm

Norman, J. (1988). *Chinese*. Cambridge, England: Cambridge University Press.

Ramsey, S. R. (1987). *The languages of China*. Princeton, NJ: Princeton University Press.

Taylor, I., & Taylor, M. M. (1995). *Chinese, Korean and Japanese*. Amsterdam: John Benjamins Publishing.

Teng, X., & Weng, Y. (2001). Bilingualism and bilingual education in China. In N. K. Shimahara, I. Z. Holowinsky, & S. Tomlinson-Clarke (Eds.), *Ethnicity, race, and nationality in education: A global perspective* (pp. 213–233). Mahwah, NJ: Lawrence Erlbaum Associates.

U.S. Census Bureau. (2003). *Census 2000, public use microdata sample, United States, technical documentation*. Washington, DC: Author.

Wiley, T. G. (2001). On defining heritage languages and their speakers. In J. K. Peyton, D. A. Ranard, & S. McGinnis (Eds.), *Heritage languages in America: Preserving a national resource* (pp. 29–36). Washington, DC & McHenry, IL: Center for Applied Linguistics and Delta Systems.

Wiley, T. G. (in press). Chinese "dialect" speakers as heritage language learners: A case study. In O. Kagan (Ed.), *Heritage languages: Festschrift for Russell Campbell*. Mahwah, NJ: Lawrence Erlbaum Associates.

Wong, S. C., & Lopez, M. G. (2000). English language learners of Chinese background. In S. L. Mckay & S. C. Wong (Eds.), *New Immigrants in the United States* (pp. 263–305). Cambridge, England: Cambridge University Press.

Yan, M. M. (2006). *Introduction to Chinese dialectology*. Munich: LINCOM Europa.

6

Motivation and Achievement in Chinese Language Learning: A Comparative Analysis

Xuehong Lu
State University of New York–Buffalo

Guofang Li
Michigan State University

This chapter presents a comparative analysis of the effect of different motivational factors (integrative, instrumental, and situational) on heritage and non-heritage college students' Chinese learning in mixed classrooms. Data for this study include questionnaires collected among Chinese heritage students (n=59) and non-Chinese heritage students (n=61, including 19 Asian non-Chinese and 42 non-Asian non-Chinese students) enrolled in Chinese language classes. Quantitative results indicate that both integrative and instrumental motivations are important to students' self-confidence in their language proficiency, but integrative motivation is more important to students' overall tests scores. Contrary to previous findings, heritage language students are more influenced by instrumental motivation than non-heritage students. However, Chinese heritage language students are less influenced by situational factors (such as teacher effect, effect of mixed-classes) than non-heritage language students, especially non-Chinese, non-Asian students. Findings suggest that in addition to promoting students' integrative motivation, Chinese language teaching at college level should also include curriculum and teacher professional development that addresses students' mixed abilities and needs, and fosters individual students' sustained interest in the language.

In the past two decades, changes in U.S. demographics and market opportunities in China have generated great interest in Mandarin Chinese as a foreign language in the United States. Based on the 2000 U.S. census, the Asian American population has increased to 10.2 million, representing 3.6% of the total 281.4 million U.S. population. Chinese Americans, totaling 2.43 million, form the largest subgroup, constituting 23.7% of the Asian American population, and 0.9% of the nation's total population. California (980,642) and New York (424,774) are the two states with the largest Chinese American populations. At the same time, as the world's largest market and leading a steadily growing economy, China has become a land of opportunity for a wide array of businesses. An article in the May 9, 2005 issue of *Newsweek* magazine states that while the 20th century was called the American century, the 21st century is China's. With these changes in the United States and in China, the Chinese language is becoming increasingly important in the West and around the globe.

Lu, X., & Li, G. (2008). Motivation and achievement in Chinese language learning: A comparative analysis. In A. W. He, & Y. Xiao (Eds.), *Chinese as a heritage language: Fostering rooted world citizenry* (pp. 89–108). Honolulu: University of Hawai'i, National Foreign Language Resource Center.

Despite the growing importance of the Chinese language in the world economy, in the United States, the enrollment in Chinese learning in K–16 has been relatively low. Among the most commonly taught languages, Chinese ranked seventh after Spanish, French, Italian, German, American Sign Language, and Japanese. According to a report released by the Asia Society, only 24,000 students in grades 7–12 study Chinese, a language spoken by 1.3 billion people worldwide; in contrast, more than one million students learn French, a language spoken by only 80 million people (Asia Society, 2005).

Change in college enrollment in Chinese as a foreign language has also been reported to be small. According to the Modern Language Association report (Welles, 2004), college enrollment in Chinese as a foreign language grew from 28,456 by 20% to just over 34,000 between 1998 and 2002. This rate is relatively low compared with other foreign languages such as American Sign Language, which grew by 432.2%; Arabic, which grew by 92.3%; and Italian, which grew by 29.6%. Despite the government's continued push for expanding Chinese language instruction in the K–16 level, there are many challenges to higher educational institutions that lacked not only language resources, infrastructure, but also qualified teachers and established programs to provide quality instruction.

Another growing challenge is that, unlike previous language classes that were mostly students of Chinese heritage, the new student body is becoming increasingly diverse: It includes not only students of Chinese origin and heritage, but also a large group of students with non-Chinese backgrounds who not only differ in their cultural and linguistic backgrounds, but also in their purposes of learning the language, particularly their motivation to learn.

Mixed classrooms with heritage and non-heritage college students have also presented unprecedented pedagogical challenges. Categorized as one of the so-called "less commonly taught" foreign languages in the United States, the Chinese language shares many pedagogical concerns with some other foreign languages. One difficulty in teaching Chinese in the US is that it is taught in a foreign language (FL) setting, because authentic language input may not be readily available outside the classroom for most students. Additionally, with a character-based logographic language, Chinese language learners must be highly motivated since persistence and determination are indispensable to cope with the stress of a difficult language (Okada, Oxford, & Abo, 1996; Root, 1999). In fact, Chinese was rated by the ACFTL guidelines as one of the most difficult languages (Hadley, 2001), and Chinese character learning is considered the most daunting task of learning Chinese (Everson, 1998). This situation is further complicated when one teaches Chinese as a foreign language in a mixed classroom setting which contains a number of non-heritage learners, whose Chinese language proficiency and understanding of the Chinese culture might be at different levels in comparison with their heritage fellow students. Some important questions arise: Since the two groups of learners come from such different cultural and linguistic backgrounds, would the presence of the two groups in the same classroom affect each other's motivation in learning the language? Would the presence of heritage learners—that is, students with a "Chinese background"—make Chinese language classes more intimidating for non-heritage learners and therefore decreases their motivation to learn? Or vice versa, would the presence of students with non-Chinese background make the classes less interesting and challenging for heritage learners and hence affects their motivation to learn as well? Though research to date has suggested that motivation is the most important factor that affects language learning, most of these studies have focused on the study of motivation among a more homogeneous group. Few studies have explored and compared how motivation affects foreign language learning between heritage and non-heritage students in mixed classrooms.

The goal of this study is to bridge this gap in research on motivation and foreign language learning by comparing heritage and non-heritage college students in mixed Chinese classrooms in two universities in Western New York. Specifically, this study addresses the following four research questions:

1. Do heritage and non-heritage learners differ in terms of motivational factors such as integrative and instrumental orientations towards learning Chinese?

2. Is there a relationship between integrative and instrumental motivations and learning outcomes as measured by teacher assessments?

3. How do differences in learner traits (i.e., students' perceptions of their own abilities) influence their motivation to learn?

4. How do differences in situational motivation influence the two groups of students' Chinese learning?

Previous research on motivation and second/foreign language learning

Research on second and foreign language education has long associated motivation with language learning (e.g., Gardner, 1979, 1985; Gardner & Lambert, 1959). Motivation, defined as the intentions, desires, goals, and needs that determine human and animal behavior, is believed to be one of the most important affective factors that influence foreign and second language learning. In second and foreign language education, motivation is identified as the learner's orientation with regard to the goal of learning the target language. Motivation affects the extent to which language learners persevere in learning, what kinds of learning behavior they exert, and their actual language attainment (Ellis, 1997). Crookes and Schmidt (1991) argue that there are four determinants of motivation: interest (that sustains learners' curiosity), relevance (that satisfies learners' needs), expectancy (that promises learners the possibility of success), and reward (that results in positive outcome). These four elements are inter-related and no single determinant would become a motivating force. Ho (1998) points out that motivation to learn a language is not a single condition of the learner but the sum of a wide range of factors that are expressed in the behavior shown by the learner in the classroom.

Gardner (1985, 2001) theorizes in his well-cited socio-educational model that there are two motivational orientations: *instrumental* and *integrative*. Instrumental orientation signifies an interest in learning the second/foreign language for pragmatic reasons such as getting a better job or requesting a higher pay, reading technical materials, passing required exams, meeting the requirements for school or university graduation, or translation work. Integrative orientation reflects a genuine interest in learning the second language in order to come closer psychologically to the other language community. The integratively motivated individual is one who is motivated to learn the second/foreign language, has a desire or willingness to identify with the other language community, and tends to evaluate the learning situation positively (Gardner, 2001). According to Gardner, integrativeness involves emotional identification with target cultural group, a favorable attitude toward the language community, and an openness to the cultural group and other groups in general (i.e., an absence of ethnocentrism).

Early research on second language learning suggested that integrative motivation was more conducive to better language attainment as integrative motivation typically underlies successful acquisition of a wide range of registers and a native-like pronunciation (Finegan, 1999). However, later research on motivation in foreign language settings shows that both forms of motivation are important and in some situations or instances, instrumental motivation was even more important for successful foreign language achievement (Kachru, 1994; Lukmani, 1972; Norris-Holt, 2001). For example, Rahman (2003), in his study of Bangladeshi college students' orientation and motivation toward English learning, finds that students focus on English for its utilitarian value (e.g., getting a good job, going abroad for further study, reading books, and traveling) and integrative motivation was not a dominant motivational orientation.

Similar findings can also be found in studies in the U.S. context. Kondo (1998) studied second generation Japanese university students' motivation to take Japanese courses. In this study, students' motivation is very much related to students' subjective value (valence) they placed on the language as well as their belief about their own ability to reach the target level of proficiency. Their short-term goals were to pass the Japanese courses with good grades. However, many also had long-term goals of becoming better Japanese speakers. In a study of Chinese heritage language students' motivation in taking college Chinese courses, Wen (1997) concluded that the motivation for many students beginning to learn the Chinese language was both intrinsic and instrumental. The integrative motivation was to better understand their heritage language and culture, and appreciate Chinese art and literature. At the same time, the students' motivation was also instrumental in that they took the language classes because the fulfilling requirements were less demanding than other five-unit courses. The contradictory findings from early and later studies suggest that the two motivational orientations may not be clear-cut or dichotomous. Each orientation needs to be investigated within the specific learning contexts and situations.

Extending Gardener's socio-educational framework, Dörnyei (1990, 1994, 1996) argues that research on motivation and second/foreign language learning should consider the social and pragmatic dimensions of motivation. These dimensions include the personal traits of the learner and the situational factors in which the learning occurs, that is, they reflect who learns what and where. In his motivational model, he classifies motivational factors into three levels: the language level (reactions and attitudes toward the target language which can be instrumental and/or integrative), the learner level (socio-cognitive factors such as need for achievement and self-confidence), and the learning situation level (which is related to a specific language course, a teacher, or a peer group situation). Agreeing with Dörnyei's extension, Gardner (2001) in his revised socio-educational model also points out that in addition to examining integrative and instrumental orientation, it is important to consider individual differences in learners' motivational orientation in learning a language, especially in language anxiety (i.e., feelings and concerns in using the language in the classroom and other contexts) and attitudes toward the learning situation including formal and informal learning contexts (e.g., types of classrooms).

In sum, a wide array of factors affects students' motivation in foreign language learning. In this study, our analysis of Chinese heritage and non-Chinese heritage students' motivation in Chinese learning considers both integrative and instrumental motivation as well as learner traits and situational factors. In terms of personal traits, we examine learners' language anxiety or confidence level in the four language skills such as reading, writing, speaking, and listening. In terms of the situational factors, we investigate students' attitudes towards teacher effect (teacher's instructional approach, teacher feedback, and teacher's efficacy), course style (teacher-centered or student-centered classes), class level (e.g., introductory, intermediate, and advanced) and class composition (e.g., homogeneous or mixed classes with students from diverse cultural and linguistic backgrounds and different levels of Chinese proficiency). The following (Figure 1) is the theoretical model we use to guide our study of the direct and competitive effect of each of the two motivations on Chinese language achievements, as well as motivations' indirect effect on achievements, through the learner's personal characteristics and situational factors.

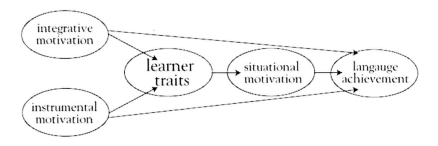

Figure 1. Theoretical model for language achievement

Method

The purpose of this study was to investigate the relationship between various motivations, learners' situational factors, and language proficiency achievements among heritage and non-heritage Chinese language students of college level in a mixed classroom setting. A questionnaire survey was used for data collection for this study.

Subjects

The sample for this study included 120 students from nine Chinese college classes at two universities in Western New York. The 120 students could be considered anything but homogenous. Since the Chinese language program at these sites placed various students in mixed classrooms, the students enrolled had varied in Mandarin Chinese skills, from zero (FL students) to advanced (HL and continued Chinese students). The participants' Chinese language proficiency was classified by their instructional levels.

Based on their cultural/linguistic heritage, we classified the students in three categories: (a) Chinese heritage (CH) students with various amounts of Chinese exposure from family members and communities in the Mainland China, Taiwan, Hong Kong, or South Pacific countries (n=59); (b) Asian non-Chinese students (ANC) such as those from Japan, Korea, and Vietnam (n=19); and (c) Non-Asian, non-Chinese (NANC) students (European and African Americans whose native language is English; n=42).

Fifty-nine students whose parents had a Chinese-speaking background made up the Chinese Heritage (CH) learners group. These CH students include 1.5 and 2.0 generation Chinese students with limited proficiency as well as students who were raised in families of Chinese origin living in the Southeast Asian areas. All these students have some form of exposure to Chinese and can speak or understand Cantonese or other Chinese dialects and they were enrolled in classes to study Mandarin, the standard Chinese language.

The Asian, Non-Chinese group (ANC) consisted of 19 students whose parents had no Chinese language background but had an Asian language background, such as Korean, Japanese, and a few Southern Pacific Asian countries. Korean and Japanese languages and cultures are closely connected with Chinese. Both Japanese Kanji and the traditional Korean writing system use many Chinese characters, even though the pronunciations are completely different.

Forty-two students whose parents had no Chinese language background and who were born in the United States made up the Non-Asian, non-Chinese group (NANC). The NANC students are those college students of European origin and a few African Americans. Some have already learned one or more foreign languages. For others, Chinese is their first foreign language. Unlike the students in the CH and ANC groups, the NANC students have a wider range of age in the Chinese language classes, while the other two groups of students fall between 18 to 24 years of age.

Instrument

The instrument used for this study consisted of a three-part questionnaire (see the Appendix). The first part of the questionnaire measured the independent variables: integrative orientation, instrumental orientation, learning contexts or situational factors, and learners' expectations for future studies in the language. Eighteen questions on integrative and instrumental orientation were adapted from the Attitude/Motivation Test Battery (AMTB) by Gardner (1985). Fourteen questions on learning contexts or situational factors (teacher effect, course style, grade level, and class composition), were developed based on Dörnyei's (1994) theoretical framework on situational motivation. In order to better understand how the situational factors influence learners' motivational orientation, we also added six questions on learners' expectations for Chinese language learning in their future studies. A 7-point Likert scale was used for questions in this section.

The second part of the questionnaire consisted of 16 questions on students' learning situational scale which were also based on Dörnyei's (1994) theoretical framework. The students were asked to check the level best describing their attitudes toward their learning contexts. A 5-point scale was used for this section. The third section included 29 questions to gather demographic information about the respondents, racial and ethnic backgrounds, family social economic status, language usage at home, and so forth. In this section, four questions were included to measure students' self-perception of their Chinese language abilities in four skill areas such as reading, writing, listening, and speaking. These questions were conceptualized and developed by the researchers. In addition to the information collected through the questionnaire, students' GPA upon their entry into the Chinese classes was also collected.

In addition to the questionnaire, the final course grades were also used to measure students' learning outcomes. Though the final course grades data were collected from the different levels of the Chinese programs and final exams for each level were different in course content, a similar grading scale for the was used at all levels, which allowed the a consistent and reliable set of scores across classes for analysis.

Procedure

The questionnaire survey was administered during Fall 2005, and the interviews were conducted during the same semester. We asked the administration and faculty at each of the two campuses to assist in the data collection. The instructors distributed questionnaires in their Chinese classes and the participants returned them after completion. The data was analyzed using SPSS 14.0 for Windows. Major statistical techniques used in the study include (a) Descriptive analysis of motivation scores, (b) Independent samples *t*-test of instrumental and integrative motivation, (c) ANOVA correlation analysis of dependent and independent variables, and (d) factor analysis on situational motivation.

Results

The objectives of this study were to examine (a) whether heritage (CH) and non-heritage learners (ANC and NANC) differ in terms of motivational factors such as integrative and instrumental orientations towards learning Chinese; (b) the relationship between integrative and instrumental motivations and learning outcomes as measured by teacher assessments; (c) differences in learner traits (i.e., students' perceptions of their own abilities) that influence their motivation to learn; and (d) differences in situational motivation that influence the two groups of students' Chinese learning. In the following, the results on instrumental, integrative, and situational motivation as well as personal traits among the three groups of students are presented.

Comparative results on integrative and instrumental orientation

A descriptive analysis of motivation scores on integrative and instrumental motivation in the survey across the three groups indicates that in terms of integrative orientation, there is no significant difference across the three groups. The mean score of the Chinese was 38.29 ($SD=6.256$, $n=59$); the ANC (Asian non-Chinese) group was 36.37 ($SD=6.702$, $n=19$); and the NANC (non-Asian non-Chinese) students was 36.52 ($SD=6.504$, $n=42$). According to one-way analysis of variance, no significant differences were observed: F (2, 119)=1.202, $p=.304$. In terms of instrumental motivational orientation, the mean score of the Chinese was 33.08 ($SD=6.966$, $n=59$); the ANC group was 27.21 ($SD=7.277$, $n=19$); and the NANC students was 25.19 ($SD=7.134$, $n=42$). At the univariate level, significant differences among the three groups were observed: F (2, 119)=16.352, $p<.001$. In order to further understand the motivational differences between the Chinese heritage and the NANC heritage students, independent t tests were conducted. While no significant difference was seen in integrative orientation ($t=1.374$, $p=.173$), significant difference was found in instrumental orientation ($t=5.557$, $p<.001$).

Comparative results on learning outcomes

In terms of learning outcomes, our analysis shows that although CH students had a lower GPA (M=3.144) than the ANC group (M=3.3509) and NANC group (M=3.3582) while entering the program, they do perform better on the final teacher assessment in Chinese. The 2005 final assessment results show a significant difference: F (2, 119)=3.736, $p=.027$. The mean scores of their final assessment among the three groups are: CH (M=91.98), ANC (M=90.37), and NANC (M=86.57).

A covariate analysis indicates that there is a strong correlation between integrative motivational orientation and final assessment scores ($r=.219$, $p=.016$), but a weak correlation between instrumental orientation and final assessment results ($r=0.122$, $p=.185$). A further breakdown analysis among the three groups, however, shows significant differences across groups. Among the Chinese heritage (CH) students, neither instrumental ($r=.137$, $p=.577$) nor integrative motivation ($r=.115$, $p=.386$) is strongly correlated to final assessment scores. The analysis among the NAC group also yields similar results. Even more, a negative correlation is found between instrumental motivation and final assessment results ($r=-.192$, $p=.431$). With regard to the NANC group, the results suggest that though instrumental motivation is not correlated to higher test scores ($r=.148$, $p=.349$), integrative motivation is significantly correlated to higher test scores ($r=.349$, $p=.024$). We speculate that the reason for the differential results may in part due to smaller sample sizes in the subgroups (with ANC group being the smallest and NANC group the second smallest). Therefore, there is less statistical power to detect significant differences in sub-group analysis than large group analysis.

Comparative results on personal traits

In this study, we attribute personal traits to students' perception of their own abilities in reading, writing, speaking, and listening in Chinese. We hypothesize that, due to Chinese heritage language students' familiarity with Chinese language and culture, they would have more self-confidence in all four language skills than non-Chinese heritage students. Therefore, they will do better in the language assessment than the other two groups.

The analysis also demonstrates a strong correlation between instrumental motivation, integrative motivation, and students' self-confidence in all four language skills. As we predicted, Chinese heritage students display consistently higher self-evaluation of their Chinese reading, writing, listening, and speaking abilities than the non-Chinese heritage students. ANC students are more confident in their Chinese reading and writing abilities than the NANC students, but less confident in their listening and speaking skills.

The results of three groups indicate that, for the Chinese heritage students, instrumental motivation is not correlated with their confidence in any of the four language skills. Interestingly, integrative motivation is highly correlated to their perceptions on their listening and speaking abilities, but *not* their reading or writing skills (see Table 1).

Table 1. Correlations between integrative motivation and self-perception of four skills among Chinese heritage students

		integrative	selfListen	selfSpeak	selfRead	selfWrite
integrative	Pearson correlation	1	.466**	.345*	.186	.224
	sig. 2-tailed		.000	.011	.183	.106
	N	59	54	54	53	53
selfListen	Pearson correlation	.466**	1	.683**	.542**	.415**
	sig. 2-tailed	.000		.000	.000	.002
	N	54	54	54	53	53
selfSpeak	Pearson correlation	.345*	.683**	1	.358**	.258
	sig. 2-tailed	.011	.000		.008	.062
	N	54	54	54	53	53
selfRead	Pearson correlation	.186	.542**	.358**	1	.842**
	sig. 2-tailed	.183	.000	.008		.000
	N	53	53	53	53	53
selfWrite	Pearson correlation	.224	.415**	.258	.842**	1
	sig. 2-tailed	.106	.002	.062	.000	
	N	53	53	53	53	53

** Correlation is significant at the 0.01 level (2-tailed).
* Correlation is significant at the 0.05 level (2-tailed).

For the ANC group, the analysis suggests that there is no strong correlation between instrumental or integrative motivation and their self-confidence. In some incidents, instrumental motivation is negatively correlated to their perception of their listening abilities ($r=-.036$, $p=.888$).

The analysis of the NANC group showed mixed results. Instrumental motivation is not correlated to their confidence in any of their four language skills. Integrative motivation seems to be highly correlated to their confidence in listening, speaking, and writing, but not in reading (see Table 2).

Table 2. Correlations between integrative motivation and self-perception of four skills among NANC students

		integrative	selfListen	selfSpeak	selfRead	selfWrite
integrative	Pearson correlation	1	.396*	.357*	.169	.441**
	sig. 2-tailed		.018	.035	.331	.008
	N	42	35	35	35	35
selfListen	Pearson correlation	.396*	1	.820**	.506**	.523**
	sig. 2-tailed	.018		.000	.002	.001
	N	35	35	35	35	35
selfSpeak	Pearson correlation	.357*	.820**	1	.357*	.458**
	sig. 2-tailed	.035	.000		.035	.006
	N	35	35	35	35	35
selfRead	Pearson correlation	.169	.506**	.357*	1	.716**
	sig. 2-tailed	.331	.002	.035		.000
	N	35	35	35	35	35
selfWrite	Pearson correlation	.441**	.523**	.458**	.716**	1
	sig. 2-tailed	.008	.001	.006	.000	
	N	35	35	35	35	35

** Correlation is significant at the 0.01 level (2-tailed).
* Correlation is significant at the 0.05 level (2-tailed).

Comparative results on situational motivation

In order to better understand the impact of situational motivation on Chinese language learning, a factor analysis was first conducted to generate meaningful factors. Thirteen questions were included in the correlation matrix and factor extraction. Principal component analysis was also performed to extract factors that had eigenvalues of greater than 1.0. Four factors emerged: (a) effect of teacher (e.g., teacher's instructional approach, feedback, and efficacy), (b) effect of course style (e.g., teacher-centered or student-centered classes), (c) effect of class level (e.g., grade levels such as introductory, intermediate and advanced), and (d) effect of class composition (e.g., homogeneous or mixed classes with students from diverse cultural and linguistic backgrounds and different levels of Chinese proficiency). The means and standard deviation of the four factors were calculated. The results show that the highest mean for the teacher effect factor was (M=.813), followed by effect of mixed classes (M=.740), effect of class level (M=.614), and then by course style (M=.606).

Following the factor analysis, a bi-variate analysis was used to determine the effect of situational factors and students' motivation patterns, as well as their desire for future studies. The analysis including all students suggests that there is a strong correlation between teacher effect and students' integrative (r=.587, p<.001) and instrumental motivation (r=.315, p<.001). There is some correlation between effect of course style and integrative motivation (r=.186, p=.042), but not instrumental motivation (r=.150, p=.101). Students' desire for future studies was also highly correlated with teacher effect ($r=.227$, $p=.013$), but not with course style ($r=.089$, $p=.334$).

Separate analysis of the three groups suggests significant differences with these factors across the groups. As Table 3 demonstrates, among the Chinese heritage students, there were strong correlations between teacher effect and their instrumental and integrative motivation, but effect of class composition was weakly correlated to their instrumental motivation, but not to integrative motivation. Neither teacher nor class composition effect was correlated to their desire for future studies or their test scores (see Table 3).

Table 3. Correlations between situational factors and motivation among Chinese heritage students

		integrative	instrumental	effectTeacher	effectClass	futureSum	gradeF05
integrative	Pearson correlation	1	.596**	.668**	.106	.296*	.063
	sig. 2-tailed		.000	.000	.425	.023	.638
	N	59	59	59	59	59	59
instrumental	Pearson correlation	.596**	1	.523**	.255	.498**	.007
	sig. 2-tailed	.000		.000	.051	.000	.955
	N	59	59	59	59	59	59
effectTeacher	Pearson correlation	.668**	.523**	1	.432**	.075	.129
	sig. 2-tailed	.000	.000		.001	.575	.328
	N	59	59	59	59	59	59
effectClass	Pearson correlation	.106	.255	.432**	1	−.074	.045
	sig. 2-tailed	.425	.051	.001		.577	.736
	N	59	59	59	59	59	59
futureSum	Pearson correlation	.296*	.498**	.075	−.074	1	−.150
	sig. 2-tailed	.023	.000	.575	.577		.256
	N	59	59	59	59	59	59
gradeF05	Pearson correlation	.063	.007	.129	.045	−.150	1
	sig. 2-tailed	.638	.955	.328	.736	.256	
	N	59	59	59	59	59	59

** Correlation is significant at the 0.01 level (2-tailed).
* Correlation is significant at the 0.05 level (2-tailed).

For the Asian non-Chinese students, teacher effect was highly correlated with both their instrumental and integrative motivation, but not to their expectations for further studies or their test scores. Class composition effect did not have correlations with their instrumental or integrative motivation, or their desire for future studies, but was important for their test scores (see Table 4).

Table 4. Correlations between situational factors and motivation among ANC students

		integrative	instrumental	effectTeacher	effectClass	futureSum	gradeF05
integrative	Pearson correlation	1	.675**	.818**	.367	.410	.106
	sig. 2-tailed		.002	.000	.123	.081	.665
	N	19	19	19	19	19	19
instrumental	Pearson correlation	.675**	1	.569*	.208	.151	−.115
	sig. 2-tailed	.002		.011	.393	.536	.639
	N	19	19	19	19	19	19
effectTeacher	Pearson correlation	.818**	.569*	1	.228	.360	.139
	sig. 2-tailed	.000	.011		.349	.130	.571
	N	19	19	19	19	19	19
effectClass	Pearson correlation	.367	.208	.228	1	−.075	.496*
	sig. 2-tailed	.123	.393	.349		.759	.031
	N	19	19	19	19	19	19
futureSum	Pearson correlation	.410	.151	.360	−.075	1	−.409
	sig. 2-tailed	.081	.536	.130	.759		.082
	N	19	19	19	19	19	19
gradeF05	Pearson correlation	.106	−.115	.139	.496*	−.409	1
	sig. 2-tailed	.665	.639	.571	.031	.082	
	N	19	19	19	19	19	19

** Correlation is significant at the 0.01 level (2-tailed).
* Correlation is significant at the 0.05 level (2-tailed).

Among the NANC students, Table 5 shows that teacher effect is strongly correlated to integrative motivation, but not instrumental motivation. The effect of mixed classes did not have any correlations with either integrative or instrumental motivation. It seems to be highly related to teacher effect. Though their desire for future learning is significantly correlated to integrative motivation, teacher effect, class composition effect as well as their test scores, class composition effect has the lowest among all the factors. Apparently, their desire for future learning was correlated to integrative motivation. Interestingly, their test scores did not have strong correlations with teacher or class effects, but did with their desire for future learning (see Table 5).

Table 5. Correlations between situational factors and motivation among NANC students

		integrative	instrumental	effectTeacher	effectClass	futureSum	gradeF05
integrative	Pearson correlation	1	.551**	.445**	.219	.489**	.336*
	sig. 2-tailed		.000	.003	.164	.001	.030
	N	42	42	42	42	42	42
instrumental	Pearson correlation	.551**	1	.240	.096	.169	.164
	sig. 2-tailed	.000		.126	.545	.285	.298
	N	42	42	42	42	42	42

continued…

Table 5. Correlations between situational factors and motivation among NANC students (cont.)

		integrative	instrumental	effectTeacher	effectClass	futureSum	gradeF05
effectTeacher	Pearson correlation	.445**	.240	1	.460**	.344*	.192
	sig. 2-tailed	.003	.126		.002	.026	.224
	N	42	42	42	42	42	42
effectClass	Pearson correlation	.219	.096	.460**	1	.312*	.189
	sig. 2-tailed	.164	.545	.002		.044	.232
	N	42	42	42	42	42	42
futureSum	Pearson correlation	.489**	.169	.344*	.312*	1	.552**
	sig. 2-tailed	.001	.285	.026	.044		.000
	N	42	42	42	42	42	42
gradeF05	Pearson correlation	.336*	.164	.192	.189	.552**	1
	sig. 2-tailed	.030	.298	.224	.232	.000	
	N	42	42	42	42	42	42

** Correlation is significant at the 0.01 level (2-tailed).
* Correlation is significant at the 0.05 level (2-tailed).

Discussion

The findings of this study suggest that both integrative and instrumental motivations are important to college students' Chinese learning. Similar to previous research conclusions, the results of this study also indicate that the instrumental and integrative orientations are not dichotomous or mutually exclusive in the college students' Chinese learning (Finegan, 1999). How each orientation plays a role in students' language learning should be understood within the specific context and against students' particular cultural and linguistic backgrounds.

Consistent with previous research (Wen, 1997; Yang, 2003), in this study, integrative orientation is important for all three groups of learners including the Chinese heritage learners. For the CH learners, this suggests that motivation to learn the language correlates with intrinsic interest in Chinese culture and the desire to understand one's own cultural heritage. For ANC and NANC students who are outside of the Chinese culture, the desire to interact with Chinese speakers and become associated with authentic Chinese language and culture is important for their success in learning the language. However, there is difference in terms of instrumental motivation among the three groups of students. Chinese heritage students reported higher instrumental motivation in their language learning than the Asian non-Chinese students and the non-Asian, non-Chinese students. The differences may be attributed to Chinese heritage students' cultural and linguistic backgrounds who might think that the Chinese courses are less demanding for them. It is possible that they may choose to take Chinese classes just for easy grades or passing the FL language requirements. This might also be true to the Asian non-Chinese students who are also more instrumentally motivated than the non-Asian, non-Chinese students.

Interesting differences are also observed in the students' self-confidence in learning. Though both instrumental and integrative motivations are important to students' confidence level and their overall test results, how the two motivational orientations play out in the three groups of students vary greatly. Among the Chinese heritage students, neither instrumental nor integrative motivation matters to their self-confidence. This is probably due to their Chinese cultural and linguistic backgrounds which have already afforded them confidence in their language abilities and their familiarity with the language also contributed to their high test scores among the three groups. In contrast, for the Asian non-Chinese groups, it seems that the more they are motivated, the less they are confident in their language abilities. This might be related to their first language and cultural interference. Although their first language (e.g., Japanese and Korean) might be similar to Chinese in terms of the orthographic system, the more they study Chinese, the more differences they may find between the two languages. For both Asian non-Chinese and non-Asian non-Chinese students, integrative motivation is significant in fostering their confidence in their language abilities. That is, the more they want to learn about Chinese culture, the more confident they are in their language learning.

One thing worth noting here is that integrative motivation plays an important but different role in students' self-confidence in the four language skills. For the Chinese heritage students, for example, integrative motivation is important for their perception of their listening and speaking abilities, but not reading and writing abilities. This may be related to their desire to be able to communicate in Chinese and speak as fluently as native-Chinese speakers, but due to their limited exposure to Chinese reading and writing while growing up in the American context, they are less developed in their Chinese literacy skills. The non-Asian, non-Chinese students also demonstrated a similar tendency. That is, they are more motivated to learn the language and they pay more attention to their oral communication skills rather than the literacy skills such as reading and writing. For this group of students, their lack of confidence in literacy skills such as reading may be related to the orthographic difference between their first language (e.g., English and Chinese).

In terms of situational factors, the findings suggest that teacher effect and the effect of mixed classes exert the most important influence on the students' motivation to learn. Teacher quality seems to be related not only to students' integrative motivation but also to instrumental motivation. This suggests that teacher quality and how they conduct their classes is of paramount significance to students' success in learning. Mixed classes, however, only affect students' integrative motivation. This may be related to the fact that through mixed classes, non-Chinese students are exposed to Chinese heritage students who are from the target language culture, and therefore they become more motivated to learn the target language. On the other hand, the Chinese heritage students are exposed to students of other ethnic backgrounds who are motivated to learn their language and culture. The experience validates their perception and value of their heritage language and culture, and therefore further motivates them to learn the language and culture.

There are, however, significant differences across the groups in terms of their desire for continued study in the language. For Chinese heritage students and Asian non-Chinese, neither teacher nor class effect matters. For the non-Chinese, non-Asian students, teacher effect, not class effect, seems to have a determining role in their continued interest in the learning Chinese. It might be that for the Chinese and Asian students, their cultural backgrounds already enable them to have the intrinsic motivation to learn the language. But for the non-Chinese, non-Asian students, who do not have the intrinsic culture factor to learn the language, the Chinese language teacher might become the bridge for understanding the Chinese culture. Their continued interest in the language is highly dependent on how well the teacher motivates them to want to learn more about the language and culture.

Pedagogical implications

The findings of this study have significant implications for college Chinese instruction in mixed classes. First, the results show that integrative motivation is important to all students but the importance of instrumental motivation varies. These results suggest two important orientations for college Chinese instruction. One is that in all courses, cultural studies should be an important part of the language curriculum. Since all students have the desire to learn Chinese culture and become part of the Chinese cultural community, it is important that the curriculum is aligned with students' integrative motivation. The other orientation is that since students are more diversified in their instrumental motivation, it is necessary for Chinese language teachers to recognize the specific types of instrumental motivation among the different groups of students in order to help students achieve success in language learning.

The results also show that the different motivations play different roles in students' confidence in their Chinese reading, writing, speaking, and listening abilities. These findings suggest that for students who come from different backgrounds and have different motivational orientations, differential instruction is necessary to address students' different needs (Hall, 2002; Holloway, 2000). Though all students are motivated to communicate in Chinese, students from different cultural backgrounds differ in their reading and writing abilities. Hence, for Chinese teachers, it is also important to address the students' different needs to improve their reading and writing skills, in addition to paying particular attention to listening and speaking skills instruction. According to the findings, Chinese teachers need to pay particular attention to Chinese heritage students' literacy development even though they can communicate relatively well in speaking and listening. For Asian non-Chinese students, teachers should help them overcome first language interference and help them particularly with listening and speaking skills. And for the non-Asian, non-Chinese students, particular attention needs to be paid to their sustained interest in the Chinese culture, and to helping them overcome distinct orthographic differences between their first language and Chinese, particularly in reading.

A third implication of this study is that there is a need to consider situational factors such as teacher quality and class structure in students' motivation to learn Chinese. As our study suggests, though teacher or class effect is not that important to Chinese or Asian students, it is of paramount importance to non-Chinese, non-Asian students. Hence, teacher quality, which also affects how the teacher organizes his/her class structure, is crucial for students' sustained interest in Chinese learning. Given this, more teacher professional development in improving their pedagogical practices is necessary to improve students' Chinese learning in the program. Workshops such as how to be culturally responsive in instruction and how to address individual students' motivational orientation and learning needs will be particularly helpful in teacher development.

Lastly, the findings have implications for Chinese program reform. Since the three groups of students showed very diverse motivational orientations and different achievement patterns, it seems that college Chinese or FL program can be established by dual/triple/multiple tracks with students of similar first language backgrounds in a similar track. In such a program design, extracurricular activities will be promoted and provided for students of different backgrounds to come together to build a community of learners. With increasing interests in the Chinese language in the United States, such program design will allow teachers to build instruction based on students' cultural and linguistic backgrounds to address their diverse needs and to overcome the problems associated with diverse motivational orientations.

References

Asia Society. (2005). *Expanding Chinese-language capacity in the United States: What would it take to have 5 percent of high school students learning Chinese by 2015?* New York: Asia Society.

Crookes, G., & Schmidt, R. (1991). Motivation: Reopening the research agenda. *Language learning, 41,* 469–512.

Dörnyei, Z. (1990). Conceptualizing motivation in foreign-language learning. *Language Learning, 40*(1), 45–78.

Dörnyei, Z. (1994). Motivation and motivating in the foreign language classroom. *Modern Language Journal, 78,* 273–284.

Dörnyei, Z. (1996). Moving language learning motivation to a larger platform for theory and practice. In R. L. Oxford (Ed.), *Language learning motivation: pathways to the New Century* (pp. 71–80). Honolulu: University of Hawai'i Press.

Ellis, R. (1997). *The study of second language acquisition.* New York: Oxford University.

Everson, M. E. (1998). Word recognition among learners of Chinese as a foreign language: Investigating the relationship between naming and knowing. *Modern Language Journal, 82,*194–204.

Finegan, E. (1999). *Language: Its structure and use* (3rd ed.). Forth Worth, TX: Hartcourt Brace.

Gardner, R. C. (1979). Social psychological aspects of second language acquisition. In H. Giles and R. St. Clair (Ed.), *Language and social psychology* (pp. 193–220). Oxford, England: Blackwell.

Gardner, R. C. (1985). *Social psychology and second language learning: The role of attitudes and motivation.* London: Edward Arnold.

Gardner, R. C. (2001, March). *Language learning motivation: The student, the teacher, and the researcher.* Unpublished keynote presentation at the Texas Foreign Language Education Conference, University of Texas at Austin.

Gardner, R. C., & Lambert, W. E. (1959). Motivational variables in second-language acquisition. *Canadian Journal of Psychology, 13,* 266–272.

Gardner, R. C., & Lambert, W. E. (1972). *Attitudes and motivation: Second language learning.* Rowley, MA: Newbury House.

Hadley, A. O. (2001). *Teaching language in context* (3rd edition). Boston, MA: Heinle & Heinle.

Hall, T. (2002). *Differentiated instruction.* Wakefield, MA: National Center on Accessing the General Curriculum. Retrieved September 4, 2006, from http://www.cast.org/publications/ncac/ncac_diffinstruc.html

Ho, M. (1998). Cultural studies and motivation in foreign and second language learning in Taiwan. *Language, Culture, and Curriculum, 11*(2), 165–182.

Holloway, J. H. (2000). Preparing teachers for differentiated instruction. *Education Leadership, 8*(1), 14–18.

Kachru, B. (1994). World Englishes and applied linguistics in second language acquisition. In R. K. Agnihotri & A. L. Khanna (Eds.), *Socio-cultural and linguistic aspects of English in India* (pp. 13–40). London: Sage.

Kondo, K. (1999). Motivating bilingual and semibilingual university students of Japanese: An analysis of language learning persistence and intensity among students from immigrant backgrounds. *Foreign Language Annals, 32*(1), 77–88.

Lukmani, Y. M. (1972). Motivation to learn and language proficiency. *Language Learning, 22,* 261–273.

Norris-Holt, J. (2001). Motivation as a contributing factor in second language acquisition, *The Internet TEFL Journal, VII*(6), 1–4. Retrieved August 28, 2006, from http://itesjl.org/Articles/Norris-Motivation.html

Okada, M., Oxford, R. L., & Abo, S. (1996). Not all alike: Motivation and learning strategies among students of Japanese and Spanish in an exploratory study. In R. Oxford (Ed.), *Language learning motivation: Pathways to the new century (Technical Report #11;* pp. 105–19). Honolulu: Second Language Teaching and Curriculum Center, University of Hawai'i.

Rahman, S. (2003). Orientations and motivation in English language learning: A study of Bangladeshi students at the undergraduate level. *Asian EFL Journal, 7*(1), 1–25.

Root, E. (1999). *Motivation and learning strategies in a foreign language setting: A look at a learner of Korean.* Unpublished doctoral dissertation, Department of English as a Second Language, University of Minnesota, Minneapolis.

Welles, E. B. (2004). Foreign language enrollments in United States institutions of higher education, Fall 2002. *ADFL Bulletin, 35*(2/3), 7–25.

Wen, X. (1997). Motivation and language learning with students of Chinese. *Foreign Language Annals, 30*(2), 235–250.

Yang, J. S. R. (2003). Motivational orientations and selected learner variables of East Asian language learners in the United States. *Foreign Language Annals, 36*(4), 45–56.

Appendix: Chinese language learning assessment questionnaire

[optional]: respondent's name (in English): _____ (in Chinese): _____

ID Number: _____

Chinese course being taken: _____ name of the teacher: _____

Part I. We would like to know the reasons why you learn Chinese, and your opinion about the effectiveness of the Chinese class you are taking. Please check one answer for each question.

SA=strongly agree   **A**=agree   **SWA**=somewhat agree
SWD=somewhat disagree   **D**=disagree   **SD**=strongly disagree
NA=not applicable

I take Chinese classes because:	SA	A	SWA	SWD	D	SD	NA
1. It will allow me to be at ease with people who speak Chinese.	☐	☐	☐	☐	☐	☐	☐
2. I need the course to fulfill the university requirements.	☐	☐	☐	☐	☐	☐	☐
3. I enjoy to converse with varied people in the language.	☐	☐	☐	☐	☐	☐	☐
4. It will make me a knowledgeable person.	☐	☐	☐	☐	☐	☐	☐
5. It will enhance my understanding of Chinese culture and society.	☐	☐	☐	☐	☐	☐	☐
6. I think it will be useful in getting a good job.	☐	☐	☐	☐	☐	☐	☐
7. I will be able to participate more freely in the activities of Chinese cultural groups.	☐	☐	☐	☐	☐	☐	☐
8. It will enable me to compete effectively in the global economy because China is growing fast.	☐	☐	☐	☐	☐	☐	☐
9. I will be able to enjoy Chinese classics, literature, music, and films.	☐	☐	☐	☐	☐	☐	☐
10. Learning Chinese will please my parents.	☐	☐	☐	☐	☐	☐	☐
11. I want to communicate better with my Chinese friends.	☐	☐	☐	☐	☐	☐	☐
12. I think I can get an easy and good grade.	☐	☐	☐	☐	☐	☐	☐
13. It fulfills my personal interests.	☐	☐	☐	☐	☐	☐	☐
14. I will feel ashamed if I could not speak Chinese.	☐	☐	☐	☐	☐	☐	☐
15. It can help me to better understand the globalization and internationalization of higher education.	☐	☐	☐	☐	☐	☐	☐
16. My partner (boyfriend/girlfriend) is from the country.	☐	☐	☐	☐	☐	☐	☐
17. I enjoy the experience when surpassing myself in studying Chinese	☐	☐	☐	☐	☐	☐	☐
18. I enjoy the pleasure when I get from hearing Chinese spoken by native speakers.	☐	☐	☐	☐	☐	☐	☐

I like my Chinese class because:

	SA	A	SWA	SWD	D	SD	NA
19. I enjoy speaking Chinese with my classmates.	☐	☐	☐	☐	☐	☐	☐
20. The course material is interesting.	☐	☐	☐	☐	☐	☐	☐
21. The teacher makes learning fun.	☐	☐	☐	☐	☐	☐	☐
22. The course tasks are at the proper level for me.	☐	☐	☐	☐	☐	☐	☐
23. The teacher's feedback is encouraging.	☐	☐	☐	☐	☐	☐	☐
24. The class activities are helpful.	☐	☐	☐	☐	☐	☐	☐
25. My grade in Chinese has improved since I started.	☐	☐	☐	☐	☐	☐	☐
26. The online material is helpful and enhances learning.	☐	☐	☐	☐	☐	☐	☐
27. The TA tutoring session helps improve my Chinese.	☐	☐	☐	☐	☐	☐	☐
28. Learning is student-centered and interactive.	☐	☐	☐	☐	☐	☐	☐
29. The team-work or paired-work is fun and helpful.	☐	☐	☐	☐	☐	☐	☐
30. The teacher keeps me informed about the Program.	☐	☐	☐	☐	☐	☐	☐
31. The class offered in a mixed classroom setting with heritage learners and non-heritage learners.	☐	☐	☐	☐	☐	☐	☐
32. I can learn Chinese culture in/out side the classroom.	☐	☐	☐	☐	☐	☐	☐

My future plan for learning Chinese:

	SA	A	SWA	SWD	D	SD	NA
33. I intend to take more advanced Chinese classes.	☐	☐	☐	☐	☐	☐	☐
34. I intend to minor in Chinese.	☐	☐	☐	☐	☐	☐	☐
35. I intend to enroll in a study abroad program to China.	☐	☐	☐	☐	☐	☐	☐
36. I plan to work in China.	☐	☐	☐	☐	☐	☐	☐
37. I plan to travel to China.	☐	☐	☐	☐	☐	☐	☐
38. I plan to live in China.	☐	☐	☐	☐	☐	☐	☐

Part I. We would like to know your situation and what you feel in each of the following situations. Please simply tick or put an X on the level of your situation for each of the following:

example: I know (a lot of __ __ __ **X** __ very little) of Chinese culture.

1. I think learning Chinese is (easy __ __ __ __ __ very difficult).

2. I think learning Chinese is (boring __ __ __ __ __ fun).

3. I (really like __ __ __ __ __ don't like) the sound of Chinese.

4. I (don't want __ __ __ __ __ want) to study abroad someday.

5. I will (often __ __ __ __ __ never) need to use Chinese in my daily life.

6. I will (never __ __ __ __ __ often) need to use Chinese for my future job.

7. If I had choice I (would __ __ __ __ __ would not) study Chinese.

8. My parents (want __ __ __ __ __ don't want) me to study Chinese.

9. Most of my friends (enjoy __ __ __ __ __ dislike) learning Chinese.

10. Speaking Chinese is (not important __ __ __ __ __ very important).

11. I think my strategies of learning the language are (efficient __ __ __ __ __ not efficient).

12. Chinese will be (very likely __ __ __ __ __ not likely) to be the dominant language in the world.

13. I am (aware __ __ __ __ __ not aware) of what roles China have played in the world.

14. I am (aware __ __ __ __ __ not aware) of the development of technology and economy in China.

15. I (know __ __ __ __ __ don't know) how Chinese culture, customs, and religions were developed.

16. I am (aware __ __ __ __ __ not aware) of the usefulness of Chinese in the society of the future.

Part III. We would like to know some of your background information. Please answer each of the following questions to the best of your knowledge. Again, all personal information will be kept confidential and no other party has access to it.

your gender: ☐ male ☐ female

your birth-date: ____ month, _____ day, _____ year

your age: _____

your birth place: _____ city, _____ country

residence in childhood: _____

residence now: _____

your major at University at Buffalo: _____

your current GPA: _____

your SAT score for entering the University: _____

your GPA at high school: _____

your current annual family income:
 ☐ less than $10,000 ☐ $10.000–$24,999
 ☐ $25,000–$39,999 ☐ $40,000–$54,999
 ☐ $55,000–$69,999 ☐ $70,000–$89,999
 ☐ $90,000–$109,999 ☐ over $100,000

nationality: ☐ USA ☐ China ☐ other _____

race/ethnicity: ☐ Chinese ☐ other Asian ☐ White ☐ Black ☐ Hispanic☐ other

What is your native language? _____

Which language was spoken in your home as a child? _____

Which languages were spoken in your neighborhood when you were a child? _____

_____

Do you consider yourself to be
- ☐ a gifted language learner
- ☐ an above average language learner
- ☐ an average language learner
- ☐ a poor language learner

If you had to describe your knowledge of Chinese now, which of these statements would be most appropriate?

listening:	☐ basic	☐ working knowledge	☐ fluent
speaking:	☐ basic	☐ working knowledge	☐ fluent
reading:	☐ basic	☐ working knowledge	☐ fluent
writing:	☐ basic	☐ working knowledge	☐ fluent

Are you going to minor in Chinese? ☐ no ☐ yes
courses taken: _____, _____, _____,

Have you been to a study abroad program in China? ☐ no ☐ yes
from _____/_____ to _/_____

Have you been to China? ☐ no ☐ yes
from _____/_____ to _/_____ for_____

Chinese is my _____ language in speaking.
☐ first and best ☐ second ☐ third or later

Chinese is my _____language in writing.
☐ first and best ☐ second ☐ third or later

I came to the US _____
- ☐ before I was 5.   ☐ between 5 and 11.   ☐ between 12 and 18.
- ☐ after I was 18.   ☐ when I was born.

I started to learn Chinese when I was at the age of _____.

I have studied Chinese for _____ (number) ☐ semesters/☐ years.

Right now, I spend approximately _____ hours on Chinese outside class every week.

I am a ☐ freshman ☐ sophomore ☐ junior ☐ senior ☐ graduate

I take Chinese rather than another language because _____

_____

_____.

7

An Identity-Based Model for the Development of Chinese as a Heritage Language

Agnes Weiyun He
State University of New York at Stony Brook

NFLRC
monographs

Based on the characteristics of the Chinese as a Heritage Language (CHL) learner and the nature of CHL learning and drawing insights from Language Socialization, Second Language Acquisition, and Conversation Analysis, this article proposes an identity theory of CHL development. It posits that CHL development takes place in a three-dimensional framework with intersecting planes of time, space, and identity. Temporally, CHL development recontextualizes the past, transforms the present, and precontextualizes the future. As such, it fosters rooted world citizenry with appreciation of and competence in Chinese language and culture. Spatially, it transforms local, independent communities into global, interdependent communities. The degree to which a learner's CHL develops is dependent upon the degree to which s/he is able to find continuity and coherence in multiple communicative and social worlds in time and space and to develop hybrid, situated identities and stances.

The learner of Chinese as a heritage language

Jason Chen is a 19 year old in a beginning level CHL class in a university. He can speak Cantonese, understands Mandarin, but does not know how to read and write in Chinese. He was born in Canton and immigrated with his family to Queens, New York when he was 3. Before he started Kindergarten at 6, he spoke Cantonese at home with his parents, his grandmother, and his aunt, all of whom speak Cantonese, comprehend Mandarin, and have very limited command of English. He had some knowledge of English from watching TV and from the children he played with outside the home who spoke a mixture of English, Vietnamese, Cantonese, Fujianese, Chaozhou dialect, and Mandarin. When Jason first started school, his teacher thought his English was weak and placed him in extra help sessions taught by teacher aids who were bilingual in Cantonese and English. It didn't take him long to pick up English language skills. Very soon, Jason was speaking English fluently and became one of the highest achieving students in his class, all the way through high school. However, as his abilities in English grew, his interaction with his family became less and less frequent or substantive. Since a time he no longer recalls, he has been speaking English to his parents and his aunt at home too; the only person he still speaks Cantonese to is his grandmother, with whom he keeps a minimum level of

He, A. W. (2008). An identity-based model for the development of Chinese as a heritage language. In A. W. He, & Y. Xiao (Eds.), *Chinese as a heritage language: Fostering rooted world citizenry* (pp. 109–121). Honolulu: University of Hawai'i, National Foreign Language Resource Center.

communication. In his own words, "I love my family. But I don't talk to them. Well I'd like to talk to them, but there's such a language barrier." At some point during his formative years, his parents sent him to a community-based weekend Chinese language school, where he was taught Mandarin. He went for a year but felt "the teacher was just totally boring" and he "didn't learn anything." His best friends are Bob, his roommate at the dorm who is from a Jewish family background, and Jim, a transfer student from Korea who shares his interest in business and finance, basketball, and video games. He is also seriously dating a girl from a Mandarin-speaking family background. When asked why he is taking CHL, Jason said, "I am Chinese. I feel stupid not knowing the language. Plus I'd like to do business in China, some day."[1]

Jason Chen would be a rather typical student in a university-level CHL classroom. Following Valdés' (2001, p. 38) definition of heritage learner, I define the CHL learner broadly as a language student who is raised in a home where Chinese is spoken and who speaks or at least understands the language and is to some degree bilingual in Chinese and in English. More specifically, I focus on learners who see Chinese "with a particular family relevance" (Fishman, 2001, p. 169) and who are English-dominant with no or very limited reading/writing ability in Chinese. In other words, I focus on CHL *development*; I do not consider CHL maintenance as can be seen in the case of advanced level CHL students who have obtained native or near native proficiency in all areas of the language and who take courses in literature in Chinese to maintain or further expand their language skills.

One might initially think that to learn one's heritage language is to (re)establish similarities with members of one's heritage culture and/or to (re)establish differences from members of mainstream American culture. However, as can be seen in Jason's case, to learn CHL appears not merely to inherit one's heritage language and maintain one's heritage cultural identity but also to transform the heritage language (in terms of changes in dialect, script, accent, discourse norms, etc.) and re-create one's identity. When Jason walks into the CHL classroom, he brings with him linguistic and behavioral patterns that were formed when he was 6 or 12 and that remain active or that await to be reactivated; he brings with him richly textured experiences interacting with his Cantonese-speaking family members, his English-, Vietnamese-, Cantonese-, Fujianese-, Chaozhou dialect-, and Mandarin-speaking neighbors, his English-speaking but multi-ethnic peers and teachers, his English- and Mandarin-speaking girl friend. He brings with him ways of speaking and being that mirror those of these diverse groups of people. He brings with him memories of his past experience learning CHL as well as expectations and anticipations about the verbal and non-verbal behavior of his present CHL teacher and CHL classmates. He also brings with him dreams of working in China some day and ideas of what a Chinese-American means. In a nutshell, Jason embodies elements that are both hetero-temporal and hetero-spatial. He has learned and is still learning to cope with, to understand, to accept or reject, to model or modify the language and cultural behaviors of every community he has encountered throughout his life span. Learning CHL will enable him to inherit some of the "Chineseness" from his family and his neighborhood but will also enable him to become a very different kind of Chinese-American from his family and his neighbors.

This chapter locates learner identity as the center piece rather than the background of heritage language development. Identity is to be understood in association with its verb form,

---

[1]   This chapter is a condensed version of "Toward an identity theory of the development of Chinese as a heritage language," which appeared in *The Heritage Language Journal* (2006), 4(1), retrievable from http://www.heritagelanguages.org/

to *identify*, and thus as identification. In other words, identity is treated not as a collection of static attributes or as some mental construct existing prior to and independent of human actions, but rather as a process of continual emerging and becoming, a process that identifies what a person becomes and achieves through ongoing interactions with other persons (Bucholtz & Hall, 2004; He, 1995; Ochs, 1993). In the words of Lemke (2002, p. 72), "What else is an *identity* but the performance, verbally and nonverbally, of a possible constellation of attitudes, beliefs, and values that has a recognizable coherence by the criteria of some community?" In this sense, the identity of the HL speaker is to a large measure forged through his/her speech. This article explores the challenges and opportunities CHL development presents to the construction and negotiation of CHL learner identities and conversely how identity formation and transformation is symbiotic with CHL development. The overall purpose is thus to formulate an identity-based model for CHL development.

Theorizing CHL development

It is becoming a widely held view that heritage language is an extremely valuable resource, both for the individual and for society. Heritage language development can lead to academic and economic benefits, can be an important part of identity formation, and enables the heritage language speaker to benefit from deeper contact with family, community, and the country of origin (Krashen, Tse, & McQuillen, 1998; Peyton, Ranard, & McGinnis, 2001; Wong Fillmore, 1991). Chinese is being taught as a heritage language to a drastically increasing number of students at all levels throughout the United States (ACTFL). While there has been some empirical research (He, 2000a, 2001, 2003a, 2004a, 2005; Li, 2005; Tse, 1998, 2000, 2002; X. Wang, 1996), CHL has received little attention in terms of theory building thus far (but see S. Wang, 2005). Very little is known about either the rate or the route of CHL development.

In this article, my overall objective is to tentatively propose a theory of CHL development which aims to account for what is already known about CHL development from existing empirical work and also to predict what will be observed. It is hoped that future research will test the hypotheses derived from the theory so as to either confirm or disconfirm and modify it. In other words, as a form of "hermeneutic reasoning" (Gadamer, 1975; Habermas, 1971), the theory will be presented in a way that is falsifiable. It will be a theory, like any other theory, that remains open to a potentially endless journey of understanding, interpretation, testing, and modification.

An identity theory of CHL development can be located within the partial convergence of three strands of research: (a) Language Socialization; (b) Second Language Acquisition (SLA) theories, specifically the Acculturation Model and Accommodation Theory; and (c) Conversation Analysis. In what follows, I first sketch these strands of work that have served as sources of theoretical inspiration and discuss their relevance to our current purposes, then outline an identity theory with its associated hypotheses, and finally discuss its potentials and limitations.

Theoretical predecessors

Language socialization

Grounded in ethnography, Language Socialization, as a branch of linguistic anthropology, focuses on the process of becoming a culturally competent member through language use in social activities. As originally formulated by Ochs and Schieffelin (Ochs, 1990, 1996; Ochs & Schieffelin, 1984; Schieffelin & Ochs, 1986a, 1986b, 1996), Language Socialization is concerned with (a) how novices (e.g., children, language learners) are socialized to be competent members in the target culture through language use, and (b) how novices are socialized to use language. It analyzes the organization of communicative practices through which novices acquire socio-cultural knowledge and relates the grammatical, discursive, and non-verbal details of interaction to the construction of social and cultural ideologies that define a community.

The theory of Language Socialization rests on a theory of indexicality. Indexicality, as a number of linguistic anthropologists such as Ochs (1990), Duranti and Goodwin (1992), and Wortham (2003) argue, is central to the linguistic and cultural organization of social life, something that constitutes language as a context-bound, interactively-accomplished phenomenon. From sociolinguistics, among other fields, we have learned that a single linguistic form may index some contextual dimension (e.g., honorific forms such as 您 "nin" or 老人家 "laorenjia" in Chinese can index social and affective relationships between the speaker and the addressee or between the speaker and the referent). Or, a set of linguistic forms may index some contextual dimension. As isolated linguistic features often have a wide range of indexical possibilities (e.g., mispronouncing 大灰狼 "da hui lang [big grey wolf]" as 大飞狼 "da fei lang [big flying wolf]" can index speech by a child, a non-standard dialect speaker, a foreign language speaker, or a creative speaker), it is often the case that a combination of several indexes narrows the indexical scope in terms of identities of and relations between the language users, and/or dispositions of the language users, and/or the activities at hand (e.g., duplication of syllables along with high pitch might index a child Chinese speaker).

In the framework of Language Socialization, indexicality is conceived of as a property of speech through which sociocultural contexts (e.g., identities, activities) are constituted by particular stances and acts which in turn are indexed through linguistic forms (Ochs, 1990, 1992, 1993). That is to say, from a LS perspective, the indexical relationship between linguistic forms and sociocultural contexts is often achieved indirectly, instead of directly (i.e., one or more linguistic forms indexing some contextual dimension). Major sociocultural dimensions include social identities of the participants, relationships among participants, affective dispositions of participants (feelings, moods, and attitudes of participants toward some proposition), epistemological dispositions of participants (beliefs or knowledge vis-à-vis some proposition, e.g., the source of their knowledge or the degree of certainty of their knowledge), social/speech acts and activities, and genre. Ochs (1990) argues that among these dimensions—*affective and epistemological dispositions*—are the two contextual dimensions which are recurrently used to constitute other contextual dimensions. Hence this two-step indexical relationship can be illustrated in this way,

LINGUISTIC FORMS→ AFFECT/STANCE →CONTEXTUAL FEATURES (e.g., identity).

For example, in the Chinese heritage language classrooms that I have studied, in terms of linguistic forms, teachers in these classrooms consistently use three-phased directives to moralize their commands for the students to act according to the teacher's wishes (He, 2000a), namely,

ORIENTATION→ EVALUATION→ DIRECTIVE.

Specifically, the teacher first orients the students to some state of affairs which in turn renders the students' behavior problematic, then formulates negative consequences which may result from the students' problematic behavior, and only then does she issue a directive to correct the behavior. Thus, rather than simply issuing directives, the teacher weaves cultural values and ideology in the prefaces so as to warrant the directives for desirable behavior.

Moralized directives thus index both an affective disposition and social identity. They directly index affective dispositions of being moral and authoritative and indirectly index the social identity of the speaker—that of a parent or a teacher, as in the Chinese culture parent/teacher roles are largely defined in terms of or constituted by moral and authoritative dispositions. It is thus the teacher's and the parents' prerogative as well as responsibility to socialize the students/children into the various virtues that regulate all human conduct.

Although "teacher" is a universal social role, the communicative practices as teachers vary considerably across cultures and societies (see He, 2003a). In other words, there is not a one-to-one mapping relationship between three-phased moralized directives (language forms) and the social identity of the teacher (cultural context). Instead, the relation of moralized directives to the identity of the Chinese teacher is constituted and mediated by the relation of language forms to stances (e.g., moral and authoritative), activities and other social constructs. As such, students in these classes come to understand teacher-related meanings in part through coming to understand certain recurrently displayed stances (e.g., upholding moral values such as filial piety).

As argued elsewhere (He, 2003b), the Language Socialization approach to indexicality provides a systematic account of how language relates to cultural context. In the diaspora situation of teaching/learning a heritage language in the adopted culture, it is possible that the CHL learners may fail to achieve the identity of "a CHL community member" through failure to act and feel in some way expected, desired or preferred by the CHL community or through the failure of the CHL community to ratify the CHL learner's displayed acts and stances. With Language Socialization, we can examine how different displays of and reactions to certain acts and stances construct different identities and relationships. It also allows us to examine the construction of multiple yet compatible/congruent identities, blended and blurred identities in multilingual, multicultural, immigrant contexts.

SLA theories

Two theories from SLA are of particular relevance to the building of a theory of CHL development with reference to leaner identity—the Acculturation Model (Schumann, 1978a, 1978b) and the Accommodation Theory (Giles, 1977; Giles & Byrne, 1982). Both theories are concerned with accounting for successful language acquisition in terms of the relationships between the language learner's social group and the target language community. The central premise of the Acculturation Model is that second language acquisition is a form of acculturation and the degree to which a learner acculturates to the target language group will control the degree to which s/he acquires the second language. Acculturation is determined by the degree of social and psychological distance between the learner and the target language culture. Variables that create such distance include the following: whether the target language and the native language groups view each other as socially equals, whether the target culture and the native culture are congruent with each other, and whether both communities have positive attitudes toward each other, leaner motivation, and ego boundaries (Schumann, 1978b). This model treats social and psychological distance as significant but static and fixed. It does not consider the role of interaction between the language learner and the target language speaker.

The Accommodation Theory shares the Acculturation Model's concern with motivation and learner identity, but its primary objective is to investigate how inter-ethnic communication and its associated social and psychological stances shape SLA. While the Acculturation Model treats social and psychological distance as an a priori given, the Accommodation

Theory considers inter-ethnic group relationships as subject to constant negotiation during the course of each interaction and are thus dynamic and fluctuate along with the shifting, evolving view of identity held by each group vis-à-vis the other. This theory considers the level of learner motivation to be a reflex of how s/he defines himself/herself in ethnic terms, which, in turn, is governed by a number of variables: (a) identification with the his/her own social group, (b) inter-ethnic comparison, (c) perception of ethno-linguistic vitality (whether the learner sees his social group as holding a low or high status and as sharing or excluded from power), (d) perception of inter-ethnic boundaries (whether the learner sees his social group as culturally and linguistically separate from the target language group or as culturally and linguistically related), and (e) identification with other social categories (whether the learner identifies with some social categories [occupational, religious, gender] and as a consequence whether s/he holds adequate or inadequate status within his/her social group).

Accommodation Theory suggests that ethnic identity is an important aspect of variability in SLA. It also encompasses language acquisition and language use within a single framework (Firth & Wagner, 1997; Kasper, 1997). It accounts for the learner's variable linguistic output as follows: Learners are continually modifying their speech with others so as to reduce or accentuate the linguistic and social differences between them depending on their assessment of the interactive situation. With this theory, it is then possible to explain the development of a new dialect, accent, or script. For example, Jason Chen from our earlier scenario may speak Cantonese to his grandmother to reduce differences and maintain communication, speak newly acquired Mandarin to his girlfriend and write to her using the simplified script to enhance intimacy, imitate a standard northern accent when speaking Mandarin to differentiate himself from his parents and his aunt, and so forth.

Conversation analysis

The third and final strand of work that has directly inspired the identity theory is Conversation Analysis (He 2000b, 2004b; Markee, 2000; Sacks ,1992; Sacks, Schegloff, & Jefferson, 1974; Schegloff, 1991). Conversation Analysis sees language and interaction as a most notable and noticeable cultural and social form, often explicitly linked to and in some contexts even criterial of identity (Sacks, 1992). Identity, from the CA perspective, inheres in actions and in language use, not in people. As the product of situated social action, identities take on an emergent quality and may shift and recombine, moment-by-moment, to meet new circumstances. In this view, CHL can then be seen as a form of social action, which produces cultures and membership in groups. Learner identities are achieved through the interaction with other individuals and experience in various social spaces including the space of families, ethnic, and other socioculturally defined groups, and various social institutions such as schools and work places (He, 1995, 1997, 2004a).

The body of research from CA that directly addresses the problem of identity construction can be found in Sacks' work on "membership categorization" (Sacks, 1992, that is, how people do descriptions of participants. Sacks noted that when people use descriptions, they employ categories to label themselves, others, and also objects. These categorizations are "inference-rich" (Sacks, pp. 40–48) in that when a particular category is used, members of a society rely on their local knowledge of what it means to be labeled with such a category. That is to say, when categories are used and interpreted, participants always tie them to specific characteristics and behaviors which are presumed to be known about the category. Sacks also observed that any feature of a person could be used for membership categorization and that several categories can be applied for the same person (e.g., a Chinese American, a student, a female, a daughter). What is of interest is the procedures via which participants select membership categories.

Conversation Analysis compels us to pay attention to the interactional, moment-by-moment production of identity and motivation, rather than learners' overall, general goals as suggested by the SLA theories. It enables us to look at how identity (and thus motivation) emerges from interaction itself—how meanings are communicated, expressed, oriented to, received, negotiated, and modified. Unlike the case of foreign/second language learning where the learner is clearly a member of his/her "native culture" who is attempting to learn the norms and rules of the "target culture" as enacted and (re)constituted by the target language he/she is learning, the learner of a heritage language appears to have a multi-faceted identity as someone who is both similar to and different from members of the target culture since he/she is socio-historically connected with the target culture and yet experientially displaced from it.

To conclude this section, Language Socialization provides a theory of indexicality which views language as a resource for developing specific, multiple and fluid discourse patterns, stances, and values which in turn index various social and cultural identities. It prompts us to understand the meanings and connections that learners make between CHL learning and their everyday lives and to look at CHL development as social practice rather than a set of language skills to be acquired—practice that is shaped by and also shapes learner identities.

The Acculturation Model and Accommodation Theory from Second Language Acquisition research highlight the importance of motivation in language development and view motivation as deriving from learner identity. They further unpack learner identity in terms of concrete sets of relationships between the learner, his/her own social group, the target language speaker, and the target social group. Accommodation Theory shows great promise as it implies that the degree to which a learner acquires a second language has to do with the learner's ongoing, evolving assessment of him/herself with regard to his/her own social group and the target language/dialect group.

Conversation Analysis, furthermore, enables us to see that language development is rooted in learners' co-construction of participation frameworks, situated tasks, and interactionally achieved identities. It provides the analytical resources to examine how learner identity may be established, sustained, or altered in actual, real-time, moment-by-moment interaction. These three analytical perspectives, though diverse in their origins, converge in their concern with the role of identity as it is shaped by and shapes language use. Having considered language development as a socially indexical practice, learner identity as a crucial driving force for language learning, and the interactional production of learner identity, we are now ready to propose an identity theory of CHL development.

Toward an identity theory of CHL development

I have argued thus far that the question of identity may be a key to CHL development. An emphasis on learner identity as a prime dynamic force in CHL development can bring into focus the significance of cultural as well as language factors to conceptualizing the evolving tensions and transformations both within the learner and between the learner and the multiple worlds which s/he inhabits. As discussed earlier, identity, when seen as a process, is also identification, or positioning. It rests on two fundamental constitutive features—temporality and spatiality.

First, construction of identity involves a process that extends through time (Heidegger 1962) and involves multiple timescales (Lemke, 2002). On a macro level, cultural/social identities are historically emergent. As such, they presuppose assumptions about the origins of specific groups, their evolution through various historical periods, their arrival at the present stage, and their projected and perceived destinations in the future. On a micro level, identities are dynamically and fluidly negotiated, validated, challenged or changed as social interaction unfolds in real time. Second, construction of identity involves a process that extends in space. It is connected with a specific territory endowed with meanings. The spatiality of identity construction may apply to demographic identities such as ethnic groups in an indirect, indexical manner. For example, traditionally, Chinese-American ethnic identification was located in largely self-contained enclaves of Chinatown. Nowadays, Chinese Americans no longer occupy a contiguous geographical space, but they do define themselves and are defined by others partly in reference to their or their parents/ancestors' homelands (Chang, 2003).[2]

An identity theory of CHL development may thus read like this: CHL development takes place in a three-dimensional framework with intersecting planes of time, space, and identity. Temporally, CHL development recontextualizes the past, transforms the present, and precontextualizes the future. As such, it fosters rooted world citizenry with appreciation of and competence in Chinese language and culture. Spatially, it transforms local, independent communities into global, interdependent communities. The degree to which a learner's CHL develops is dependent upon the degree to which s/he is able to find continuity and coherence in multiple communicative and social worlds in time and space and to develop hybrid, situated identities, and stances.

The following 10 hypotheses can be formulated accordingly:

Along the temporal dimension

1. **Rootedness Hypothesis.** The degree of success in CHL development correlates positively with the learner's desire to be rooted in his/her heritage culture and to accentuate similarities with members of the CHL community. This explains why CHL students in university CHL classes often claim that they disliked taking Chinese lessons when they were young and did not have the desire to remain connected with their family background; whereas now that they are fully grown and ready to embrace their cultural heritage from the past, they are eager to learn CHL seriously.

2. **Benefits Hypothesis.** The degree of success in CHL development correlates positively with the learner's envisaged benefits and rewards (social and economic) in the future.[3] In today's world, Mandarin Chinese is clearly the language of literacy linked to not only literary activities but also economic opportunities. Learning the language well makes practical, functional sense.

3. **Interaction Hypothesis.** The degree of success in CHL development correlates positively with the learner's desire to communicate successfully in a moment-by-moment fashion. Existing research, though limited, has confirmed our hunch that strong long-term motivations may not lead to success in CHL learning (Tse, 2002). A very important aspect of motivation comes from the reward of communicating in situated activities (e.g., understanding a comic strip in magazine or a letter from the grandparents, being able to talk to relatives or to travel independently in

---

[2]   From an ecological perspective, language development can also be seen as both temporal and spatial positioning (Kramsch, 2002).

[3]   This is also known in SLA as the instrumental motivation (Gardner & Lambert, 1972).

Chinese speaking worlds). This hypothesis is particularly applicable to children CHL learners when the Rootedness Hypothesis and the Benefits Hypothesis are indeterminate.

Along the spatial dimension

4. **Positive-Stance Hypothesis.** The degree of success in CHL development correlates positively with the positive stance the English-speaking community has towards the Chinese language. For a long time, China was in the economic dark ages and Chinese language was not considered important in American schools. But that is not the case anymore. With more and more students learning Chinese as a foreign language, CHL students will feel inspired and compelled to master the language, especially in contexts and on campuses where cultural tolerance and diversity is promoted and celebrated.

5. **By-Choice Hypothesis.** The degree of success in CHL development correlates positively with the frequency with which the learner's family uses CHL by choice. It has been observed anecdotally that when families use CHL by necessity (i.e., parents speak CHL because their English is limited), learners are likely to see CHL as limiting rather than enriching. By contrast, when parents speak CHL because they choose to, learners see a model of the development/maintenance of CHL "where the motive is linguistic, cognitive, and cultural enrichment—the creation of citizens of the world" (Hakuta, 1985, pp. 229–230). This perhaps also explains to some extent why there seems to be pride for school-attained CHL on the one hand and sometimes uneasiness about home-acquired CHL on the other.

6. **Diverse-Input Hypothesis.** The degree of success in CHL literacy development correlates positively with the extent to which the learner has access to rich and diverse CHL input. Input includes not only various reading and A/V materials at home and school but also spoken and cultural input from interacting with Chinese speaking family members as well as from frequent visits to places where Chinese is used natively (e.g., parents' home towns in China, Taiwan).

7. **Discourse-Norms Hypothesis.** The degree of success in CHL development correlates positively with the extent to which the discourse norms (ways of speaking, patterns in turn-taking, allocation of speech roles, preferences in conversational topics, etc.) in the CHL-speaking contexts (home, classroom, or community) are sensitive to the discourse norms in the English-speaking community.

Along the identity dimension

8. **Enrichment Hypothesis.** The degree of success in CHL development correlates positively with the extent to which the learner has created a niche (linguistic, social, cultural) in the English-speaking community. This explains why adult CHL learners tend to be more enthusiastic about and committed to CHL learning than children, as the former have found their own place, so to speak, in the English speaking world, a place where they see themselves as linguistic and social equals to others and where they feel free to ground, enrich, and expand their experiences. It can be predicted that children who speak CHL only before school age are more likely to develop a negative attitude towards CHL when they start school than early bilinguals (those using two languages from infancy). The former group see CHL as holding them back and see CHL as the cause for not understanding

English (and its various ramifications); whereas the latter, who are already comfortable with English, do not see the need to resist CHL in order to position themselves fittingly in the English speaking world.

9. **Multiplicity Hypothesis.** Neither in the temporal nor spatial sense is identity singular, unitary, or non-contradictory. The CHL learner's identity is complex in that s/he assumes multiple identifications that may be overlapping and/or competing. The salience of various identifications varies contextually and relationally (Lo & Reyes, 2004). The degree of success in CHL development correlates positively with the ease with which the learner is able to manage differences and discontinuities presented by multiple speech roles in multiple, intersecting communities.

10. **Transformation Hypothesis.** As the CHL learner copes with the multiple linguistic codes in the contexts of family, peer groups, and school institutions, s/he is engaged in a double process of socialization into given speech communities and of acquisition of literacy as a means of asserting personal meanings that have the potential to transform the speech community. In other words, CHL can be used both to inherit heritage practices and to transform the very practices that motivated CHL learning in the first place.

Discussion

This chapter has taken as its anchor position that heritage language development is grounded in the learner's participation in social practice and continuous adaptation to the unfolding, multiple activities and identities that constitute the social and communicative worlds which s/he inhabits. A theory that is oriented to learner identity has been tentatively put forth to describe and predict the key variables responsible for CHL development. While the identity theory presented here might be relevant or applicable to heritage languages in general, at the present time, it is intended to address CHL. Depending upon the learner's developmental stage, variables important to CHL children learners, for example, may be different from those important to CHL adult learners. By the same token, some hypotheses may be primary and others come into play in cases where the primary hypotheses are indeterminate (e.g., the patterns in which CHL is used in the family may become a crucial variable when some other variables such as the stance of the English speaking community toward the Chinese language constitute neither a clearly positive nor a clearly negative influence).

Finally, the proposed theory is yet to specify the route of CHL development (cf. Lynch, 2003). For example, is it the case that CHL follows a natural sequence of development with variations in the rate of development of specific lexcio-grammatical and discourse features and in the level of proficiency achieved? Do classroom CHL learning and naturalistic CHL learning at home follow the same developmental path? Only when these and other related important questions are addressed may we have a comprehensive picture of CHL development.

References

Bucholtz, M., & Hall, K. (2004). Language and identity. In A. Duranti (Ed.), *A companion to linguistic anthropology* (pp. 369–394). Oxford, England: Blackwell.

Chang, I. (2003). *The Chinese in America: A narrative history.* New York: Penguin Books.

Chen, P. (1999). *Modern Chinese: History and sociolinguistics.* New York: Cambridge University Press.

Duranti, A., & Goodwin, C. (1992). *Rethinking context*. New York: Cambridge University Press.

Firth, A., & Wagner, J. (1997). On discourse, communication, and (some) fundamental concepts in SLA research. *The Modern Language Journal, 81*, 285–300.

Fishman, J. A. (2001). 300-Plus Years of heritage language education in the United States. In J. K. Peyton, D. A. Ranard, & S. McGinnis (Eds.), *Heritage languages in America. Preserving a national resource* (pp. 81–89). McHenry, IL: Center for Applied Linguistics.

Gadamer, H-G. (1975). *Truth and method*. New York: Seabury Press.

Gardner, H., & Lambert, W. (1972). *Attitudes and motivations in second language learning*. Rowley, MA: Newbury House.

Giles, H. (Ed.). (1977). *Language ethnicity and intergroup relations*. New York: Academic Press.

Giles, H., & Byrne, J. (1982). An intergroup approach to second language acquisition. *Journal of Multilingual and Multicultural Development, 3*, 17–40.

Habermas, J. (1971). *Knowledge and human interest*. Boston: Beacon.

Hakuta, K. (1985). *Mirror of language*. New York: Basic Books.

He, A. W. (1995). Co-constructing institutional identities: the case of student counselees. *Research on Language and Social Interaction, 28*(3), 213–231.

He, A. W. (1997). Learning and being: identity construction in the classroom. *Pragmatics and Language Learning, 8*, 201–222.

He, A. W. (2000a). Grammatical and sequential organization of teachers' directives. *Linguistics and Education, 11*(2), 119–140.

He, A. W. (2000b). Discourse analysis. In M. Aronoff & J. Rees-Miller (Eds.), *The handbook of linguistics* (pp. 428–445). Oxford, England: Blackwell.

He, A. W. (2001). The language of ambiguity: Practices in Chinese heritage language classes. *Discourse Studies, 3*(1), 75–96.

He, A. W. (2003a). Novices and their speech roles in Chinese heritage language classes. In R. Baley & S. Schecter (Eds.), *Language socialization in bilingual and multilingual societies* (pp. 128–146). Clevedon, England: Multilingual Matters.

He, A. W. (2003b). Linguistic anthropology and language education. In S. Wortham & B. Rymes (Eds.), *Linguistic anthropology of education* (pp. 93–119). Westport, CT: Praeger.

He, A. W. (2004a). Identity construction in Chinese heritage language classes. *Pragmatics, 14*(2/3), 199–216.

He, A. W. (2004b). CA for SLA: Arguments from Chinese language classes. *The Modern Language Journal, 88*(4), 568–582.

He, A. W. (2005). Discipline, directives, and deletions: Grammar and interaction in Chinese heritage language classes. In C. Holten & J. Frodesen (Eds.), *The power of context in language teaching and learning: A Festschrift for Marianne Celce-Murcia* (pp. 115–126). Boston: Thomson Heinle.

Heidegger, M. (1962). *Time and being* (John Macquarrie & Edward Robinson, Trans.). New York: Harper.

Kasper, G. (1997). "A" stands for acquisition: A response to Firth and Wagner. *The Modern Language Journal, 81*, 307–312.

Kramsch, C. (Ed.). (2002). *Language acquisition and language socialization: Ecological perspectives*. New York: Continuum.

Krashen, S., Tse, L., & McQuillan, J. (1998). *Heritage language development*. Culver City, CA: Language Education Associates.

Lemke, J. (2002). Language development and identity: Multiple timescales in the social ecology of learning. In C. Kramsch (Ed.), *Language acquisition and language socialization* (pp. 68–87). New York: Continuum.

Li, D. (2005, November). Attitudes, motivations and identities in learning Chinese as a heritage language at the post-secondary level. Unpublished paper presented at the Annual ACTFL/CLTA Conference, Balitmore, MD.

Lo, A., & Reyes, A. (2004). Language, identity and relationality in Asian Pacific America: An introduction. *Pragmatics, 14*(2/3), 115–125.

Lynch, A. (2003). The relationship between second and heritage language acquisition: Notes on research and theory building. *Heritage Language Journal, 1*(1). Retrieved June 23, 2007, from www.heritagelanguages.org

Markee, N. (2000). *Conversation analysis*. Mahwah, NJ: LEA.

Ochs, E. (1988). *Culture and language development*. Cambridge, England: Cambridge University Press.

Ochs, E. (1990). Indexicality and socialization. In J. W. Stigler, R. Shweder, & G. Herdt (Eds.), *Cultural psychology: Essays on comparative human development* (pp. 287–308). Cambridge, England: Cambridge University Press.

Ochs, E. (1992). Indexing gender. In A. Duranti & C. Goodwin (Eds.), *Rethinking context* (pp. 335–358). New York: Cambridge University Press.

Ochs, E. (1993). Constructing social identity. *Research on Language and Social Interaction, 26*, 287–306.

Ochs, E. (1996). Linguistic resources for socializing humanity. In J. J. Gumperz & S. L. Levinson (Eds.), *Rethinking linguistic relativity* (pp. 407–437). Cambridge, England: Cambridge University Press.

Ochs, E., & Schieffelin, B. B. (1984). Language acquisition and socialization: Three developmental stories. In R. Schweder & R. LeVine (Eds.), *Culture theory: Essays on mind, self and emotion* (276–320). Cambridge, England: Cambridge University Press.

Peyton, J., Ranard, D. A., & McGinnis, S. (Eds.). (2001). *Heritage languages in America: Preserving a national resource*. McHenry, IL: Center for Applied Linguistics.

Sacks, H. (1992). *Lectures on conversation* (Vols. 1 & 2). Cambridge, MA: Blackwell.

Sacks, H., Schegloff, E. A., & Jefferson, G. (1974). A simplest systematics for the organization of turn-taking for conversation. *Language, 50*, 696–735.

Schegloff, E. A. (1979). The relevance of repair to syntax-for-conversation. *Syntax and semantics, 12*, 261–286.

Schegloff, E. A. (1991). Reflections on talk and social structure. In D. Boden & D. H. Zimmerman (Eds.), *Talk and social structure* (pp. 44–70). Cambridge, England: Polity Press.

Schieffelin, B., & Ochs, E. (Eds.). (1986a). *Language socialization across cultures.* New York: Cambridge University Press.

Schieffelin, B., & Ochs, E. (1986b). Language socialization. *Annual Review of Anthropology 15,* 163–191.

Schieffelin, B., & Ochs, E. (1996). The microgenesis of competence. In D. Slobin, J. Gerhardt, A. Kyratzis, & J. Guo (Eds.), *Social interaction, social context, and language* (pp. 251–264). Mahwah, NJ: Lawrence Erlbaum.

Schumann, J. H. (1978a). The pidginization process: A model for second language acquisition. Rowley, MA: Newbury House.

Schumann, J. H. (1978b). The acculturation model for second language acquisition. In R. Gingras (Ed.), *Second language acquisition and foreign language teaching.* Arlington, VA: Center for Applied Linguistics.

Tse, L. (1998). Ethnic identity formation and its implications for heritage language development. In S. Krashen, L. Tse, & J. McQuillan (Eds.), *Heritage language development* (pp. 15–29). Culver City, CA: Language Education Associates.

Tse, L. (2000). The effects of ethnic identity formation on bilingual maintenance and development: An analysis of Asian American narratives. *International Journal of Bilingual Education and Bilingualism, 3,* 185–200.

Tse, L. (2002). Heritage language literacy: A study of US biliterates. *Language, Culture, and Curriculum, 14*(3), 256–268.

Valdés, G. (2001). Heritage language students: Profiles and possibilities. In J. K. Peyton, D. A. Ranard, & S. McGinnis (Eds.), *Heritage languages in America. Preserving a national resource* (pp. 37–80). McHenry, IL: CAL.

Wang, S. (2005, November). Biliteracy resource system of intergenerational language and culture transmission: A conceptual framework for heritage language learning. Unpublished paper presented at the Annual ACTFL/CLTA Conference, Balitmore, MD.

Wang, X. (Ed.). (1996). *A view from within: A case study of Chinese heritage community language schools in the U.S.* Washington, DC: National Foreign Language Center.

Wong Fillmore, L. (1991). When learning a second language means losing the first. *Early Childhood Research Quarterly, 6,* 323–346.

Wortham, S. (2003). Linguistic anthropology of education. In S. Wortham & B. Rymes (Eds.), *Linguistic anthropology of education* (pp. 1–29). Westport, CT: Praeger.

The Learner Language

8

Effects of Print Input on Morphological Awareness Among Chinese Heritage Language Learners

Keiko Koda
Chan Lü
Yanhui Zhang
Carnegie Mellon University, Pennsylvania

NFLRC monographs

This chapter explores how the quality and quantity of print input shape morphological awareness among school-age Chinese heritage language (CHL) learners. Morphological awareness pertains to the ability to analyze a word's morphological structure. The significance of this ability lies in its capacity for enabling learners to dissect, identify, and manipulate morphemes in printed words, and in so doing, assisting them in inferring the meaning of unfamiliar characters and accessing stored character information. Although a tacit grasp of morpheme structures and functions stems from oral language development, their explicit understanding necessitates considerable print exposure and experience. The primary goals of the chapter are three-fold: (a) to identify the major properties of the Chinese characters explicitly taught in a widely-used textbook series (Grade 1–6) specifically designed for CHL students; (b) to compare the character properties in the CHL textbooks with those introduced in a textbook series used in China (Shu, Chen, Anderson, Wu, & Xuan, 2003); and (c) to examine how the input properties available to CHL students relate to their morphological awareness. Our analysis suggests that input properties appear to have a powerful impact on the formation of morphological awareness.

Words are building blocks in any form of verbal communication, and as such, word knowledge is integral to language comprehension and production. Understanding how this knowledge develops, therefore, is anything but inconsequential. Previous research illuminates several important facts about this knowledge: (a) the knowledge is multi-dimensional; (b) its development entails multiple encounters with a word in its variety of uses in context; (c) recognizing new information about the word associated with a particular use in input is, in itself, an acquired competence; (d) the acquisition of this competence is greatly expedited by morphological awareness; and (e) both morphological awareness and word knowledge evolve through cumulative experience with print input. Consequently, systematic examinations of the two key factors—print input and morphological awareness—should shed substantial light on word-knowledge development.

Koda, K., Lü, C., & Zhang, Y. (2008). Effects of print input on morphological awareness among Chinese heritage language learners. In A. W. He, & Y. Xiao (Eds.), *Chinese as a heritage language: Fostering rooted world citizenry* (pp. 125–135). Honolulu: University of Hawai'i, National Foreign Language Resource Center.

This chapter explores how the quality and quantity of print input affect morphological awareness among Chinese heritage language (CHL) students in the US. In this context, "CHL students" refers to school-age children who use Chinese (Mandarin and related dialects) as the primary means of communication at home, learn English as the language of instruction, and pursue additional literacy in Chinese as a heritage language. Typically, they attend a local elementary school during the week, and are enrolled in a weekend community school. Clearly, their heritage-language literacy is subservient to the school literacy in English, and occurs with substantially less expectation and heavily restricted print input. "Morphological awareness" is defined as the ability to analyze, identify, and manipulate morphemes in words. Although a tacit understanding of morpheme structures and functions emerges from the use of spoken language, their explicit grasp develops primarily through decoding and encoding morphological information in print (e.g., Bialystok, 2001; Carlisle, 2003; Kuo & Anderson, 2008). Hence, systematic analysis of the print input available to CHL students serves as a critical first step in probing the nature of their morphological awareness.

Background

Roles of morphological awareness in word learning

Of late, interest in morphological awareness has risen sharply among reading researchers. Its facilitative benefits can be best understood through its capacity for enabling children to analyze a word's internal structure to identify its morphological constituents. Since morphemes provide grammatical, syntactic, and semantic information, this ability is essential in identifying a word's grammatical category, inferring the meaning of an unfamiliar word, and accessing stored lexical information (Carlisle, 2003; Koda, 2005; Ku & Anderson, 2003). Although morphological awareness facilitates all modes of word learning, the nature of its contribution varies from one learning mode to another because each mode involves its own unique operations.

Intentional learning, for example, entails establishing linkages among three lexical elements—meaning, sound, and grapheme—in the words to be memorized. On the surface, such linkage building appears simple, involving only a single holistic bond connecting each element. In actuality, however, for "intentionally-learned" words to be serviceable, multiple features in a word's grapheme must be identified and linked, through multiple bonds, with their corresponding lexical and sub-lexical elements. To illustrate, when using an intentionally-learned word in context, children commonly fail to recognize its proper usage, because they tend to attend only to the core semantic information of the word, and disregard the syntactic cue available in the grapheme, such as "slow*ness*" and "slow*ly*" (McKeown, 1993; Scott & Nagy, 1997). Obviously, single holistic bonds are insufficient for efficient use of intentionally-learned words in context. As an enabler for intraword analysis, morphological awareness offers vital assistance in multiple bond building in intentional word learning.

In contrast, incidental learning occurs as a by-product of other activities, such as reading and studying, and lexical inference is integral to this mode of learning. Because lexical inference requires identifying known morphological elements in an unknown word, it relies critically on the ability to analyze the intraword morphological structure. According to Nagy and Anderson (1984), roughly 60% of the new words children encounter in printed school material is structurally transparent, multi-morphemic words, such as *unladylike*; their meanings can be easily constructed by dissecting the words into their morphological constituents. Thus, in principle, the meaning of more than half the new words children encounter in school could be deduced on the basis of morphological information. Here again, morphological awareness plays a crucial role in learning words in context.

Morphological awareness is a multi-faceted construct, consisting of a number of component capabilities. As such, it develops gradually over time as its diverse facets mature at disparate rates according to their own timetables. In English, for example, children are sensitized to inflectional morphemes in structurally transparent words well before schooling (Berko, 1958; Carlisle, 2003), but the productive use of inflectional information does not occur until Grade 2 or 3 (Bear, Invernizzi, Templeton, & Johnston, 1996). Further, understanding of derivational morphemes develops over an even longer period of time—between Grades 4 and 8 (Ku & Anderson, 2003; Tyler & Nagy, 1989, 1990). Hence, as noted above, while a tacit grasp of morpheme structures and functions stems from oral language use, their explicit understanding necessitates considerable print exposure and experience. The section that follows explains precisely how this awareness evolves through experiential exposure to print input.

Role of input and experience

Recent psycholinguistic theories hold that linguistic knowledge and processing skills both emerge progressively through the continuous detection and abstraction of regularities implicit in input. Connectionist theory, as a case in point, offers plausible explanations of how co-occurring patterns are detected and identified as corresponding elements, and then internalized as linked units. Its main contention is that the internalization of the established relationships can occur through cumulative experience of mappings of the elements to be linked—that is, for example, mapping particular linguistic functions (e.g., plural marking) onto their corresponding forms (e.g., plural marker /s/ and /z/ in spoken words and "-s" in print). The more frequently a particular pattern of mappings are experienced, the stronger the connection holding the linked elements together. The theory thus describes knowledge acquisition as a gradual transition from deliberate efforts to automatic execution, rather than as an all-or-nothing process. Accordingly, knowledge is seen as a dynamic, ever-changing, state, rather than a static entity.

In this view of learning, knowledge acquisition is predicated upon statistical probabilities wherein the elements to be linked co-occur. For example, when the letter "t" appears at the first position in a word, the letter most likely to be activated is "h," simply because the probability that "t" will be followed by "h" is 50 times higher than that for any other letter (Adams, 1990). Put simply, the connection linking the letters "t" and "h" at the word initial position is substantially stronger than any other letter combination. Eventually, it is this connection strength that explains efficiency in input processing in real-life communication. In the input-driven accounts, therefore, input characteristics (input frequency and regularity, in particular) and learner experience are the key determinants of learning outcomes. As Ellis (2002) puts it, "rules" of language, at all processing levels, are structural regularities evolving from learners' "lifetime analysis of the distributional characteristics of the language input" (p. 144).

In brief, the input-driven view of learning defines language learning as a process of detecting and abstracting structural regularities in input. It thus assigns the significant role to input and experience in explaining and predicting eventual learning outcomes. Logic suggests then that morphological awareness can be seen as a learning outcome, shaped through input processing experience in a particular language, and therefore, its eventual form can be identified through careful analysis of the morpheme properties of the language under consideration—Chinese, in this case.

Morphological awareness in Chinese

Properties of Chinese morphemes

In Chinese, morphemes are graphically encoded at two levels: radicals and characters (see, e.g., Chen, Allport, & Marshall, 1996; Shu & Anderson, 1997). "Radicals" refers to the recurrent stroke patterns used in compound characters. Over 80% of the characters currently in use are compound characters consisting of two functionally identifiable radicals: one providing semantic information and the other conveying phonological information (Zhang, 1994). The majority of radicals are single-unit characters, many of which are taught in early grades. Therefore, when these characters reappear as radicals in compound characters in a later grade, their information—either phonological or semantic—should be accessible in children's lexical memory. Character learning thus relies on the knowledge of the single-unit characters which turn to radicals because it provides the visual and functional bases for character segmentation, radical identification, and radical information extraction.

There are approximately 1,100 phonetic radicals. As noted above, many of them are single-unit characters, and therefore, their respective pronunciation is used as the reading of the compound characters containing them (Shu & Anderson, 1999). Hence, in theory, compound characters can be pronounced by extracting the phonological information from the phonetic radical. In contrast, semantic radicals, roughly 190 in use, provide a guide to the meaning of compound characters (Shu & Anderson). As an illustration, the meaning of characters containing the "water" radical relates to water in one way or another, as can be seen in the characters for 湖 "lake," 池 "pond," 洋 "ocean," 洪 "flood," 泳 "swim," all sharing this radical. Although semantic radicals are useful for categorizing semantically-related characters, their information is generally too broad, as evident in the "water" radical, to allow character meaning construction by itself. Semantic radical information is thus helpful only when other input sources, such as neighboring characters and surrounding sentences, provide sufficient semantic constraints on the meaning of the character to be inferred. Moreover, when single-unit characters serve as a semantic radical, only an aspect of their original meaning is captured. For instance, when the character for "gold" 金 is used as a semantic radical, it indicates that the characters containing this radical refer to something metallic, as in 链 "chain," 铠 "armor," 钢 "steel," and 针 "needle." It is important, therefore, for learners to understand that a subtle change in meaning occurs when single-unit characters are used as a semantic radical.

As noted above, Chinese morphemes are encoded at the two—lexical and sub-lexical—levels. Because of their meaning-bearing function, semantic radicals are often considered as equivalent to single morphemes (e.g., Nagy & Anderson, 1999; Packard, 2000; Shu & Anderson, 1997;). Since the meaning of characters—single-unit or compound—is also associated with their grapheme holistically, characters themselves are also treated as morphemes (e.g., Taft & Zhu, 1995). Because of the dual-level encoding, character recognition relies on semantic information extraction both at the character (lexical) and radical (sub-lexical) levels. Skilled readers are, in fact, capable of such parallel information extraction during character recognition (Taft & Zhu, 1995; Zhou & Marslen-Wilson, 1994). Although radical information is insufficient for character meaning construction, logographic readers tend to turn to semantic radicals when encountering unfamiliar characters in context. It has been reported that successful character meaning inference is achieved through the integration of character-internal (semantic radical) and character-external (adjacent characters and surrounding sentences) information (e.g., Ku & Anderson, 2003; Mori & Nagy, 1999; Shu, Anderson, & Zhang, 1995).

Based on these properties, we contend that morphological awareness in Chinese should entail an explicit understanding that (a) most characters can be decomposed into two or more graphic components; (b) one of the graphic components in a compound character provides partial information on the character's meaning; (c) the meaning of characters sharing the same graphic component may be related; (d) semantic radical information only captures an aspect of the original meaning of the character serving as the radical; and (e) many characters can be combined to form a new word. As in English, the varying facets of Chinese morphological awareness develop at disparate rates during the school years (Ku & Anderson, 2003; Shu & Anderson 1999). Within the input-driven theory of learning, we argue that these facets are shaped through cumulative exposure to and experience with print input. It is imperative, therefore, that the nature of print input—through which morphological awareness is shaped in Chinese—be systematically analyzed.

Properties of school Chinese

Shu and colleagues (2003) examined the major properties of the characters explicitly taught in elementary schools in China based on an extensive analysis of a textbook series (grades 1 to 6) widely used in China (hereafter referred to as "Chinese" textbooks). The features they analyzed include (a) types of characters (e.g., pictographic, ideographic, semantic-phonetic compound), (b) visual complexity (number of strokes), (c) spatial structure (placement of radicals in compound characters), (d) phonetic regularity (consistency between the phonetic radical and the character's pronunciation), (e) phonetic consistency (congruence of the phonological information provided by the same phonetic radical), (f) semantic transparency (degree of semantic radical's contribution to the character meaning), (g) independent and bound components (lexical status of radicals), and (h) phonetic and semantic families (number of characters sharing the same radical).

Their analysis revealed that (a) larger numbers of characters are taught in the first three grades; (b) that these "early" characters tend to be of high frequency and visually simple, but phonologically and semantically opaque; and (c) that characters introduced at the upper grades tend to be of low frequency and visually complex, but phonetically regular and semantically transparent. These results indicate that native Chinese speaking children (hereafter referred to as "Chinese" students) are initially taught structurally simple characters conveying familiar concepts, and then introduced to structurally more complex, and conceptually less familiar characters. Importantly, moreover, their analysis also showed that the majority of the radicals (90% of the phonetic radicals and 92% of the semantic radicals) are single-unit characters, many of which are taught as independent characters in the initial two grades. Clearly, these "basic" characters (a particular sub-set of characters which are used as radicals in compound characters) serve as building blocks in learning a large number of compound characters. The mastery of the "basic" characters in the early grades, therefore, is critical for character-knowledge development. Collectively, these and other findings suggest that the input available to Chinese children is logically organized, allowing them to first establish a solid functional base with the "basic" characters, and then learn the rules for assembling and dissembling those characters (serving as radicals) through cumulative exposure to a large number of structurally transparent compound characters. Hence, the input promotes systematic expansion of character knowledge through radical-based, componential, approaches to character learning.

Analysis

Properties of school Chinese as a heritage language

Following the procedures used in the Shu et al. (2003) study, we analyzed the properties of the characters introduced in a textbook series (Grades 1 to 6) specifically designed for CHL students (Zhong Wen, 1997, hereafter referred to as "heritage textbooks"), which has been widely used in weekend Chinese schools in the United States. The textbooks are distributed by the Embassy of China in the United States. Table 1 presents the major properties of the characters introduced in the Heritage textbooks and those in the Chinese textbooks (Shu et al., 2003). The most striking difference was found in the total numbers of characters introduced in the two textbook corpora: 940 and 2,570 in the Heritage and the Chinese textbooks, respectively. CHL students are thus exposed to only 36% of the characters taught to their native speaking counterparts. The numbers of semantic-phonetic compound characters are similarly contrasting: 514 (CHL) and 1,850 (Chinese) in the two corpora. Given that semantic-phonetic compounding is the most dominant character formation type, and also that the school textbooks are virtually the only source of print input available to the vast majority of CHL students, these quantitative indices make it plain that CHL literacy learning indeed occurs with heavily restricted print input.

Table 1. Major properties of the characters introduced in the grade 1–6 "heritage" and "Chinese" textbooks

		grade 1	grade 2	grade 3	grade 4	grade 5	grade 6	total
total number of characters	heritage (US)	124	141	152	149	185	189	940
	Chinese (China)	436	709	541	358	323	203	2570
number of semantic-phonetic compounds	heritage (US)	28 (.23)	74 (.53)	98 (.64)	101 (.68)	104 (.56)	109 (.58)	514 (.55)
	Chinese (China)	196 (.45)	496 (.70)	411 (.76)	300 (.84)	278 (.86)	164 (.81)	1845 (.72)
number of single-unit characters	heritage (US)	82 (.66)	32 (.23)	24 (.16)	18 (.12)	31 (.17)	25 (.13)	212 (.23)
	Chinese (China)	113 (.26)	50 (.07)	27 (.05)	11 (.03)	10 (.03)	8 (.04)	219 (.09)
number of semantically transparent characters	heritage (US)	20 (.71)	62 (.84)	78 (80)	82 (.81)	95 (.91)	103 (.86)	440 (.86)
	Chinese (China)	159 (.81)	246 (.86)	370 (.90)	267 (.89)	256 (.92)	151 (.92)	1449 (.78)
number of phonologically consistent characters (%)	heritage (US)	12 (.42)	33 (.45)	58 (.59)	61 (.60)	69 (.66)	49 (.45)	282 (.55)
	Chinese (China)	112 (.57)	177 (.62)	284 (.69)	201 (.67)	189 (.68)	120 (.73)	1083 (.59)
visual complexity	heritage (US)	5.54	7.56	8.36	8.85	8.98	8.56	7.96
	Chinese (China)	7.37	9.22	9.80	10.29	10.57	10.56	9.635

As noted above, character learning largely depends on the mastery of the "basic" characters in the initial grades, because they reappear as radicals in compound characters introduced in later grades. Our analysis revealed that CHL and Chinese students are taught almost identical numbers of single-unit characters over the 6 years (216 and 219, respectively). Their distributions, however, are different between the two textbook corpora. While in the "Chinese" textbooks, nearly 75% (163/219) of the single-unit characters are taught in the first two grades, the single-unit characters introduced in these grades constitute a little over 50% (114/216) in the heritage textbooks. According to Shu et al. (2003), moreover, roughly 60% of the single-unit characters introduced in Grades 1 and 2 are the "basic" characters. As shown in Table 2, however, of the 114 single-unit characters in the CHL Grade 1 and 2 textbooks, only 42 are the "basic" characters, which constitute meager 22% of the semantic radicals. This implies that the input available to CHL students, particularly in the early grades, is far from sufficient for establishing the critical functional base required for identifying and manipulating radicals in learning compound characters in the later grades.

Despite the quantitative differences, there are similarities between the two textbook corpora. For example, mirroring the real-life frequency distributions, semantic-phonetic compounds are by far the most dominant character type in both corpora. In specific, in the "Heritage" Grades 2–6 textbooks, the proportions of semantic-phonetic compounds range from 53% (Grade 2) to 68% (Grade 4) with the mean proportion of 60%, and those in the "Chinese" textbooks vary from 70% (Grade 2) to 86% (Grade 5) with the mean proportion of 79%. Moreover, the majority of the semantic radicals in both "Chinese" and heritage textbooks are semantically transparent (78% and 86%, respectively), conveying the information closely related to the whole-character meaning. These similarities indicate that despite the heavily restricted quantity, the input quality in the heritage textbooks may provide CHL students a workable foundation sufficient for uncovering semantic radicals' basic properties—both structural and functional.

Table 2: Single-unit characters reappearing as radicals in compound characters in CHL textbooks

	grade 1	grade 2	grade 3	grade 4	grade 5	grade 6	total
# of single-unit charactersfuture semantic radicals	36	6	4	5	5	3	59
# of single-unit charactersfuture phonetic radicals	60	19	19	13	26	14	151

To sum up, our analysis demonstrates that the characters explicitly taught to CHL students are heavily limited in quantity. In particular, the total number of the "basic" characters introduced in the initial grades is severely restricted, making it difficult for CHL students to establish the functional base for using radical information in learning and processing compound characters. On the other hand, in both "Chinese" and "Heritage" corpora, semantic-phonetic compound characters are by far the most dominant character formation type, and the vast majority of them are structurally and functionally transparent. Such transparency presumably helps sensitize CHL students to the basic properties of radicals in compound characters. Beyond these, however, the restricted "sample" size, in all likelihood, prohibits CHL students from refining their rudimentary understanding of semantic radical (morpheme) forms and functions, and as a consequence, their morphological awareness is likely to remain "basic."

Predicting morphological awareness in Chinese as a heritage language

Based on the morpheme (characters/radicals) property analysis described above, we made several predictions regarding the morphological awareness among CHL students. Two assumptions underlie the predictions: (a) for the majority of CHL students, the heritage textbooks are the major source of print input; and therefore, (b) the properties of the textbook characters are largely responsible for the formation of their morphological awareness. It is important to note that other variables, such as instructional methodology and teacher beliefs, also contribute to the formation of morphological awareness and character knowledge. The exclusion of these and other variables, by no means, indicates that they have been ruled out as factors. We are focusing on print input simply because our goal is to explore a possible causal connection between input properties and morphological awareness within the well-articulated, input-driven, theory of learning.

Based on the analysis above, we predicted morphological awareness in CHL students to have the following characteristics:

- Because they are exposed to a proportionally larger number of compound characters, they are sensitized to the segmental nature of characters.

- Because the majority of compound characters in their input are structurally regular, they develop a basic understanding of the structural constraints on radicals in compound character formation.

- Inasmuch as most radicals are functionally transparent, they also understand the primary function assigned to each radical in a compound character.

- They become aware of how semantic radical information relates to the whole-character meaning.

Beyond these, however, it is unlikely that CHL students can refine and adjust their morphological awareness to detailed properties of semantic radicals shared only a sub-set of characters. Hence, it is highly improbable that their morphological awareness will allow systematic expansion of character knowledge through radical analysis and manipulation.

Measuring morphological awareness in Chinese as a heritage language

We tested the predictions described above using the data collected in a related study (Koda et al., this volume). The study involved 59 Grades 3 to 5 CHL students (all speakers of Mandarin or a related dialect) attending a weekend Chinese school. Through paper-and-pencil, multiple-choice tests, diverse facets of morphological awareness were measured, including (a) sensitivity to the structural constraints on radicals in compound character formation (radical formation); (b) ability to identify the semantic radical in a semantic-phonetic compound character (radical form); (c) understanding of the functional relationship between the semantic radical and the whole character meaning (radical meaning); and (d) sensitivity to a subtle change in meaning when a "basic" character is used as an independent character and when it serves as a semantic radical (radical explanation).

The results are presented in Table 3. As evident, CHL students performed well above the chance level (25%) on all tasks, but one (radical explanation). The highest response accuracy was found in the radical formation task designed to measure CHL students' sensitivity to the structural constraints on radicals. As predicted, however, their performance declined considerably in the tasks requiring knowledge of the semantic content of radicals (radical form and radical meaning). These results clearly suggest that although a grasp of the structural properties of radicals can evolve with heavily restricted input, a clear understanding of their functional properties necessitates substantially more input than is currently available to CHL students. The lowest scores, moreover, occurred in the task assessing CHL students' sensitivity to a detailed property of semantic radicals (radical explanation). Obviously, the formation of such subtlety requires both knowledge of substantially more "basic" characters and increased exposure to a wider variety of compound characters. Presumably, the heritage textbooks do not provide the input—in both quality and quantity—necessitated for the acquisition of this and other highly refined awareness facets.

Table 3: Means and standard deviations (in parentheses) of the morphological awareness subtest scores (% correct) in the four-task test

morphological awareness facets					
task requirements	tasks	overall (N=59)	grade 3 (N=23)	grade 4 (N=20)	grade 5 (N=16)
structural violation detection	radical formation	.88 (.12)	.88 (.12)	.86 (.12)	.89 (.12)
semantic analysis	radical meaning	.46 (.21)	.52 (.16)	.44 (.20)	.43 (.26)
	radical form	.55 (.21)	.59 (.17)	.49 (.19)	.56 (.26)
detailed semantic analysis	radical explanation	.25 (.15)	.24 (.17)	.24 (.13)	.28 (.15)

Taken as a whole, these findings lend support to the hypothesized connection between print input and morphological awareness. As predicted, CHL students seem sensitized to the structural properties of radicals in compound characters; but without sufficient knowledge of the "basic" characters, it appears that they are unable to build the functional foundation based on which they can fine-tune their awareness to accommodate detailed properties of semantic radicals.

Conclusions

This chapter explored the nature of print input available to CHL students, as well as its relation to their morphological awareness. The findings demonstrated that (a) the input available to CHL students is heavily limited in quantity, but similar in its distributional and other qualitative properties to that available to native Chinese-speaking children; (b) despite the quantitative restrictions, the input provides CHL students a sufficient foundation for forming sensitivity to the basic properties of semantic radicals; (c) the foundation, however, is far from sufficient for categorizing and abstracting detailed properties of semantic radicals; and as a result, (d) CHL students are unable to develop the skills to utilize radical information efficiently in learning and processing novel characters. Clearly, the quality and quantity of print input have a powerful and predictable impact on the formation of morphological awareness. Given the potential utility of these findings, further explorations are highly desirable. Future research, for example, should more directly examine the specific ways in which CHL students' underdeveloped morphological awareness affects the formation of diverse character learning competencies. Systematic probing of the dynamic interconnections among input, morphological awareness, and word knowledge development could yield significant new insights into the unique nature of literacy development among heritage language learners.

References

Adams, M. J. (1990). *Beginning to read.* Cambridge: MIT Press.

Bear, D. R., Invernizzi, M., Templeton, S., & Johnston, F. (1996). *Words their way: Word study for phonics vocabulary, and spelling instruction.* Upper Saddle River, NJ: Merrill.

Berko, J. (1958). The child's learning of English morphology. *Word, 14,* 150–177.

Bialystok, E. (2001). *Bilingualism in development: Language, literacy, and cognition*. New York: Cambridge University Press.

Carlisle, J. F. (2003). Morphology matters in learning to read: A commentary. *Reading Psychology, 24,* 291–322.

Chen, Y. P., Allport, D. A., & Marshall, J. C. (1996). What are the functional orthographic units in Chinese word recognition: The stroke or the stroke pattern? *The Quarterly Journal of Experimental Psychology, 49A,* 1024–1043.

College of Chinese Language and Culture, Jinan University. (1997). *Zhong Wen*. Guangzhou: Jinan University Press.

Ellis, N. C. (2002). Frequency effects in language processing: A review with implications for theories of implicit and explicit language acquisition. *Studies in Second Language Acquisition, 24,* 143–188.

Koda, K. (2005). *Insights into second language reading*. Cambridge, England: Cambridge University Press.

Ku, Y., & Anderson, R. C. (2003). Development of morphological awareness in Chinese and English, *Reading and Writing, 16*(5), 399–422.

Kuo, L., & Anderson, R. C. (2008). Conceptual and methodological issues in comparing metalinguistic awareness across languages. In K. Koda & A. M. Zehler (Eds.), *Learning to read across languages* (pp. 39–67). New York: Routledge.

McKeown, M. G. (1993). Creating effective definitions for young word learners. *Reading Research Quarterly, 28,* 16–31.

Mori, Y., & Nagy, W. E. (1999). Integration of information from context and word elements in interpreting novel Kanji compounds. *Reading Research Quarterly, 34,* 80–101.

Nagy, W. E., & Anderson, R. C. (1984). How many words are there in printed school English? *Reading Research Quarterly, 19,* 304–330.

Nagy, W. E., & Anderson, R. C. (1999). Metalinguistic awareness and literacy acquisition in different languages. In D. Wagner, B. Street, & R. Venezky (Eds.), *Literacy: An international handbook* (pp. 155–160). New York: Garland Publishing.

Packard, J. (2000). *The morphology of Chinese: A linguistic and cognitive approach*. New York: Cambridge University Press.

Scott, J., & Nagy, W. (1997). Understanding the definitions of unfamiliar verbs. *Reading Research Quarterly, 32,* 184–200.

Shu, H., & Anderson, R. C. (1997). Role of radical awareness in the character and word acquisition of Chinese children. *Reading Research Quarterly, 32,* 78–89.

Shu, H., & Anderson, R. C. (1999). *Learning to read Chinese: The development of metalinguistic awareness*. In A. Inhuff, J. Wang, & H. C. Chen (Eds.), *Reading Chinese scripts: A cognitive analysis* (pp. 1–18). Mahwah, NJ: Lawrence Erlbaum Associates.

Shu, H., Anderson, R. C., & Zhang, H. (1995). Incidental learning of word meanings while reading: A Chinese and American cross-cultural study, *Reading Research Quarterly, 30,* 76–95.

Shu, H., Chen, X., Anderson, R. C., Wu, N., & Xuan, Y. (2003). Properties of school Chinese: Implications for learning to read. *Child Development, 74*, 27–47.

Taft, M., & Zhu, X. (1995). The representation of bound morphemes in the lexicon: A Chinese study. In L. B. Feldman (Ed.), *Morphological aspects of language processing* (pp. 109–129). Hillsdale, NJ: Lawrence Erlbaum Associates.

Tyler, A., & Nagy, W. (1989). The acquisition of English derivational morphology. *Journal of Memory and Language, 28*, 649–667.

Tyler, A., & Nagy, W. (1990). Use of English derivational morphology during reading. *Cognition, 36*, 17–34.

Zhang, H. C. (1994). Some studies on the recognition of Chinese characters. In Q. Jing, H. Zhang, & D. Peng (Eds.), *Information processing of Chinese language* (pp.1–11). Beijing: Beijing Normal University Press.

Zhou, X., & Marslen-Wilson, W. (1994). Words, morphemes and syllables in the Chinese mental lexicon. *Language and Cognitive Processes, 10*, 545–600.

9

Literacy Development in Chinese as a Heritage Language

Keiko Koda
Yanhui Zhang
Carnegie Mellon University, Pennsylvania

Chin-Lung Yang
University of Hong Kong

NFLRC
monographs

This chapter addresses biliteracy development among school-age Chinese Heritage Language (CHL) students. These children typically use Chinese (Mandarin or a related dialect) at home, receive primary literacy instruction in English at school, and pursue ancillary literacy in Chinese in a weekend school. As such, their primary literacy tends to build on underdeveloped oral proficiency, and secondary literacy reflects heavily restricted print input and experience. Their literacy learning thus lacks sufficient linguistic resources in both languages. Despite these inadequacies, however, many children succeed in their primary literacy, and some even in heritage-language literacy. Based on theories of cross-language transfer, reading universals, and metalinguistic awareness, the chapter explores, through an integrative framework of biliteracy development, what additional resources may be available to these children, and how such resources might offset the limited linguistic support. The chapter also presents a brief summary of a preliminary study conducted as partial validation of the proposed framework.

Over the past half century, unprecedented numbers of children and youth have undergone schooling in languages other than their mother tongue. In order to succeed academically in school, these children must develop literacy skills in the societal language, in which they may or may not be proficient. Understanding how they develop reading skills is thus exceedingly important. Many of the children, moreover, pursue additional literacy in their mother tongue, a non-societal language, without adequate print input and experience. Their literacy learning thus involves more than one language, and occurs with restricted linguistic resources. As such, it adds further complexities to monolingual reading development among societal-language speakers learning to read in a single language. Despite its vital significance, however, little information is available regarding the challenge in literacy learning among school-age heritage-language learners.

In an effort to reduce this void, this chapter addresses issues surrounding biliteracy development through a systematic integration of theories in two major research fields: reading

Koda, K., Zhang, Y., & Yang, C.-L. (2008). Literacy development in Chinese as a heritage language. In A. W. He, & Y. Xiao (Eds.), *Chinese as a heritage language: Fostering rooted world citizenry* (pp. 137–149). Honolulu: University of Hawai'i, National Foreign Language Resource Center.

and second language acquisition. Specifically, it explores the development of morphological awareness and reading skills among school-age Chinese heritage language (CHL) learners. In this context, morphological awareness is operationally defined as the ability to identify, analyze, and manipulate morphological information in print. The significance of this ability lies in its capacity for assisting the learner in identifying the grammatical category of words, inferring meanings of unfamiliar words, and accessing stored lexical information. Hence, morphological awareness is directly, and possibly causally, related to reading development. Since the formation of this awareness necessitates both adequate oral language proficiency and print processing experience, the vital question is what happens to morphological awareness—and subsequently reading development—when neither is sufficient. In this regard, biliteracy development in CHL students offers a unique opportunity to isolate impacts of these factors on their morphological awareness. Inasmuch as these children use their mother tongue at home, receive primary literacy instruction in English at school, and pursue ancillary literacy in Chinese in a weekend school, their primary literacy builds on underdeveloped oral proficiency, and secondary literacy occurs with heavily restricted print input. Hence, inadequate linguistic resources characterize their literacy learning in both languages.

Most critically, however, despite the inadequate linguistic support, many of the children succeed in their primary literacy, and some in both. Logic suggests that other resources must be available to these children, compensating for the insufficient linguistic resources. Second-language research has long recognized that previously established competencies transfer across languages in virtually all aspects of learning. This implies that when learning to read in two languages, reading acquisition in one language could be enhanced, through cross-language transfer, by resources available in another language. Systematic examinations of such competence sharing should yield significant insights into biliteracy development.

Background

Reading is a complex, multi-dimensional construct involving a large number of sub-component operations, each demanding diverse processing skills. In second-language reading, the complexity increases exponentially, because virtually all operations involve two languages. To understand reading development in a second language, therefore, it is essential to clarify what the "dual-language involvement" means, and how it affects literacy learning in two languages. To address these critical issues, brief summaries of the relevant theories are useful. First, theory of language transfer is vital because it clarifies the mechanism of competence sharing across languages. The concept of reading universals is equally important, because it specifies the reading properties—and associated competencies—invariant across languages. Since the universally demanded competencies, when transferred, should provide substantial facilitation in any language, the theory establishes the basis for identifying the competencies shared across languages. Finally, morphological awareness is directly relevant to the current conceptualization because it plays a critical role in reading acquisition in all languages, and thus is a prime candidate for such resource sharing.

Cross-language transfer

Transfer has long been a major theoretical concept in second-language research. Despite its centrality, there is little agreement as to what constitutes transfer, partially because of the constantly shifting views of second-language learning—what is learned and how it is learned. Traditionally, for example, transfer has been regarded as a learner's reliance on first-language knowledge to compensate for insufficient second-language knowledge. This belief implies that transfer tends to cease once second-language linguistic knowledge develops, and, more critically, that after sufficient second-language knowledge is attained, first-language knowledge plays a minimum role in explaining individual differences in second-language learning.

Although once influential, this view of transfer is no longer uniformly endorsed. In the Functionalist theory, as an illustration, language is viewed as a set of relations between forms and functions (Van Valin, 1991), and its acquisition is seen as the internalization of these relationships (MacWhinney & Bates, 1989). The language children are learning provides a solid basis for building representations, abstracting patterns, and linking particular forms with their corresponding functions. Under these premises, second-language learning is conceptualized as the process of establishing an additional set of form-function relationships in a new language. In this view, consequently, what transfers is not static transformational rules, as traditionally conceived, but rather, the internalized form-function relationships which have evolved gradually through input processing experience.

Similarly, in second-language reading, a clear consensus as to what actually transfers has yet to emerge, in part because of the polarized views of reading. One faction perceives reading as an indivisible whole, while the other considers it as a constellation of separate components. Proponents of the holistic view posit that since language is acquired as a whole through communication, and communicative use of language is intrinsic in reading, reading is also learned holistically as a meaning-making process (Goodman, 1967, 1969). They contend, moreover, that the ultimate goal of reading is meaning construction, regardless of language, and therefore, there should be little difference in the reading process across languages. The early transfer research, taking this view, focused on two primary issues: the interrelationship between first- and second-language reading abilities (e.g., Cummins, 1979, 1991; Cummins, Swain, Nakajima, Handscombe, & Green, 1981; Legaretta, 1979; Skutnabb-Kangass & Toukomaa, 1976; Troike, 1978) and the conditions that either inhibit or facilitate reading skill transfer from the first to the second language (e.g., Clarke, 1988; Devine, 1987, 1988). By defining reading as a single, unitary construct, these early transfer studies generally disregarded the component skills involved in underlying efficient print information processing. As a result, little attention is given to what precisely is transferred from one language to another, and how the transferred skills contribute to second-language reading development.

In more recent studies, however, reading is seen as a constellation of closely related, yet separate, mental operations—each necessitating a unique set of sub-skills (e.g., Carr & Levy, 1990). Since this view incorporates multiple skills, it allows the tracing of possible relationships between corresponding skills in the languages involved, as well as functional interconnections among different skills both within and across languages. Biliteracy studies consistently indicate that phonological skills are closely connected between two alphabetic languages (e.g., Abu-Rabia, 1995; Da Fontoura & Siegel, 1995; Durgunoglu, Nagy, & Hancin, 1993; Gholamain & Geva, 1999). A similar cross-linguistic relationship also has been reported in studies involving two typologically unrelated languages, Chinese and English (Bialystok, McBride-Chang, & Luk, 2005; Wang, Perfetti, & Liu, 2005). Although the scope of these studies has been limited, focusing almost exclusively on decoding skills, the approach holds strong promise for examining inter-lingual connections in a variety of component skills and their relation to second-language reading development.

Reading universals

For a theory of transfer to inform biliteracy development, it must clarify how prior literacy experience affects second-language learning to read. Such clarification is only possible through systematic comparisons of literacy experiences across languages. The notion of reading universals is vital in this regard because it specifies the learning-to-read requisites imposed on all learners in all languages.

According to the universal grammar of reading proposed by Perfetti and associates (Perfetti, 2003; Perfetti & Dunlap, 2008; Perfetti & Liu, 2005), reading is a dynamic pursuit embedded in two interrelated systems: a language and the writing system that encodes the language. Inevitably, learning to read requires a linkage of the two, which entails the acquisition of skills to map between spoken language elements and graphic symbols (e.g., Fowler & Liberman, 1995; Goswami & Bryant, 1992; Nagy & Anderson, 1999). In learning to read, therefore, children must first recognize which language elements are encoded in the writing system (the general mapping principle), and then, deduce precisely how these elements are encoded (the mapping details). For example, children learning to read English must understand that each letter represents a distinct sound (the alphabetic principle), and then, gradually work out the details of sound-symbol correspondences (the mapping details).

To successfully grasp general mapping principles, children must gain several basic insights that (a) print relates to speech; that (b) speech can be segmented into a sequence of sounds; and most critically, that (c) these segmented sounds systematically relate to the graphic symbols in the writing system. Since these insights do not involve language-specific details, once developed in one language, they should be readily available in another language. This, however, is not necessarily the case for mapping details, because their acquisition requires substantial print input and experience in the language in which literacy is learned. The acquired mapping details, therefore, should differ systematically in diverse languages to the extent that sound-symbol, as well as morpheme-symbol, relationships vary. What is common across languages in this task lies only in the task itself. This, in turn, implies that prior literacy experience fosters an explicit understanding of what is to be accomplished in the task, which may expedite the process by allowing learners to be more reflective and strategic.

The clear implication is that biliteracy development entails repeated processes to the extent that the literacy experiences in two languages are similar. Such similarities should allow bilingual learners to usefully exploit the competencies accumulated through prior literacy experience, thereby facilitating reading development in an additional language. Thus, in essence, the concept of reading universals, properly incorporated, significantly contributes to theories of biliteracy development.

Roles of morphological awareness in learning to read

Morphological awareness refers to the ability to analyze a word's morphological structure. In learning to read, as noted above, children must understand how language elements are encoded in the writing system. Morphological awareness contributes to this process by enabling children to segment words into their morphological constituents. Beyond the initial stage of learning, moreover, morphological awareness also plays a prominent role in reading. To illustrate, it promotes analytical approaches to word learning and processing in context (Bialystok, 2001; Carlisle, 2003; Koda, 2000, 2002, 2005; Ku & Anderson, 2003). Since concept of word segmentation bolsters the capacity for identifying familiar elements in an unfamiliar word, the awareness allows children to extract partial information from familiar components. Without this competence, lexical inference is seriously hampered, and word learning becomes excessively challenging. Lacking lexical inference ability, reading comprehension is also acutely impaired.

Morphological awareness is a multi-faceted construct, consisting of a range of capabilities reflecting the properties of morpheme functions and structures in a particular language. For example, in English, word formation generally entails the addition of affixes—either before or after base morphemes—in reasonably systematic and linear fashion. In contrast, the basic unit of character formation in Chinese is radicals, which refer to recurrent stroke patterns (e.g., Chen, Allport, & Marshall, 1996; Shu & Anderson, 1997). In forming characters, moreover, radicals are combined through procedures markedly different from those used in English. For example, the most dominant formation type, phonetic-semantic compounding, involves a non-linear integration of two radicals, to which a distinct function—providing phonetic or semantic information—is assigned. Thus, in short, the basic principles of word formation vary considerably across languages. It follows then that children learning to read two typologically different languages must develop distinct morphological awareness closely attuned to the grapheme-morpheme relations in each language.

Framework for cross-language competence sharing

Previous studies have yielded a number of significant insights directly relevant to cross-language competence sharing and its potential role in learning to read in additional languages. Listed below are the critical contentions drawn from the theories described above. They serve as the fundamental premises underlying the current framework within which the specific contributions generated by transferred competencies in biliteracy development are systematically conceptualized:

- Reading is embedded in two interrelated systems: a language and its writing system. Therefore, learning to read inevitably requires all learners in all languages to make links between the two.

- Through its capacity for enabling children to analyze a word's internal structure, morphological awareness underlies the requisite linkage building.

- The awareness is a multi-faceted construct, involving a number of capabilities differentially reflecting the morpheme properties of a particular language.

- The acquisition of the awareness facets closely attuned to the detailed, language-specific, properties necessitates substantial print input and processing experience.

- Once developed, morphological awareness, and other literacy-related, competences transfer across languages.

Under these premises, the current framework gives rise to three specific hypotheses regarding the role of competence sharing via transfer in reading development in Chinese as a heritage language. First, the fundamental awareness facets—such as the concept of word segmentation, as well as recognition of the basic structural regularities—do not entail details of language-specific properties. In principle, therefore, they can develop quickly and serve as a basis for forming more refined facets both within and across languages. It can be hypothesized, therefore, that CHL students develop a basic understanding of the major structural properties of morphemes (radicals) even with heavily restricted input.

Second, the concept of word segmentation and other fundamental awareness facets alone, however, are insufficient for the formation of more refined awareness, because the formation of the latter, language-specific, facets necessitates substantial print input and processing experience. In the absence of adequate input, morphological awareness in Chinese among CHL student is likely to remain fundamental. Lacking the awareness facets closely attuned to the detailed functional properties of Chinese radicals, their awareness is of little use in reading comprehension. Consequently, it can also be hypothesized that Chinese reading skills develop independent of morphological awareness.

Lastly, once successfully acquired, reading skills in primary literacy in English should be available—through reverse transfer—to compensate for less-developed reading skills in Chinese. Since comprehension skills develop gradually throughout the primary-school years, older students generally possess not only a greater number of transfer-ready skills, but also more higher-order skills, than younger cohorts. Thus, a third and final hypothesis is that Chinese reading comprehension skills among older CHL students are qualitatively different from those among younger students.

The study

The hypotheses presented above were partially tested in an exploratory study, comparing morphological awareness and reading comprehension sub-skills among Grades 3 to 5 CHL students. The following three research questions guided the study:

1. Do different facets of morphological awareness among school-age CHL students increase over time?

2. Do different reading comprehension sub-skills among CHL students increase over time?

3. Does morphological awareness affect reading sub-skills development in Chinese as a heritage language?

Fifty-nine CHL students from a weekend Chinese school in the Greater Pittsburgh area participated in the study. These children attended Grades 3 to 5 English-medium classes in local public schools during the week, and Grades 3 to 5 Chinese language classes in the weekend school. Two sets of paper-and-pen tests, designed to measure disparate facets of morphological awareness and distinct reading comprehension sub-skills, were administered in class as part of instructional activities. The specific tasks and the construct each task was purported to measure are listed below.

Morphological awareness tasks

Five multiple-choice tasks were adopted from Li, Anderson, Nagy, & Zhang's 2002 study with slight modifications:

1. **Radical meaning** measured children's understanding that the meaning of the whole character can be inferred based on the information provided by its semantic radical. In the task, students were presented with a two-character word, in which one of the characters was given in Pinyin. It required students to choose an appropriate character from four compound characters which share the same phonetic radical, to substitute the Pinyin.

2. **Morpheme discrimination** checked the awareness that some compound words containing the same character do not necessarily share the same meaning. In the task, students were presented with four two-character words sharing one character. They were asked to select the word whose meaning is different from the others.

3. **Radical form** assessed students' discernment of how the meaning of a compound character relates to the meanings of its semantic radical. Students were required to identify the semantic radical in a compound characters.

4. **Radical formation task** tested sensitivity to the structural constraints on radical combinations in forming compound characters. In this task, students were

presented with four different placements of two graphic components as the radicals of a compound character, and asked to select the most legitimate placement of the four.

5.   **Radical explanation** evaluated students' understanding of subtle changes in meaning when a single-unit character is used as a radical.

Reading comprehension tasks

The reading comprehension test comprised eight grade-appropriate (both lexically and syntactically) passages adapted from children's story books in Mainland China. Each passage was approximately 400 characters in length. After reading each passage, students were asked to answer five multiple-choice comprehension questions, each of which was designed to measure a specific comprehension sub-skill:

1.   **Vocabulary choice** measured the ability to identify a context-appropriate, two-character compound word. The task required students to select one word from a pool of four two-character words, sharing one character in common, to fill in the blank in the reading passage.

2.   **Lexical inference** assessed the ability to infer the meaning of a word using contextual information. In the task, students were required to select the best sentence, out of four possibilities, describing the target word.

3.   **Co-referential resolution** evaluated the ability to identify the referent of a pronoun across sentences.

4.   **Text-based inference** measured the ability to infer an unstated text segment based on the information presented in the text.

5.   **Gist detection** probed the ability to grasp the main idea of the passage.

Development of morphological awareness

Morphological awareness sub-test scores are presented in Table 1. The data demonstrated that CHL students performed well above the chance level (25%) on all tasks but one (radical explanation), showing no signs of random performance. Hence, despite the heavily restricted print input, seemingly, CHL students are sensitized to the basic properties of semantic radicals by the time they reach the third grade. The data also showed that response accuracy varied widely across tasks, ranging from 24% to 89%. Of the five tasks, the highest accuracy rates occurred in radical formation, designed to measure students' understanding of physical placement of the radicals in compound characters. Accuracy rates declined considerably in the tasks requiring semantic analysis of character components (radical meaning, morpheme discrimination, and radical form), and the lowest scores were found in radical explanation—the task assessing sensitivity to subtle changes in meaning when a single-unit character is used as a semantic radical. These findings clearly suggest that diverse awareness facets mature at disparate rates. Specifically, sensitivity to radicals' structural properties appears to develop more rapidly than recognition of their functional properties.

Importantly, however, the data also demonstrated that virtually no difference existed in morphological awareness among the three grade groups. The finding is astonishing because first-language studies consistently suggest that major growth of morphological awareness occurs between Grades 2 and 6 among native English-speaking children (Carlisle, 2003; Ku & Anderson, 2003), as well as their Chinese counterparts (Ku & Anderson, 2003; Shu & Anderson, 1999). The present findings thus suggest that although CHL students are successful in acquiring the basic awareness facets with heavily limited character input, they seem unable to fine-tune those facets to accommodate details of their grapheme-morpheme relations. Consequently, their morphological awareness appears to remain basic throughout the school years.

Table 1.   Means and standard deviations (in parentheses) of the morphological awareness sub-test scores (% correct)

facet	overall (N=59)	grade 3 (N=23)	grade 4 (N=20)	grade 5 (N=16)
radical meaning	.46(.21)	.52(.16)	.44(.20)	.43(.26)
morpheme discrimination	.41(.21)	.46(.22)	.40(.22)	.37(.19)
radical formation task	.88(.12)	.88(.12)	.86(.12)	.89(.12)
radical form	.55(.21)	.59(.17)	.49(.19)	.56(.26)
radical explanation	.25(.15)	.24(.17)	.24(.13)	.28(.15)

Development of reading comprehension sub-skills

Reading comprehension sub-skill scores are listed in Table 2. Unlike morphological awareness, clear differences existed in comprehension performance across grade levels. Grade 5 students outperformed the younger cohorts on all five sub-skills. However, performance of Grades 3 and 4 students did not differ in any of the tasks with one major exception (coreference). Performance variations were also observable across tasks. Students in all grades scored higher on gist detection. This finding was unexpected because gist detection is supposedly more demanding than the vocabulary and coreference questions, because it was purported to assess the ability to integrate locally constructed meanings (phrases and sentences). Post-hoc analyses revealed, however, that the gist questions may have inadvertently induced a much simpler operation, that is, identifying the passage topic by locating a key word or a sentence introducing the passage topic. Even so, the mean accuracy rate of the gist questions was only 39%, pointing up the serious challenge CHL students face in reading Chinese passages for comprehension.

Table 2.   Means and standard deviations (in parentheses) of the reading comprehension sub-test scores (% correct)

facet	overall (N=59)	grade 3 (N=26)	grade 4 (N=17)	grade 5 (N=16)
vocabulary	.36 (16)	.34 (15)	.29 (09)	.45 (25)
coreference	.44 (25)	.29 (22)	.46 (24)	.57 (28)
lexical inference	.33 (18)	.29 (15)	.27 (16)	.42 (24)
text inference	.33 (22)	.30 (19)	.24 (18)	.46 (28)
gist	.39 (24)	.35 (22)	.32 (21)	.49 (30)
total	.37 (21)	.31 (19)	.32 (18)	.48 (27)

Table 3 presents correlations between morphological awareness and reading comprehension. As predicted, no systematic relationship existed between the two constructs in the Grades 4 and 5 data, implying that reading skills among CHL learners may develop independently of morphological awareness. Interestingly, however, the correlation was significant in the Grade 3 data. Given the small sample size, it is unclear as to what the discrepant correlational patterns really mean. Clearly, further studies are needed to disentangle the conflicting information regarding the functional connection between reading comprehension sub-skills and morphological awareness.

In view of the minimum variation in morphological awareness among the three grade groups, as well as no systematic relationship between morphological awareness and reading comprehension, it is highly unlikely that the stronger comprehension performance among Grade 5 students is attributable to their morphological awareness or other component skills in Chinese. Further, the acquisition of comprehension sub-skills measured in the study requires substantial text processing experience. Yet, the majority of participants indicated that they rarely read Chinese books outside of Chinese classes, again implying that the improved comprehension among Grade 5 students does not stem from Chinese literacy experience. What, then, is responsible for their improved comprehension sub-skills? It seems reasonable to suggest that their performance gains may be attributable to more solidly-established reading skills in English. Without data on the students' English literacy, the conjecture, howsoever plausible, cannot be substantiated. Because of their potential utility, this and other related speculations should be tested empirically in future studies.

Table 3.   **Correlations among morphological awareness and reading comprehension**

	reading comprehension		
	grade 3 (N=23)	grade 4 (N=17)	grade 5 (N=14)
morphological awareness	.49*	.01	.22

* $p<.05$

Implications for theory of biliteracy development

Several important implications can be drawn from the results of the study. First, heritage learners' performance on the morphological awareness tasks—non-random but varied—indicates that they are sensitized to the basic formation regularities in Chinese characters, but not to detailed functional properties of semantic radicals. Hence, it seems reasonable to suggest that although the basic awareness facets develop rapidly even with heavily limited print input and experience, these facets remain basic throughout the school years, without evolving into more refined understanding of language-specific properties. Because it is the latter facets that promote character knowledge expansion and reading comprehension, future research should focus on the factors affecting their acquisition.

Second, given that even Grade 3 students are capable of detecting and using characters' structural regularities, it also seems likely that CHL learners benefit greatly from explicit instruction on the functional and distributional properties of radicals. Moreover, it will be extremely beneficial to determine to what extent such metalinguistic training compensates for heavily limited character input and exposure in character knowledge development among CHL learners.

Third, the study revealed that reading comprehension performance among Grade 5 students was considerably stronger than that among younger cohorts. CHL students, moreover, scored higher on the questions addressing global comprehension than those requiring in-depth analysis of local information. These patterns of performance clearly suggest the involvement of non-language-specific factors—presumably unaffected by limited print exposure and experience—in heritage literacy learning. It is highly plausible that primary literacy in English may have contributed to the attainment of global comprehension sub-skills particularly among Grade 5 students. Undoubtedly, systematic examinations of cross-linguistic relationships in comprehension sub-skills will shed substantial light on biliteracy theory and practice.

In short, literacy learning in a heritage language differs from that in the first language in that it occurs with heavily restricted linguistic resources. It is also distinct from that in a second language because it typically builds on adequately developed oral language competence. Hence, their literacy learning experiences offer a unique opportunity to dissect the specific contributions stemming from the two dominant factors—oral language proficiency and print experience—both regarded as critical for reading acquisition. Systematic explorations of literacy development of heritage language learners will likely offer significant new insights into the critical intersection between language development and literacy learning.

Implications for literacy instruction for heritage language learners

Weekend-school programs can play a crucial role in encouraging heritage language learners to develop literacy skills in their heritage languages (Cummins, 2005). Our study findings suggest that weekend heritage language schools can provide a metalinguistic foundation necessary for literacy development in the language. It has been reported that metalinguistic foundation building is closely associated with formal schooling experience (Park, 2004). Our study has shown that weekend heritage language schools can also serve this function.

In addition, the findings further indicate that the limited print input inhibits CHL students from fine-tuning their basic awareness facets. Although more research-based information is needed to determine any specific recommendations for instructional interventions, the present findings point up three fundamental principles, which, properly incorporated, could substantially improve the effectiveness of literacy instruction: (a) promoting children's ability to detect the structural and functional regularities in characters; (b) ensuring early mastery of the basic characters—those serving as radicals in compound characters; and (c) engaging children in semantic information extraction from characters and radicals in print.

Summary and conclusions

This study explored the development of morphological awareness and reading comprehension sub-skills among Grades 3 to 5 CHL students. Three findings are particularly illuminating. First, CHL students performed well above the chance level on the tasks designed to measure disparate facets of morphological awareness, suggesting that they have become sensitized to the basic properties of Chinese morphemes (radicals) even with heavily restricted input. Second, no systematic increment occurred in morphological awareness across grade levels. With limited print input and exposure, morphological awareness among CHL student appears to remain fundamental. Lacking the awareness facets closely attuned to the language-specific morphological properties, seemingly, their awareness is of little use in reading comprehension. The generally weak correlations between morphological awareness and reading comprehension seem to suggest their developmental dissociation. Finally, as predicted, reading comprehension in Chinese is significantly better among older, than younger, students. Given that (a) there was virtually no increment in morphological awareness; (b) that no systematic connection existed between morphological awareness and reading comprehension; and (c) that the comprehension gains were observed only among Grade 5 students, it seems reasonable to attribute the superior performance of older learners to more firmly established reading skills in English, which become available through reverse transfer. Taken together, these findings suggest a strong possibility that literacy in an additional language can be facilitated by metalinguistic and other related competencies developed through prior literacy learning. Given its potential impacts on biliteracy theory construction, cross-language competence sharing should be more directly addressed in future studies.

References

Abu-Rabia, S. (1995). Learning to read in Arabic: Reading, syntactic, orthographic and working memory skills in normally achieving and poor Arabic readers. *Reading Psychology, 16*(4), 351–394.

Bialystok, E. (2001). *Bilingualism in development: Language, literacy, and cognition.* New York: Cambridge University Press.

Bialystok, E., McBride-Chang, C., & Luk, G. (2005). Bilingualism, language proficiency, and learning to read in two writing systems. *Journal of Educational Psychology, 97*(4), 580–590.

Carlisle, J. F. (2003). Morphology matters in learning to read: A commentary. *Reading Psychology, 24,* 291–322.

Carr, T., & Levy, B. (1990). Writing system background and second language reading: A component skills analysis of English reading by native speaker-readers of Chinese. In T. Carr & B. Levy (Eds.), *Reading and its development: Component skills approaches* (pp. 375–421). San Diego, CA: Academic Press.

Chen, Y. P., Allport, D. A., & Marshall, J. C. (1996). What are the functional orthographic units in Chinese word recognition: The stroke or the stroke pattern? *The Quarterly Journal of Experimental Psychology, 49*(A), 1024–1043.

Clarke, L. (1988). Invented versus traditional spelling in first graders' writings: Effects on learning to spell and read. *Research in the Teaching of English, 22*(3), 281–309.

Cummins, J. (1979). Linguistic interdependence and the educational development of bilingual children. *Review of Educational Research, 49*(2), 222–251.

Cummins, J. (1991). Interdependence of first- and second-language proficiency in bilingual children. In E. Bialystok (Ed.), *Language processing in bilingual children* (pp.70–89). New York: Cambridge University Press.

Cummins, J. (2005). A proposal for action: Strategies for recognizing heritage language competence as a learning resource within the mainstream classroom. *Modern Language Journal, 89,* 585–590.

Cummins, J., Swain, M., Nakajima, K., Handscombe, J., & Green, D. (1981). *Linguistic interdependence in Japanese and Vietnamese students.* Report prepared for the Inter-America Research Associates, June. Tronto: Ontario Institute for Studies in Education.

Da Fontoura, H., & Siegel, L. (1995). Reading, syntactic, and working memory skills of bilingual Portuguese-English Canadian children. *Reading and Writing, 7*(1), 139–153.

Devine, J. (1987). General language competence and adult second language reading. In J. Devine, P. Carrell, & D. Eskey (Eds.), *Research in reading English as a second language* (pp. 73–87). Washington, DC: Teachers of English to Speakers of Other Languages.

Devine, J. (1988). The relationship between general language competence and second language reading proficiency. In P. Carrell, J. Devine, & D. Eskey (Eds.), *Interactive approaches to second language reading* (pp. 260–277). New York: Cambridge University Press.

Durgunoglu, A. Y., Nagy, W. E., & Hancin, B. J. (1993). Cross-language transfer of phonemic awareness. *Journal of Educational Psychology, 85,* 453–465.

Fowler, A. E., & Liberman, I. Y. (1995). The role of phonology and orthography in morphological awareness. In L. B. Feldman (Ed.), *Morphological aspects of language processing* (pp. 157–188). Hillsdale, NJ: Erlbaum.

Gholamain, M., & Geva, E. (1999). The concurrent development of word recognition skills in English and Farsi. *Language Learning, 49,* 183–217.

Goodman, K. (1967). Reading: A psycholinguistic guessing game. *Journal of the Reading Specialist,* 6(4), 126–135.

Goodman, K. (1969). A psycholinguistic approach to reading: Implications for the mentally retarded. *Slow Learning Child: The Australian Journal on the Education of Backward Children, 16*(2), 85–90.

Goswami, U., & Bryant. P. (1992). Rhyme, analogy, and children's reading. In P. B. Gough, L. C. Ehri, & R. Treiman (Eds.), *Reading acquisition* (pp. 49–63). Hillsdale, NJ: Lawrence Erlbaum Associates.

Koda, K. (2000). Cross-linguistic variations in L2 morphological awareness. *Applied Psycholinguistics, 21*(3), 297–320.

Koda, K. (2002). Writing systems and learning to read in a second language. In W. Li, J. S. Gaffiney, & J. L. Packard (Eds.), *Chinese children's reading acquisition: Theoretical and pedagogical issues* (pp. 225–248). Boston: Kluwer Academic.

Koda, K. (2005). *Insights into second language reading: A cross-linguistic approach.* NY: Cambridge University Press.

Ku, Y-M., & Anderson, R. C. (2003). Development of morphological awareness in Chinese and English. *Reading and Writing: An Interdisciplinary Journal, 16,* 399–422.

Legarretta, D. (1979). The effects of program models on language acquisition of Spanish speaking children. *TESOL Quarterly, 13,* 521–534.

Li, W. L., Anderson, R. C., Nagy, W., & Zhang, H. C. (2002). Facets of metalinguistic awareness that contribute to Chinese literacy. In W. L. Li, J. S. Gaffney, & J. L. Packard (Eds.), Chinese children's reading acquisition (pp. 87–106). Dordrecht, The Netherlands: Kluwer Academic Publishers.

MacWhinney, B., & Bates, E. (Eds.). (1989). *The crosslinguistic study of sentence processing.* New York: Cambridge University Press.

Nagy, W. E., & Anderson, R. C. (1999). Metalinguistic awareness and literacy acquisition in different languages. In D. Wagner, R. Venezky, & B. Street (Eds.), *Literacy: An international handbook* (pp. 155–160). Boulder, CO: Westview Press.

Park, E. C. (2004). The relationship between morphological awareness and lexical inference skills for English language learning with Korean first-language background. *Dissertation Abstracts International, 65*(05). (UMI No. 3131518).

Perfetti, C. A. (2003). The universal grammar of reading. *Scientific Studies of Reading, 7,* 3–24.

Perfetti, C. A., & Dunlap, S. (2008). Learning to read: General principles and writing system variations. In K. Koda & A. M. Zehler (Eds.), *Learning to read across languages: Cross-linguistic relationships in first- and second-language literacy development* (pp. 13–38). New York: Routledge.

Perfetti, C. A., & Liu, Y. (2005). Orthography to phonology and meaning: Comparisons across and within writing systems. *Reading and Writing, 18,* 193–210.

Shu, H., & Anderson, R. C. (1997). Role of radical awareness in the character and word acquisition of Chinese children. *Reading Research Quarterly, 32,* 78–89.

Shu, H., & Anderson, R. C. (1999). *Learning to read Chinese: The development of metalinguistic awareness.* In A. Inhuff, J. Wang, & H. C. Chen (Eds.), *Reading Chinese scripts: A cognitive analysis* (pp. 1–18). Mahwah, NJ: Lawrence Erlbaum.

Skutnabb-Kangass, T., & Toukomaa, P. (1976). *Teaching migrant children's mother tongue and learning the language of the host country in the context of socio-cultural situation of the migrant family.* Helsinki: The Finnish National Commission for UNESCO.

Troike, R. C. (1978). Research evidence for the effectiveness of bilingual education. *NABE Journal, 3,* 13–24.

Van Valin, R. D., Jr. (1991). Functionalist linguistic theory and language acquisition. *First Language, 11,* 7–40.

Wang, M., Perfetti, C. A., & Liu, Y. (2005). Chinese-English biliteracy acquisition: Cross-language and writing system transfer. *Cognition, 97,* 67–88.

10

NFLRC
monographs

Home Literacy Environment in CHL Development

Yun Xiao
Bryant University, Rhode Island

Through a survey that involved 127 Chinese heritage language (CHL) learners in three American universities, this study reveals substantial correlation between CHL learners' home literacy environment and their HL literacy development. Significant differences are found across the instructional levels: namely, the higher the instructional level, the richer the CHL home literacy environment. Compared with the mainstream dominant language, however, the CHL home literacy environment is bleak, where HL reading materials and literacy activities are, in most of the cases, inadequately constructed for its stimulation or attainment. The findings of the study suggest that interventions in HL learners' homes, communities, and mainstream schools are needed to protect CHL from being retarded or eroded.

In foreign language classrooms, HL learners have been characterized as having prior background knowledge in their home languages but their linguistic skills are skewed in one way or another (United States Department of Education, 1999). Specifically, they may be able to engage in oral communication on informal and familiar topics but do not have the needed literacy skills in reading and writing. In other words, the HL learner may be, to some extent, bilingual but not bi-literate (Dai and Zhang, this volume; Hendryx, this volume; Koda et al., this volume). To understand the role of learners' prior home language background in CHL learning, the researcher has conducted two consecutive studies, which compared the linguistic performance of CHL learners with that of their non-heritage counterparts (Xiao, 2004, 2006). The results of both studies showed that CHL students performed significantly better than their non-heritage counterparts in listening and speaking, but not in reading and writing.

These CHL students were either born in this country or immigrated with their parents from China or Taiwan at a young age. Like other immigrant children, they communicated orally with their family members in HL at home and were simultaneously exposed to home literacy materials and practices. With their parents' high expectation of maintaining their heritage roots, many of them were, at some point of their lives, sent to Sunday/weekend community HL schools to receive Chinese literacy instruction.

From the perspective of literacy development in multicultural settings, Au (1993) has suggested that literacy learning begins in the home but not in school. When home and school

Xiao, Y. (2008). Home literacy environment in CHL development. In A. W. He, & Y. Xiao (Eds.), *Chinese as a heritage language: Fostering rooted world citizenry* (pp. 151–166). Honolulu: University of Hawai'i, National Foreign Language Resource Center.

literacy practices were closely matched, children did well. Studies in reading research have shown that children's access to reading materials and the amount of reading activities are critical in developing their literacy in reading and writing (McQuillan, 1998; Neuman, 1999). Through immersion in meaningful texts, children incidentally learn the language and are highly motivated to read (Elley, Cutting, Mangubhai, & Hugo, 1996). Thus, the impact of reading materials at home and the extent of family reading have been shown to be significant and substantial for learners' literacy development (Ortiz, 1986).

Ample evidence has shown that, in the United States, mainstream middle-class families provide their children with extensive literacy experiences, print-rich environments, storybook readings, schoolwork completion, coloring and drawing, and so forth (Neuman, 1999). It was estimated that the mean number of children's books in an American home was 137 (McQuillan, 1998), and that a typical middle-class child entered first grade with approximately 1,000 hours of being read to (Adams, 1990). This type of mainstream literacy experience has been found not only in the United States but also elsewhere, where school is an extension of home, and home is the hub of literacy resources. Shu, Li, Anderson, Ku, and Yue (2002) conducted a home literacy study in China, which investigated the association of Chinese children's home literacy environment and their school performance at grade levels. The study indicated that Chinese parents were heavily involved in their children's literacy development and provide ample literacy activities and reading materials at home. Moreover, those children who had better access to books at home and more shared reading activities with their parents had higher literacy skills and better performance in school.

Such findings are also supported by Tse's (2001) study of adults learning their heritage languages in the United States. This study investigated 10 highly HL-literate US-raised immigrant adults (in Spanish, Cantonese, and Japanese) for their HL literacy access and experience. In the participants' homes, the researcher found a total of 36 types of HL books, texts, newspapers, games, poetry, and so forth, and a total of 37 types of literacy activities such as independent or group reading, language brokering, game playing, and functional writing. The study revealed that there was a strong association between adults' HL environment and their HL literacy attainment. Namely, adult immigrants, who had access to rich HL literacy resources in their homes and immediate communities, attained higher levels of HL literacy.

However, such rosy pictures have not been found in immigrant HL children's studies in the US. Instead, an extensive literature confirmed that these children's HL literacy was lost after they entered mainstream schools (Wong Fillmore, 1991), where they were swept away by "an abrupt shift" from HL to dominant language (Bougie, Wright, & Taylor, 2003, p. 349) and encountered an intense disconnection between home and school literacy practices (McCarthey, 1997). These studies revealed that, to gain acceptance, immigrant children typically dropped their HL and made English their primary language (Li, 2003, 2006; Pease-Alvarez, Garcia, & Espinosa, 1991). Li (2003) reported that many Chinese immigrant children experienced discontinuity between home and school, and that their home literacy was incongruent with the school practices and was not valued by their school teachers (p. 194). As a result, many of them were struggling with reading and writing in Chinese, although they were fluent in the oral language (Li, 2006).

To understand the role of home environment for Chinese immigrant children learning English as a second language, Xu (1999) examined six kindergartners' home literacy resources and their English and Chinese literacy experiences through home visits and interviews. The study revealed a remarkable disparity in literacy materials and activities between English and Chinese. While the former were abundant, the latter were minimal. The children's parents were found to engage their children in extensive English literacy activities, with minimal attention being paid to Chinese literacy. To grasp every opportunity for their children to learn English, the parents and sometimes grandparents demonstrated interest in learning English by reading books to or being read to by their children. Although they agreed that their HL was important, the parents believed that their children must have good English to go to college and have college degrees to obtain decent jobs. In such home environments, the children's oral use of Chinese gradually decreased and was eventually replaced by English. Such data confirm previous findings about the experience of HL learners: They speak or hear the heritage language spoken at home and in their immediate communities, but, in most of the cases, do not receive formal instruction in the heritage language during elementary or secondary grades. As a result, they are only literate in English but not in their heritage languages (Valdés, 2005, p. 413).

As is evident from the discussion so far, home/community environment is crucial to young children, and adults as well, in their literacy attainment. When given access to rich print environment and the opportunity to meaningful reading and writing activities, be it primary, secondary, or HL, the learner well develops the target literacy. Although the studies discussed above cover a range of language learning settings, little is known about how home literacy environment influences the HL development of college students. As the literature reveals, these students typically acquire their HL (as a means of communication) at a young age, lose it after entering mainstream schools, and re-learn it as a foreign language after entering colleges or universities. In other words, these students revisit their HL after they experience a "subtractive form of bilingualism" (Lambart, 1975, p. 67) in grade schools, in which they went through the mainstreaming process to become monolingual English speakers.

In this vein, research should show the consequences or causes of the HL erosion or attainment, and their various associated contributing factors. As a token, the present study investigates one factor by answering the following general question: How does college Chinese students' home literacy environment affect their HL attainment? For data collection and analysis, this inquiry breaks down into four specific research questions:

1. How many Chinese reading materials are available to CHL learners in their homes?
2. How often do parents engage in parent-child HL literacy-related activities in their homes?
3. How often do CHL learners engage in HL literacy-related studies in their homes?
4. How does parents' level of Chinese education affect the learners' HL advancement?

Method

Participants

One hundred and thirty HL students enrolled in the Chinese language programs in three American universities participated in the survey. After eliminating three participants, who selected "Chinese (ethnicity)" in the questionnaire but did not indicate any Chinese dialects being spoken in the home, 127 participants' data were analyzed. Of them, 78 were 1st-year students, 31 were 2nd-year students, and 18 were 3rd-year and up. For data analysis, the 1st-year students were defined as beginning-level, 2nd-year as intermediate, and 3rd-year and up as advanced. As is evident from the number of participants at each instructional level, there was substantial attrition across the instructional levels; namely, the enrollment of CHL students drastically decreased starting from the intermediate level. Therefore, at the advanced level, only a handful of students were available for the study.

Data collection and analysis

Data were collected through a survey during 15 minutes of class time at the end of spring semester 2005. The survey was composed of 18 questions (see Appendix), three of which (questions 12, 14, and 16) were intended to ascertain the participants' HL background by asking if any of the Chinese dialects was spoken in their homes. Accordingly, they were not analyzed for the study. The questionnaire adopted the model developed by Shu et al. (2002), which was composed of four parameters: home literacy resources, parent-child literacy-related activities, learners' independent literacy-related activities, and parents' education. The model used in Shu's study, which investigated children learning Chinese as L1 in China, was adapted to fit the context and needs of the present study. To avoid compartmentalizing the participants' thoughts within individual parameters, the survey questions were randomly ordered. Moreover, while most of the questions asked about participants' recent HL learning experience, the rest concerned their childhood experience at home and in weekend HL schools. To explore their insights, 10 participants (5 at the lower level and 5 at the higher level) on the University of Massachusetts at Amherst campus were selected for one-on-one interview with the researcher. The interviews were semi-structured, which sought in-depth information based on answers to the survey questions.

Data were analyzed using the four parameters and parameter-specific ratings contained in the survey: CHL home literacy resources, parent-child CHL literacy-related activities, learners' independent CHL literacy-related activities, and parents' Chinese education. Statistical tests including a two-way ANOVA in the general linear model were conducted to determine the significance of variable differences.

Results

Results of home Chinese literacy resources

Questions 1 and 2 in the survey sought information about the participants' HL home literacy resources, which included Chinese books, newspapers, and magazines. Question 1 asked how many Chinese books were in the home for parents and for children (participants), and were grouped in five categories for the data analysis: *very low* (0–2 books), *low* (3–10 books), *medium* (11–25 books), *high* (26–50 books), *very high* (50 books and up). Question 2 asked how many types of HL newspapers and/or magazines were in the home on a regular basis, which were also grouped into five categories for the data analysis, such as *very low* (0), *low* (1 type), *medium* (2 types), *high* (3 types), *very high* (3 types and up). By consolidating the results of both questions 1 and 2, disparity was found between parents and children, and among the instructional levels in the quantity of reading materials possessed, that is, participants' parents had many more books than their children across the instructional levels, and higher-level participants had more books than their lower-level counterparts. Specifically, half of the advanced-level participants (50%) had *high* to *very high* numbers of books, and only a few of the beginners (5.13% of the total) had *high* to *very high* numbers of books (see Figure 1).

Figure 1 compares the participants' home literacy resources across the three instructional levels. As shown in the figure, the higher the instructional level was, the more HL reading materials the participants had in their homes. Results of Two-Way ANOVA revealed that instructional level had significant main effects on CHL home literacy resources: $F(2, 6)=1.3E + 17$, $p<0.001$. One-on-one interviews further showed that the instructional-level difference rested not only in quantity but also in quality of the CHL home literacy resources. When asked what kind of Chinese books/newspapers/magazines there were in their homes, the beginning students mentioned Chinese posters, menus, character cards, picture-books, and so forth. On the other hand, the advanced students additionally named some of the Chinese classics, such as *Xī Yóu Jì* (*The Journey to the West*) and *Hóng Lóu Mèng* (*Dreams of the Red Chamber*), and some popular Chinese newspapers widely circulated in this country, such as *Dà Jìyuán ShíBào* (*The Epoch Times*) and *Shìjiè Rì Bào* (*Chinese World*). However, when asked if they had level-graded Chinese recreational literature readings at home similar to those they saw in English, the answer was unanimously "No."

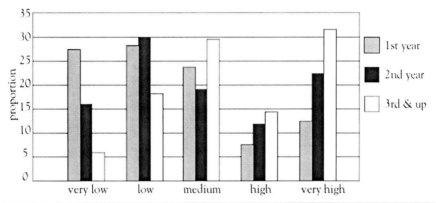

Figure 1. Comparison of participants' home literacy resources by instructional level

Results of parent-child CHL literacy activities

The results of parent-child home CHL literacy activities, which included booking reading, character writing, game/song/card practices, and written communications at home, were analyzed by onset age and frequency.

Results of parent-child CHL home literacy activities by onset age
Question 3 asked the participants when their parents/family started to read Chinese books/materials to them, and question 9 asked when their parents started to teach them how to write Chinese characters. Both questions were grouped in five categories for the data analysis: *never, 1–3 years old, 3–5 years old, 5–7 years old,* and *after 7 years old.* The results showed that almost half of the parent-child CHL home literacy activities started around 1–5 years old and dwindled after that (see Figure 2).

Results of Two-Way ANOVA showed that starting age had significant main effect, F (4, 8)=3.90, $p<0.05$, on parent-child literacy-related activities. In one-on-one interviews, most of the interviewees reported that, when they were little, their parents would teach them how to write the Chinese names of the family members and some simple Chinese characters, sing Chinese songs, and read character cards/books with picture illustrations. Such activities were drastically reduced once they started kindergarten or first grade. When asked why, the typical answer was, "Well, my parents just wanted me to concentrate on English and school work." Some of them even assumed themselves responsible for helping their parents, by saying, "My parents wanted me to learn enough English to finish college and to help them. They don't speak much English and often need my help even when they go to see a doctor." (In the researcher's teaching practice, it was not uncommon that a CHL student asked to be excused from class to accompany his/her parent(s) to see a doctor or serve a court function.)

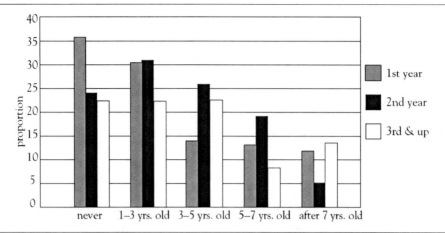

Figure 2.   Comparison of parent-child literacy-related activities by starting age

Results of parent-child CHL home literacy activities in book reading and character writing by frequency

Questions 4 and 10 asked how often the participants' parents/family engaged in literacy activities such as reading Chinese books/materials and writing Chinese characters. Both questions were rated on five scales: *never, occasionally, sometimes, often,* and *every day.* The results showed that the majority of the beginning students (75.64% of the total) had minimal (*never* to *occasional*) literacy activities with their parents, while a few of them (12.82%) had substantial (*often* to *every day*) activities of this sort. On the other hand, half of the advanced-level participants had minimal (*never* to *occasional*) literacy activities with their parents, and over one third of them (38.89%) had substantial (*often* to *every day*) activities of this sort (see Figure 3).

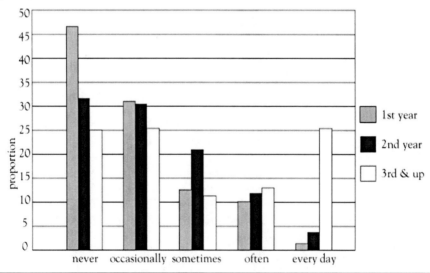

Figure 3.   Comparison of parent-child literacy activities by frequency

Results of Two-Way ANOVA showed that frequency, and the interaction of frequency and instructional level had significant effects on parent-child literacy activities: $F(4, 12)=143.86$, $p<0.001$ for frequency; $F(8, 12)=67.77$, $p<0.001$ for the interaction. Such results indicate that advanced students had significantly more book/material reading and character writing with their parents than their lower-level counterparts. One-on-one interviews revealed that, besides instructional level, participants' early experience in formal Chinese education contributed to the disparity in their home literacy activities. For those who were born in the United States or came to the United States as an infant and never had formal HL literacy instruction in mainstream schools, "Chinese was too hard to read and write," and accordingly their parents tended to be half-hearted with their HL literacy activities once they started mainstream schools. Conversely, for those who started kindergarten or grade school in China/Hong Kong/Taiwan before they arrived in the US, "Chinese was not that difficult," and their parents tended to be more enthusiastic to continue with their HL literacy activities. Some of them even believed that Chinese language skills might qualify them for China-related careers in the future. One of them, who took the Business Chinese—an advanced Chinese course—from the researcher, said it all: "I called my Dad for help almost every day. Otherwise, I cannot finish your homework. My goal is to get a job in a company which does business with China."

Results of parent-child Chinese game activities

Question 17 asked if the participants' parents/family did any Chinese fun activities with them at home, such as Chinese Character games, puzzles, jingles, chess, cards, and songs. The results showed that approximately one third of the beginning and intermediate students never had such activities, while all of the advanced students did. Out of the six activities specified in the survey, Chinese chess and songs were more favored than the others, especially by beginning students. When asked in the one-on-one interviews what kind of Chinese chess or songs they played or sang at home, girls tended to say, "I don't play chess. I sing with my Mom some simple songs, such as *Bǎobao kuài shuìjiào* (*My sweet baby, have a good sleep*)." But boys would say, "I do not sing that stuff. I like Chinese chess. Sometimes I play *Májiàng* (a traditional Chinese rummy game with small tiles) with my parents" (see Figure 4).

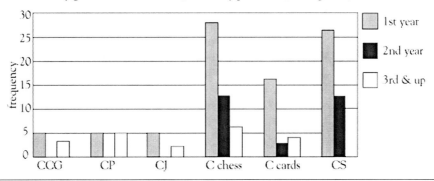

Figure 4. Comparison of parent-child game activities by instructional level

Results of home written communication

Questions 13 and 15 asked what language the participants used when communicating in writing with their parents and with their siblings. The scales for each question were: *English*, *Chinese*, and *mixed* (Chinese with English). The results showed that only three beginning students had no written communications at all with their parents, and among the others there were noticeable differences in language use across the instructional levels. Specifically, while 19% of the beginning students used *Chinese* or *mixed* when communicating with their parents, around 56% of the advanced students used *Chinese* or *mixed*. Moreover, while 10% of the beginning students used *Chinese* or *mixed* when communicating with their siblings, around 44% of the advanced students used *Chinese* or *mixed* (see Figure 5).

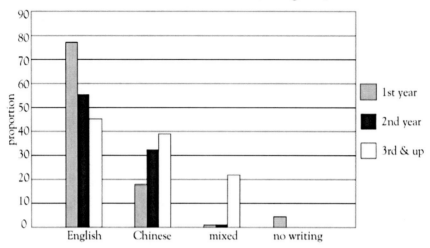

Figure 5.   Comparison of participant-parent written communication by instructional level

Results of Two-Way ANOVA showed that language use, and the interaction of language use and instructional level, had significant main effects on participant-parent home written communication: $F(2, 6)=88.65$, $p<0.001$ for language use; $F(4, 6)=36.76$, $p<0.001$) for the interaction. Such results revealed that, in their home written communication, the participants used significantly more English than Chinese across the instructional levels, and beginning students used significantly more English than their advanced counterparts.

One-on-one interviews revealed that beginning students tended to write to family members, especially siblings, in English, with two exceptions: (a) when parent(s) had difficulty reading English, and (b) when there was a need to write simple intimate messages such as *Māma nǐhǎo* (Hello, Mom), *Bàba nǐhǎo* (Hello, Dad) or greeting cards such as *Shēngrì kuàilè* (Happy birthday), *Xīnnián hǎo* (Happy new year). Otherwise, they chose to use English. When asked why, the answer was, "It is so much easier to write in English than in Chinese." However, advanced students reported that they could write simple notes or letters in Chinese with their family members.

Results of participants' independent HL literacy-related activities at home

Questions 7, 8, and 11 asked participants about the time spent on independent Chinese studies at home per day, which included reading Chinese books, newspapers, and journals, watching Chinese TV or movies, and writing characters. The results showed that, on average, around 45% of the beginning students, 36% of the intermediate students, and 18% of the advanced students did not have any Chinese studies at home. However, over 50% of the advanced students had such activities for 0.5 hour and up per day, while only around 20% of the beginning students did so (see Figure 6).

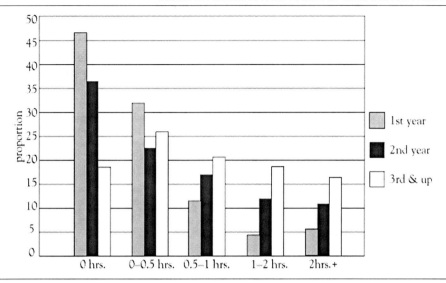

Figure 6. Participants' time length of Chinese study at home per day

Results of Two-Way ANOVA showed that time length of Chinese study, and the interaction of time length and instructional level were significant variables: $F(4,24)=10.64$, $p<0.001$ for time; $F(8,24)=5.75$, $p<0.001$ for the interaction. Namely, advanced students spent more time on Chinese studies at home than their lower-level counterparts. In one-on-one interviews, when asked, "What do you do for your Chinese studies at home?" the typical answer was "I do homework from my Chinese class," which meant that, in most of the cases, the independent Chinese studies were not voluntary but assigned tasks.

Results of participants' CHL studies in Chinese community schools
Results of participants' CHL studies in community schools included starting age and frequency. Question 5 asked how old the participants were when they started HL community schools (i.e., Sunday/Saturday/evening/summer schools) to learn Chinese. The rating was on five scales: *never, 1–3 years old, 3–5 years old, 5–7 years old*, and *after 7 years old*. Question 6 asked how often they learned Chinese in such schools. The rating was on four scales: *never, occasionally, sometimes*, and *often*.

The results showed that, on average, around 40% of the participants never went to community HL schools to learn Chinese. For those who did, the starting age was mostly around 3 years old. In one-on-one interviews, those who went to community schools reported that they normally studied there for 2–3 hours per week for 1 or 2 years and dropped out after kindergartens or grade schools started. In addition, not a single person continued such studies after entering college. When asked why, the typical answer was "I hated going to Chinese Sunday school. It was boring!" When asked what they did in Chinese Sunday schools, the answer was, "we learned *pinyin* (the phonetic symbols of the Chinese sound system), wrote names, characters strokes, some simple characters; sang children's songs; and read kids' stories."

Results of parents' Chinese education

Question 18 asked the participants about their parents' education obtained in China/Hong Kong/Taiwan, under the assumption that the higher the level of Chinese education their parents had, the higher the level of CHL attainment the participants would have. However, the results did not confirm such an assumption in that the majority of the parents had senior high or college and higher Chinese education, without noticeable difference across the instructional levels (see Table 1). One-on-one interviews revealed that, in general, parents' focus was largely on their children's English proficiency and school work, no matter how much Chinese education they had themselves.

Table 1.   Response to the question, "Can you tell me the education your parents obtained in China/Hong Kong/Taiwan?"

participant's instructional level	parents	parents' education level			
		junior &under	junior high	senior high	college & up
beginning	N=156	6	26	61	62
intermediate	N=62	0	14	16	32
advanced	N=35	0	4	13	19
total	N=253	6 (2.37%)	44 (17.39%)	90 (35.57%)	113 (44.66%)

Summary and discussion

This study began with an examination of HL linguistic issues and learners' home literacy practices in various settings, and sought to answer the question of how Chinese college students' home resources and activities affected their HL literacy development. The data revealed that a large number of Chinese immigrant homes possessed zero to minimal HL reading materials and that level-appropriate HL recreational literature readers, so abundant in English and the leading foreign languages in the US., were barely existent in their homes. Significant differences were, however, found across the instructional levels; namely, advanced learners had significantly more reading materials than their beginning counterparts. In addition, advanced students had, besides the basic and functional materials, exposure to some Chinese classical literacy works and popular Chinese newspapers in this country. Such findings indicate substantial relevance between CHL learners' home literacy practices and their HL literacy advancement, which confirms the previous findings that children's access to reading materials and the amount of reading activities were critical in developing their literacy in reading and writing (McQuillan, 1998; Neuman, 1999).

The results of parent-child HL literacy-related activities showed that, in general, Chinese parents did not invest much time or effort on HL literacy activities with their children; however, significant differences were found across the instructional levels. While the majority of the beginning learners had 0-mimial parent-child interaction in Chinese book reading and character writing, advanced learners had significantly more activities of this sort. In addition to literacy activities at home, most of the participants had experience in receiving Chinese literacy instruction in weekend HL schools, but such experience did not show significant advantage in their HL literacy development. The data showed that learners typically started Chinese community schools at a very young age and dropped out once their kindergartens or grade schools started. This confirms the previous finding that there was "an abrupt shift" from HL to dominant language in early HL education (Bougie et al., 2003).

Chinese game activities, which are rich in both linguistic and cultural content, were found not very popular among the CHL learners, except for those less culture/language-demanding ones such as simple Chinese songs or chess. In terms of written communication at home, the results show that participants typically used significantly more English than Chinese when communicating with their family members. However, advanced students used significantly more Chinese than their lower-level counterparts; in addition, the content of the writing was differentiated. While the advanced learners could compose notes or letters in Chinese, the beginning learners only wrote sketchy greeting cards.

The participants' independent Chinese studies at home, such as book reading, TV watching, and character writing, revealed that a considerable amount of CHL learners did not engage in such activities, especially at the beginning level. However, advanced learners spent significantly more time on such activities than their lower-level counterparts. Interestingly, parents' Chinese education was not found to exert significant impact on their children's CHL literacy development. Instead, most of the parents were reported to be concerned more about their children's English proficiency and school work rather than their children's HL literacy development, no matter how much Chinese education they themselves had. Obviously, minority immigrant parents view their primary responsibility as preparing their children for the mainstream skills with which to compete for desirable social and economic roles in the dominant culture when they grow up (Ogbu, 1978).

To sum up, the present data reveal that, compared with the dominant language in this country and elsewhere, the CHL home environment is, in most of the cases, linguistically deprived, where HL reading materials and literacy activities are inadequately constructed for its stimulation or attainment, especially for beginners. This confirms the previous findings that immigrant children's HL is typically eroded or lost (Li, 2003; Pease-Alvarez et al., 1991; Wong Fillmore, 1991).

The findings suggest that interventions at learners' home, community, and mainstream school are needed to protect HL from being retarded, eroded, or blocked within its ethnic culture, or, worse, completely lost. The interventions can presumably include (a) increasing learners' access to level-appropriate HL reading materials, (b) enhancing parents' involvement in their children's HL literacy development, and (c) placing HL learners in a multilingual and multicultural mainstream curriculum. Under the impact of globalization, multilingualism, and multiculturalism, students' social and economical roles in their adult life will change, and so will the role of mainstream schools, which are preparing the students to live in the changing world. By this token, mainstream teachers should, among other things, build up the connections between school and the homes for non-mainstream HL students, appreciate their heritage values, and have a working knowledge of their home language and culture.

Moreover, both HL parents and children should be receptive to the message about the new developments, potentials, and values of their home language and culture in the changing world. Parents should also be provided with instructional guidance to help with their children's HL literacy development. In addition, homes, community and school libraries should invest in non-mainstream HL reading materials, which are, however, hardly existent in the market at the present time. CHL researchers and teaching practitioners are thus duty-bound to develop level-appropriate, informative, and interesting reading materials in a timely fashion, such as graded Chinese recreational literature readers and their like.

Currently, pre-college CHL learning takes place in two major settings: mainstream primary/secondary schools and community HL schools. Based on data from the Asia Society Report 2005, the Chinese enrollment in community schools is six times that of mainstream schools (i.e., 150,000 students for the former and 24,000 for the latter in 2003). With regard to this striking contrast, many questions can be raised, and solutions need to be sought. One question is: Why do the CHL learners who have a head start in the community HL schools typically quit learning Chinese upon entering the mainstream schools? To date, mainstream schools have not gone un-criticized for this, but the community schools have. The present data show that the Chinese community schools are not yet a full-fledged education system but transient gap filler between home and mainstream school. They are characterized by mini-operation (2 to 3 hours per week), insufficient funding provision (makeshift classrooms and facilities), and out-of-date traditional teaching practices (instructors are mostly untrained volunteers). The majority of the interviewees in this study complained about boredom and lack of age-/level-appropriate tasks in Chinese community schools. Their experience was supported by Wang's 4-year study (2004), in which she found that Chinese community schools adopted a *Hanzi* (Chinese character) acquisition approach and that students were asked to copy and memorize *Hanzi* over and over again in class, with the instruction seldom going beyond sentences. She concluded with an alarming message that "there was no sense of progress or achievement. Students basically stay at the same level, unable to move forward in their HL proficiency or literacy" (p. 368). Given the significant new role they are assumed to play in strengthening, maintaining, and developing students' heritage language (Cummins, 2005), research should probe into various issues involved in this system, and substantial improvements are needed to achieve the optimum goal.

As illuminated in the current debates, the existing language acquisition theories do not adequately account for the development of heritage language, which is legitimately a L1 but pedagogically treated as a L2. Developmentally, HL does not take the path or rate of either L1 or L2 (He, 2006; this volume). While L1 acquisition is about the ultimate uniform success of a native linguistic system, L2 acquisition is about the restructuring of the learner's interlanguage system. HL acquisition is about the maintenance or relearning of a HL, but little is known what teaching approach is most workable in this setting. Lynch (2003) contends that the HL learners who arrive at the foreign language classrooms seem not entirely L1 speakers or L2 speakers of their HL. Valdés suggests that the HL speaker is an am-bilingual or L1/L2 user, namely, a dual language user (2005, p. 414). These theories are definitely interesting and worthy of further debate and research. Future CHL research should, on one hand, promote the HL development and, on the other, illuminate L2A theories by exploring various issues surrounding learners' early childhood HL experience, school-age HL erosion/loss, and adulthood HL relearning.

References

Adam, M. (1990). *Beginning to read*. Cambridge, MA: MIT Press.

Au, K. H. (1993). *Literacy instruction in multicultural settings*. New York: Harcourt Brace College Publishers.

Bougie, E., Wright, S. C., & Taylor, D. M. (2003). Early heritage-language education and the abrupt shift to a dominant-language classroom: Impact on the personal and collective esteem of Inuit children in Arctic Quebec. *International Journal of Bilingual Education and Bilingualism*, 6(5), 349–373.

Cummins, J. (2005). A proposal for action: Strategies for recognizing heritage language competence as a learning resource without the mainstream classroom. *The Modern Language Journal*, 89(4). 585–592.

Elley, W., Cutting, B., Mangubhai, F., & Hugo, C. (1996). *Lifting literacy levels with storybooks: Evidence from the South Pacific, Singapore, Sri Lanka and South Africa*. Unpublished paper presented at the International Literacy Conference, Philadelphia, PA.

Lambart, W. E. (1975). Culture and language as factors in learning and education. In A. Wolfgang (Ed.), *Education of immigrant students. Symposium Series 5.* (pp. 55–83). Toronto: Ontario Institute for Studies in Education.

Li, G. (2003). Literacy, culture, and politics of schooling: Counternarratives of a Chinese Canadian family. *Anthropology & Education Quarterly, 34*(2), 182–204.

Li, G. (2006). *Culturally contested pedagogy: Battles of literacy and schooling between mainstream teachers and Asian immigrant parents* (SUNY series, Power, Social Identity, and Education). Albany: State University of New York Press.

Lynch, A. (2003). The relationship between second and heritage language acquisition: Notes on research and theory building. *Heritage Language Journal 1*(1), 11–17. Retrieved date from http://www.heritagelanguages.org

McCarthey, S. J. (1997). Connecting home and school literacy practices in classroom with diverse population. *Journal of Literacy Research, 29*(2), 145–182.

McQuillan, J. (1998). *The literacy crisis: False claims, real solutions.* Portsmouth, NH: Heinemann.

Neuman, S. B. (1999). Books make a difference: A study of access to literacy. *Reading Research Quarterly, 34*(3), 286–311.

Ogbu, J. U. (1978). *Minority education and caste: The American system in cross-cultural perspective.* New York: Academic Press.

Ortiz, V. (1986). Reading activities and reading proficiency among Hispanic, black, and white students. *American Journal of Education, 95,* 59–76.

Pease-Alvarez, L., Garcia, E. E., & Espinosa, P. (1991). Effective instruction for language-minority students: An early childhood case study. *Early Childhood Research Quarterly, 6,* 347–361.

Shu, H., Li, W., Anderson, R., Ku, Y. M., & Yue, X. (2002). The role of home-literacy environment in learning to read Chinese. In W-L. Li, J. S. Gaffney, & J. L. Packard (Eds.), *Chinese children's reading acquisition: Theoretical and pedagogical issues.* (pp. 207–224). Boston: Kluwer Academic Publishers.

Tse, L. (2001). Heritage language literacy: A study of US biliterates. *Language, Culture and Curriculum, 14*(3), 256–268.

United States Department of Education (1999). *Standards for foreign language learning in the 21st century.* Washington, DC.: National Endowment for the Humanities (NFAH).

Valdes, G. (2005). Bilingualism, heritage language learners, and SLA research: opportunities lost or seized? *The Modern Language Journal, 89*(3), 410–426.

Wang, C. S. (2004). Biliteracy resource eco-system of intergenerational language and culture transmission: An ethnographic study of a Chinese-American community. Unpublished doctoral disseration, University of Pennsylvania, Philadelphia.

Wong Fillmore, L. (1991). When learning a second language means losing the first. *Early Childhood Research quarterly, 6,* 323–346.

Xiao, Y, (2004). L2 acquisition of Chinese topic-prominent constructions. *Journal of the Chinese Language Teachers Association, 39*(3), 65–84.

Xiao, Y. (2006). Heritage learners in foreign language classroom: Home background knowledge and language development. *Heritage Language Journal, 4*(1), 47–57

Xu, H. (1999). Young Chinese ESL children's home literacy experiences. *Reading Horizons, 40*(1), 47–64.

Appendix

your Chinese class _____   your gender: **M   F**

your home language (circle only one)   **Chinese   Non-Chinese**

Dear student: You are invited to answer the following questions, which will help us better understand the various curricular challenges involved in programs designed to meet your needs. This is not a test. Your participation is highly appreciated. 謝謝!

Directions: Please read the following questions and circle only one answer for each entry:

1. How many *Chinese* books are there in your home?
   for your parents: 0–2   3–10   11–25   26–50   50 and above
   for you and your siblings: 0–2   3–10   11–25   26–50   50 and above

2. How many kinds of *Chinese* newspapers and/or magazines do your family read on regular basis?
   0   1   2   3   3 and above

3. *When* did your parents/family start to read Chinese books/materials to you?
   never   1–3 years old   3–5 years old   5–7 years old   after 7 years old

4. *How often* did your parents/family teach you how to read Chinese books/materials?
   never   occasionally   sometimes   often   every day

5. *How old* were you when you went to Sunday/Saturday/evening/summer schools to learn Chinese?
   never   1–3 years old   3–5 years old   5–7 years old   after 7 years old

6. *How often* did you learn Chinese in Sunday/Saturday/evening/summer schools?
   never   occasionally   sometimes   often

7. When you are at home, *how much time* do you spend reading Chinese books, newspapers, and journals per day?
   0   0–1/2 hour   1/2–1 hour 1 –2 hours   2 hours and above

8. When you are at home, *how much time* do you spend watching Chinese TV or movies per day?
   0   0–1/2 hour   1/2–1 hour 1–2 hours   2 hours and above

9. *When* did your parents start to teach you how to write Chinese characters?
   never   1–3 years old   3–5 years old   5–7 years old   after 7 years old

10. *How often* did your parents/family teach you how to write Chinese characters?
    never   occasionally   sometimes   often   every day

11. When you are at home, *how much time* do you spend writing characters per day?
    0   0–1/2 hour   1/2–1 hour 1 –2 hours   2 hours and above

12. What language do your family use when interacting with each other?
    English   Chinese (i.e., Mandarin, Cantonese...)

13. What language do your parents use when communicating with you in writing?
    English   Chinese

14. What language do your parents use when communicating with you in speaking?
    English   Chinese (i.e., Mandarin, Cantonese...)

15. What language do your siblings use when communicating with you in writing?
English   Chinese

16. What language do your siblings use when communicating with you in speaking?
English   Chinese (i.e., Mandarin, Cantonese...)

17. Do your parents/family do the following activities with you (circle as many as you like)?
Chinese Character games   Chinese puzzles   Chinese jingles
Chinese chess   Chinese cards   Chinese songs

18. Can you tell me the education your parents obtained in China/Hong Kong/Taiwan?
junior high   senior high   college and above

11

NFLRC
monographs

Developing a Chinese Heritage Language Corpus: Issues and a Preliminary Report

Tao Ming
Hongyin Tao
University of California, Los Angeles

This chapter reports on the construction of a Chinese heritage language (HL) corpus and discusses its significance for Chinese HL learning and teaching. The corpus under construction so far comprises about 1,000 samples of written essays and narratives, with a total of about 200,000 characters. Based on this dataset, we devised a coding system with 10 major categories and 36 subcategories for HL learner errors. We also conduct a case study on the use of the perfective marker le, which shows that a previous estimate of heritage learners' grammatical acquisition is inaccurate. Finally, we discuss the important role that corpora can play in the accurate description of heritage learner language, for compiling adequate teaching materials, in addressing the important question of oral and written fluency, as well as for sound language assessment.

This chapter reports on the construction of a Chinese heritage learner language (CHL) corpus and discusses the significance of such infrastructures. With increasing enrollment of heritage learners in language programs at U.S. institutions of higher learning, heritage language (HL) education is fast becoming a field of its own, drawing from research and practice in linguistics, psychology, and language education. Research on Chinese heritage learners dates back to Christensen and Wu (1993) and Wang (1996), although the terms "false beginners" and "semi-natives" instead of "heritage learners" were often used then. More recent studies on CHL can be found in, for example, Shen and Bear (2000) and the papers in Tao (2006). An overview of the literature shows that most of the recent studies deal with character and literacy issues (Ke, 1998; Tse, 2001; Xiao, 2006), while others focus on issues of learner motivation, community, and identity (He, 1997, 2001, 2003, 2006; Weger-Guntharp, 2006).

A common theme in these studies appears to center on the differences between heritage language (HL) and foreign language (FL) learners and the unique pedagogical and assessment challenges that HL poses (McGinnis, 1996). What urgently needs to be done next, we believe, involves a number of key areas. The first area concerns a precise understanding of the basic properties of Chinese as a heritage language. What characterizes Chinese heritage learner language? What types of errors that learners tend to make? How are different types of structures acquired by different types of CHL learners and why? There are so far only sporadic

Ming, T., & Tao, H. (2008). Developing a Chinese heritage language corpus: Issues and a preliminary report. In A. W. He, & Y. Xiao (Eds.), *Chinese as a heritage language: Fostering rooted world citizenry* (pp. 167–187). Honolulu: University of Hawai'i, National Foreign Language Resource Center.

studies investigating a few of these issues, systematic investigations are lacking. In this respect, Campbell and Rosenthal (2000), to our knowledge, is the first to theorize about the systematic linguistic differences between HL learners and FL learners. Of relevance is their assertion that FL learners "have the ability to produce and comprehend a high percentage (estimated 60% to 65%) of the grammatical structures at all level" (p. 169), whereas HL learners "have acquired 80% to 90% of the grammatical rules that govern words, phrase, sentence, and discourse production and recognition" (p. 167). The differences between the two groups of learners, based on Campbell and Rosenthal's estimation, are quite striking. However, to what extent can we be sure of these differences? So far, limited empirical research has been conducted to verify/refute the estimations given by Campbell and Rosenthal. In this paper, we will explore the use of the Chinese perfective aspect marker *le* in a case study to test this hypothesis. We will use this example to show why corpus construction is important for a better understanding of patterns of heritage language acquisition.

Second, there are generally no well-grounded benchmark standards to gauge HL learner proficiency. In the U.S. foreign/second language teaching community, the best known standards are the ACTFL proficiency guidelines (e.g., Breiner-Sanders, Swender, & Terry, 2001). However, ACTFL guidelines do not make explicit distinctions between FL and HL learners, and as such their application is limited as far as HL is concerned. Recognizing the need for HL assessment standards, there have been calls for action to address this issue (see, e.g., the UCLA 2001 report), but progress remains slow.

 The approach adopted in this study is corpus based, one that emphasizes the importance of large-scale empirical studies in HL acquisition, especially the construction and exploitation of computer corpora. Generally speaking, computer corpora are principled collections of large scale linguistic data that are usually digitized for easy access and quick processing (Biber, Conrad, & Reppen, 1998). Ever since the COBUILD project and the publication of such works as the *Collins COBUILD English Language Dictionary* (Sinclair, 1987) and the *Collins COBUILD English Grammar* (Sinclair, 1990), the first corpus-based dictionary and grammar for learners, the contribution of corpora to language study and teaching has been increasingly recognized, and corpus-based studies and pedagogical materials have been dramatically increased, for English at least (Biber et al., 1998; Biber, Johansson, Leech, Conrad, & Finegan, 1999; Hunston, 2002; Kennedy, 1998; McEnery & Wilson, 2001; McEnery, Xiao, & Tono, 2005; Meyer, 2002; Partington, 1996; Sinclair, 1991; Stubbs, 1996, 2001; Tognini-Bonelli, 2001). Corpus-based linguistic research has contributed greatly to comprehensive and accurate descriptions of native and learner language, with new insights into both language structure and use.

Large scale data in a corpus is particularly useful in enabling the researcher and the teacher to break away from the constraints of relying solely on individual intuition and personal reflections. Not surprisingly, then, an increasing number of corpora have been constructed for linguistic investigation and language teaching. In the area of Chinese corpus construction, a number of well known corpora have been built. For example, both the Lancaster Corpus of Mandarin Chinese (LCMC; McEnery & Xiao, 2004) and the Academia Sinica Balanced Corpus of Modern Chinese (Huang & Chen, 1992) have been in wide use. However, the variety of corpora is limited. This is especially the case in learner corpus and language teaching. To our knowledge, the only known Chinese learner corpus is the L2 Chinese Interlanguage Corpus (LCIC) developed by the Beijing Language and Culture University (Chu, Chen, Zhang, Wei, Zhang, & Zhu, 1995). This corpus, however, as with many others, remains largely unavailable for public use. To fill the gap, the present project, by constructing a large-scale CHL learner corpus, aims to make a contribution towards remedying the scarcity situation of Chinese learner language data and contribute to Chinese language pedagogy in general.

In the remainder of the paper, we will first present the scope of the corpus project, followed by a description of the data source. We will then discuss the encoding and segmentation schema and the error categories for this corpus. Finally, we will present sample data in the use of the aspect marker *le* as a demonstration of the utility of a HL corpus.

Data source

The source of our heritage language corpus consists mainly of compositions and essays from students enrolled in the HL track of the elementary Chinese classes locally known as Chinese 1A, 2A, and 3A at a west coast university. In the university curriculum system, Chinese 1A, 2A, and 3A constitute a three-quarter-sequence of elementary-level heritage track classes. According to the course descriptions, students who finish this sequence qualify for the 1-year foreign language requirement. (A non-heritage track parallel this sequence is also offered at the elementary level.) Most of the participants in this study are junior undergraduate students, who range in age from 17 to 23. Before being admitted into the HL track, these students were required to take a placement test that serves to provide information about the students' language background. Students who scored 3 or 4 points in spoken test on a scale of 4 were placed into the elementary HL track regardless of their performance in the written test. Students speaking other dialects such as Cantonese or Shanghai dialect but not fluent Mandarin were denied staying in the HL track. The result of the placement test reveals that the participants in this project are close to advanced foreign language learners in terms of the speaking ability and listening comprehension. However, the participants' ability in other language skills such as writing and grammar varies from some scoring over 80 to others under 30 on a scale of 100. The results of the written placement tests show that the majority of the participants (91%) have very limited proficiency in written Chinese. As detailed later, except for the Frog Stories and Pear Stories, which are in-class assignments, all the compositions and essays are collected from after-class assignments. The frequency of the written assignment is once a week. We began to collect data from the second quarter (class 2A) of the academic year, that is, winter quarter 2006. All the collected data are raw data as the written assignments were collected before they were corrected by the instructors.

There are several reasons for collecting written samples from the heritage learners. First, reading and writing are known to be the main issues for heritage learners (Peyton, Ranard, & McGinnis, 2001; Wang, 1996); collecting written data will provide direct material for tackling HL learner problems. Second, written data is relatively easier to collect than many other types of data (e.g., conversation with transcription). Initial collection of written data will provide the necessary basis for future coding and processing of the heritage learner corpus.

According to our survey conducted in Fall 2006, 85% of the students in the heritage track were born in the US as second-generation immigrants; the remainder were born either in mainland China or Taiwan, and most of them arrived before the age of five. Among them, 73% have been to Chinese language schools before college; and 65% of their parents are from Taiwan.

So far we have collected around 1,000 samples with an average of 200 characters each, resulting in a collection of 200,000 characters. The topics of the sample compositions are diverse, ranging from argumentative to narrative topics. We intend to cover a variety of text types. The following table presents detailed information regarding the topics of the essays we have collected or plan to collect, as well as the size of the corpus under construction.

As indicated in Table 1, topics 1, 2, and 3 are narratives; topics 4, 5, and 6 are descriptive; and topics 7 and 8 are argumentative. Owing to the students' varying degrees of language proficiency, however, the nature of the language samples is not always conforming to the expected characteristics of the genres as one might find in writings by skilled native speakers.

Table 1.   List of topics

	topic and stimuli	estimated length in # of characters	# of compositions	total # of characters
1	frog, where are you?	350	200	70,000
2	a most memorable trip	200	200	40,000
3	the pear story	350	200	70,000
4	brief introduction to a selected book	200	200	40,000
5	my hometown	200	200	40,000
6	on friendship	200	200	40,000
7	to rent an apartment or buy a house?	200	200	40,000
8	is the post office still indispensable?	200	200	40,000
9	a letter to your friend	200	200	40,000
10	how to stay healthy?	200	200	40,000
	total	2,300	2,000	460,000

Coding and markup

Encoding and segmentation

There are two Chinese character systems currently used in the Chinese classroom—traditional and simplified. Students in our language classes have the option to choose either one. To meet the requirements of text analysis software tools such as Concordance (Watt, 1999) and Wordsmith Tools (Scott, 1999), we choose Unicode (UTF–8) to encode the texts since Unicode is a superset of both GB (the simplified system) and Big5 (the traditional system) and works with different varieties of Chinese. We also use ICTCLAS, a Chinese part of speech (POS) tagger developed by the Institute of Computing Technology, the Chinese Academy of Sciences (Zhang, Yu, Xiong, & Liu, 2003). One of the most accurate programs freely available today, ICTCLAS is capable of word segmentation, part-of-speech tagging, and recognition of unknown words.

Error tagging of the pilot corpus

Our CHL corpus focuses on what we believe to be inappropriate uses (or "errors") of linguistic forms. In data analysis, these "errors" are categorized as over- and underuse of specific linguistic features in various subtypes. Our use of the notion "error" is a loose one; that is, we are using it without making any explicit theoretical assumptions of a fixed standard against which the learner data is compared. Overall, our guiding principle of data coding is to start with the most prominent error types that are deemed to be most relevant for studying learner language. We selected 100 compositions on a variety of topics out of the corpus to form a mini-corpus for the pilot study. The total number of characters of the mini-corpus amounts to around 20,000. At the moment, the errors identified so far based on the mini-corpus can be divided into 10 broad categories, including those on verbs or verb phrases, nominals, and sentences. These error types are presented below, under the assumption that a fine-grained system can be devised and more coding categories can be added later:

ScriPt (character) Errors (SPE)

VerB or verb phrases Errors (VBE)

NomiNal Errors (NNE)

CLassifier Errors (CLE)

Preposition Phrase-related Errors (PPE)

Word Order Errors (WOE)

AdJective Errors (AJE)

ADverb Errors (ADE)

PRonoun Errors (PRE)

SentenCe (sentential) Errors (SCE)

We hope that the error type identified here, while crude, will be useful for future research in this area. In the next section, we discuss these errors and their subtypes.

Categorization of learner errors

SPE   Errors on characters are labeled as SPE, which is subcategorized into three subcategories: phonologically related script errors (SPE1), graphemic script errors (SPE2), and semantic related script errors (SPE3).[1] According to Shen and Bear (2000), phonologically based script errors refer to errors where an invented script form is used by the learner because of sound similarities with the target character which bears no resemblance to the invented script in terms of shape or meaning. The following presents an example where the parenthesized character is the target form.

(1)   我看了一些烹饪就学了新的东西我一（以）前都不知道。

It is a well-known fact that Chinese is rich in homophones. Correct context is needed to disambiguate what character is used by the learner. CHL learners are found to tend to use simpler characters to replace more complex ones, as demonstrated in example (1). Sometimes, the learner substitutes characters with similar pronunciations, as illustrated in (2), where the intended word is 喜.

(2)   我希望(喜欢)这本书的故事。

Graphemic script errors (SPE2) in Shen and Bear (2000) are defined as errors in which the inappropriately-used character resembles the intended character in shape. In (3), an incorrectly used character 运 is used to substitute the intended character 动, with the two characters sharing the same radical 云.

(3)   可是，一只运（动）物飞山来，打王朋的头，所以，他的头疼死了。

Semantic script errors (SPE3) are used to mark errors where the target character and the incorrectly-used character are related to each other in meaning. Sometimes, the erroneous character might resemble the target character in shape or sound or both. In the following example, 觉 is used in place of 睡, an error type that is likely due to the semantic affinity of the two characters.

---

[1]   See Shen and Bear (2000) for more detailed categorization of script errors.

(4)   晚上的时候，王朋觉（睡）着了的时候，青蛙跑出去。

VBE Errors in this verbs or verb phrases, including overuse and underuse, are further divided into several subcategories. For instance, VBE1 is used to mark aspect related errors on verbs or verb phrases where an aspect marker is incorrectly used.

(5)   旁边有一个很大的树，小张想他的小动物可以爬上那棵树，所以他跑上去看（了）一看。他在树上的时候，一个很聪明的动物飞（了）出去。

In (5), the learner did not use the perfective aspect marker *le* to mark a peak event (Chang 1986; Li & Bayley, this volume), which is a typical case of what we call underuse of aspect markers. Overuse of an aspect marker by CHL learners is also observed, as demonstrated in (6).

(6)   我知道如果我去买这本书，你会学了很多东西，比较健康一点，也会成高兴了一点。

We will explore this issue further in the case study later in this chapter. VBE2 marks learner's failure to use a resultative verb complement (RVC; Li & Thompson, 1981).

(7)   我看了一些烹饪就学（到）了新的东西我一前都不知道。

As suggested in (7), the learner fails to use the resultative verb complement 到 to indicate the endpoint of the action denoted by the verb 学. Unlike English, VRCs are very productive in Chinese. Their main function is to convert a verb which does not have a natural endpoint into a telic verb which has an inherent endpoint (Xiao & McEnery, 2004). VBE3 is a label for errors where the learner fails to use the potential complement form and replaces it with a modal verb.

(8)   每个人都能看懂 (看得懂) 这本书，所以你不一定要是中国人才能用上（用得上）这本书。什么样的人都可以用这本书去学中文。

VBE4 is used to mark verb omissions which may otherwise not be omitted. Chinese differs from English in that a repeated English verb may be omitted or replaced with a pro-verb such as *do* and its variants, whereas Chinese verbs in many cases have to be repeated due to the lack of pro-verbs. Example (9) provides such a case, where a required reiteration of the verb 吃 is missing.

(9)   如果你要好好地培养你的身体，你应该天天运动，跑步和吃健康的饭。捎去开餐买菜，捎去吃炸的东西和少（吃）油油的菜。

In this example, the missing verb 吃 is found in the first part of the same sentence. VBE5 refers to the misuse of modal verbs. For example, CHL learners tend to overuse the model verb 要, as exemplified in (10), where a different modal verb or no modals may be used.

(10)   我一定要觉得健康是最重要的，要不然，将来生活会难的很多。

VBE6 refers to the non-typical collocation of a verb with its arguments.

(11)   你的健康最重要因为你的身体是在这世界上最重要的事。如果你不好好地培养（保养）你的身体，你就会死掉。

In (11), the verb 培养 cannot co-occur with the noun phrase 你的身体. VBE7 is to tag errors where the learner confuses the transitivity of verbs (intransitives for transitives and vice versa). For example, an intransitive verb 走 in (12) is used transitively.

(12) 我还记得我在飞机上梦见我本来还没走（离开）台湾，每天还看得到我的爷爷，奶奶，外公，外婆，舅舅，阿姨。

Verb reduplication errors are marked with VBE8. A reduplication error is illustrated in (13), in which the learner used the simple form 玩 to replace its reduplicated form玩玩 or 玩一玩

(13) 王朋真高心，所以他睡觉的时候想一想他的青蛙因为他明天要跟青蛙和狗好好玩。

NNE Errors in nominals are rather limited because Chinese nouns do not have rich morphology to indicate grammatical categories such as number, gender, and case. Three types of noun-related errors are observed in the mini-corpus. The first type (NNE1) subsumes errors in which an unintended noun is used whose meaning is not congruent with the context.

(14) 别的烹饪书没有这儿个品质（特点），只会教你怎么做那些菜。

The second type of noun errors refers to errors where a single-character (monosyllabic) noun is used to replace a double-character (or multi-syllabic) noun.

(15) 王中华看间了他的小动物很伤心，因为它不想伤他们的婚姻，但是他还要拿回一只小动物，可是小动物送他它的大儿子当礼(礼物)，所以中华就带小动物的儿子回家，永远也没有看间小动物了。

Finally, the third nominal error type (NNE3) has to do with the change from a noun to a locative. Learners often fail to distinguish between a nominal for a concept and a nominal for a location, under-marking the latter, for example,

(16) 王朋看进去一棵树，因为他以为青蛙跳进树(里面)了。

In this example, a locative marker里面, which changes a nominal referent (树) to a location, would make it more appropriate.

CLE Two types of errors in classifiers are found in the mini-corpus. Errors in the first category (CLE1) are related to incorrectly used classifier (17) and errors in the second category (CLE2) arises from the lack of an obligatory classifier (18).

(17) 小张对面有一个(棵)死的树。他搞熟他的小狗它应该不说话。

(18) 因为飞机票太贵，我们只买了火车票。我们从一(个)国家到别的国家就坐火车。

PPE Errors in preposition encompass two different categories. PPE1 is to mark an error where an inappropriate preposition is used.

(19) 声音在（从）树的后面来的，所以他们安安静静的走过去。

PPE2 is to mark an error resulting from failure to deploy an obligatory preposition.

(20) 我在台湾留了两个多月，(从)暑假开始到暑假过了。

WOE Errors in word order are divided into five subcategories. WOE1 is to tag errors originating from the misplacement of a relative clause.

(21) 王朋跟小狗去外面，一边走路一边教。他们两个去一个地方有很多运物和很多树。

Relative clauses (RC) in Mandarin Chinese differ from their English counterpart in that the RC is placed before the head noun. The author of (21) inappropriately placed the relative clause 有很多运物和很多树 after the head noun 一个地方, perhaps due to English interference. WOE2 is to tag errors arising from misplacement of a locative phrase.

(22) 王朋先找青蛙在地下，但是他被一只小运物打死了。

Unlike English, Chinese in general deploys a locative preposition phrase before a verb. The learner producing (22) incorrectly placed the location after the verb. WOE3 is to index the misplacement of a time phrase, as shown in (23).

(23) 有一次，我们差一点没买到从英国到法国的票，只有五点钟的车。所以我起了床早上三点半，走到火车站。

It is observed in the mini-corpus that CHL learners sometimes misplace an instrument phrase, as illustrated by 用角 in (24), which is marked with WOE4.

(24) Deer 把那个小孩干跑了用角。

Misplacement of adverbs is tagged with WOE5. The adverb 很快 in the following example is inappropriately placed at the end of the sentence.

(25) 那只 lu 跑了个小时以后就（很快地）把王中华丢进了一条小河里去了很快。

AJE Among the subtypes of adjective errors, AJE1 marks an error where an inappropriate adjective is used, which causes incongruence in meaning between the adjective and the noun that it modifies.

(26) 我也觉得这本书很有意思因为他的作者教你做比较健壮（健康）的菜。

AJE2 refers to errors where a degree modifier of an adjective is incorrectly used.

(27) 小王一点儿（有一点儿）生气，可是一下子就好了。

The learner in (27) uses the degree phrase 一点儿 to modify the adjective, which caused ungrammaticality. AJE3 is to mark incorrect duplication of adjectives.

(28) 黑洞里头有一双大大白白的眼睛。

ADE ADE1 is to mark errors where an obligatory adverb is not used, and ADE2 marks errors where an inappropriate adverb is used resulting in semantic anomalies. This is illustrated in (29) and (30), respectively.

(29) 因为他就可以有一只青蛙，还有它（也）可以常常来看其他的青蛙。

(30) 当我们离开了我们的父母，我们会很吃力（努力地）去找别人来照顾我们。

PRE PRE1 refers to cases of ambiguous pronoun reference, as exemplified in (31).

(31) 小河虽然很冷，可是他不怕，因为他听到他的小动物的叫。他一看就看到小动物跟他的对象。

The last occurrence of the pronoun 他 in (31) is ambiguous because it is difficult to identify the antecedent of the pronoun. PRE2 marks errors on pronouns where a mandatory pronoun is missing.

(32) 有一天他找到一只小动物，他觉得（它）很可爱，想把它带回家养。

As shown in (32), the parenthesized pronoun is needed. However, the learner fails to produce the obligatory pronoun. Besides underused errors, overuse of pronouns is also observed in the mini-corpus. Overuse errors are marked with PRE3.

(33) 古时候有一个很爱动物的小孩，他的名字叫王中华。他住在一个小乡里，每天他可以去树林召动物。有一天他找到一只小动物，他觉得很可爱，他想把它带回家养。

Overuse of pronouns is a commonly observed phenomenon in CHL learners' written discourse. The reason might be attributable to the negative transfer from English where subject is almost obligatory in each clause.[2] PRE3 is utilized to indicate mismatches between the antecedent and a pronoun.

(34) 因为青蛙爸爸喜欢小白和小狗，他给他们一只小青蛙孩子。小白和小狗谢谢爸爸，他（们）高兴地回家。

The antecedent of the pronoun in (34) is 小白和小狗, which is plural. However, the learner in (31) used a singular pronoun 他 to refer back to the plural antecedent.

SCE Sentential errors subsume three subcategories. SCE1 refers to multiple errors which lead to ungrammatical sentences.

(35) 我一念一点就笑很多。我的脸也会很红。

The sentence produced by learner in (35) is very difficult, if not impossible, to understand due to the multiple grammatical errors and the absence of a logical connector. SCE2 tags sentential errors owing to problematic use of conjunctions.

(36) 我想是因为我坐飞机会晕跟因为我吃坏了肚子，所以我一下了飞机就了。

The learner producing (36) tried to explain why she vomited after disembarking from the plane, with two reasons. The problem is that she used two tokens of the causal conjunction 因为, which is linked by an NP conjunction 跟. It is also worth mentioning that learners tend to overuse the conjunct word 和. 和 is often used by learners not only to connect two nominal phrases but also other grammatical elements such as adjectives, verb phrases, and even two sentences. SCE3 is to tag incomplete sentences. Incomplete constructions often make it very difficult for the reader to understand what the learner wants to convey, as shown in (37).

(37) 我是在小学先看得这本书。我的朋友说这本书很所以我就看了。今天我想介绍一下这本书。

It is obvious that the author of (37) does not finish in the middle of the second sentence as it is impossible to end a clause with an adverb 很. SCE4 is to mark errors in punctuation. Again, misuses of punctuation can be either overuses or absences of punctuation marks. An instance of missing punctuation is exemplified in (38), where the quotation marks are missing after the verb 说.

(38) 小张再说(：")小动物，你在那里呀?（"）他说以后一个很大的动物好像一个羊拿走小张！

For a summary of the categories discussed above, see the Appendix A.

---

[2]   For in-depth discussion on the use of pronouns, see W. Li (2006).

Obviously this is by no means an exhaustive list of the codes needed to tag a HL corpus. Absent from this list, for example, are discourse level errors. As important as they are, however, we have not been able to tag them because of the amount of work it entails. The categories listed above need to be refined and changed as more data is collected and coded.

We note that our approach to error coding (see Appendix B for a sample) can be characterized as minimalistic. That is, we code errors only when there is an obvious deficit; we do not strive for "better uses," that is, with the change of certain elements the language may sound better than what is minimally required. An example is given in (39).

(39) 王朋跟小狗去外面，一边走路一边教。

For this example, we would code two errors instead of three. The two errors are the script error (SPE1) for 教/叫 and the missing pronoun/noun error before (小狗/它) 一边走路一边教. We would not code a missing adverb here: 王朋跟小狗(一起)去外面, even though using such an adverb in this context would make the utterance sound better. A different case is given in (40).

(40) 王朋觉得找青蛙很重要因为他要跟青蛙玩。

Here, a comma before the adverbial clause headed by 因为 would make the overall organization clearer; however, as this is not a fundamental mistake we did not code errors of this type.

Also, a question arises as to how to tag the errors with maximum accuracy. Tagging errors manually for the categories listed above is laborious and susceptible to mistakes. In our experience the corpus tagging tool kit (ACWT) developed by Tao (2005) can help reduce this problem. As an input/tagging program, ACWT cannot identify the errors for the researchers intelligently; however, after entering all the proposed error tags to ACWT, the sample texts can be tagged semi-automatically with human intervention, and the level of accuracy is improved considerably. Finally, whenever possible, the tagged errors are checked by at least two researchers in order to maximally reduce the amount of coding errors. We expect this process to be ongoing throughout the life of the project.

A preliminary case study of the perfective marker *le*

To show the utility of the CHL corpus, we now present some preliminary data based on a subset of the CHL corpus under construction. We look into HL learners' use of the perfective aspect marker *le*. The sample material consists of 128 in-class compositions from Chinese heritage learners enrolled in Chinese 3A, a last session in a 3-quarter elementary course. The topic of the composition is the well-known story, "Frog, Where are You," initiated by a team of psycholinguistic researchers (Berman & Slobin, 1994). The story is shown in 24 pictures without verbal description. In the story, a boy loses his frog and finds it after a series of adventurous encounters with some animals. The participants were asked to write down the story in their own words. If they did not know the characters they wanted to use, they were allowed to use pinyin as replacement. The allocated time was one hour. The average length of the sample compositions is 400 characters. Altogether, 128 compositions were collected and the total number of characters collected is approximately 50,000.

This case study focuses on the overuse and underuse of the perfective aspect marker *le*.[3] The overuse errors are divided into two categories, namely, (a) errors resulting from the

---

3   This case study does not distinguish between verbal final *le* and sentence final *le* for two reasons: (a) the number of verbal final *le* is very low, accounting for only 5% of all occurrences; and (b) this case study

incompatibility between lexical aspects and grammatical aspects, and (b) errors related to syntactic constraints and discourse constraints. The lexical aspect is used to characterize the internal temporal contour in a verb as explicated by Vendler and others. According to Vendler (1967), verbs (or verbs with its accompanying elements) can be divided into four broad categories on the basis of lexical aspect. Achievement verbs encode situations which have natural endpoint but no inherent duration. In other words, the beginning and ending of an event presented by an achievement overlap with each other; examples of such verbal expressions include *die, fall,* and *win a game.* Accomplishment verbs characterize situations that also have natural endpoints; they differ from achievement verbs in that they present situations which imply duration. Examples of such include *write a letter, run a mile,* and *build a house.* Activity verbs such as *walk, run,* and *swim* present situations with duration, consisting of successive phases over time and with an arbitrary endpoint. State verbs such as *love, know,* and *want* encode situations which have no natural endpoint, and which are not dynamic (i.e., continuing without additional energy being applied). Having specified the verb lexical aspect types, let us now examine their relation with the perfective marker *le.*

According to Yang (1995), the perfective aspect marker *le* may not co-occur with verbs featuring States and Activities. In examples (41) and (42), the perfective aspect marker *le* is misplaced with a State and an Activity verb respectively.

(41) 从前美国麻州住了一个男孩, 叫王大中。

(42) 我看了一个地老su dong (鼠洞).

For overuses involving syntactic constraints, see (43).

(43) 小男孩起床的时候, 发现了王朋不见了。

In this case, *le* can not be placed after a main verb which takes a subordinate clause. Errors of this type are considered syntactically related. The use of *le* is also constrained by discourse factors. For instance, Chang (1986) reported that *le* can be "used as an explicit marker for the peak event in a discourse segment" (p. 265). The error in the following sentence is a case of failure to follow this discourse constraint on the use of *le.*

(44) 他们爬到了一个石头上，看到一个动物，吓一跳。

In (44), the perfective aspect marker *le* is inappropriately placed after the verb in the first event, which is not a peak event in this sequence. On the other hand, it would be needed after 吓 in 吓一跳, a peak event in the sequence, but it is missing in the sample. So together this constitutes a violation of the discourse constraint as discussed by Chang (1986).

The underuse errors also fall into two broad categories: those related to lexical aspect and those related to syntactic and discourse constraints. The former co-occurs mainly with Accomplishment and Achievement verbs, and underuse errors are seldom observed on State and Activity verbs. The following is an example where an obligatory *le* fails to occur after an Accomplishment verb.

(45) 他们两个去一个地方有很多运物和很多树。

Besides those resulting from the incongruence between lexical aspect and the perfective aspect marker *le,* underuse errors also occur in some syntactic environments where an obligatory *le* is

strives to understand the characteristics of CHL learners by comparing its findings with Yang, Huang, & Sun, (1999) and Yang, Huang, & Chao, (2000) where verbal final *le* and sentence final *le* is not maintained.

missing. For example, in the past tense context, the use of *le* is mandatory in BA constructions (Yang, 1995).

(46)   我又不小心，把东西玩坏，东西一坏了，小王就开始飞。

The learner who produced (46) failed to place an obligatory *le* in the BA construction.

Analogous to overuse errors, discourse factors also play a role in underuse errors. According to Chang (1986), if a discourse unit consists of several sequenced events, the last event (peak event) is the most important one and it must be marked as such with the perfective aspect marker *le*. Examinations of the extracted data reveal that some CHL learners failed to observe this constraint. In addition to (44) discussed earlier, the following is another case.

(47)   他pa过一块大木头，pa过一块大石头，发现一窝qingwa。

In the above excerpt, there are three sequenced events. In principle, it is possible to mark each and every event with a token of *le*. However, the learner of this extract did not mark any of them, especially the peak event at the end of the sequence. In other cases, just as in (44), the learner incorrectly chose to mark an earlier event instead of the final peak event with *le*. Here is another example.

(48)   小狗来到了河边，爬到石头上，看到一个dong物。

Using the error system devised here, we mark all the aforementioned errors discussed with VBE1. With the marking in place, we utilize a text analysis software Concordance (Watt, 1999) to extract all sentences containing an error on the use of *le*. Overall 1,217 instances are extracted for this case study. The number refers to the sum of both sentences where *le* is used (including overuses) and sentences in which an obligatory *le* is missing. Among them, 184 sentences were identified to contain an error, whether it is an overuse or an underuse. Thus the overall error rate is 15.1%. The errors were marked by the two investigators separately and the inter-rater reliability was 98.4%. The following table presents the distribution of errors on the use of *le* with respect to the total use. It is worth pointing out that the reported errors do not concentrate on essays from a few learners; they are found to be distributed across different learners.

Table 2.   Percentage of errors

error type	total	% of total use (1217)
overuse	47	3.8%
underuse	137	11.3%
total	184	15.1%

Table 3 compares the overuse (redundant) and underuse (missing) cases in regard to the total number of errors.

Table 3.   Proportions of errors

error type	#	%
overuse	47	26%
underuse	137	74%
total	184	100%

Clearly the vast majority of errors are of the underuse type. That is, compared with underuse errors, the overuse errors are relatively lower and CHL learners err in places where additional markers need to be provided, perhaps due to complex syntactic and discourse requirements.[4] This shows that corpus data can be useful in providing an accurate picture of HL learner deficits.

Our corpus data is also relevant at another level. Recall that in assessing HL learners' grammatical knowledge, Campbell and Rosenthal (2000) contend that "[HL learners] have acquired 80% to 90% of the grammatical rules that govern words, phrase, sentence, and discourse production and recognition." Our corpus-based findings concerning aspect marking show that, although the general tendency stated in Campbell and Rosenthal is compatible with the Chinese data, their estimation number is a bit too high.[5] Furthermore, our data suggests that there is a clear distinction between underuse and overuse cases, and it is the overuse that shows the HL learners relatively higher level of proficiency.

When we examine of the overuse of *le* in the corpus data, we find interesting differences between HL learners and learners taking Chinese as a foreign language (CFL). Our discussion is focused on the comparison of the findings in our study and those in a comparable study (Yang et al., 1999). To compare with their findings, we first excluded those cases where an obligatory *le* fails to show up and focus instead on those non-obligatory cases where an overuse occurs. The results are reported in Table 4.

Table 4.   Error percentage on overuse of *le*

total	# of overuse	%
1080	47	4.4%

Using narrative writing assignments by English speaking learners of Chinese as a foreign language in the L2 Chinese Interlanguage Corpus (LCIC) developed by the Beijing Language and Culture University (Chu et al., 1995), Yang et al. (1999) report that CFL learners have more or less the same error rate in the overuse of the aspect marker *le*, ranging from 17% to 27%, and no significant improvement is reported even for advanced learners. One reason for this error might be that CFL learners are more likely to treat the perfective aspect marker as a tense marker thus overusing it in the past tense context (Sun, 1993; Zhao, 1997), whereas CHL learners have the language intuition (though not always at a high level of proficiency) which enables them to avoid such errors.

Finally, we discuss the underuse of the aspect marker *le* in comparison with Yang et al. (2000) where the underuse of aspect markers is studied. In their written assignments (120 articles), Yang et al. found that CHL learners in their study tended to make more mistakes on its overuse and the underuse instances are much smaller than overuse cases. Our data shows that the opposite is true for CHL learners, as evidenced by the fact that the majority of mistakes on

---

[4]   This statement is made with the caveat that further analysis needs to be done on the basis of the two separate *le* types.

[5]   One reviewer pointed out that Campbell & Rosenthal's estimation refers to the speaking competence of heritage learners and their acquisition of grammatical rules in spoken language; as such there is no comparability between the results reported in this case study and the number in their estimation. However, we note that Campbell & Rosenthal's estimation is not exclusively based on spoken language, as evidenced by the statement that "The following description of what we believe to be the competencies and knowledge that average/typical HL students bring to university foreign language programs" (2006, p. 167). There is no explicit statement from them saying that their estimation should not be applied to written language.

the use of *le* concentrates on its underuse. Yang et al. also report that beginning and intermediate CFL learners tend to make more mistakes on the overuse of aspect markers whereas advanced and high advanced CFL learners tend to err more in their underuse. In other words, CHL learners in our study behave in a way similar to advanced learners in the deployment of the aspect marker *le*. The finding reported here is not surprising considering the fact that CHL learners in this study could speak Chinese rather fluently before they enrolled in the Chinese class, and their preexisting knowledge on the use of *le* is well shaped by its regular use in the verbal interaction with their Chinese speaking family members at home.[6]

From this brief comparison it may be concluded that CHL learners differ systematically from CFL learners in the deployment of the aspect marker *le*. This is concrete evidence that in the area of Chinese grammar CHL learners and CFL learners need to be treated differently. Thus, even though our database is still very small and our coding system is quite crude, it is quite clear that a well constructed corpus with systematically coded information can help to achieve a more accurate description of the heritage learner's level of proficiency as well as areas of deficits.

Concluding remarks

The CHL corpus under construction constitutes an important infrastructure for Chinese HL study. We have decided to focus on written data as a way of getting it started in corpus construction because of the relevance of the written data to reading and writing skills, two of the most pressing areas of HL learning. Other types of data, especially oral data, should be recognized as equally important. Our error coding system is obviously very preliminary and further improvements are needed, but a coding system, such as the one being developed here, can help us in revealing error types that may otherwise be overlooked. Finally, our case study further shows that a HL corpus has the potential to contribute to Chinese language learning and teaching in significant ways. Before closing, we would like to touch upon the last point briefly.

First, a heritage language corpus (or different corpora), if constructed properly, can reveal accurately the characteristics of Chinese heritage learner language and raise the awareness of problems in heritage language development. More accurate data, in the long run, will help improve Chinese language instruction in general. At the moment, only small-scale studies have been conducted, usually focusing on a small range of phenomena. We stress the importance of systematic study with large amounts of data. With a CHL learner corpus, we anticipate that a large variety of topics can be explored and meaningful comparisons with CFL learner data can be conducted. It may, for example, provide important insights into research topics such as script/orthography learning, word order transfer, lexical use, discourse connection, anaphora patterns, and so forth. Adequate data collection can be achieved obviously with a large number of student participants recruited, but also with learners of diverse backgrounds, of different proficiency levels, as well as under different communicative contexts. This pilot study is just one step toward achieving this goal.

Second, corpus-based studies of CHL can also contribute significantly to the development of adequate pedagogical materials. Currently, appropriate Chinese textbooks for Chinese HL learners are still severely lacking. A few widely circulated Chinese textbooks in American universities, for example, are mainly designed for CFL learners. Our teaching experience tells

---

[6]   Zhao (1997) found that errors in the underuse cases account for only 2% to 5% of the total errors. Apparently, Zhao's finding also suggests that CFL learners tend to make more mistakes on the overuse of *le* although the study is based on spoken data.

us that these textbooks are unsuitable for CHL learners for obvious reasons. A database of CHL learner language will provide critical information regarding what needs to be emphasized and what should be prioritized in pedagogical materials. At a minimum, the error information as revealed in the corpus will open a window into the difficulties and troubles of Chinese heritage learners, which in turn may provide crucial information for the development of effective pedagogical materials tailored to the needs of different types of Chinese heritage learners.

At a more theoretical level, a CHL learner corpus is also important in shedding light on the important question of what constitutes different levels of (oral and written) fluency in Chinese. Again, here we do not have well-grounded benchmark materials and the widely used standards or guidelines (typically for FL learners) do not accord well with the CHL reality. In our view, only a variety of carefully planned and well constructed CHL learner databases can provide the needed foundation for developing such benchmark materials.

Finally, constructing CHL learner corpora is important for sound language assessment. Without well-established benchmark materials, the effectiveness of language assessments is bound to be limited, if it exists at all, when it comes to evaluating learner proficiency and progress. Currently at most U.S. institutions of higher learning, rarely are heritage learners evaluated on the basis of results from empirical research (for an early case study, see McGinnis, 1996). Much is impressionistic, and idiosyncratic practices abound. HL corpora can be critical in providing quantitative information that can be incorporated in the service of such activities as placement tests, exit tests, and other types of proficiency assessment.

We hope to have presented a convincing case for heritage language corpus building and that more efforts will be put from the field of Chinese heritage language in the creation and sharing of valuable corpus resources.

References

Berman, R. A., & Slobin, D. I. [in collaboration with A A. Aksu-Koc, M. Bamberg, L. Dasinger, V. Marchman, Y. Neeman, P. C. Rodkin, E. Sebastian, C. Toupin, T. Trabasso, & C. von Stutterheim] (1994). *Relating events in narrative: A crosslinguistic developmental study*. Hillsdale, NJ: Lawrence Erlbaum.

Biber, D., Conrad, S., & Reppen, R. (1998). *Corpus linguistics: Investigating language structure and use*. Cambridge, England: Cambridge University Press.

Biber, D., Johansson, S., Leech, J., Conrad, S., & Finegan, E. (1999). *Longman grammar of spoken and written English*. London: Longman.

Breiner-Sanders, K. E., Swender, E., & Terry, R. M. (2001). *Preliminary ACTFL proficiency guidelines—writing*. Washington DC: ACTFL Inc. Retrieved January13, 2007, from http://www.actfl.org/files/public/writingguidelines.pdf

Campbell, R. N., & Rosenthal, J. W. (2000). Heritage languages. In J. W. Rosenthal (Ed.), *Handbook of undergraduate second language education* (pp. 165–84). Mahwah, NJ: Lawrence Erlbaum Associates.

Chang, V. W. (1986). *The particle le in Chinese narrative discourse: An interactive description*. Unpublished doctoral dissertation, University of Florida.

Christensen, M., & Wu, X. (1993). An individualized approach for teaching false beginners. *Journal of Chinese Language Teachers Association, 27*(2), 91–100.

Chu, C., Chen, X., Zhang, W., Wei, P., Zhang, W., & Zhu, Q. (1995). *Hanyu zhongjieyu yuliaoku xitong* [Corpus of Chinese Interlanguage] (CCI 1.0). Beijing: Beijing Language and Culture University. Retrieved August 18, 2006, from www.blcu.edu.cn/kych/H.htm

Freedman, A., & Medway, P. (Eds.). (1994). *Learning and teaching genre.* Portsmouth, NH: Boynton/Cook.

He, A. W. (1997). Learning and being: Identity construction in the classroom. *Pragmatics and Language Learning, 8,* 201–222.

He, A. W. (2000). Grammatical and sequential organization of teachers' directives. *Linguistics and Education, 11*(2),119–140.

He, A. W. (2001). The language of ambiguity: Practices in Chinese heritage language classes. *Discourse Studies, 3*(1), 75–96.

He, A. W. (2003). Novices and their speech roles in Chinese heritage language classes. In R. Baley & S. Schecter (Eds.), *Language socialization in bilingual and multilingual societies* (pp. 128–146). Clevedon, England: Multilingual Matters.

He, A. W. (2006). Toward an identity theory of the development of Chinese as a heritage language. In H. Tao (Ed.), *The Heritage Language Journal, Special Issue on Chinese as a Heritage Language, 4*(1). Retrieved August 15, 2006, from http://www.heritagelanguages.org

Huang, C., & Chen, K. (1992). A Chinese corpus for linguistics research. In *Proceedings of the 1992 International Conference on Computational Linguistics* (COLING–92; pp. 1214–1217). Nantes, France: Association for Computational Linguistics.

Hunston, S., & Francis, G. (1998). Verbs observed: A corpus-driven pedagogic grammar. *Applied Linguistics, 19*(1), 45–52.

Hunston, S., & Francis. G. (1999). *Pattern grammar.* Amsterdam: John Benjamins.

Hunston, S. (2002). *Corpora in applied linguistics.* Cambridge, England: Cambridge University Press.

Ke, C. (1998). Effects of language background on the learning of Chinese characters among foreign languages students. *Foreign Language Annals, 31*(1), 91–100.

Kennedy, G. (1998). *An introduction to corpus linguistics.* London: Longman.

Li, C., & Thompson, S. A. (1981). *Mandarin Chinese: A functional reference grammar.* Berkeley: University of California Press.

Li, W. (2006). Incorporating topic chains into pedagogical grammar of Chinese (把话题链纳入汉语教学语法体系—汉语语篇特点在外语教学中的体现). *Journal of Chinese Language Teachers Association, 41*(1), 31–56.

McCarthy, M. (1991). *Discourse analysis for language teachers.* Cambridge, England: Cambridge University Press.

McEnery, T., & Wilson, A. (2001). *Corpus linguistics* (2nd ed.). Edinburgh: Edinburgh University Press.

McEnery, T., & Xiao, Z. (2004, May 24–30). The Lancaster corpus of Mandarin Chinese: A corpus for monolingual and contrastive language study. In *Proceedings of the Fourth International Conference on Language Resources and Evaluation (LREC) 2004* (pp. 1175–1178). Lisbon.

McEnery, T., Xiao, Z., & Tono, Y. (2005). *Corpus based language studies.* London: Routledge.

McGinnis, S. (1996). Teaching Chinese to the Chinese: The development of an assessment and instructional model. In J. E. Liskin-Gasparro (Ed.), *Patterns and policies: The changing demographics of foreign language instruction* (pp. 107–121). Boston, MA: Heinle and Heinle.

Meyer, C. F. (2002). *English corpus linguistics: An introduction*. Cambridge, England: Cambridge University Press.

Partington, A. (1996). *Using corpora for English language research and teaching*. Amsterdam: John Benjamins.

Peyton, J. K., Ranard, D., & McGinnis, S. (2001). *Heritage languages in America: Preserving a national resource*. McHenry, IL: Delta Systems and Center for Applied Linguistics.

Scott, M. (1999). *WordSmith Tools*. Oxford, England: Oxford University Press.

Shen, H. H., & Bear, R. D. (2000). Development of orthographic skills in Chinese children. *Reading and Writing: An Interdisciplinary Journal, 13*, 197–236.

Sinclair, J. M. (Ed.). (1987). *Collins COBUILD English language dictionary*. London: Collins.

Sinclair, J. M. (Ed.). (1990). *Collins COBUILD English grammar*. London: Collins.

Sinclair, J. M. (1991). *Corpus, concordance, collocation*. Oxford, England: Oxford University Press.

Stubbs, M. (1996) *Text and corpus analysis: Computer-assisted studies of language and culture*. Oxford, England: Blackwell.

Stubbs, M. (2001). *Words and phrases: Corpus studies of lexical semantics*. Oxford, England: Blackwell.

Sun, D. (1993). Waiguo xuesheng xiandai Hanyu le de xide guocheng chubu fenxi [A preliminary analysis of the acquisition of modern Chinese le by foreign language learners). *Yuyan Jiaoxue yu Yuanjiu (Language Teaching and Research), 2*, 65–75.

Tognini-Bonelli, E. (2001). *Corpus linguistics at work*. Amsterdam: John Benjamins.

Tao, H. (2005). *A corpus worker's toolkit (ACWT)*. Software and Manual, Department of Asian Languages and Cultures, University of California, Los Angeles.

Tao, H. (Ed.). (2006). *The Heritage Language Journal. Special Issue on Chinese as a Heritage Language, 4*(1). Retrieved August 15, 2006, from http://www.humnet.ucla.edu/humnet/ealc/

Tse, L. (2001). Heritage language literacy: A study of US biliterates. *Language, Culture and Curriculum, 14*(3), 256–268.

University of California, Los Angeles (2001). *Heritage language research priorities conference report*. Retrieved from August 16, 2006, from www.cal.org/heritage

Valdés, G. (2000). The teaching of heritage language: an introduction for Slavic-teaching professionals. In O. Kagan & B. Rifkin (Eds.), *The learning and teaching of Slavic languages and cultures* (pp. 375–403). Bloominton, IN: Slavica Pub.

Vendler, Z. (1967). Verbs and times. In Z. Vendler (Ed.), *Linguistics in philosophy* (pp. 97–121). Ithaca: Cornell University Press.

Wang, X. (Ed.). (1996). *A view from within: A case study of Chinese heritage community language schools in the United States*. Washington, DC: The National Foreign Language Center.

Watt, R. J. C. (1999). Concordance [computer software]. Scotland: University of Dundee.

Weger-Guntharp, H. (2006). Voices from the margin: Developing a profile of Chinese heritage language learners in the FL Classroom. In H. Tao (Ed.), *The Heritage Language Journal, Special issue on Chinese as a heritage language*, (4)1, 29–46. Retrieved July 21, 2007, from http://www.heritagelanguages.org.

Xiao, Y. (2006). Heritage learners in foreign language classroom: Home background knowledge and language development. In H. Tao (Ed.), *The Heritage Language Journal, Special Issue on Chinese as a Heritage Language*, 4(1), 47–56. Retrieved August 16, 2006, from http://www.heritagelanguages.org

Xiao, R. Z., & McEnery, T. (2004). *Aspect in Mandarin Chinese: A corpus-based Study*. Amsterdam: John Benjamins.

Yang, S. (1995). *The aspectual system of Chinese*. Unpublished doctoral dissertation, University of Victoria.

Yang, S., Huang, Y., & Sun, J. (1999). Hanyu zuowei dier yuyan de ti biaoji xide (the Acquisition of Chinese Aspect Marking in Chinese as a Second Language). *Journal of the Chinese Language Teachers Association, 34*, 31–54.

Yang, S., Huang, Y., & Chao, X. (2000). Hanyu xide guocheng zhong de Biaoji buzu xianxiang (The Phenomenon of Under-marking of Chinese Aspect). *Journal of the Chinese Language Teachers Association, 35*, 87–116.

Zhang, H., Yu, H., Xiong, D., & Liu, Q. (2003, July). HHMM-based Chinese lexical analyzer ICTCLAS. In *Proceedings of the 2nd SIGHAN Workshop/41th ACL* (pp. 184–187). Sapporo, Japan. Retrieved February 12, 2007, from http://www.nlp.org.cn/project/project.php?proj_id=6.

Zhao, L. (1997). Liuxuesheng le de xide guocheng kaocha ji fenxi (The Examination and Analysis of the Acquisition of *le* by Chinese as Foreign Language Learners). *Yuyan Jiaoxue yu Yuanjiu (Language Teaching and Research), 2*, 4–10.

Appendix A: Examples of the coded error types

script errors (SPE)	SPE1	phonologically related script errors	我一（以）前都不知道。
	SPE2	graphemic script errors	一只运（动）物飞山来。
	SPE3	semantic script errors	王朋觉（睡）着了的时候。
verb errors (VBE)	VBE1	aspect errors	也会成高兴了一点。
	VBE2	resultative verb complement	看了一些烹饪就学（到）了新的东西。
	VBE3	no potential complement form	中国人才能用上（用得上）这本书。
	VBE4	verb omission	捎去吃炸的东西和（吃）油油的菜。
	VBE5	misuses of modal verbs	我一定要觉得健康是最重要的。
	VBE6	collocation errors	培养（保养）你的身体。
	VBE7	transitivity	还没走（离开）台湾。
	VBE8	verb reduplication error	因为他明天要跟青蛙和狗好好玩(玩一玩/玩玩).
noun errors (NNE)	NNE1	inappropriate nouns	烹饪书没有这儿个品质（特点）。
	NNE2	multi- vs. single-character (syllable)	送他它的大儿子当礼(礼物)
	NNE3	failure to change a referent to a location	他以为青蛙跳进树(里面)了。
classifier errors (CLE)	CLE1	missing obligatory classifier	从一(个)国家到别的国家
	CLE2	inappropriate classifier	一个（棵）死的树
preposition errors (PPE)	PPE1	inappropriate preposition	声音在（从）树的后面来的
	PPE2	missing pp parts	(从)暑假开始到暑假过了
word order errors (WOE)	WOE1	misplacement of relative clauses	他们两个去一个地方有很多运物和很树。
	WOE2	misplacement of a locative	王朋先找青蛙在地下
	WOE3	misplacement of time	所以我起了床早上三点半
	WOE4	misplacement of instrument	DEER把那个小孩干跑了用角。
	WOE5	misplacement of adverb	那只LU跑了个小时以后就（很快地）把王中华丢进了一条小河里去了很快。
adjective errors (AJE)	AJE1	inappropriate adjective	做比较健壮（健康）的菜
	AJE2	modifier of adjective	小王一点儿（有一点儿）生气
	AJE3	incorrect duplication	一双大大白白的眼睛
adverb errors (ADE)	ADE1	missing adverb	因为他就可以有一只青蛙，还有它（也）可以常常来看其他的青蛙。
	ADE2	inappropriate adverb	很吃力（努力地）去找别人来照顾我们
pronoun errors (PRE)	PRE1	ambiguous pronoun reference	他一看就看到小动物跟他的对象。
	PRE2	missing mandatory pronoun	他觉得（它）很可爱

	PRE3	overuse of a pronoun	有一天他找到一只小动物，他觉得很可爱，他想把它带回家养。
	PRE4	unmatched number	小白和小狗谢谢爸爸，他（们）高兴地回家。
sentential errors (SCE)	SCE1	multiple errors	我一念一点就笑很多。
	SCE2	inappropriate conjunctions	我想是因为我坐飞机会晕跟因为我吃坏了肚子。
	SCE3	incomplete sentences	我的朋友说这本书很所以我就看了。
	SCE4	punctuation errors	小张再说(：")小动物，你在那里呀?（"）

Appendix B: Sample error coding

今天，妈妈爸爸真好，送<VBE1>王朋一只青蛙。王朋真高心<SPE1>，所以他睡觉的时候想一想<VBE1>他的青蛙因为他明天要跟青蛙和狗好好玩<VBE8>。可是，王朋水<SPE1>的时候，青蛙跳出<VBE1>窗户，所以王朋起来一<SPE1>后，青蛙不在房间了。王朋觉得找青蛙很重要因为他要<VBE5>跟青蛙玩，也要<VBE5>跟<PPE1>朋友看看他的青蛙。他找青蛙在他的房间里面<WOE2>，看进<SPE1>他的衣服和他的衣柜。王朋也<ADE2>以为他的小狗吃下<VBE2>了他的青蛙，所以他很生气，可是王朋快<ADE2>知道没吃到青蛙了<SCE1>。

王朋跟小狗去外面，<PRE2>一边走路一边教<SPE1>。他们两个去<VBE1>一个地方<WOE1>有很多运<SPE3>物和很多树。王朋先找青蛙在地下<WOE2>，但是他被一只小运<SPE3>物打死<VBE1>。然后，王朋看进去一棵树<SCE1>，因为他以为青蛙跳进树<NNE3>了。可是，一只运<SPE3>物飞山<SPE1>来，打<VBE1>王朋的头，所以，他的头疼死了。小狗也被其他的运<SPE3>物打了。王朋找<VBE2>青蛙在山旁边<WOE2>，可是一只很大的运物<SPE3>很生气。这只运<SPE3>物拿起王朋来<SCE1>，方<SPE1>进河里面。王朋和小狗很怕，可是王朋快知道他们在最好的地方找青蛙<SCE1>。他们看到青蛙和他的家人，就有内人和小孩子<SCE1>。

王朋和他的小狗跟青蛙的家人谈一谈<VBE1>。他们走的时候，青蛙给<VBE1>王朋一个小孩子因为他知道王朋回<SPE1>单<SPE1>一个好爸爸。王朋真高心<SPE1>，因为他就可以<VBE5>有一只青蛙，还有<SCE2>/<SCE4>它<PRE4>可以常常来看其他的青蛙<VBE1>。

12

Heritage Language Development, Maintenance, and Attrition Among Recent Chinese Immigrants in New York City

Gisela Jia
Lehman College, The City University of New York

This study investigated Chinese Heritage Language (CHL) development, maintenance, and attrition among recent Chinese immigrants (n=85) in New York City. Participants were young adults, with age of arrival in the United States (US) ranging from 4 to 20 years, and with at least 5 years of residence in the US. Participants retrospectively rated their CHL speaking, reading and writing skills for each two-year interval of their residence in the US and reported their cultural identity and their CHL use in various situations. Several findings emerged. (1) With an increasing exposure to English and a steady growth of English skills, heritage language skills continuously declined over the years. (2) CHL reading and writing skills experienced larger scale attrition than speaking skills. (3) Those who immigrated to the US at younger ages, from lower income families, and with a stronger Chinese cultural identity, showed significantly higher self-rated CHL proficiency. The nature of these predictive relations is discussed.

In the United States (US), heritage language (HL) speakers refer to those whose home or ancestral language is other than English, including those whose ancestors lived in this country prior to its establishment and those who have arrived in the subsequent generations (Alliance for the Advancement of Heritage Languages). According to the 2000 U.S. census, there are 28.4 million first generation immigrants, constituting 10.4% of the U.S. population. Among them, 7.2 million were born in Asia. Chinese Heritage Language (CHL) speakers constitute a heterogeneous group. Some are born in the US or immigrate to the US at young ages. They continue to be raised in Chinese-speaking homes, growing up able to understand or speak at least one Chinese dialect with various levels of proficiency. They tend to be called *CHL learners* (Valdés, 2001) as most of them have below native level Chinese proficiency and often are engaged in continued learning of Chinese. Others immigrate to the US at older ages with more developed Chinese skills and maintain native level or close to native level Chinese proficiency even after years of exposure to English. In the current article, an inclusive term *CHL speakers* will be used to refer to all speakers of Chinese as home language, regardless of their Chinese proficiency levels.

Jia, G. (2008). Heritage language development, maintenance, and attrition among recent Chinese immigrants in New York City. In A. W. He, & Y. Xiao (Eds.), *Chinese as a heritage language: Fostering rooted world citizenry* (pp. 189–203). Honolulu: University of Hawai'i, National Foreign Language Resource Center.

The reality of globalization has made it indisputable that bilingualism is a valuable asset for both nations and individuals. A primary approach to increase the level of bilingualism is to promote the conservation and development of the HL. As Chinese is the third most frequently spoken language in U.S. homes (by 2 million people; Shin & Bruno, 2003), CHL speakers have much to offer to this process. In the US, due to the strong dominance of English language and the limited resources for other languages, immigrant children, even those predominantly HL users before schooling, show rapid decline of HL skills (Fishman, 1991; Krashen, 1998; Wong Fillmore, 1991). However, the same children then try to (re)learn their HL in foreign language classrooms in high schools or colleges. Clearly, in this scenario, we are not making the most efficient use of educational resources.

To combat the rapid loss of HL skills among early generations of immigrants, we need systematic research findings generated from a coherent research agenda. Lynch (2003) pointed out that the construction of such an agenda may follow the framework of second language acquisition (SLA) research. For SLA research conducted with immigrant populations, two general purposes have been to describe how the learning of various aspects of English language (for immigrants in English-speaking countries) proceeds, and to uncover the variables that explain the different levels of attainment in English (Gass & Selinker, 2001). Adopting the same framework in HL research, researchers need to describe the processes of HL development, maintenance, and attrition, and explain the varying HL skills among HL speakers.

Previous research

Describing changes in CHL Levels

Once young children with Chinese as their home language (whether U.S.- or foreign-born) become exposed to English (usually through schooling), what happens to their Chinese? Studies have shown that when these children become young adults, the overwhelming majority of them have English as their dominant language with native level or close to native level proficiency (Jia, Aaronson, & Wu, 2002), as well as a weaker native language (albeit with varying degrees of proficiency). This finding has been obtained from other HL groups, such as Korean (Flege, Yeni-Komshian, & Liu, 1999), Vietnamese (McDonald, 2000) and Spanish (Bialystok & Miller, 1999; Jia, Aaronson, Young, Chen, & Wagner, 2005). However, such a snapshot of their HL level as young adults does not reveal much about the processes that lead to this point. Indeed, we have little knowledge in processes of CHL proficiency change (He, 2006, this volume). Available findings mostly concern Spanish HL speakers. For example, Spanish HL speakers who are exposed to English at a young age gradually switch their dominant language from Spanish to English (e.g., Eilers & Oller, 2003). As a result, over several generations, they become monolingual English speakers as other language groups do (Rumbaut, Massey, & Bean, 2006). Along with this dominant language switch, growth of basic HL skills still takes place (e.g., knowledge in concrete nouns and verbs of high frequency; Jia, Kohnert, Collado, & Aquino-Garcia, 2006;Kohnert, Bates, & Hernandez, 1999). In a longitudinal study of 10 first generation Chinese immigrant children and adolescents in the US, parental reports also have shown such a decline at a more general level of language proficiency (Jia & Aaronson, 2003).

Explaining variability in CHL levels

At the explanatory level, previous studies with various HL groups have shown that HL abilities vary considerably among individual adult HL speakers (e. g., Hendryx, this volume;

also see studies cited in Kondo-Brown, 2003). This has promoted an inquiry into the causes of such variations in HL proficiency. Several relevant variables have emerged.

Age of arrival

For first generation immigrants, age of arrival in the US has been discovered as an important predictive variable of HL maintenance and attrition. A number of long-term attainment studies have documented a dominant language shift among the younger arrivals of first generation immigrants. In these studies, participants were adults who began their English exposure at different ages and had a substantial English exposure (e.g., a minimum of 5 years of residence in the US plus a minimum of 2 years of English schooling in the US), when their English proficiency had relatively stabilized. In comparison to older arrivals, younger arrivals (usually with age of English exposure younger than 9–12 years), showed higher English than HL proficiency in pronunciation (Flege, Munro, & Mackay, 1995; Yeni-Komshian, Flege & Liu, 2000), in lexical retrieval (McElree, Jia, & Litvak, 2000), and in detection of morphosyntactic violations (Jia et al., 2002; Jia et al., 2005). In a 3-year longitudinal study of 10 native Chinese speakers who immigrated to the US between ages 5 and 16 years, Jia & Aaronson (2003) demonstrated that the younger arrivals (with arrival ages younger than 9 years), but not the older arrivals, switched their preferred language from Chinese to English within a year of English immersion, used more English than Chinese even when they were more proficient in Chinese, and gradually shifted to English dominance in language skills. This process co-occurred with younger arrivals' more rapid gains in English than older arrivals. The same study also documented that such age differences were related to the different HL levels and different cultural and peer preferences associated with different arrival ages.

Cultural identity

The level of identity with heritage culture is another variable that predicts HL proficiency. In several ethnographical studies, in-depth interviews with HL users suggest that a stronger ethnic identity is associated with higher levels of HL skills. Cho (2000) studied 114 young adult second-generation Korean immigrants and first generation early arrivals. Those with higher Korean HL proficiency expressed a stronger connection with their ethnic group, and a higher degree of acceptance of Korean values, ethnicity, and manners. In a study of six Hawai'i-based second-generation Japanese undergraduate students, Kondo-Brown (Kondo, 1997) found that the more advanced Japanese HL speakers showed stronger ethnic and cultural identity orientation and attitudes. Tse (2000) examined published narratives of 38 adult Asian Americans. Narrators described strong associations between an ethnic group and its HL, so that attitudes toward an ethnic group influenced their interest in developing and maintaining their HL, thus their HL abilities. He (2006, also this volume) proposed an identity-based model of HL development that positions ethnic identity as the corner stone of HL development.

Socioeconomic status

One previously studied variable that has yielded mixed results is socioeconomic status (SES). Available findings are mostly from Spanish HL speakers. Among Mexican-Americans in Texas, those with lower SES used Spanish more than those with higher SES who were more assimilated to the mainstream English culture (Sánchez, 1983). However, Amastae (1982) found that middle-class Mexican-Americans in Texas tend to value Spanish language skills more than those of lower class. There may exist generational effects, in the sense that, first generation immigrants as studied in Sánchez, have a strong desire to assimilate into the mainstream English culture due to a sense of insecurity about their social status. Therefore, their HL use is more confined by their English skills; those with lower SES levels need to use HL more, simply because they cannot function easily with English. Immigrants of later generations mostly feel settled to whatever their social class is. Subsequently, those of higher SES with more resources develop a stronger awareness of the importance of heritage culture and language, than those of lower SES.

Present study

Among the heterogeneous population of CHL speakers, the current study focused mostly on those who were foreign-born and are referred to as first generation immigrants ($n=78$). They arrived in the US as young adults, ranging in age at arrival from 4 to 20 years, and with at least 5 years of residence in the US. In addition, seven other U.S.-born participants were also included. Their systematic exposure to English only began at the age of 4 years. Previous studies have shown that their language profile resembled that of younger arrivals among the foreign-born (e.g., Jia et al., 2002; Yeni-Komshian et al., 2000). For the data analysis of this study, all participants will be referred to as recent immigrants. The focus on recent immigrants stems from the observations that HL loss starts from this group immediately after English exposure, and that the group also shows tremendous internal variability in their HL change trajectories. In adopting the framework of SLA research as suggested by Lynch (2003), the current study is intended to contribute to the description and explanation of various patterns of CHL change (i.e., development, maintenance and attrition) among recent Chinese immigrants.

As previously mentioned, few empirical findings exist concerning the changes of CHL proficiency *over time* once immersion to English takes place through immigration and schooling. As part of the beginning effort to fill in this gap, the current study, using a retrospective self-report measure, charted the changes of CHL skills among 85 recent Chinese immigrants during their first decade of contact with English in New York City. The findings offer a rudimentary but empirically based picture of the developmental trends of CHL after systematic exposure to English begins. As participants reported their CHL abilities separately for speaking, reading, and writing, as well as their English abilities in all three aspects, we can examine how CHL developmental trends vary across three language proficiency domains, and view the trends in the context of English acquisition.

At the explanatory level, the current study examined several variables that may predict CHL proficiency:

- As previously mentioned, the longitudinal findings of Jia & Aaronson (2003) offer an in-depth view of age-related differences in HL and English ability changes among the recent Chinese immigrants. However, the sample size was relatively small ($n=10$). To complement the longitudinal study, the current study involved a larger group of CHL users from similar backgrounds as those in the longitudinal study. Participants retrospectively rated their CHL ability changes over the first decade of their English immersion. The findings, though obtained with a different methodology, can be used to verify the reliability of the findings from the longitudinal study.

- As previously mentioned, several studies have documented a relation between cultural identity and HL levels (Cho, 2000; Kondo, 1997; Tse, 2000). The current study also explored the role of cultural identity in CHL development and maintenance. If cultural identity emerges as a significant predictor of CHL proficiency, the contention that stronger cultural identity leads to higher HL levels, drawn from the previous ethnographic studies, would receive further empirical support, particularly in a quantitative form. Nevertheless, such a predictive validity still does not determine a causal relation that is suggested in reports of the previous ethnographical findings.

- Previous studies have yielded mixed findings about the relation between SES and HL levels. It is hypothesized that the relation may vary depending on the generation status of the immigrants. To examine the role of SES in HL development and maintenance among CHL speakers, the current study included several SES indicators (i.e., family income, parents' educational levels, and English abilities) as potential predictive variables of CHL skills. If the previous analysis of an interaction effect between immigrant generation and SES status is valid, then lower SES levels should predict more CHL use, as well as a higher CHL level.

Method

Participants

Participants were 85 heritage speakers of Mandarin Chinese who learned English as their second language in the US. There were 49 females (58%) and 36 males (42%). When data were collected, their average age was 21 (range: 16–30). The majority of the participants (n=78) were born outside of the US, and immigrated to the US before age 20. To ensure basic level of systematic exposure to English, all selected participants had lived in the US for at least 5 years (range: 5–16 years; average: 10 years) and had received a minimum of 2 years of education in the US. Their age of arrival in the US varied from 4 to 20 years old (average: 12 years). Seven other participants were born in the US but their systematic exposure to English did not begin until they went to English-speaking schools at age 4. Participants were college and high school students living in New York City (NYC).

Data collection

Self-rated Chinese and English proficiency
As part of a Language Background Questionnaire (LBQ) developed by the author and colleagues (Jia et al., 2002), participants self-rated their Chinese and English proficiency in speaking, reading,and writing along a 1–7 (1=*not at all*; 7=*native-like*) point scale. They did so for each 2-year segment of the entire time period from their arrival in the US (or the beginning of their systematic exposure to English for those born in the US) to the time of the study. Self-rating is a convenient method to yield quantitative information on bilinguals' global linguistic skills, and has been shown to correlate significantly with results of various language tests (e.g., Jia et al., 2002).

Predictive variables of Chinese proficiency
Information on several potential predictive variables of CHL proficiency was also obtained with the LBQ. The predictive variables are classified into the following groups:

Age and time variables. As in studies on SLA in the immigration context, three time-related variables were included in this study: age of arrival in the US, the number of years of education in the US, and the number of years of residence in the US. In this sample population, these three variables tended to be significantly correlated with each other, namely, those who immigrated at younger ages tended to have stayed at the US longer and to have received more years of education in the US.

Socioeconomic status (SES). Participants reported their approximate annual household income, by selecting from 14 income levels, ranging from $5,000 to $200,000. Participants reported the highest education level each of their parents had obtained. As done for their own HL and English abilities, participants also rated each of their parents'

English abilities in the aspects of speaking, reading, and writing. They did not do so for their parents' HL abilities as there was little variability.

Cultural identity and preference. Participants were asked to indicate the culture with which they identified, and the culture that they preferred. They selected from one of three choices: *native culture, American culture,* or *both* (i.e., identify equally with both cultures or showed no preference of one over the other). In data analysis, the three choices were coded with lower to higher numeric values in the order of American culture, both, and native culture. Therefore, a significant positive correlation between HL proficiency and cultural identity or preference indicates an association of a stronger native cultural identity and better HL skills.

Language environment. Similar to self-ratings of language proficiency, participants reported, for each 2-year segment of their U.S. residence, the percentage of time that they spoke HL to people around them (i.e., family members they lived with, including mother, father, and siblings, and friends in school/at work or when hanging out), the percentage of time that they used HL in leisure reading (books, magazines/newspapers), leisure writing (not for school or work purposes), and for watching TV and movies.

The 2-year rating segment for language abilities and language environment was chosen based upon pilot testing with some Chinese-English bilinguals. The interval was not too short (e.g., as opposed to one year) to substantially increase the amount of time needed to fill out the questionnaire nor was it too long (e.g., as opposed to 5 years) to miss subtler fluctuations in the value of a relevant variable.

Chinese grammaticality judgment task

To assess the concurrent validity of the self-rated Chinese proficiency, a Mandarin listening grammaticality judgment task was administered to measure participants' Chinese grammatical sensitivity. Grammaticality judgment tasks allow good control of important parameters in the sentence stimuli (i.e., the number of sentences testing each grammatical structure, sentence length and error position). This task has been widely adopted by psycholinguists to study bilingual language proficiency (Bialystok & Miller, 1999; Birdsong & Molis, 2001; Flege et al., 1999; Jia et al., 2002). The current task included 112 Mandarin sentences testing seven grammatical structures. The task was meant to be basic, and groups of monolingual Mandarin-speaking children older than 10-years scored over 90% correct. The Mandarin grammatical structures were perfective aspect, durative aspect, experiential aspect, present tense, *ba*-construction, verb-copying, and topic prominence. Each structure was tested with eight correct and eight incorrect sentences. Each sentence contained eight words, and for each structure, grammatical errors occurred equally often at each serial position (beginning, middle, and end of a sentence) with the same frequency.

Procedures

Participants attended the study individually in a quiet room on two university campuses. The LBQ was filled out in a paper-and-pencil format. A researcher was available while participants were working on the questionnaire. Sentences in the grammaticality judgment task were presented aurally to the participants using customized software. After participants heard each sentence, they pressed a designated "yes" or "no" key on the computer keyboard to indicate their judgment of its grammaticality. Each sentence was presented once, and responses were automatically recorded.

Data processing

The concurrent validity of the self-assessed language proficiency was examined by correlating scores on the grammaticality judgment task and self-assessed Chinese proficiency in speaking, reading, and writing at the time of the study. There were significant bivariate correlations between the two proficiency indicators. A higher score on the grammaticality judgment task predicted significantly higher self-assessed Mandarin speaking ability, $r=.35$, $p<.001$, reading ability, $r=.40$, $p<.001$, and writing ability, $r=.30$, $p<.001$. Given that the grammaticality judgment task tested the sensitivity to only a limited number of grammatical structures, and the self-assessments reflected global proficiency in speaking, reading, and writing, the significant correlations indicated sufficient concurrent validity of the self-assessed HL proficiency at the time of the study.

Results

Change of self-reported Chinese and English skills over time

The self-reported HL speaking, reading, and writing skills at multiple 2-year intervals were averaged across participants and are indicated in Figures 1 and 2. Over the years of English immersion, all three aspects of self-reported English proficiency increased steadily over time, whereas self-reported HL proficiency declined continuously. Average HL speaking ability started just below 7, indicating close to native-like ability in reference to adult monolingual HL speakers. Then, it dropped to between scales 5 and 6 at the time of the study, indicating an above medium level proficiency. Average HL reading and writing abilities started from between the scales of 5 and 6, and had dropped to between 3 and 4 by the time of the study, indicating medium level reading and writing abilities.

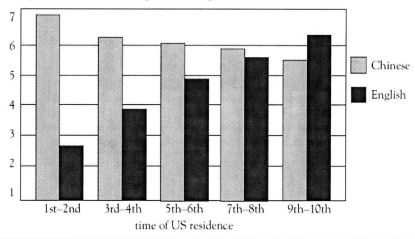

Figure 1. Self-rated Chinese and English speaking proficiency of all participants

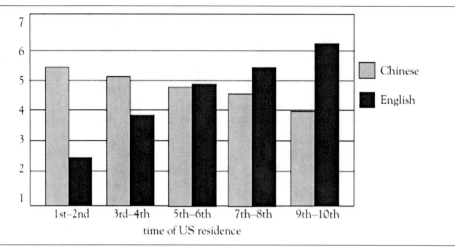

Figure 2. Self-rated Chinese and English reading proficiency of all participants

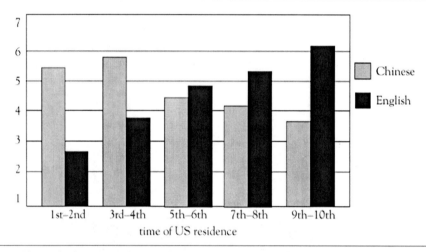

Figure 3. Self-rated Chinese and English witing proficiency of all participants

Predictive variables

The relation between self-assessed current HL proficiency and the main predictive variables investigated were first examined with bivariate correlation analyses. The outcome variables are self-assessed current HL speaking, reading, and writing abilities at the time of the study. (Performance on the grammaticality judgment task was not used as an outcome variable because the range of performance was smaller than the self-ratings, limiting the amount of variance to be accounted for by the explanatory variables.) After the correlation analyses, variables bearing significant correlations with the outcome variables were entered into a hierarchical regression analysis to examine how the relevant variables in combination explain HL proficiency variance.

Simple bivariate correlation analysis

Age/time variables. Higher self-assessed current HL speaking, reading, and writing proficiency was associated with an older arrival age in the US, a briefer length of residence in the US, and fewer years of education in the US (Table 1). Because these three predictive variables were significantly correlated with each other (i.e., those with younger arrival age had stayed longer and had more years of education in the US), partial correlation analyses were conducted to examine the unique contribution of the variables to the HL proficiency. Age of arrival remained a significant predictor when the other two variables were controlled, but not vice versa. Therefore, arrival age alone was used in later hierarchical regression analysis.

Table 1.   Bivariate correlations between predictive variables and self-rated Chinese proficiency

age/time variables (years)	speaking	reading	writing
age of arrival	.58***	.76***	.70***
length of stay	−.38***	−.55***	−.49***
us education	−.48***	−.65***	−.57***
SES variables			
family income	−.32*	−.48**	−.35**
mother's educational level	−.09	−.39**	−.21
father's educational level	−.08	−.32**	−.14
mom English ability	−.28*	−.52***	−.35**
dad English ability	−.34**	−.52***	−.37**
cultural preference and identity			
cultural identity	.27*	.35**	.30**
cultural attraction	.15	.21	.22
language environment variables			
speak to father	−.44***	−.38**	−.31**
speak to mother	−.50***	−.43***	−.35**
speak to sibling	−.55***	−.65***	−.42**
speak to friends (in school/at work)	−.32**	−.45***	−.28*
speak to friends (hanging out)	−.43***	−.58***	−.45***
watching tv/movie	−.25*	−.34**	−.19
leisure reading (books)	−.56***	−.57***	−.35**
leisure reading (newspapers/magazine)	−.33**	−.57***	−.36**
leisure writing	−.32**	−.54***	−.44***
father speak to you	−.36**	−.37**	−.31**
mother speak to you	−.26*	−.23	−.20

*$p<.05$, **$p<.01$, ***$p<.001$

SES variables. As indicated in Table 1, higher self-assessed HL ability was associated with lower SES indicated by some variables. Higher self-assessed HL reading ability was predicted by significantly lower levels of family income, parental education and parental English abilities. Higher self-assessed HL speaking and writing abilities was predicted by significantly lower levels of family income and parental English abilities.

Cultural preference and identity. Stronger identification with Chinese culture predicted significantly higher self-assessed HL speaking, reading, and writing abilities. Cultural preference was not associated with HL proficiency (Table 1).

Language environment variables. Self-reported language use in the form of retrospective data for multiple 2-year segments was averaged across all intervals to obtain a general score for that aspect of language environment. Among the 33 pairs of bivariate correlations between language environment and self-rated language proficiency (11 language environment variables x 3 aspects of HL proficiency); 30 were significant (Table 1). More specifically, more HL use in these aspects (averaged across the years of English immersion) predicted significantly higher self-assessed HL speaking, reading, and writing proficiency. To reduce the amount of environmental variables to be entered to the hierarchical regression analysis, a factor analysis was conducted. Variables that clustered on one factor would be averaged for the regression analysis. Further, factor analysis revealed latent constructs existing among these environmental variables, offering a deeper view of participants' HL language environment. The factor analysis was conducted using the Principal Component Model with Varimax rotation. Two factors were extracted. Loaded on one factor were four variables: participants speaking HL to mother and father, and mother and father speaking HL to participants. The other seven variables, indicating HL use with siblings, friends, and self (watching TV and movies, leisure reading and writing) loaded on a separate factor. Subsequently, two composite language environment scores were derived; each was the average value of the variables involved in a factor.

Hierarchical regression analysis

Results from these bivariate correlation analyses need to be further processed in order to understand the unique and combinatory contributions of the predictive variables of self-assessed current HL proficiency. For example, though stronger identity with Chinese culture predicted higher self-rated Chinese proficiency, the relation may be largely mediated by age of arrival, in the sense that those who were exposed to English at an older age, tended to identify more strongly with Chinese culture, and maintained more Chinese language skills. In the hierarchical regression analysis, variables were entered into a regression equation according to their hypothesized causal priority to reduce confounding effects (Cohen, West, Aiken, & Cohen, 2002). That is, no variable entered later can be a possible cause of a variable entered earlier. Therefore, arrival age was entered first, SES variables second, followed by cultural identity, and then language environment. The outcome variables were the self-assessed HL speaking, reading, and writing abilities at the time of the study.

For self-assessed HL speaking ability, arrival age explained 21.2% of the variance. Adding language use with parents increased adjusted R^2 to 28.3%, a significant amount of change ($p<.05$). No other variable, entered in the sequence previously specified, led to a significant amount of R^2 change.

For self-assessed HL reading ability, arrival age explained 49.4% of the variance. Adding family income increased the adjusted R^2 to 53.9%, a significant amount of increase ($p<.05$). Adding cultural identity increased the adjusted R^2 to 56.1%, a marginally significant amount of increase ($p=0.055$). No other variable, added in the sequence previously specified, led to a significant amount of R^2 change.

For self-rated HL writing ability, arrival age explained 49.9% of the variance. Adding family income increased the adjusted R^2 to 54.3%, a significant amount of increase ($p<.05$). Adding cultural identity increased the adjusted R^2 to 56.3%, a marginally significant amount of increase ($p=0.058$). Adding language use with siblings, friends, and self increased the adjusted R^2 to 58.3%, a marginally significant amount of increase ($p=.095$). No other variable, added in the sequence previously specified, led to a significant amount of R^2 change.

Summary and discussion

The current study sought to (a) describe how HL proficiency changed with increasing amount of English immersion among a group of recent Chinese immigrants in New York City, and (b) uncover the predictive variables of HL proficiency among these HL speakers. In the following, the findings are discussed in relation to those from other HL groups, from a longitudinal study of CHL speakers, and from other relevant studies.

Over the course of English immersion, the English abilities of these CHL speakers showed a steady increase. In a conjunction study of Russian and Spanish HL speakers in New York City (Jia, Aaronson, Young, Chen, & Chen, in preparation), a similar trend and rate of growth was also observed in both groups. However, both CHL speakers and Russian HL speakers showed a significant amount of HL attrition, whereas Spanish speakers experienced less attrition and even some growth of their HL skills.

Such group differences are consistent with some existing findings in the field. As mentioned earlier, across different HL groups, HL speakers who were exposed to English at a young age switch their dominant language from HL to English (e.g., Jia et al., 2005; Yeni-Komshian et al., 2000). However, some groups experience more significant attrition than others. For example, among Spanish HL speakers who were exposed to English as a young age, basic lexical proficiency in Spanish continued to grow over the years of English immersion (Jia et al., 2006; Kohnert et al., 1999) whereas Chinese HL speakers experience less HL growth and more attrition (though with large individual differences). The level to which HL is accessible in the communities may be responsible for such language group differences. In New York City, Spanish speakers congregate in larger communities than Chinese and Russian speakers do. Larger communities offer a richer HL environment through media (e.g., radio and TV channels), auditory and visual language materials (e.g., rented videos with movies and shows, and newspapers), and the use of HL in interpersonal interactions (e.g., stores).

Findings from the current study also indicate that the levels of HL development, maintenance, and attrition also varied across the proficiency domains. In comparison to speaking abilities, reading and writing abilities started at a lower level and experienced larger scales of attrition. This is consistent with numerous observations (e.g., Hendryx, this volume) that CHL learners in college Chinese language classrooms are more likely to be able to speak than read or write Chinese. Further, while they do better than non-heritage Chinese learners in acquiring Chinese listening and speaking skills, they do not show an advantage in acquiring reading and writing skills (Xiao, 2006). The reason is two-fold. On one hand, there are smaller environmental demands on Chinese reading and writing than speaking skills. On the other hand, less Chinese print input is available in the environment than oral input. Supporting this point, findings from the study of Tse (2001) and Xiao (this volume) indicated that stronger HL reading and writing skills among adult bilinguals or college CHL learners were associated with more HL print materials available at home. Further, in the current study, participants indicated considerably more CHL spoken than read in everyday living across the years of English immersion.

In the current study, several variables were found to predict CHL proficiency. Age of arrival in the US, indicating the age of systematic exposure to English, was a significant predictor of self-rated CHL speaking, reading and writing proficiency. Namely, those who were exposed to English at a younger age developed and maintained lower levels of HL. To illustrate this result, the CHL participants were divided into a younger arrival group (with age of arrival<=12 years) and an older arrival group (with age of exposure>=13 years). The pattern of decreasing use of HL over time observed in the total group of Chinese speakers mainly occurred in the younger arrival group. The same pattern was observed in a parallel study of Russian HL speakers.

These findings of arrival age related differences buttress the phenomenon of dominant language switch among younger arrivals documented in long-term attainment studies (e.g., Jia et al., 2002; Yeni-Komshian et al., 2000) by adding a time dimension to the shift. The findings are also highly consistent with the longitudinal findings from a smaller sample of first generation Chinese immigrant children and adolescents (Jia & Aaronson, 2003). Many researchers argue that such an arrival age effect is mediated through differential language environment that immigrants of various ages are exposed to, and language environment is further mediated by the different HL levels and cultural preferences associated with arrival age (e.g., Jia et al., 2002; Jia & Aaronson, 2003). Supporting this point, in the current study, across all the time points of English immersion, a younger arrival age predicted significantly less CHL use in various aspects of language environment. These findings mirror the results obtained from the longitudinal study (Jia & Aaronson, 2003).

In the current study, after the arrival age effect was statistically controlled, several other variables further explained a significant or marginally significant amount of variance in CHL proficiency. Lower family income predicted significantly higher self-assessed current Chinese reading and writing abilities. Further, lower family income was also associated with lower educational levels and poorer English abilities of parents. Though the latter two variables did not emerge as significant predictors in the hierarchical analysis, their predictive power may be partially carried by family income. As mentioned earlier, previous findings of the relation between SES and HL use among Mexican Spanish HL speakers are mixed (Amastae, 1982; Sánchez, 1983). It is hypothesized that there may be a generational effect, in the sense that lower SES may lead to more HL use among the first generation but not among the second generation immigrants. The current findings confirm the part of the hypothesis about first generation immigrants. According to the hypothesis, first generation immigrants all have a strong desire to assimilate into the mainstream English culture due to a sense of insecurity about their social status. Those with higher income, higher educational levels, and better English abilities assimilate more successfully, and subsequently use English less. Supporting the point that language environment mediated the relation between family income and HL proficiency, in the current study, across all the years of English immersion, lower family income predicted significantly more CHL use in all situations.

Future study may focus on the literacy activities of CHL families of various income levels, and ascertain as well as probe in greater depth the relation between SES and CHL use. Further, the current findings may seem contradictory to the By-choice hypothesis derived from the Identity-Based Model of CHL development proposed by He (2006; also this volume). According to the By-choice hypothesis, more HL use by choice, not by necessity, predicts better learning, because learners see HL as enriching rather than limiting. This hypothesis is reasonable, but can only be tested when all other differences among families (e.g., SES, amount of language use) are controlled, leaving language by choice versus necessity as the only variable distinguishing families. Such a control can be more easily achieved by studies with an experimental design rather than a correlational design, which is used in most HL studies, including the current one.

In the current study, cultural identity predicted a marginally significant amount of variance in self-rated HL reading and writing abilities. In several ethnographic studies, a stronger native culture and ethnic identity has been found to relate to more HL use and higher proficiency among Korean Americans (e.g., Cho, 2000), Japanese Americans (e.g., Kondo, 1997), and Asian Americans in general (Tse, 2000). In the current study, a stronger identification with Chinese culture was associated with higher self-rated Chinese reading and writing abilities.

Although this correlation does not determine a causal relation, such a finding is required in the first place in order to ascertain a causal relation. Further, this relation may be mediated through language environment, in that a stronger cultural identity leads to more HL use. Supporting this point, in the current study, a stronger identity with Chinese culture predicted significantly more CHL use in most of the language environmental aspects measured.

Up to this point of discussion, the predictive power of language environment in CHL proficiency has been shown through age of arrival, family income, and cultural identity. However, above and beyond these mediating effects, language environment further explained a significant amount of CHL proficiency variance in the current study. More CHL use with parents predicted significantly higher CHL speaking proficiency. More CHL use with siblings, friends, and by self predicted marginally significantly higher self-rated CHL writing proficiency. As this portion of language environment variance is independent of arrival age, family income, and cultural identity, one wonders what variables caused these environmental differences that then might have led to variation in HL proficiency. There are a host of variables, not examined in the current study, that have been shown to play a role in HL development and maintenance mediated by language environment. Some possibilities include CHL use at the community level (e.g., in churches and other organizations; e.g., Cho, 2000), and CHL reading materials available at home (e.g., Xiao, this volume). There are likely other functioning factors that are elusive to empirical investigations, such as motivation. Lu and Li (this volume) empirically demonstrated a relation between CHL proficiency and the concurrent motivation in learning Chinese among college CHL or Chinese as a foreign language learners. He (2006; also this volume) also hypothesized that a learner's desire to communicate successfully in a moment-by-moment fashion generates CHL learning. A retrospective study like the current one can hardly yield reliable data on motivation in CHL learning over the years of U.S. residence. Research with experimental or longitudinal designs and innovative measures is needed to quantify motivation and ascertain a causal relation between motivation and CHL proficiency.

In the current study, independent of the relation between language environment and CHL levels, factor analyses indicated that the various language environment variables clustered in two groups. CHL use with parents formed a unique factor, whereas CHL use with siblings, friends, and self (i.e., listening to radio and watching TV, leisure reading and writing) formed a separate factor. This indicates that CHL speakers tend to (largely unconsciously) divide up their language environment into one with parents, and one with all other people and themselves. This confirms anecdotal reports from many Chinese immigrant parents that their children may use HL with them, but mostly use English on other occasions, including with their siblings.

In sum, the current findings indicate that significant and variable CHL loss occurs among recent Chinese immigrants. Those with younger ages of exposure to English, and from higher income families, constitute the most vulnerable population. Reading and writing abilities are the language proficiency domains most subject to attrition. The predictive power of age of English exposure, family income, and cultural identity in HL proficiency is mediated by language environment. Language environment also demonstrates an independent predictive power of CHL proficiency in that more use of CHL is associated with higher CHL proficiency. Therefore, increasing the presence of CHL in immigrant homes and the communities is crucial to CHL development and maintenance. Then, to maximize the use of the available CHL resources, parents and their children need to be more aware of the advantages afforded by bilingualism, and foster an appreciation of HL cultural values and attitudes.

References

Alliance for the Advancement of Heritage Languages (2006). AAHL website. Retrieved September 30, 2006, from http://www.cal.org/heritage/about/

Amastae, J. (1982). Language shift and maintenance in the lower Rio Grande valley of southern Texas. In F. Barkin, E. Brandt, & J. Ornstein-Galicia (Eds.), *Bilingualism and language contact: Spanish, English and Native American languages* (pp. 261–277). New York: Teachers College Press.

Bialystok, E., & Miller, B. (1999). The problem of age in second-language acquisition: Influences from language, structure, and task. *Bilingualism: Language and Cognition, 2,* 127–145.

Birdsong, D., & Molis, M. (2001). On the evidence for maturational constraints on second language acquisition. *Journal of Memory and Language, 44,* 235–249.

Cho, G. (2000). The role of heritage language in social interactions and relationships: Reflections from a language minority group. *Bilingual Research Journal, 24*(4). Retrieved September 30, 2006, from http://brj.asu.edu/v244/articles/ar4.html

Cohen, J., West, S. G., Aiken, L., & Cohen, P. (2002). *Applied multiple regression/correlation analysis for the behavioral sciences.* Lawrence Erlbaum Associates, Mahwah, NJ

Eilers, R., & Oller, K. (2003). Language and literacy in bilingual children: The Miami experience. *Symposium presented at the Society for Research in Child Development Biennial Meeting,* Tampa, Florida.

Fishman, J. (1991). *Reversing language shift: Theoretical and empirical foundations of assistance to threatened languages.* Clevedon, England: Multilingual Matters.

Flege, J. E., Munro, M. J., & Mackay, I. R. A. (1995). Factors affecting strength of perceived foreign accent in a second language. *Journal of the Acoustical Society of America, 97,* 3125–3134.

Flege, J. E., Yeni-Komshian, G. H., & Liu, S. (1999). Age constraints on second-language acquisition. *Journal of Memory and Language, 41,* 78–104.

Gass, S. M., & Selinker, L. (2001). *Second language acquisition: An introductory course.* Mahwah, NJ: Lawrence Erlbaum Associates.

He, A. W. (2006, Fall). Toward an identity theory of the development of Chinese as a heritage language. *Heritage Language Journal, 4*(1). Retrieved February 7, 2007, from http://www.heritagelanguages.org

Jia, G., & Aaronson, D. (2003). A longitudinal study of Chinese children and adolescents learning English in the US. *Applied Psycholinguistics, 24,* 131–161.

Jia, G., Aaronson, D., & Wu, Y. H. (2002). Long-term language attainment of bilingual immigrants: Predictive factors and language group differences. *Applied Psycholinguistics, 23,* 599–621.

Jia, G., Aaronson, D., Young, D., Chen, S., & Chen, J. (in preparation). *Heritage language development, maintenance and attrition among recent Chinese-, Spanish- and Russian-speaking immigrants in New York City.*

Jia, G., Aaronson, D., Young, D., Chen, S., & Wagner, J. (2005). Bilingual Mandarin-, Russian- and Spanish-English speakers' grammatical proficiency in their two languages. In M. Minami, H. Kobayashi, M. Nakayama, & H. Sirai (Eds.), *Studies in language sciences, Vol. 4* (pp. 160–171). Tokyo, Japan: Kurosio Publishers.

Jia, G., Kohnert, K., Collado, J., & Aquino-Garcia, F. (2006) Action naming in Spanish and English among sequential bilinguals. *Journal of Speech, Language and Hearing Research, 49*, 588–602.

Kohnert, K. J., Bates, E., & Hernandez, A. E. (1999). Balancing bilinguals: Lexical-semantic production and cognitive processing in children learning Spanish and English. *Journal of Speech, Language, and Hearing Research, 42*, 1400–1413.

Kondo, K. (1997). Social-psychological factors affecting language maintenance: Interviews with Shin Nisei University students. *Linguistics and Education, 9*, 369–408.

Kondo-Brown, K. (2003, Spring). Heritage language instruction for post-secondary students from immigrant backgrounds. *Heritage Language Journal, 1*(1). Retrieved September 30, 2006, from http://www.heritagelanguages.org

Krashen, S. (1998). Heritage language development: Some practical arguments. In S. Krashen, L. Tse, & J. McQuillan (Eds.), *Heritage language development* (pp. 3–13). Culver City, CA: Language Education Associates.

Lynch, A. (2003, Spring). The relationship between second and heritage language acquisition. *Heritage Language Journal, 1*(1). Retrieved September 30, 2006, from http://www.heritagelanguages.org

McDonald, J. L. (2000). Grammaticality judgments in a second language: Influences of age of acquisition and native language. *Applied Psycholinguistics, 21*, 395–423.

McElree, B., Jia, G., & Litvak, A. (2000). The time course of conceptual processing in three bilingual populations. *Journal of Memory and Language, 42*, 229–254.

Rumbaut, R. G., Massey, D. S., & Bean, F. D. (2006). Linguistic life expectancies: Immigrant language retention in southern California. *Population and Development Review, 32*(3), 447–460.

Sánchez, R. (1983). *Chicano discourse: Socio-historic perspectives.* Rowley, MA: Newbury House.

Shin, H. B., & Bruno, R. (2003). Language use and English-speaking ability: 2000. Census 2000 Brief. Retrieved September 30, 2006, from http://www.census.gov

Tse, L. (2000). The effects of ethnic identity formation on bilingual maintenance and development: An analysis of Asian American narratives. *International Journal of Bilingual Education and Bilingualism, 3*(3), 185–200.

Tse, L. (2001). Heritage language literacy: A study of US biliterates. *Language, Culture and Curriculum, 14*(3), 256–268.

Valdés, G. (2001). Heritage language students: Profiles and possibilities. In J. Peyton, J. Ranard, & S. McGinnis (Eds.), *Heritage languages in America: Preserving a national resource* (pp. 37–80). McHenry, IL: The Center for Applied Linguistics and Delta Systems.

Wong Fillmore, L. (1991). When learning a second language means losing the first. *Early Childhood Research Quarterly, 6*, 323–346.

Xiao, Y. (2006). Heritage learners in the Chinese language classroom: Home background. *Heritage Language Journal, 4*(1). Retrieved February 7, 2007, from http://www.heritagelanguages.org

Yeni-Komshian, G. H., Flege, J. E., & Liu, S. (2000). Pronunciation proficiency in the first and second languages of Korean-English bilinguals. *Bilingualism: Language and Cognition, 3*, 131–149.

13

The (Re)acquisition of Perfective Aspect Marking by Chinese Heritage Language Learners

Li Jia[1]
University of Texas, San Antonio

Robert Bayley
University of California, Davis

NFLRC
monographs

The acquisition of tense and aspect has been widely studied in European and Asian languages. However, participants in most studies of Asian languages have either been children acquiring an L1 or university students acquiring an L2 in an academic setting. Relatively few studies have investigated children who are in the process of reacquiring Mandarin after shifting to English as their predominant language or acquiring Mandarin as a heritage language. This study investigates the (re)acquisition of the Mandarin perfective aspectual marker -le by 36 children and adolescents in a Chinese heritage language school in the southwestern United States. Results of several different measures indicate that participants who were born in China outperformed their U.S.-born counterparts, as did participants who reported using primarily Mandarin at home. Results for age show a more complicated picture, with younger speakers outperforming older speakers on a narrative-retelling task, but older speakers outperforming younger speakers on cloze and sentence completion tasks. Finally, results of multivariate analysis of the narratives show that use of perfective verbal suffix -le is significantly constrained by its position in the sentence and by whether it is optional or obligatory. The implications of these results for heritage language maintenance are explored.

The acquisition of tense and aspect in second languages has been widely studied in European languages, including English, French, Italian, and Spanish (e.g., Andersen, 1991; Andersen & Shirai, 1996; Ayoun & Salaberry, 2005; Bardovi-Harlig, 1999, 2000; Bayley, 1994, 1999; Collins, 2002; Salaberry, 2001). Studies of both first and second language acquisition of aspect marking in non-European languages have also been conducted, among them Shirai and Kurono (1998) on Japanese, and P. Li (1990), P. Li and Shirai (2002), Duff and D. Li (2002), and Wen (1995, 1997) on Mandarin. Most studies of Asian languages examined children who were acquiring the language as an L1, or university students who were acquiring a second language in an academic setting. Few studies have investigated children who are in the process of re-acquiring Mandarin after shifting to English as their predominant language or acquiring

---
[1]   Names are listed in reverse alphabetical order. Both authors contributed equally to this study.

Jia, L. & Bayley, R. (2008). The (re)acquisition of perfective aspect marking by Chinese heritage language learners. In A. W. He, & Y. Xiao (Eds.), *Chinese as a heritage language: Fostering rooted world citizenry* (pp. 205–222). Honolulu: University of Hawai'i, National Foreign Language Resource Center.

Mandarin as a heritage language (but see He, 2000, 2003). In this study, we investigate the (re)acquisition of the Mandarin perfective aspectual marker -le by 36 children and adolescents who either initially acquired Mandarin as an L1 or were acquiring it as a heritage language. Both groups of speakers were enrolled in language classes at the same site, the Lu Xun Chinese Heritage School (a pseudonym) in the southwestern US. The results of several different measures indicate that, as expected, participants who were born in China outperformed their U.S.-born counterparts, as did participants who reported using primarily Mandarin at home. Results for age show a more complicated picture, with younger speakers outperforming older speakers on a narrative-retelling task, but older speakers outperforming younger speakers on cloze and sentence completion tasks. Finally, the results of multivariate analysis of elicited narratives show that use of perfective verbal suffix -le was significantly constrained by its position in the sentence and by whether it is optional or obligatory.

The chapter is organized as follows: First, we outline Mandarin aspectual categories, with a particular focus on the verbal suffix -le. We then review previous work on the first and second language acquisition of Mandarin aspectual categories. The following section outlines the methods of the present study. We then present the results for the three tasks. Finally, we discuss the implications of the results for maintenance of Chinese specifically and for maintenance of heritage languages more generally.

Mandarin aspectual categories

Mandarin Chinese, unlike English and other Indo-European languages, does not possess overt tense markers indicated by inflectional suffixes. Rather, temporal relations are indicated by temporal adverbials or by the context. Mandarin does, however, grammaticalize aspect by markers such as -zhe, -ne, and zai to express imperfectivity, and -le to express perfectivity. The main Mandarin markers of grammatical aspect are conveniently summarized by Duff and Li (2002) and Erbaugh (1992), as shown in Table 1.

Table 1.   Grammatical aspect markers in Mandarin

perfective	LE	bounded, perfective	verbal suffix	ta kan-LE yi ge dianying he see-LE one cl movie 'He saw a movie.'
	GUO	experiential	verbal suffix	ta kan-GUO neige dianying he see-GUO that movie 'He has seen that movie.'
imperfective	ZAI	progressive (foregrounded)	adverb	ta ZAI kan dianying he ZAI watch movie 'He is watching a movie.'
	ZHE	stative, durative (backgrounded); progressive situation (esp. in writing)	verbal suffix	ta kan-ZHE dianshi chi fan he watch-ZHE tv eat rice 'He ate while watching tv.'
	NE	progressive (in colloquial speech); durative	verbal suffix	wo (ZAI) chi fan-NE I (ZAI) eat rice-NE 'I'm eating.'

sources: Duff and Li (2002, p. 419), Erbaugh (1992, p. 389)

Perfective aspect marker -le

The form and meaning of the perfective aspect marker -le, the focus of this study, are among the more complex questions of Chinese linguistics. Indeed, -le has been the most intensively discussed of all the Chinese aspect markers (see, e.g., Kwan-Terry, 1979; Lu, 1975; Rohsenow, 1978; Shi, 1989; Thompson, 1968; Wang, 1965). Grammatically, *-le* indicates a completed action, but the completion of such action has no relationship to the time of speaking, so it is possible to use *-le* in the following situations (all examples are taken from the data for the present study)[2]:

(1) Description of a past action

小	男孩	找	了	他	的	衣服	和	靴子。
xiao	nanhai	zhao	-le	ta	de	yifu	he	xuezi
little	boy	search	PFV	3sg	NOM	clothes	and	boots

The little boy searched his clothes and boots (for the frog).

(2) Description of a present perfect action

小	男孩	回	到	了	家。
xiao	nanhai	hui	dao	-le	jia
little	boy	back	arrive	PFV	home

The little boy has arrived home.

(3) Description of a future action

看	了	电影	他	会	很	兴奋。
kan	-le	dianying	ta	hui	hen	xingfen
watch	PFV	movie	3sg	can	very	excited

He will be very excited after he watches the movie.

For language learners, acquisition of perfective *-le* is complicated by the existence of the homophonous sentence final particle *le*, which, among other functions, may indicate a currently relevant state (CRS) rather than perfectivity (C. Li & Thompson, 1981), e.g.,

(4)

然后	这	个	蜜蜂	就	出	来	了。
ranhou	zhe	ge	mifeng	jiu	chu	lai	le
then	this	CL	bee	soon	exit	come	CRS

Then the bee came out right away.

The situation is further complicated because both particle *le* and verbal suffix *-le* may be sentence final.

(5)

孩子	他	醒	了。
haizi	ta	xing	-le
child	3sg	awake	PFV

The child woke up.

(6)

孩子	已经	醒	了。
haizi	yijing	xing	le
child	already	wake	CRS

The child is already awake.

---

[2] The following abbreviations are used in the morpheme by morpheme glosses in the examples: CL, classifier; CRS, Currently Relevant State (*le*); NOM, nominalizer (*de*); PFV, perfective aspect (*-le*); 1pl, first person plural pronoun; and 3sg, third person singular pronoun.

Grammatical and lexical aspect

Most studies of the role of aspect have used Vendler's (1967) categories: achievement (or punctual) verbs, accomplishment (or telic) verbs, activity verbs, and stative verbs, which can be characterized as a continuum from most to least prototypically perfective. Thus, achievement verbs (e.g., *jump, fall*) are [+dynamic, +telic, +punctual], while stative verbs (e.g., *see, hear*) are [–dynamic, –telic, –punctual (or +durative)]. P. Li and Bowerman (1998), however, discuss two additional Chinese lexical aspectual categories: mixed telic-stative verbs, which "indicate either the process of a telic action or the state resulting from that process, depending on their aspect markers" (p. 316), for example, *chuan* (put on, wear), and semelfactive verbs, or verbs that "encode a punctual but not a resultative situation, for example, *tiao* (jump) and *zhayan* (blink)" (p. 330). However, in their L1 data, they did not code mixed telic-stative verbs.

There has been considerable disagreement among scholars about Chinese lexical aspectual categories. Smith (1991), for example, insists that the resultative verb construction (RVC; e.g., *zou-dao-le*, walk-arrive-*le*) belongs to accomplishment verbs. Tai (1984), however, claims that Chinese does not have accomplishment verbs. Secondly, P. Li and Shirai (2000) label the RVC structure as a subcategory of achievement verbs, which is consistent with Tai's position. In this chapter we follow Tai and combine achievement and RVCs.

The perfective aspect marker *-le* can be used after verbs of all lexical aspectual categories, as shown in examples 7 through 11.

(7)   Achievement verbs
    蜜蜂   窝   掉   到   了   地   上。
    mifeng wo   diao   dao   -le   di   shang
    bee   hive   fall   arrive PFV   ground on
    The beehive fell to the ground.

(8)   Mixed telic-stative verbs
    他   拿   了   一   个   青蛙。
    ta   na   -le   yi   ge   qingwa
    3sg take/hold PFV one CL   frog
    He is holding (as a result of having taken) a frog.

(9)   Semelfactive verbs
    小   男孩   叫   了   他   的   青蛙   好   几   声。
    xiao nanhai jiao -le ta   de   qingwa hao ji   sheng
    little boy   call PFV 3sg NOM frog   good several voice
    The little boy called his frog several times.

(10)   Activity verbs
    小   男孩   和   他   的   狗   游泳   了。
    xiao nanhai he ta   de   gou youyong -le
    little boy   and 3sg NOM dog swim   PFV
    The little boy and his dog swam.

(11) Stative verbs

小	男孩	又	有	了	一	只	青蛙。
xiao	nanhai	you	you	-le	yi	zhi	qingwa
little	boy	again	have	PFV	one	CL	frog

The little boy had another frog.

As we would expect, however, *le* is more common with verbs that are prototypically perfective, such as achievement verbs. In fact, we see distributional imbalance, not only in Chinese, but cross-linguistically, where forms used to express certain aspectual meanings, whether imperfective or perfective, tend to be used most frequently with verbs of lexical aspectual classes that are prototypically imperfective or perfective (for further details on distributional imbalance, see Andersen, 1991, and Shirai & Andersen, 1995).

Research on the acquisition of Chinese aspectual marking

A number of scholars have examined the acquisition of Chinese aspectual marking, both in L1 and L2. In an experimental study, P. Li (1990), for example, studied the L1 acquisition of aspectual marking by 135 2 to 6-year-old children in Beijing. He tested the children's performance in the three modalities of comprehension, production, and imitation. Li used picture stories with a focus on contrasting perfective and imperfective aspect to test the children's understanding and use of the two aspects. Results showed that "resultative and telic verbs occurred almost exclusively with the perfective -*le*" and that "[t]he occurrence of -*le* with process and punctual verbs dropped drastically" when the children reached 6 years old (p. 107).

In a further study of the L1 acquisition of lexical and grammatical aspect, Li and Bowerman (1998), using the same methods as Li (1990), found that children were sensitive to the association between telic verbs and the perfective aspect marker -*le*. However, the results provide no indication that children were sensitive to the difference between stative and activity verbs or between semelfactive and activity verbs in their use or understanding of aspect markers. The results of both Li (1990) and Li and Bowerman (1998) support Slobin's (1985) basic child grammar hypothesis that the contrast between process and result is important in children's early acquisition of temporal morphology.

Other studies include Erbaugh (1985, 1992), who examined the acquisition of -*le* by four Mandarin-speaking children in Taipei. The results of a longitudinal study indicated that between 80 and 90% of the examples of -*le* refer to an event in the immediate past, and thus pertain to the action-completing function of the verbal suffix.

The acquisition of both perfective aspect marker -*le* and particle *le* has also attracted attention in second language acquisition. Wen (1995), for example, studied the acquisition of particle *le* by English-speaking college students in the United States. The speakers in her study acquired perfective aspect marker -*le* before the sentence-final particle *le* and were found to have experienced acquisition difficulties and transferred their L1-based default value to their L2 Chinese. In a later study, Wen (1997) investigated the acquisition of -*le* and the other two aspect markers, -*guo* and –*zhe*, by university level English-speaking learners. The results indicated that "the learners acquired the perfective aspect marker -*le* and the past experience marker -*guo* before the durative aspect marker -*zhe*" (1997, p. 1). In addition, Wen found the process of acquiring the aspect markers was meaning-based, that is, the learners acquired these aspect markers by relying more on the time adverbial expressions and lexical aspect. This was particularly true for learners at a lower proficiency level.

Duff and Li (2002), in a pilot study of adult English speakers learning Mandarin, examined developmental trends in speakers' form/function analysis of -le and past time/perfective aspect in oral narratives. They used longitudinal and cross-sectional data and adopted a coding scheme that distinguishes the speakers' correct suppliance, zero suppliance (under-suppliance), and over-suppliance of -le in contexts of obligatory, optional, and ungrammatical usage. The results indicate a shift from non-suppliance of -le early in acquisition to an over-suppliance of -le owing to the generalization and transfer of their L1 tense-marking. As a result, non-targetlike interlanguage use of -le with particular lexical items occurs in the narratives, such as *shuo-le 'say,' *zhi dao-le 'know,' and *wen-le 'ask' followed by direct/indirect speech.

In a second study of acquisition and use of Mandarin perfective aspect, Duff and Li (2002) found that native speakers used -le far more frequently and correctly in both obligatory and optional contexts than non-native speakers did, with -le produced about four times as often in obligatory than in optional contexts. They also found that native speakers produced longer narratives than non-native speakers.

The present study

Based on our review of the Chinese aspectual system and the literature on acquisition, we investigate the following four questions:

1. What trend will emerge from the acquisition of the perfective aspect marker -le by the participants at different age levels and with different length of study in the heritage language school?

2. Do grammatical and lexical features in children's use of -le interact?

3. What are the relationships among children's length of stay in the United States, years of attendance at the Chinese heritage language school, and use of perfective aspectual marking?

4. How do the children's home language environments affect the use of perfective aspectual marking?

Methods

The community

The data were collected at the Lu Xun Chinese Heritage School, founded by a group of parents from the Chinese community in 1998. The purpose of having such a school is to provide an opportunity for students to maintain Chinese language and to learn about Chinese culture. The school board is composed of parent volunteers and most of the teachers have had teaching experience (Jia, 2006). As in China, literacy instruction uses simplified characters and the Hanyu Pinyin system of romanization. The textbooks, which are published in China, are especially written for overseas Chinese children.

During the 2002–2003 school year when we collected the data, about 60 students were enrolled in five different level classes. Students met in the spring and the fall semesters, each consisting of 16 class sessions on Sunday afternoons. These students were assigned to different levels by their language proficiency rather than by their age or length of residence in the US.

Participants

Thirty-six students participated in the study, representing different levels of experience at the heritage language school. Participants ranged in age from 5 to 15 and included 18 U.S.-born Chinese who were in the process of acquiring Mandarin as a heritage language, and 18 who were born in China but came later with their parents to the United States. According to the parents, the Mandarin proficiency of the late arrivals had been diminishing owing to the influence of English. Although speaking Chinese is required at the language heritage school and at home at the will of the parents, not all students avail themselves of opportunities to speak Mandarin. Besides going to the Chinese heritage school, some students are sent back to China during summer by their parents. General information of the participants is summarized in Table 2.

Table 2. Speakers' demographic characteristics

age	birthplace		students' home language			parents' home language		gender		years at HL school			total
	CHINA	US	M	B	E	M	B	F	M	1	2	3+	
5–7	2	4	1	4	1	4	2	5	2	4	2	0	6
8–10	6	5	5	6	0	5	6	6	5	3	5	3	11
11–13	4	3	2	4	1	4	3	4	3	0	1	6	7
14–15	6	6	3	2	7	3	9	8	3	3	2	7	12
total	18	18	11	16	9	16	20	23	13	10	10	16	36

notes: M=Mandarin; B=English/Mandarin; E=English; HL school=heritage language school

Tasks and data elicitation

In addition to the demographic information summarized in Table 2, we collected three types of data. First, in order to obtain comparable narrative data from all participants, we asked students to look at and then retell the story of Mercer Mayer's (1969) wordless picture book, *Frog where are you?*, an elicitation device that has been widely used in studies of first and second language acquisition of numerous languages ranging from frequently studied languages such as English, German, and Spanish to less commonly studied languages such as Basque, Walpiri (an Australian indigenous language), and West Greenlandic (for bibliographies of studies using the "frog story" see Berman & Slobin, 1994, and Strömqvist & Verhoeven, 2004).

Second, 24 students who were in their second year at the school or beyond, divided evenly by birthplace and age group, were given a multiple choice cloze test consisting of 15 sentences and 20 verbs and asked to fill in the blanks with -*le*, Ø, or another appropriate aspect marker, for example, -*zhe*, *zai*, or -*guo* (see Appendix A). Sentences were presented in Chinese characters, with *pinyin* supplied for difficult words that students might not know.

Third, the 24 students who participated in Task 2 were presented with 10 pictures and 10 sentences describing the pictures and asked to complete the sentences with -*le* or Ø (Appendix B). As in Task 2, sentences were presented in Chinese characters, with *pinyin* supplied when necessary.

Data reduction

Narrative data were transcribed in standard *Hanyu Pinyin* orthography. All potential sites of aspectual marker -*le* were identified. In addition, we identified all instances of the homophonous sentence-final particle *le*. In preparation for variable rule analysis, following Duff and Li (2002), we coded broadly, as follows:

Dependent variable. -*le* used grammatically, -*le* used ungrammatically, -*le* absent where expected or allowed. A reliability check was conducted by the first author and another native Mandarin speaker with a strong background in linguistics. The agreement rate exceeded 95%.

Position of -le in the sentence. Sentence final; postverbal within sentence.

Sentence final

孩子	他	醒	了。
haizi	ta	xing	-le
child	3sg	awake	PFV

The child is awake.

Postverbal within the sentence

小	狗	看见	了	蜜蜂	窝。
xiao	gou	kanjian	-le	mifeng	wo
little	dog	see	PFV	bee	hive

The little dog saw the beehive.

Optionality. -le required in standard Mandarin; -le optional in standard Mandarin.

Required

男孩	听	见	了	一	个	声音。
nanhai	ting	(jian)	le	yi	ge	shengyin
boy	hear		PFV	one	CL	noise

The boy heard a noise.

Optional

小	男孩	爬	上	(了)	石头,	抓住	了	个	树枝。
xiao	nanhai	pa	shang	(-le)	shitou	zhuazhu	-le	ge	shuzhi
little	boy	climb	up	PFV	rock	hold	PFV	CL	branch

The little boy climbed up the rock and took hold of a branch.

The optional"-le" occurs after the verb "climb" in this example, which is grammatically acceptable when the action "hold" follows as part of the series of actions (for similar example see notes in Duff & Li, 2002).

Lexical aspect. Punctual; telic-stative; semelfactive; activity, stative. For examples see (7) to (11).

Grounding. Foreground; background.

那	男孩	睡着	了,	小	青蛙	跑	了。
na	nanhai	shuizhao	-le	xiao	qingwa	pao	-le
that	boy	sleep	PFV	little	frog	run	PFV

The boy fell asleep while his frog ran away.

Here, the verb "fell asleep" is background, while the verb "run away" is foregrounded.

Birthplace/age of arrival of student. US, China, arrived in US at age 5 or earlier (that is, while they were still acquiring major features of their L1 grammatical system); China, arrived in US at age 6 or older.

Age of student. 5–7; 8–10, 11–13, 14–15.

Number of years at the Lu Xun Chinese Heritage Language School. 1, 2, 3 or more.

Language use at home (student). Mandarin primarily or exclusively, Mandarin and English, English primarily or exclusively.

Language use at home (parents). Mandarin primarily or exclusively, Mandarin and English.

In distinguishing between perfective aspect marker *-le* and CRS sentence-final particle *le*, we followed Li and Thompson (1981), who distinguish between the two homophonous forms on the basis of use. Table 3 summarizes the distinction.

Table 3.   Function and use of verbal suffix *-le* and sentence-final particle *le*

function	use
verbal suffix *-le* **to indicate the entirety of an action**	When an event is bounded • by being a quantified event • by being a definite or specific event • by being inherently bounded in the meaning of the verb • by being the first event in a sequence
sentence-final particle *le* **to indicate a currently relevant state (CRS)**	When the state of affairs *le* represents • is a changed state • corrects a wrong assumption • reports progress so far • determines what will happen next • is the speaker's total contribution to the conversation at that point

Analyses

Two types of analyses were undertaken. First, to test for the influence of the multiple linguistic and social factors that might potentially constrain a speaker's use of *-le*, we performed multivariate analysis on the narrative data using the Variable Rule Program (VARBRUL) (Sankoff, Tagliamonte, & Smith, 2005), a specialized application of the statistical procedure known as logistic regression (Bayley, 2002). VARBRUL enables the analyst to model simultaneously the influence of factors, such as the position of *-le* in the sentence or years in the United States, at multiple levels and estimates the importance of each factor relative to other factors in the same group. Factors with a "weight" of between .50 and 1.0 are said to favor use of the variable that has been defined as the application value, or the value that counts as an application of the rule being investigated, in this case the appropriate use of *-le*. Factors with a weight between 0 and .50 are said to disfavor the application of the rule being investigated. The closer the weight is to 1.0 or to 0, the stronger the influence of the particular factor, whether favorable or unfavorable. VARBRUL weights, however, must be interpreted in light of the input value, or corrected mean. The input value is the overall likelihood that a variant will be used, for example, that a speaker will use *-le* appropriately, regardless of the presence or absence of any other factor in the environment. Finally, the VARBRUL program contains a routine for testing the significance of factor groups and eliminating those factor groups that do not contribute significantly to the observed variation.

Results from the cloze task and the sentence completion task were analyzed with one-way ANOVAs.

Results

Overall, results indicate that speakers born in the US as well as speakers born in China, used *-le* appropriately in the majority of obligatory contexts, although as expected, the performance of students born in China exceeded the performance of students born in the US. Both groups of speakers, however, used *-le* very infrequently in optional contexts. Somewhat surprisingly, results from the narrative and sentence completion tasks suggest that use of *-le* in obligatory contexts declines with age. However, results on the cloze task do not follow the same pattern.

Rather, the older students outperformed the younger on the cloze task. Finally, in contrast to other studies, lexical aspect did not prove to be a significant influence on the use of -le. In the following sections, we report on the results from each of the three tasks.

Task 1. Narratives

Narrative length
Speakers born in China, many of whom arrived in the United States after the age of six, produced narratives that were significantly longer than those of the U.S.-born speakers, whether expressed in terms of the number of characters (or morphemes) or clauses. Table 4 shows the results for the U.S.- and China-born students.

Table 4. Narrative length (task 1)

	born in China (n=18)			born in US (n=18)			
	mean	range	sd	mean	range	sd	t
length (characters)	463.83	298–911	135.40	299.0	181–452	72.98	–4.546*
length (clauses)	47.72	28–98	15.02	29.5	20–43	6.38	–4.730*

* p<.000

VARBRUL analysis
The 36 narratives that were obtained via story retelling and examined here yielded 549 possible sites of -le, 484 sites where -le is required in standard Mandarin and 65 where it is optional. The very few examples where -le was used in a context where it is ungrammatical, which amounted to less than 1.5% of the data, were not included in the analysis. Multivariate analysis with VARBRUL indicates that use of -le is constrained by the position of the perfective suffix in the sentence and optionality among the linguistic factor groups considered. Neither lexical aspect nor grounding achieved statistical significance. Among the social factors, use of -le is significantly constrained by home language use, the student's birthplace, and age. Full results are given in Table 5. Note that factors within groups that did not differ significantly from one another have been combined.

Table 5. Use of -le by Chinese heritage language learners

factor group	factor	n	% -le	VARBRUL weight
position of -le	sentence final	200	83	.779
	postverbal in sentence	349	43	.327
optionality	obligatory	484	63	.556
	optional	65	15	.156
birthplace x age	China 5–10	130	80	.709
	China 11–15	143	60	.521
	United States	276	46	.386
home language	Mandarin	186	74	.613
	Mandarin/English, English	363	49	.442
total	input	549	58	.603

notes: Factors within groups that did not differ significantly from one another have been combined. Chi-square/cell=0.7368; log likelihood=–282.623; all factor groups significant at p<.05.

As shown in Table 5, the position of -le in the sentence proved to be the most important linguistic constraint. In the "frog" narratives, students were far more likely to use -le when it was sentence-final (.779) than when it was attached to a verb within the sentence (.327). The result may be explained by the fact that the sentence-final position is more salient than post-verbal position within the sentence. However, this result contrasted with Teng's (1999) findings, where verbal *-le* was more frequently used and acquired earlier than sentence-final *-le*. Students were also far more likely to use *-le* in obligatory contexts (.556) than in optional contexts (.156), a result that conforms to Erbaugh's (1992) findings for L1 acquisition.

With respect to the social factors, as expected, children who reported using primarily Mandarin at home were more likely to use *-le* in both obligatory and optional contexts (.613) than students who reported using a combination of English and Mandarin or English predominantly (.442). Note that students who used a combination of English and Mandarin at home and students who used mostly English at home did not differ in their use of *-le* in the narrative-retelling task. This result conforms to other studies of minority language maintenance and shift, the results of which show that home language use is the best predictor of language maintenance (Hakuta & Pease-Alvarez, 1994; Pease-Alvarez, Hakuta, & Bayley, 1996).

In addition, the initial analysis showed that students who were born in China and acquired Mandarin as an L1 (.601) outperformed students who were born in the US (.404). However, the results of the initial run also showed that birthplace and age interacted. Hence we created a new factor group, birthplace by age. The results of the run with the interactive factor group, reported in Table 5, showed that 5 to 10-year-old China-born students used *-le* appropriately 80% of the time (.709), compared to 60 percent for 11 to 15-year-olds (.521), and only 46% for the U.S.-born students (.386), who did not differ from one another according to age.

Task 2. Cloze test

The youngest students did not participate in this task owing to their low proficiency level in reading and writing. The task was in the form of multiple choice cloze test consisting of sentences where *-le* was prohibited or required as in examples (12) and (13).

(12)   Prohibited (X)

我们	常常	看	X	电影。
women	changchang	kan	X	dianying
1pl	often	see		movie

We often go to the movies.

(13)   Required (了)

老师	讲	了	二十	分钟。
laoshi	jiang	*-le*	ershi	fenzhong
teacher	talk	PFV	twenty	minute

The teacher talked for twenty minutes.

As in the narrative-retelling task, the China-born students outperformed the U.S.-born students. However, a closer examination of the results of a one-way ANOVA indicates the groups differed significantly only on the sentences in which *-le* is ungrammatical ($p<.000$). Although the China-born students did outscore the U.S. born students on sentences that require *-le*, with a mean of 7.58 versus 5.67 for the U.S.-born students, the difference did not reach statistical significance ($p<.084$). In addition, as we have noted, the results for age differed from the results of the narrative-retelling task. On Task 2, the mean for 8 to 10-year-old students was 9.25 (out of a possible 20). The means for the 11 to 13-year-olds and the 14 to 15-year-olds were 14.625 and 17, respectively. Further analysis revealed that the difference between groups was significant at $p<.000$.

Task 3. Sentence completion

Again, the youngest students, most of whom had been at the school for less than a year, did not participate in the illustrated sentence completion task, which included sentences where -le is obligatory as well as sentences where -le is prohibited and a small number of sentences where it is optional. On this task, as on all of our other measures, the China-born students outperformed their U.S.-born counterparts.

In contrast to the results for the verbal cloze in Task 2, the results for age were similar to the results on the narrative-retelling task. For verbs that require -le, the youngest students, those aged 8 to 10, scored highest ($\overline{X}=6.375$), compared to a mean of 4.875 for the 11 to 13-year-olds and a mean of 5.125 for the 14- to 15-year-olds. In the case of contexts that prohibit use of -le, however, the 11 to 13-year-olds outscored the two other age groups. A one-way ANOVA indicated that the between-group differences were significant at $p<.05$. However there was no significant difference between the groups with respect to contexts where -le is optional.

Summary of results

To summarize, variable rule analysis for the narrative-retelling indicates that for students acquiring Mandarin as a heritage language and for those who are reacquiring the language, use of -le is constrained by the position in the sentence, with -le more likely to be used in sentence-final position, and by optionality, with -le more likely to be used in obligatory than in optional contexts. The results for the narrative-retelling task also indicate that the language spoken at home has a significant influence on the use of -le. In addition, younger students are more likely to use -le than older students.

On all three tasks, students born in China outperformed students born in the US. The China-born students produced longer and more elaborated narratives and they were more likely to use -le in both obligatory and optional contexts, although use in optional contexts remained low for both groups. Finally, the results for age group on Tasks 2 and 3 appear to go in opposite directions. On Task 2, the written cloze, the older students outperformed the younger students. On the illustrated cloze task, the younger students outperformed the older on items that required -le, but the middle group (ages 11 to 13) outperformed the other two groups on items where -le was prohibited.

Discussion

The results presented here provide additional support for the importance of the home language environment for minority language maintenance. Indeed, for the students in this study, few sources of heritage language maintenance are available outside of the home and the classes they attend on Sundays. The home and the Lu Xun Chinese Heritage Language School are the primary sources of Mandarin input, combined, in some cases, with summer visits with relatives in China. Chinese is not offered as a subject in any of the schools in which the students are enrolled and their social life outside of the home, in a city in which Chinese make up only about .5% of the population, is entirely in English.

The results for the analysis of the narrative retellings are in accord with a number of previous studies. First, the results for the position of -le in the sentence are in accord with previous studies of second language acquisition that suggest that saliency at various levels plays an important role (see, e.g., Bayley, 1994; Hakuta, 1976). Second, the results for optional and obligatory contexts are in accord with Andersen's (1984) One-to-One Principle, which posits that learners will acquire first those forms where one form corresponds to one meaning. Since -*le* is by definition unnecessary in optional contexts, the students in this study for the most part simplified their learning task by omitting it from such contexts most of the time and concentrating on contexts where -*le* is required.

The results for lexical aspect, which failed to reach statistical significance, are somewhat surprising when compared with the findings in Wen (1997), who suggested that students at early stages of Chinese language acquisition look for lexical aspect and inherent word meanings. For example, the learners in her study used adjectives as predictive of the sentences where -*le* should be used, evidence of the learners' ability to equate the function of adjectives with stative verbs. In addition, the learners in both lower and more advanced levels displayed a high rate of correct use of punctual verbs such as *ting* (stop), *ying* (win), and *wang* (forget), all of which have an inherent end-point built into the meaning (Wen, 1997). Even though our study did not produce results similar to Wen's results for lexical aspect, we can suggest reasons for the difference. First, our sample is fairly small. Although we had a substantial number of participants, a number of the narrative retellings were quite short and we had only 549 tokens. Second, although the use of the frog story allowed us to collect comparable data from all participants, it also limited the number of instances of non-prototypical sites of possible -*le* use. Clearly, the effects of lexical aspect on learners' use of -*le* need to be examined with a larger corpus that includes a greater variety of speech genres.

Conclusion

This study has examined the acquisition and reacquisition of one aspect of the grammar, perfective aspect marker -*le*, by 36 U.S.- and China-born learners. Variable rule analysis of 549 tokens of the learners' grammatical or ungrammatical use of -*le* indicates that learners are more likely to use -*le* in sentence final than in postverbal position, that learners are more likely to use *le* in obligatory than in optional contexts, that learners reacquiring Mandarin favor more grammatical use than learners acquiring Mandarin as a heritage language, and that learners who regularly interact in Mandarin at home are more likely to use -*le* appropriately than those who frequently or exclusively interact in English at home. The results also suggest some decline in learners' Chinese proficiency with increasing length of time in the United States. Given the context in which the study was conducted, in a city with a small and scattered Chinese population, this last result is perhaps understandable. As learners move into adolescence, the demands on their time for school success increase and their social lives—and hence their informal verbal interactions—increasingly take place outside the home. Those outside interactions are necessarily in English. Thus, even adolescent learners whose families insist on the use of Mandarin at home have fewer opportunities for interactions in their heritage language than their younger counterparts because they are spending less time at home. The apparent decline in at least one feature of the grammar among adolescents illustrates the need to provide additional opportunities for heritage language use beyond the home and the Chinese school. Given the academic ambitions of the students studied here and their families' aspirations for them, organized language classes in the public schools would seem to be the most obvious place to begin.

References

Andersen, R. W. (1984). The one-to-one principle of interlanguage construction. *Language Learning*, *34*, 77–95.

Andersen, R. W. (1991). Developmental sequences: The emergence of aspect marking in second language acquisition. In T. Huebner & C. A. Ferguson (Eds.), *Crosscurrents in second language acquisition and linguistic theories* (pp. 305–324). Amsterdam: John Benjamins.

Anderson, R. W., & Shirai, Y. (1996). The primacy of aspect in first and second language acquisition: The pidgin-creole connection. In W. C. Ritchie & T. K. Bhatia (Eds.), *Handbook of second language acquisition* (pp. 527–570). San Diego: Academic.

Ayoun, D., & Salaberry, M. R. (Eds.). (2005). *Tense and aspect in Romance languages: Theoretical and applied perspectives*. Amsterdam: John Benjamins.

Bardovi-Harlig, K. (1999). From morpheme studies to temporal semantics: Tense-aspect research in SLA. *Studies in Second Language Acquisition, 21*, 341–382.

Bardovi-Harlig, K. (2000). *Tense and aspect in second language acquisition: Form, meaning, and use.* Oxford, England: Blackwell.

Bayley, R. (1994). Interlanguage variation and the quantitative paradigm: Past tense marking in Chinese-English. In E. Tarone, S. Gass, & A. Cohen (Eds.), *Research methodology in second-language acquisition* (pp. 157–181). Hillsdale, NJ: Lawrence Erlbaum.

Bayley, R. (1999). The primacy of aspect hypothesis revisited: Evidence from language shift. *Southwest Journal of Linguistics, 18*(2), 1–22.

Bayley, R. (2002). The quantitative paradigm. In J. K. Chambers, P. Trudgill, & N. Schilling-Estes (Eds.), *The handbook of language variation and change* (pp. 117–141). Oxford, England: Blackwell.

Berman, R., & Slobin, D. I. (1994). *Relating events in narrative: A crosslinguistic developmental study.* Hillsdale, NJ: Lawrence Eribaum.

Collins, L. (2002). The roles of L1 influence and lexical aspect in the acquisition of temporal morphology. *Language Learning, 52*, 43–94.

Duff, P., & Li, D. (2002). The acquisition and use of perfective aspect in Mandarin. In R. Salaberry & Y. Shirai (Eds.), *The L2 acquisition of tense-aspect morphology* (pp. 417–453). Amsterdam: John Benjamins.

Erbaugh, M. S. (1985). Personal involvement and the development of language for time aspect. *Papers and Reports on Child Language Development, 24*, 54–61.

Erbaugh, M. S. (1992). The acquisition of Mandarin. In D. I. Slobin (Ed.), *The crosslinguistic study of language acquisition*, vol. 3 (pp. 373–455). Hillsdale, NJ: Lawrence Erlbaum.

Hakuta, K. (1976). A case study of a Japanese child learning English. *Language Learning, 26*, 321–351.

Hakuta, K., & Pease-Alvarez, L. (1994). Proficiency, choice and attitudes in bilingual Mexican-American children. In G. Extra & L. Verhoeven (Eds.), *The cross-linguistic study of bilingual development* (pp. 145–164). Amsterdam: Royal Netherlands Academy of Arts and Sciences.

He, A. W. (2000). Grammatical and sequential organization of teachers' directives. *Linguistics and Education, 11*(2), 119–140.

He, A. W. (2003). Novices and their speech roles in Chinese heritage language classes. In R. Baley & S. Schecter (Eds.), *Language socialization in bilingual and multilingual societies* (pp. 128–146). Clevedon, England: Multilingual Matters.

Jia, L. (2006). *The invisible and the visible: Language socialization at the Chinese heritage language school.* Unpublished doctoral dissertation, University of Texas at San Antonio.

Kwan-Terry, A. (1979). Two progressive aspect markers in Chinese. In D. L. Nguyen (Ed.), *South-East Asian linguistic studies,* vol. 4 (Pacific Linguistics, Series C, No. 44; pp. 213–232). Canberra: the Australian National University.

Li, C., & Thompson, S. (1981). *Mandarin Chinese: A functional reference grammar.* Berkeley: University of California Press.

Li, P. (1990). *Aspect and Aktionsart in child Mandarin.* Unpublished doctoral dissertation, University of Leiden.

Li, P., & Bowerman, M. (1998). The acquisition of lexical and grammatical aspect in Chinese. *First Language, 18,* 311–350

Li, P., & Shirai, Y. (2000). *The acquisition of lexical and grammatical aspect.* Berlin: Mouton de Gruyter.

Lu, J. H.-T. (1975). The grammatical item *le* in Mandarin. *Journal of the Chinese Language Teachers' Association, 10*(2), 53–62.

Mayer, M. (1969). *Frog, where are you?* New York: Dial Press.

Pease-Alvarez, L., Hakuta, K., & Bayley, R. (1996). Spanish proficiency and language use in a California Mexicano community. *Southwest Journal of Linguistics, 15,* 137–152.

Rohsenow, J. S. (1978). Perfect LE: Aspect and relative tense in Mandarin Chinese. In R. L. Cheng, Y. Li, & T. Tang (Eds.), *Proceedings of symposium on Chinese linguistics 1977* (pp. 267–291). Taipei: Student Book Co.

Salaberry, R. 2001. *The development of past tense morphology in L2 Spanish.* Amsterdam: John Benjamins.

Sankoff, D., Tagliamonte, S., & Smith, E. (2005). GoldVarbX: A multivariate analysis application [computer program]. Toronto: Department of Linguistics, University of Toronto and Department of Mathematics, University of Ottawa.

Shi, Z. (1989). The grammaticalization of the particle *le* in Mandarin Chinese. *Language Variation and Change, 1,* 99–114.

Shirai, Y., & Andersen, R. W. (1995). The acquisition of tense-aspect morphology: A prototype account. *Language, 71,* 743–762.

Shirai, Y., & Kurono, A. (1998). The acquisition of tense-aspect marking in Japanese as a second language. *Language Learning, 48,* 245–279.

Slobin, D. I. (1985). Crosslinguistic evidence for the language-making capacity. In D. I. Slobin (Ed.), *The crosslinguistic study of language acquisition, Vol. 2, Theoretical issues* (pp. 1157–1256). Hillsdale, NJ: Lawrence Erlbaum.

Smith, C. (1991). *The parameter of aspect.* Dordrecht, The Netherlands: Kluwer Academic Publishers.

Strömqvist, S., & Verhoeven, L. (Eds.). (2004). *Relating events in narrative, Vol. 2, Typological and contextual perspectives.* Mahwah, NJ: Lawrence Erlbaum.

Tai, J. H.-Y. (1984). Verbs and times in Chinese: Vendler's four categories. *Parasession on lexical semantics, 20,* 289–296.

Teng, S-H. (1999). The acquisition of le in L2 Chinese. *Shijie Hanyu Jiaoxue [World Chinese Language Teaching], (1),* 56–64.

Thompson, J. C. (1968). Aspects of the Chinese verb. *Linguistics, 38,* 70–76.

Vendler, Z. (1967). *Linguistics and philosophy.* Ithaca, NY: Cornell University Press.

Wang, W. S.-Y. (1965). Two aspect markers in Mandarin. *Language, 41,* 457–470.

Wen, X. (1995). Second language acquisition of the Chinese particle le. *International Journal of Applied Linguistics, 5,* 45–62.

Wen, X. (1997). Acquisition of Chinese aspect: An analysis of the interlanguage of learners of Chinese as a foreign language. *ITL: Review of Applied Linguistics, 117/118,* 1–26.

Appendix A: Task 2

动词多项选择 (circle one from the choices given):

1. 上星期六我们 _____ (看了, 看) 一场电影。
   We watched a movie last Saturday.

2. 叔叔坚持 (insist) 要我们 _____ (吃着, 吃了) 晚饭再回家。
   Our uncle insisted that we go home after having supper with him.

3. 昨天妈妈 _____ (花了，花着) 二十美金给我们 _____ (买了, 正在买) 一些文具。
   Mother spent twenty dollars to buy us some stationery yesterday.

4. 去年爸爸带我和弟弟 _____ (回, 回了) 中国。我们 _____ (参观, 参观了) 北京很多名胜古迹 (scenic spots and historical sites)。
   Last year Father took my younger brother and me back to China, where we visited many of Beijing's scenic spots and historical sites.

5. 老师和我 _____ (谈, 谈着, 谈了) 10分钟的话。
   The teacher talked to me for ten minutes.

6. 我们家 _____ (养了, 养) 一只小花猫。
   We have kept a cat in our house.

7. 妈妈在学校门口 _____ (等, 等着, 等了) 我30分钟。
   Mother waited for me for thirty minutes at the school gate.

8. 上学期数学考试我 _____ (得了, 正得着, 得) 100分, 爸爸 _____ (表扬, 表扬了) 我。
   Last semester I scored a hundred in math, for which my father praised me.

9. 放学后, 芳芳在学校门口 _____ (上了, 上) 六路公共汽车。
   After school Fangfang got onto Bus No. 6 at the school gate.

10. 狼 _____ (相信, 在相信, 相信了) 小白羊的话, 害怕地 _____ (走了, 走)。
    The wolf believed the little sheep's words and left fearfully.

11. 云云 _____ (猜出了, 猜出) 那个字的意思, 就把手高高地 _____ (举, 举了) 起来。
    Yunyun figured out the meaning of that character and raised her hand.

12. 墙上 _____ (挂, 挂了) 一幅画。
    There is a painting hanging on the wall.

13. 天 _____ (冷, 冷了), 很多人 _____ (穿上了, 穿上) 厚厚的 (thick) 棉衣。
    It's getting cold. Many people have put on thick cotton-padded clothes.

14. 铃响了, 我们的老师 _____ (进来, 进来了)。
    The bell rang. Our teacher came in.

15. 琳琳在中餐馆 _____ (碰见了, 在碰见) 两个同学。
    Linlin met two of her classmates in a Chinese restaurant.

Appendix B: Task 3

看图后用 "了" 填空, 不需要填 "了" 处请用 "X" 标出 (Look at the pictures* before you fill the blanks with -le or mark "X" where -le does not apply):

1. 我吃 ＿＿＿＿ 晚饭就去看电视 ＿＿＿＿ 。
   I will watch TV after I finish my supper.

2. 老师讲 ＿＿＿＿ 二十分钟就让我们写 ＿＿＿＿ 作业。
   The teacher talked for twenty minutes before asking us to work on our assignments.

3. 妈妈总说 ＿＿＿＿ 我的字写得不好。
   Mother always says my handwriting is not good.

4. 明明昨天没有去看 ＿＿＿＿ 电影 (dianying), 他生病 ＿＿＿＿ 。
   Mingming did not go to the movies because he was sick.

5. 太阳就像 (xiang) ＿＿＿＿一个大火球。
   The sun is like a big fireball.

6. 奶奶常 (chang) 说 ＿＿＿＿ 她老 ＿＿＿＿ 。
   Grandma often says she is getting old.

7. 云云问 ＿＿＿＿ 老师一个问题 (wenti), 可是却把答案忘 ＿＿＿＿ 。
   Yunyun asked her teacher a question, but forgot the answer to it.

8. 我看见一只鸟突然 (turan) 从树上飞走 ＿＿＿＿ 。
   I saw that a bird left the tree suddenly.

9. 一只狗从院子里 (yuanzi li) 跑出来，把小孩吓哭 ＿＿＿＿ 。
   A dog ran out of the yard and frightened the child into crying.

10. 我忘 ＿＿＿＿ 这部动画片的名字。
    I have forgotten the name of the cartoon.

* Pictures have been omitted.

The Learning

14

Code-Switching: Ideologies and Practices

LI Wei
Chao-Jung Wu
Birkbeck, University of London

This chapter addresses the tensions and conflicts between the ideologies and practices in Chinese heritage language (CHL) schools in the United Kingdom, focusing on the use of code-switching by teachers. While "speak Chinese only" is often the stated school policy and the teachers' stated belief, in practice, both teachers and students of CHL adopt a variety of multilingual practices, particularly code-switching, as a "safe" space for managing multilingual identities. Particular attention is given to the ways in which English is used in otherwise Chinese language classrooms, and how these practices may impact on the majority versus minority language divide.

Like most Chinese Heritage Language (CHL) schools across the world, the CHL schools in the UK are community based, voluntary organisations that complement mainstream schooling by providing language- and literacy-focused teaching over the weekend. The declared objectives are to promote Chinese language and literacy to the British born generation of Chinese children. Parents and teachers of these schools insist that the best practice is to "speak Chinese only" and that is often the stated policy of the CHL schools. Yet, in practice, children attending the CHL schools use a variety of multilingual practices. Code-switching is often used to create a "safe" space for them in this specific environment. In the meantime, many of the teachers also code-switch in the classroom, against the school policies and their own beliefs. In this chapter, we aim to critically examine the conflicts between the ideologies and practices of code-switching by the teachers in the CHL schools context. In particular, we investigate the majority versus minority language divide by examining the ways in which English is used in otherwise Chinese language classrooms.

Complementary schools in the UK

Chinese Heritage Language (CHL) schools in the UK are part of the so called "complementary schools" for immigrant and ethnic minority children. Complementary schools have been an important sociopolitical, educational movement in the country for nearly half a century. They have made a major impact on thousands of children of different ethnic backgrounds, attracted public debates vis-à-vis government's involvement in

Li, W., & Wu, C.-J. (2008). Code-switching: Ideologies and practices. In A. W. He, & Y. Xiao (Eds.), *Chinese as a heritage language: Fostering rooted world citizenry* (pp. 225–238). Honolulu: University of Hawai'i, National Foreign Language Resource Center.

educational management, and challenged the dominant ideology of uniculturalism in the country. Yet, they have received relatively little attention from educational researchers.

There are three broad types of complementary schools in the UK: AfroCaribbean schools, Muslim schools, and minority ethnic or heritage language schools/classes. A brief review of the sociopolitical history of the complementary schools in the UK can be found in Li (2006). This chapter focuses on the heritage language schools. These schools are usually weekend classes and they are truly complementary in the sense that their organisers do not seek for a separate education for their children. Instead, classes are run at weekends or outside normal school hours to provide additional teaching of the community languages and cultures. There are now more this type of heritage language schools and classes than separate schools for Muslims and AfroCaribbeans combined.

Although the specific social context in which the three broad types of complementary schools were set up differs, there is one common feature—they are set up in response to the failure of the mainstream education system to meet the needs of the ethnic minority children and their communities—a fact that is often deliberately ignored by various U.K. governments (Carrington & Short, 1989; Chevannes & Reeves, 1987). Despite the public debates over pluralistic, multicultural education over the decades, the U.K. governments have made no real attempt to address the criticisms that the mainstream education system is disabling and disempowering ethnic minority children and their communities. Instead, various governments have tried to make use of the complementary schools for their own political and economic agendas. For instance, the Conservative Government under Margaret Thatcher used the example of the Chinese heritage language schools to argue that ethnic minorities were better off with "self reliance" and cut back already limited funding in the Local Education Authorities budget for bilingual classroom assistants. Complementary schools and classes were further marginalised as a result. They were, and still are, seen as a minority concern and left with ethnic minority communities themselves to deal with.

The existence, and indeed expansion, of complementary schools in the UK presents a real challenge to mainstream education and society. It also raises a number of important questions to the schools themselves. For instance, one of the principal objectives the complementary schools have set for themselves is the maintenance of linguistic knowledge and cultural identity amongst the British born generations. How successful have the complementary schools been in achieving this objective? More importantly perhaps, what is this "cultural identity" that the schools and communities wish to maintain? Do parents and children share the same idea and vision about their identities? It is often said that identity is a dynamic rather than a static concept; it is negotiable and changeable; it is conditioned by context but can be manipulated by individuals, groups and institutions for different purposes (e.g., Pavlenko & Blackledge, 2001). Complementary schools are an important social context for developing identities for the immigrant and ethnic minority children attending them. What impact this specific context has on the children's identity development is an issue worth further investigation.

With regards to pedagogy and classroom management, it is obvious and understandable that the complementary schools want to insist on using specific community languages in this particular domain. Nevertheless, the long term consequence of such compartmentalisation of community languages is an issue of concern, apart from the practical difficulty of maintaining a strict "no English" policy in the schools. In this chapter, we focus on how teachers and pupils in two Chinese heritage language schools in the UK use multilingual practices as acts of identity. A specific focus will be placed on the use of code-switching by teachers and its impact on the social positioning of the two languages—Chinese and English—and the communities and cultures that the languages represent.

CHL schools in the UK

The Chinese are one of the longest established immigrant communities in the UK. The current Chinese community in the country is developed from post-war migrants, who began to arrive in Britain in the 1950s. The vast majority of the post-war Chinese immigrants were from Hong Kong. They were Cantonese and/or Hakka speakers. Many of them were peasant and labourers, who left an urbanising Hong Kong to seek a better living in the UK. They have been engaged in largely family based catering business and other service industries. The Chinese now form the third largest immigrant community in Britain, after those of AfroCaribbean origin and from the Indian subcontinent. Over a quarter of them are now British born. A more detailed account of the current sociolinguistic situation of the Chinese community in the UK can be found in Li (1994).

There were informal reports of "home schooling," that is, children being taught by their parents and others at home, amongst the Chinese families in the 1950s and 1960s in cities such as London, Liverpool, and Manchester where there were significant numbers of Chinese settlements. The very first "Chinese schools" emerged on the basis such collectives of families providing private education to their children. The reasons for the emergence of such schools are complex. There is no doubt that racial discrimination played a role. But the fact that the vast majority of the Chinese were, and still are, engaged in service industries has led to scattered settlements right across the country. It is often said that any town or village in Britain with around 2,000 residents will have at least one Chinese takeaway. The Chinese children of these families would have little or no contact with other Chinese children if there was no Chinese complementary school.

The establishment of the Chinese schools must be seen as a major achievement of the community in their determination to support themselves. It also reflects a major failure of the mainstream schools to provide the necessary support to the Chinese children. According to the U.K. Federation of Chinese Schools and the U.K. Association for the Promotion of Chinese Education, the two largest national organisations for CHL schools, there are 221 Chinese complementary schools in the UK. They are located in major urban centres. Many families have to travel for hours to send their children to the schools. They receive little support from the local education authorities. They are entirely self-financed. Parents pay fees to send the children, and local Chinese businesses offer sponsorships and other support (e.g., paying for the hire of premises and facilities). Many of the schools use teaching materials provided free of charge by voluntary organisations in China, Hong Kong, and Taiwan. The teachers are mainly enthusiastic parents and university students from China.

In the last 10 years, a pattern has emerged. There are now four types of Chinese schools: (a) for Cantonese speaking children from Hong Kong immigrant families; (b) for Cantonese speaking children of immigrant families from Hong Kong and more recently, from Canton, mainland China; (c) for Mandarin speaking children from mainland China; and (d) for Mandarin speaking children of Buddhist families, mainly from Taiwan. Most of the schools run classes over the weekend for up to three hours. Parents play a crucial role in the schools— parents pay, parents govern, and parents teach.

A typical CHL school in the UK looks like this: It rents its premises from a local school or education centre. There is a temporary reception desk at the entrance for parents to speak to the teachers about any issues of concern. A shop is available for children to buy snacks and drinks. Space is provided for staff to have tea and coffee during the break and to have meetings. The children are grouped according to proficiency in Chinese. There are traditional Chinese dance, arts, and sports sessions before or after the language and literacy sessions. Many schools also provide English language lessons for parents.

Multilingual practices in CHL schools

A wide range of multilingual practices can be observed in the CHL schools context. Some reflect what is happening in the wide community generally, while others are conditioned by the specific context of CHL schools. For instance, an interesting phenomenon that has been observed in the Chinese community in Britain is that all the British born Chinese children have English names, a feature that is not evident in communities of other ethnic origins. Most of them do also have Chinese names. Which name, English or Chinese, the parents, teachers, and the children themselves use in the Chinese school context is something of interest.

Another issue of great significance, but again which has been neglected in research, is the internal hierarchies of language varieties and speaker groups within the Chinese community. As has been said earlier, the Chinese communities in the UK have been predominantly Cantonese and Hakka speaking until the 1990s when large numbers of Mandarin speakers began to arrive. Cantonese, by its association with the economy and culture of Hong Kong, has the highest social prestige in the community. It also has the largest population of native speakers. Hakka, on the other hand, is a language variety that is typically associated with the traditional rural life in China and Hong Kong. Many of the Hakka-speaking families in the UK originated from fishing or rice farming villages in the New Territories of Hong Kong and various islands in the South China Sea. There is no institutional support for the Hakka language and its speakers either in Hong Kong or in the UK. In fact, many children from Hakka speaking families attend Chinese schools that teach Cantonese without knowing much of the latter at all.

In an earlier study, Li (1997) reported that many Hakka speaking women married Cantonese speaking men and have learned Cantonese which they use as their primary language of communication, whereas many Hakka speaking men learn English but not Cantonese even if they have married Hakka speaking wives. With the enhanced political and economic importance of mainland China and increased numbers of mainland immigrants, Mandarin Chinese has now gained a prominent place in the U.K. Chinese community. More and more Mandarin schools are being set up and almost all Cantonese schools offer Mandarin classes as well. The hierarchies and power relations between the language varieties have significant impact on the policies and practices of the CHL schools and are worthy of further investigation.

One of the most distinctive features of being bilingual is code-switching. All bilinguals engage in code-switching of various kinds, including the mixing of languages in the same utterance and alternation between languages in conversation, according to experience, environment, and communicative purpose. Code-switching is an important identity marker and maker for bilinguals (see papers in Auer, 1998; Gumperz, 1982; and Heller, 1988). Yet, there is a widespread misunderstanding and even fear of code-switching. It is often regarded as a linguistic deficiency, caused by "semilingualism" (Hansegård, 1975). In particular, bilingual parents and teachers are discouraged from code-switching because it is often perceived to have a negative effect on children's language development. Baetens Beardsmore (2003) summarises the negative attitudes towards bilingualism and code-switching in terms of fears: parental fears, cultural fears, educational fears, and politico-ideological fears.

In a truly bilingual classroom, code-switching should be the norm; it should be encouraged and celebrated. There is a real dearth of research on the use of code-switching in the classroom. Martin-Jones (1995) reviewed research on code-switching in the classroom that appeared between the mid 1970s and mid 1990s. She pointed out that whilst the earlier research highlighted the role classroom code-switching played in the interactional work that teachers and learners did in bilingual contexts, more microethnographic work was needed to help us to grasp the importance of the sociocultural and political dimensions of bilingual classroom interaction. In this paper, we wish to examine how children use code-switching to create a social space within the heritage language school context where their multilingual identity is developed.

In the heritage language schools context, bilingual teachers face a real dilemma in terms of language choice. The objective of the schools determines that they must always use the heritage language and avoid any use of English, the majority language. Yet, avoiding code-switching means suppressing one of the most important characteristics of being bilingual. The present paper examines this dilemma from a critical perspective, focussing on the effect of code-switching on the social construction of minority versus majority languages. We will also look at how children use code-switching to negotiate their own identity positions within the complementary schools context.

The study

The present study was conducted in Chinese heritage language schools in Newcastle and Manchester, two of the major urban centres in England with large Chinese settlements. There are four Chinese schools in Newcastle, three for Cantonese speakers and one for Mandarin. In Manchester, there are five Cantonese schools and two Mandarin schools. One of the Mandarin schools is run by Buddhist monks from Taiwan. We have undertaken extensive ethnographic observations in four of the schools, two from each city and one Cantonese and one Mandarin in Newcastle and Manchester respectively. Recordings, both audio and video, were made in the classroom as well as during break time. We also interviewed a selection of teachers, parents and pupils. We were particularly interested in the multilingual practices, including code-switching, in the complementary school context. In what follows, we will first demonstrate how the "Chinese only" policy is being put into practice in the CHL classroom. We then focus on code-switching initiated by teachers, and discuss the implications of their use of code-switching in the classroom in relation to their attitudes towards code-switching. We will use examples from the Mandarin classes.

Language negotiation

It is important to remind ourselves that complementary schools exist to promote the heritage language and the school policy is to use Chinese only. Most teachers in CHL schools take the policy very seriously. The following two examples show how two different teachers put the "Chinese only" policy into practice and how pupils react to what the teachers does. Both examples are taken from the same class (Mandarin school, Level 5, in Manchester). However, there was a change of teachers between weeks, as Teacher 1 (T1) in the first excerpt had other personal commitments and had to leave the Chinese school. Teacher 2 (T2) was selected and took over the class from T1. The students and all other arrangements stayed the same. The next two examples were both excerpts from our fieldnotes.

Example 1
The class has just finished activities related to a photocopied article. The teacher is diverting pupils' attention back to the textbook.

T1: 下一课我们讲' 足球变水球' 。

Xiayike women jiang "Zuqiu bian shuiqiu."

Next lesson we're talking about "Football becomes waterball."

The class gets excited and all start talking at the same time (mostly in English), although not in very loud voice. S1 says something in English.

T1: 大家不能说英文。 XX 你还得再说一次。用中文。

Dajia buneng shuo yingwen. XX, ni haidei zaishuo yici. Yong zhongwen.

You are not supposed to speak English. XX [Chinese name], you have to say that again, in Chinese.

S1: 中国的足球不太好。

Zhongguo de zuqiu butaihao.

China's football is not very good.

T1: 女孩子有没有喜欢足球的?

Nuhaizi youmeiyou xihuan zuqiu de?

Any girl who likes football?

Girls are all quiet, and S1 puts both of his hands up and cheers. Everyone laughs and someone says "女孩子" (*nuhaizi*, girls).

S1: I just like football so much. I don't care.

Teacher then talks (in Chinese) a little bit more about football. She asks if any of the girls knows how many referees are there in a football match. How many 主裁 (*zhucai*, main referees) are there? How many of them are on the sides 边裁 (*biancai*, side referees)? The girls appear not to be interested at all. S9 even puts both of her thumbs down and makes a face to show that she dislikes the subject. The class starts to get quite noisy and all start to chat in English.

The pupils in this class had a very good relationship with T1 and responded to her very warmly. When she explained what the topic of discussion was, the pupils got quite excited. However, they expressed their excitement in English, which is in itself an identity display. The teacher stopped one of the pupils (S1) and ordered him to speak Chinese. Notice that T1 used S1's Chinese name. In the CHL schools that we studied, most of the teachers use the pupils' Chinese names only. The pupils themselves, however, call each other by their English names, although they do occasionally use their Chinese names in class. Notice that there is also an interesting display of gender identity. The girls responded rather negatively to the discussion of football. They kept quiet when the teacher asked if any of them liked football. When S1 put up his hands, the others laughed at him. He responded by making a statement in English.

Example 2
T2 asks pupils to write another 作文 (*zuowen*, composition) for homework. She says it in both Chinese and English.

S1:   What is composition?

Boy (moaning): No.

S14: 今天吗?

Jintian ma?

Today?

T2 asks pupils to do it as homework, in Chinese followed by English. All start to chat in English.

S1: What is composition?

T2 explains in a lot of English.

S14: 要几个字?

Yao jige zi?

How many words?

T2: At least 70 characters.

In contrast to what T1 does, T2 seemed at ease translating many of her own statements from Chinese to English. She also responded to the pupils' questions mostly in English, even when the pupils asked some of the questions in Chinese. On the surface, the class appeared to be somewhat out of control with T2. Both the teacher and the pupils code-switched freely between English and Chinese. T2 seemed happy to accept and to use both Chinese and English for the pupils and herself. Interestingly, some of the pupils actually "volunteered" the use of Chinese on several occasions, as S14's question in the example shows. When we interviewed T2, however, she did not appear to be aware of the amount of code-switching she used. In fact, she claimed that she did not use much English at all, whereas during observation she repeated almost everything in English and sometimes instructed only in English. The pupils, on the other hand, felt more at ease with their languages when T2 was teaching. The amount of English they used did not seem to be significantly more than that when T1 was teaching.

Let us now look at teacher's use of code-switching in more detail.

Teacher initiated code-switching

Whilst the actual amount of code-switching varies from teacher to teacher, most of them admit that they use code-switching in the classroom for various purposes. On the basis of our observations, the following uses of code-switching initiated by teachers can be identified.

Dealing with procedural issues, such as establishing pedagogical focus, eliciting response, checking comprehension, explaining, and giving feedback.

Example 3

T: 现在咱们看第七题啊。第七, 找到了吗? Number 7. 不是七页, 第七题。 OK. 我们先看看怎么做。

Xianzai zanmen kan diqi ti a. Diqi, zhaodaole ma? Number 7. Bushi qiye, diqi ti. OK. Women xian kankan zenme zuo.

Now we look at question 7. Seventh, found it? question number 7. Not page 7, seventh question. First, let's see how to do it.

Example 4

T:　他左看看右看看。四周漆黑, 鸦雀无声。漆黑是什么意思?

Ta zuo kankan you kankan. Sizhou qihei, yaque wusheng. Qihei shi shenme yisi?

He looked left and looked right. Pitch dark all round; not even a crow or sparrow can be heard. What does *qihei* mean?

P:　Dark.

T:　对了, dark. Dark as?

Duile, dark. Dark as?

Correct, dark. Dark as?

…

T:　Dark as pitch.

T:　鸦雀呢?

Yaque ne?

What about *yaque*?

P:　Crow.

T:　鸦是 crow。雀是什么?

Ya shi crow. Que shi shenme?

Ya is crow. What's *que*?

…

T:　Sparrow. Crow and sparrow, no sound.

In Example 3, the teacher uses English to draw attention of the pupils to the right pedagogical task. She has already given the instructions in Chinese, but reiterates them in English to make sure that everybody is following her. In Example 4, the teacher uses translation, from Chinese to English, to check comprehension.

Dealing with disciplinary issues

Example 5

T:　OK, 你们来分成两组? 你们俩把椅子拿过来, 这边。行了。 Why don't you move? XXX, 你怎么了?

Nimen lai, fen cheng liangzu, OK? Nimen lia ba yizi na guolai, zheibian. Xingle. Why don't you move? XXX, ni zenme la?

You come here. Form two groups, OK? You two bring the chairs here, this side. That's it. Why don't you move? XXX, what's the matter with you?

Example 5 is similar to the first two, but in this case the teacher identifies one pupil who has not followed her instructions and switches to English to ask him why he has not done so.

"Social" use – discourse markers and fillers

As in Example 3, English discourse markers and fillers were frequently used in teacher talk. They had different functions, including giving feedback, checking comprehension and eliciting response. Examples include *"OK," "That's right," "Say it again," "Good,""Anyone?,"* *"Yes,"* and *"No."*

Overall, English lexical items in otherwise Chinese utterances constituted 92% of teacher initiated code-switching that was recorded. Code-switching is observed with the following frequency of use:

Establishing pedagogical focus – 47%

Eliciting response – 25%

Checking comprehension – 32%

Feedback – 18%

Translation and explanation – 76%

Note that percentages overlap as code-switching often has multiple functions.

The examples illustrate how teachers in Chinese classes use code-switching for various pedagogical purposes. Teachers resort to English for classroom management and disciplinary issues. They also switch to English when they have failed to explain new terms and concepts in the language that they are teaching. They seem to assume that the pupils know English well and understand better in English. It would therefore be the easiest to switch to English in teaching new words and concepts. Interviews with the teachers after class confirmed these assumptions, which we will discuss further later.

While acknowledging the fact that the pupils are English dominant bilinguals, the teachers' use of code-switching as seen in the examples has a number of consequences. First, it gives English more pedagogical importance. English is the language of learning and the language of knowledge and understanding. Second, it gives English more social importance. English is the language of authority. Third, it maintains the English dominance amongst the children. Children already feel that they speak better English and are better off using English. The ways in which the teachers use English in the Chinese class reinforce the children's perceptions. Ultimately, the teachers' use of code-switching in class helps to reinforce the status of English as the dominant language of society.

Attitudes towards code-switching

In addition to the observations we carried out in the classrooms, we conducted a number of interviews with teachers and parents. The interview questions were wide ranging. Most relevant to the present chapter were questions on code-switching, which included the following:

1. Do you change from one language to another when you talk to other people who know your languages?
2. Do you mix two or more languages together?
3. (Teachers) Do you change from one language to another or mix two languages together when you teach?
4. Do you stop children from changing or mixing languages? Why (not)?
5. How do you think changing or mixing languages would affect the child's learning?
6. Why do you think you and your child change or mix languages?

As shown in Table 1, all the interviewees admitted that they used code-switching themselves. But what is their attitude towards children's code-switching?

Table 1. Summary of the responses from 12 parents (5 male, 7 female) and 7 teachers (1 male, 6 female) to the first three questions

question	yes, sometimes	yes, often	no
1	17	2	0
2	18	1	0
3	7	0	0

In response to question 4, 16 interviewees said that they did prevent children from code-switching and only three, all male parents, said that they did not. Of those who said yes, 5 were teachers, 1 male and 4 female, and they said that they would stop children from code-switching especially in the Chinese school. When further probed about the reasons for trying to stop the children from code-switching, the following were typical responses:

Yes

"It's not good."

"You shouldn't mix languages."

"They (children) get confused."

Yes *(teachers)*

"They (children) are here (at the Chinese community language school) to learn Chinese. They shouldn't mix languages."

No

"It's natural."

"You can't stop them."

When asked how they thought code-switching would affect the children's learning (question 5), the responses all pointed to the perceived negative effects.

"They get confused."

"Should concentrate on learning one language at a time."

"All the exams in (mainstream) schools are in English. They shouldn't use any other language at school."

The negative attitude was further reinforced by the (mis)perception of the reasons for code-switching (question 6).

"Their Chinese is very bad. They only know English words." (suggesting proficiency, lexical gap)

"Don't know the right words." (suggesting lexical gap)

"They can understand me better." (suggesting language preference or dominance)

The interviews revealed a conflict between the adults' own linguistic practices—most of them admitted that they used code-switching—and their perception of the negative effects on the children. In the Manchester sites, most teachers interviewed reported that they would code-switch if they felt it was necessary for them to do so. However, teachers rather accepted code-switching as "the way it is" (due to pupils' lack of Chinese or the way of life in multilingual Britain) in Chinese classrooms as a result of subtle language negotiation. Only one teacher said that she didn't code-switch much (although she did switch a little, it was clear she spoke in Cantonese most of the time) as she was not confident in her own English and she preferred her pupils to translate for her.

The following is the transcript of part of an interview we conducted with the headteacher (HT) of the Mandarin school in Manchester. "I" is the interviewer.

I: 您觉得这个学校孩子们讲英文多，因为她们的父母反正听得懂？

You reckon that the fact that their parents could understand them anyway was the cause for pupils at this school to speak more English?

HT: 有可能。有几个孩子，反倒她们父母不怎么讲中文的。她们英文就讲得多一些。可能，可能，就是家长反正也听得懂。而且家长本身听懂那个，本身她跟孩子说话，她就用英文。她会用英文。

Maybe. A few of the kids, their parents don't speak much Chinese. They'd speak a bit more English. Maybe its due to the fact that the parents could understand anyway. Not only can parents understand, they also speak English to their children. They'd use English.

I: 是吗？就是你说那样子，说得很破碎那样子。

Is that so? Like you said (earlier), they speak in a fragmented manner.

HT: 可能就是很短的话，像是："XXX, your hair's too short." 这样子。这样，孩子就变成，觉得英文是可以接受的。就…因为，孩子自然而然就会讲英文。但是如果家长完全听不懂英文，至少从中文学校有几个孩子的例子看，好像是。

Perhaps very short utterances, such as: "XXX, your hair's too short." Like that. This makes the children feel that English is acceptable. As a result, children will naturally speak English. But if parents don't understand English at all, at least, from some of the pupils at the Chinese school, it looks like...

I: 是吗？如果父母的英文很有限的话，

Yes? If the parents' English is limited ...

HT: 但是这种情况未必对她的中文学习有帮助，因为这种中文吧，都是那种吃喝拉撒睡。它不能讨论任何 serious 的问题，它不能。就她的词汇量是完全局限于日常生活的那一点儿。

But it is not necessarily helpful to their learning of Chinese, because this kind of Chinese is only related to daily trivia. It cannot be use to discuss any serious issues. It can't, because their vocabularies were limited to only daily rituals.

I: 她的父母是因为她的中文也有限吗？

Was it because their parents only had limited Chinese also?

HT: 不是，我觉得，这成年的父母，中文不会只会吃喝拉撒睡，如果她光讲中文的话。所以，我觉得这个问题就是，……我们现在带丁丁他们的时候，有时候看电视的时候，我会正八经的，serious 的语言，正八经的语言来，跟他解释这是怎么回事。就是这样子，用中文，跟他解释，这是什么，这是什么。如果要不然，你要不这样的话，他的词汇量就会局限在吃喝拉撒。在将来他就会，因为他的词汇量不能用中文来和你讨论这些讲到说，比如说升学，比如说讲到对某部电影的看法等等，他没法用中文跟你讨论。结果你不得不接受他用英文跟你讨论。这样的孩子中文就会退化到只能对付吃喝拉撒睡。

我觉得这样就不能说是中文学好了。不能好好的表达自己了。那只能表达最简单的意思。

No, I think for grown-up parents, their Chinese is not limited at daily trivia if they only speak Chinese. So, I think the problem is ... Using the experience we have with our own children, sometimes when we watch TV, I'd use serious, serious language, to explain to him what's happening. Using Chinese to explain to him what is what. Otherwise, if you don't do that, his vocabulary will become limited to daily rituals. In the future, because his vocabulary is limited, he won't be able to use Chinese to discuss with you ... for example, furthering their education, or their views about certain films. He won't be able to discuss these with you in Chinese. In the end, you'd have to accept him discussing these topics with you in English. In this case, the child's Chinese will deteriorate to only being able to deal with daily trivia. I think in that case, you cannot say that they'd learn Chinese well. They won't be able to express themselves properly, but only the simplest matters.

I: 她会把比较复杂的用英文说了。保留在英文那边。

They might say the more complicated things in English, save those for the English part.

HT: 对，对。所以除非，你家长可以做到说，跟她说些比较正八经的话题的时候，你也教她用中文怎么表达。然后你才能做到将来她这个方面也能上去。然后，还有一个例子就是，父母都不会讲英文，这女儿现在已经上到稍微大一点了，小学快毕业，上中学了。这样的年纪了,她会看不起她父母了。她觉得她父母什么都不懂。她觉得她父母跟学校打交道打不了，还得通过她翻译。她一方面觉得她很 embarrassed.另一方面，她会，更不会再去跟父母讨论这种严肃的话题，不会。所以我觉得，这个特别是。就是又一个，这样子情况的妈妈，她跟我抱怨过，他特别希望学校能，老师能帮她呀。她说：孩子都不跟我说，对我凶啊什么。就是会有这样子的问题。那我们绝大多数的家长没有这样的问题。但是一个例子。比如说尽管有些是得与父母用中文交流。但是这个交流就会非常局限于这一点儿。所以其实未必就是对学中文是一个好的东西。

That's right. So unless parents can discuss more serious topics with their children...can teach them to express themselves in Chinese, you can then help them improve on these aspects. Moreover, there is another example where neither parents can speak English. The daughter is a bit older now, finishing primary school, going into secondary school. At this age, she looks down upon her parents. She feels that her parents know nothing. She feels that her parents can't even have dealings with her school. They have to go through her as an interpreter. On the one hand, she feels embarrassed. On the other hand, she'd ..she wouldn't discuss with her parents any serious topic, no. So, I think, this situation is particularly ... The mother complained to me. She was hoping that the school, the teachers could help her. She said, "The child wouldn't even speak to me. She's ferocious to me." Things like that. Most of our parents do not have this kind of problems. But this is an example. Even though some children had to use Chinese to communicate with their parents, the communication is very limited to trivia. It is not necessarily a good thing for learning Chinese.

A few points emerged from this interview. First, children do seem to be aware of their parents/teachers' bi/multilinguality. They know that if they resort to using English, there would not be any barrier of getting their messages across. Second, parents/teacher's use of

English indicates to the children that using English or code-switching is acceptable. Third, there is a concern that communicating only in English would result in the children's Chinese being lost, even though parents' lack of English did not guarantee that children would learn and use more Chinese.

It should be pointed out that differences exist in the level of English, and the level of education generally, amongst the adult population between the Mandarin speaking and the Cantonese speaking Chinese communities in the UK. The vast majority of the Mandarin speaking adults are academics and professionals from mainland China. They tend to have higher degrees and speak fluent English. There does seem to be more English in use in the Mandarin schools than in the Cantonese schools. Most of the teachers in the Cantonese schools are parents. Many of them speak good English, but they have learned their English informally rather than formally. However, the most important difference seems to us to be the fact that the mainland Chinese Mandarin speakers' bi/multilinguality has always been a mark of achievement and something to be celebrated, whereas the Hong Kong immigrant Cantonese speakers' bi/multilinguality has been neglected and somehow become associated with social disadvantage. There are complex social, historical reasons for this contrast, but it is a fact that has huge implications for the multilingual practices amongst the Chinese communities in the UK.

Conclusion

Complementary schools are an important sociocultural as well as educational institution in the UK. They present a real challenge to society, to the educational system as a whole, and to themselves, especially with regard to teaching and learning practices. Yet, they remain understudied by sociolinguists and education researchers. This chapter highlights some of the tensions between ideologies and practices in the CHL schools in the UK. A wide range of multilingual practices are in evidence in the CHL schools. We are only able to touch upon some of them.

There is still widespread perception that code-switching leads to confusion in children, even though adult bilinguals regularly code-switch and few suggest that they are confused. The present study reveals the conflict between what the adults, particularly parents and teachers, do themselves and what they want or do not want their children to do. Despite decades of scientific research on code-switching, showing its grammatical well formed-ness and sophistication, it seems that most people are still wary of its effect on children.

The use of code-switching in complementary schools and classes is a real dilemma for teachers. A truly bilingual classroom should encourage rather than discourage code-switching. Code-switching can be used effectively as a pedagogical tool in bilingual classrooms. But the principal objective of complementary education is to teach and maintain the minority community language, not English. While maintaining a bilingual environment of the Chinese children in complementary schools, the teachers' use of code-switching as we have seen in this chapter has the effect of giving English more pedagogical as well as social importance, and indirectly helping to maintain the English dominance and enhance English as a language of authority and knowledge.

CHL schools, like most other heritage language schools, have been developed in specific, complex sociohistorical contexts. There are significant internal differences and hierarchies between the languages and speaker groups within the schools and these differences and hierarchies are reflected in the organisation and operation of the CHL schools. Much more attention is needed to understand the root of these differences and hierarchies and how they might impact on the future of the Chinese communities generally and on the CHL schools in particular.

Acknowledgments

We gratefully acknowledge the support of the Economic and Social Research Council of Great Britain for its support for the project "Investigating Multilingualism in Complementary Schools in Four Communities" (ESRC, RES–000–23–1180, team members: Angela Creese, Taskin Baraç, Arvind Bhatt, Adrian Blackledge, Shahela Hamid, Vally Lytra, Peter Martin, and Dilek Yağcıoğlu-Ali) from which this paper draws some of its examples. We wish to thank all the pupils, teachers and parents at the Chinese schools in Newcastle and Manchester for their contribution to the project.

References

Auer, P. (Ed.). (1998). *Code-switching in conversation*. London: Routledge.

Baetens Beadrdsmore, H. (2003). Who's afraid of bilingualism? In J. Dewaele, A. Housen, & W. Li (Eds.), *Bilingualism: Beyond basic principles* (pp. 10–27). Clevedon, England: Multilingual Matters.

Carrington, B., & Short, G. (1989). *Race and the primary school*. Windsor, England: NFER-NELSON.

Chevannes, F., & Reeves, M. (1987). The Black voluntary school movement. In B. Troyna (Ed.) *Racial Inequality in Education* (pp. 147–169). London: Tavistock.

Gumperz, J. (Ed.). (1982). *Language and social identity*. Cambridge, England: Cambridge University Press.

Hansegård, N. E. (1975). *Tvåspråkieghet eller halvspråkighet?* [Bilingualism or Semilingualism?]. *Invandrare och Minoriteter 3*, 7–13.

Heller, M. (Ed.). (1988). *Code-switching: Anthropological and sociolinguistic perspectives*. Berlin: Mouton de Gruyter.

Li, W. (1994). *Three generations two languages one family: Language choice and language shift in the Chinese community in Britain*. Clevedon, England: Multilingual Matters.

Li, W. (1997). Who maintains/relinquishes which language how and why? A response to Michael Clyne. *Current Issues in Language & Society, 4*(2), 148–152.

Li, W. (2006). Complementary schools: Past, present and future. *Language and Education, 20*(1), 76–83.

Martin-Jones, M. (1995). Code-switching in the classroom: Two decades of research. In L. Milroy & P. Muysken (Eds.), *One speaker, two languages: Cross-disciplinary perspectives on code-switching* (pp. 90–111). Cambridge, England: Cambridge University Press.

Pavlenko, A., & Blackledge, A. (Eds.). (2001). Negotiations of identity in multilingual contexts. Special issue of *International Journal of Bilingualism, 9*(3), 234–369.

15

NFLRC
monographs

Placements and Re-Positionings: Tensions Around CHL Learning in a University Mandarin Program

Ann M. Kelleher
University of California, Davis

This chapter presents findings from a case study concerning the pedagogic policies around the teaching of Mandarin at California Northern University (a pseudonym). Contrary to expectation, Chinese as a Heritage Language (CHL) learners were found to comprise a majority of the students in two sample classes, one each from the two tracks labeled "bilingual" and "regular." The study calls attention to the fact that CHL learners resist the simple categorization that is imposed by institutional structures and enacted through the placement process. Because current institutional policies neither meet the students' language needs nor are in accord with their evolving sense of ethnic identity, some CHL students re-place and re-position themselves within the program, seeking to resolve tensions they face as they are caught at the intersection of institutional values, program structure and their own linguistic and cultural resources.

This chapter considers the role of student agency in the placement of heritage language learners within a university dual-track Mandarin program. The site of the study is California Northern University (a pseudonym), a research university that enrolls upwards of 30,000 students.[1] The paper focuses on the tensions and conflicts that arise for Chinese as a Heritage Language (CHL) students who are enrolled in classes at the low-intermediate level, where pedagogic policy divides students into two tracks. The "bilingual" track is described as a set of accelerated courses for students who can speak Mandarin or another dialect of Chinese but cannot read or write Chinese characters; no student profile is explicitly stated for the "regular" track, implying that the classes are for students without such background. While this division appears straightforward on the surface, the categorization of students along these lines is anything but neat or simple. Two categories cannot account for the heterogeneous backgrounds of the CHL learners enrolling in the program. This study examines what happens when students' language abilities and cultural identities, both self-perceived and as evaluated by placement procedures, do not mesh well with the categories established by the institution. The study reveals that CHL students may resist department-determined placement, and, by re-

---

[1]   During the 2004–2005 academic year, when the study began, approximately 17% of the undergraduate population self-identified as Chinese-American, and Chinese-American students made up the majority of those enrolled in Mandarin classes.

Kelleher, A. M. (2008). Placements and re-positionings: Tensions around CHL learning in a university Mandarin program. In A. W. He, & Y. Xiao (Eds.), *Chinese as a heritage language: Fostering rooted world citizenry* (pp. 239–258). Honolulu: University of Hawai'i, National Foreign Language Resource Center.

positioning themselves, they have the power to constitute classrooms in ways unintended by institutional policy.

This case study adopts a sociocultural perspective on language, foregrounding those aspects of language development that are part and parcel of social practice (Norton, 2000; Schieffelin & Ochs, 1986), a perspective on language that is particularly salient for CHL learners who have developed language skills at home and in communities of Chinese speakers. Ethnographic methods are employed to examine the mutual influence institutional contexts and individuals have on each other in terms of opportunities for language development (Bourdieu, 1991; Norton, 2000). Hammersley and Atkinson (1983) characterize ethnographic research methodology as a useful approach to the initial study of complicated social phenomena; considering the relatively recent emergence of heritage language learning as a field of study in its own right, ethnography seems an apt approach. It is also a methodology that asks researchers to take into account their own positionality, considering how their personal perspectives are situated vis-à-vis their research. This type of self-reflection was particularly important for the analyses undertaken in this study.[2]

A critical linguistics perspective is brought to bear in framing the analysis, considering how social and historical conditions intersect with language policy (at the local level of a university Mandarin program), differentially constraining or enabling language development for groups of learners (Bloomaert, Collins, & Slembrouck, 2005; Tollefson, 2002). Underlying this analysis is a concern for educational equity that seeks to understand how unexpressed ideologies of the educational institution play out in ways that promote or hinder learning (Brice-Heath, 1986; Gee, 1996). Language program structures, placement, and labels have powerful effects on learners (Elder, 2000; Ramanathan, 2005; Wiley, 2001) and yet research has not yet been undertaken to consider the sociocultural consequences of the tracking and the labeling of CHL students through particular placement processes. This case study begins to fill this gap by providing a detailed view of placement process outcomes from learners' perspectives within a Mandarin program that enrolls a large and heterogeneous group of CHL students. As will be evident, the fluid identities and needs of these students defy the easy slotting presupposed by such policies.

Relevant background for this study

The definition of heritage language learner (HLL) most commonly used for university-level studies comes from Valdés (2001):

> Foreign language educators use the term to refer to a language student who is raised in a home where a non-English language is spoken, speaks or at least understands the language, and who is to some degree bilingual in that language and English. (p. 38)

The utility of this definition is that it provides a conceptual bridge between cultural connection to a language and linguistic competence (broadly defined). The definition acknowledges there are cognitive and affective ends to a metaphorical language development

---

[2]   As a long-term learner of Mandarin, I have spent a large amount of time in Chinese classrooms of different types, but my personal experience is as a foreign language learner. My understanding and the analysis presented here are permeated by the insights CHL learners across many different levels of the program at CNU kindly shared with me, both through the more formal interviews I conducted for this study and in the many informal conversations I have had with Chinese-American students (past and present) who have enrolled in Chinese classes at the university. Their perspectives radically changed my view of the program and deepened my understanding of how complex the identity "Chinese language learner" can be for Chinese-American students.

spectrum. While aspects of this definition, including the focus on proficiency or language development in the home, have been debated in the literature (Beaudrie & Ducar, 2005; Carreira, 2005), this characterization of "heritage language learner" will be used as the starting point for analysis in this study.

Heritage language learners in the university: Language and identity

The specific linguistic advantages that heritage language learners may have over their foreign language learner peers have been discussed in the literature (e.g., Carreira, 2005; Hornberger & Wang, in press; Kagan, 2005; Kondo-Brown, 2003). Yet it is also recognized that HLLs' advantages do not necessarily make them better prepared for typical college language programs, even those with separate tracks at the lower levels for HLLs (Kondo-Brown, 2003). Traditionally, foreign language courses assume a particular kind of language development that differs from the language development experiences of HLLs (Kono & McGinnis, 2001). A widespread response to HLL enrollments has been the use of accelerated, dual-track programs, where HLL students are expected to progress through introductory levels quickly, joining foreign language learners at more advanced levels. The prevalence and problematic nature of this strategy is discussed by Kondo-Brown. In particular, difficulties arise when HLLs are separated but materials and methods are not changed in ways that account for their particular strengths or needs.

The differences between heritage language learners and foreign language learners are not limited to the linguistic level. Compared to their foreign language learner peers, HLLs participate in a wider array of social contexts wherein their language abilities are judged, and a theoretical conception of motivation that relates the individual to changing social contexts is a useful tool in the study of heritage language development. A core theoretical construct that can be brought to bear in examining the differences between heritage and foreign language learners at the level of identity is Norton's (2000) notion of *investment*, which redefines the concept of *motivation* as put forth by Gardner and Lambert (1972). Norton (2000) describes investment in the following way:

> Investment…signals the socially and historically constructed relationship of learners to the target language, and their often ambivalent desire to learn and practice it…The notion presupposes that when language learners speak, they are not only exchanging information with target language speakers, but they are constantly organizing and reorganizing a sense of who they are and how they relate to the social world. (pp. 10–11)

Informed by post-structural theory, investment takes the relationship between a language learner and the language of study to be complex and changing—and importantly, as being integral to a dynamic and on-going process of identity formation—rather than Gardner and Lambert's more fixed notions[3] of *instrumental* and *integrative* motivation, constructs commonly used in SLA research (Norton, 2000). And as Dörnyei (2001) points out, Norton's reconceptualization moves discussions of motivation beyond a pervasive overemphasis on the psychology of individual difference, opening a path to relate the personal to the social context.

Bringing in context as a factor is crucial for understanding the complexity of the situation for CHL learners at the university. As Harklau (1994) shows by examining the contrasting experiences of a group of immigrant high school students in their ESL and mainstream classrooms, the fact that such language learners are boundary crossers opens them to a range of

---

[3]   Gardner and Tremblay (1994) take issue with characterizations of the model as "limited" or "limiting."

outside judgments based on language ability, differing from context to context. For CHL learners as for the ESL students in Harklau's study, what is valued in one context may be a liability in another.

In the case of CHL learners, the very semiotic resources that are extremely valuable for CHL students and their families when in the home are evaluated and labeled "shortcomings" when the students enter a university-level language classroom. A summary of the commonly observed sociolinguistic issues HLLs face is given by Wang and Green (2001). Unlike foreign language learners, they say, HLLs' abilities are characterized by use of "non-standard" varieties, a limited range of registers in their oral production, imbalance between receptive and productive abilities, and limited literacy. On the positive side, identifying and promoting awareness of these characteristic tendencies may help "legitimate" the presence of HLL students in university language classrooms where their presence has been taken to be problematic or even illegitimate (see Peyton, Ranard, & McGinnis, 2001). This is important for *Chinese* HL students whose "visible" ethnicity makes them particularly susceptible to criticism, borne of ignorance, for studying a language they are presumed to already "know." But on the negative side, there is a danger of characterizing a group of students by what they lack, and thereby failing to recognize and build upon their unique strengths.

HLL: Labels and placements

The difficulty of defining and identifying HLLs for pedagogic purposes has been widely discussed (Beaudrie & Ducar, 2005; Carreira, 2005; Draper & Hicks, 2000; Hornberger & Wang, 2008; Kagan, 2005; Valdés, 2001). In terms of the tracking and placement of CHL learners more specifically, McGinnis (1996), shows how the University of Maryland Chinese program initially adapted to increasing CHL student enrollment through a three-step process. First, a locally-developed placement test was administered to students; heritage and non-heritage students' abilities at the various levels of the program were compared. Second, three distinct types of learners, labeled "novice," "semi-native," and "native" were identified. McGinnis reports that "native" students were directed to enroll in higher-level courses (Classical Chinese or literature courses, sometimes taught in Chinese), "semi-native" students (specifically, those with spoken ability in a non-Mandarin variety of Chinese and very low or no literacy skills) were accommodated by the introduction of an "accelerated track" class, and "novice" students continued to participate in the existing program. Findings indicate that adopting the new placement testing procedures and adding the accelerated track class resulted in greater homogeneity within classes. However, McGinnis makes the point that the university also had other CHL learners with distinct profiles not accommodated by the revised program, and that further monitoring and curriculum development should be undertaken as institutional resources would allow.

In a more recent study, Carreira (2005) directly addresses HLLs' linguistic and cultural backgrounds relative to placement in tertiary-level Spanish programs. She delineates the heterogeneity of students with home language background typically enrolling in Spanish programs and shows that there are HLLs whose level of language development places them in a range not easily accommodated by a two-track system (in this case, typically a Spanish for Native Speakers track versus a foreign language track). These findings mirror those of McGinnis (1996), noted above, in that both studies emphasize the difference between three tiers of learners: second (or foreign) language learners, heritage learners, and first language learners. Carreira makes the point that separate courses should be developed for Spanish HLLs who cannot enroll in the SNS courses, a point also made by Beaudrie and Ducar (2005). If that is not possible, she argues, "foreign" language classes should be adapted to address the identity needs of such learners and to capitalize on their particular linguistic strengths.

The present study takes up these points raised by Carreira (2005) and McGinnis (1996). Given the Mandarin program at CNU with high, heterogeneous CHL student enrollments, placement procedures in transition, and a dual-track curriculum of long-standing, I examine how CHL students are distributed across the "bilingual" and "regular" tracks. Because the findings are not predicted by CNU's stated policy, I examine patterns based on the CHL students' linguistic and cultural backgrounds to explain the actual distribution. Finally, I present some views of two focal students to further clarify how the realities on the ground emerged within this context, drawing on Norton's notion of investment.

Setting and participants

The Chinese program

At the time of the study, the "bilingual" and "regular" tracks at CNU shared the same basic curriculum, based on the *Integrated Chinese* series textbooks (Liu, Yao, Shi, & Bi, 1997), designed as a "four skills" curriculum for foreign language learners. The two tracks merged after one year of study for the "bilingual" track and two years for the "regular" track. After that point, there was no separation between CHL students and foreign language learners.[4] During Winter Quarter, 2005, when data collection began, the Chinese program was structured as shown in Table 1.

Table 1.   Chinese program structure at California Northern University, 2004–2005

	- - - - - - - - "regular" track- - - - - - - -			- - - - - - - - "bilingual" track- - - - - - - -		
	fall	winter	spring	fall	winter	spring
first year	1R	2R (6 sections)	3R	1B	**2B** (4 sections)	3B
second year	4R	**5R** (2 sections)	6R	(students continue in Chinese 101)		

	- no tracking -		
	fall	**winter**	**spring**
third year	101	102 (3 sections)	103
fourth year	115	115 (1 section)	115

Class abbreviations are shown (modified for anonymity but reflect program structure), for example, 1R is first quarter of the "regular" track and 1B is first quarter of the "bilingual" track. The focal courses, 5R and 2B, are shown in bold. The number of sections offered during Winter Quarter, 2005 are shown in parentheses. The designations "second," "third," and "fourth" year refer to the pacing of the curriculum for students in the "regular" track. The accelerated, bilingual track is designed to compress two years of study into one so that after the first year, the students in the "bilingual" track move into a traditional "third year" level. The "Fourth Year" class is a repeatable, 4-unit class that focuses on literacy development using texts such as news articles and literature.

---

4   The situation beyond the early levels is outside the scope of this study, but it should be noted that, while tracking ceases, this does not mean in practice that the higher level classes are geared more toward foreign language learners, as discussed by Kondo-Brown (2003). At CNU, the students who enroll in higher levels (either by continuation from earlier levels or through direct placement) most commonly are CHL learners with more advanced ability in Mandarin developed to a great extent before reaching the university. My research indicates that it is very difficult for a student with little background to successfully work her way up through the program.

The focal classes, one section each of Chinese 2B and 5R, were described by the program as follows:

2B Accelerated Written Chinese (bilingual track). Lecture—5 hours. Prerequisite: course 1B. Continuation of course 1B. Designed to accelerate the progress of students who already know spoken Mandarin or a dialect but cannot read or write Chinese characters.

5R Intermediate Chinese (regular track). Lecture/discussion—5 hours. Prerequisite: course 4R or the equivalent. Intermediate-level training in spoken and written Chinese in cultural contexts, based on language skills developed in course 4R.

Placement procedures

The department required students with existing ability in Chinese, from home exposure, classroom study or a combination thereof, to go through a placement process when first enrolling in Mandarin classes. During the 2003–2004 academic year (and for many years prior), the department used an oral interview, including conversation, reading from the *Integrated Chinese* textbook series, and questions about exposure to Chinese or prior study as the basis for placement. In addition, students would sometimes be asked to provide a writing sample. At the start of academic year 2004–2005, the placement procedures changed to include a written placement test and a language background survey, with an oral interview used as a supplement in some cases.[5]

Data collection

The following table (Table 2) summarizes the data collected for this study, including a brief description of the data types and the corresponding collection methods.

Table 2.   Types of data collected and analyzed

source	description	method
classes	**Chinese 2B** Accelerated Written Chinese, 1 section, 20 students **Chinese 5R** Intermediate Chinese, 1 section, 21 students *Classes were selected for comparability. 2B was a few chapters behind 5R, but both classes were preparing students to move into Chinese 101 after one additional quarter of study.*	*class surveys* Demographic and language background information was collected using a revised and expanded version of the department's placement survey[6] (see survey instrument, Appendix A). *observations* Each class was observed five times and daily field notes were written.
focal students	**2B "Alan"** Male, freshman, Chinese-American, parents from Taiwan, speaks Mandarin with his parents, 8 years of Chinese school (Mandarin)	*interview* A 2.5 hour interview was conducted with Alan and there was additional follow-up by email.

---

5   While the department assigned each student to a particular level, there was no way to "force" students to enroll in the class to which they were assigned. Indeed, some students would enroll in or move to a class other than the one assigned.

6   There is evidence that students' responses were more candid than they would be on a survey used for placement purposes. One of the most interesting responses was from a student in the "bilingual" track who, in response to the question, "What are some of the major reasons you decided to study Mandarin at CNU?" wrote simply, "G.P.A. Booster." And in response to the prompt "Things I like about my Chinese classes:" wrote, "Chill, hella grls that are down to kick it wit me [sic]." He was the only student to say outright that he took Chinese to improve his grade point average.

	5R "Kelly" Female, junior, Chinese-American, parents from mainland China speak Cantonese and Mandarin, speaks Cantonese with her parents, 8 years of Chinese school (Cantonese) *Focal students were selected for demographic and language background typicality within the class.*	*interview* A 1.25 hour interview was conducted with Kelly.[7] In recorded and transcribed interviews, each student was asked to expand on their language background and reasons for taking Mandarin in college.
teachers	**2B instructor** Female, from Taiwan, first year teaching at CNU **5R instructor** Female, from Taiwan, third year teaching at CNU *Each instructor had experience teaching both the "regular" and "bilingual" classes.*	*interviews* Informal interviews were conducted with the instructors after each observation session, and a one-hour interview with the 5R instructor was also recorded and transcribed.
program director	Male, from mainland China, first tenure-track faculty member to hold this position, second year at CNU, was in the process of evaluating the program to make major structural changes	*on-going communication* Communication was maintained through conversations and email. Program director reviewed and provided feedback at multiple stages.
texts	Class textbooks and materials, an institutional research report, newsletters of a language teaching consortium affiliated with CNU, and catalog descriptions of the Chinese program	*critical discourse analysis and systemic functional linguistics* (SFL)-based analysis (Martin & Rose, 2003)

Data analysis

The range of data noted above was collected and analyzed based on an ethnographic methodological approach as outlined by Hammersley and Atkinson (1983), and drawing on the works of Glaser and Strauss (1967), Carspecken (1996), and Watson-Gegeo (1988, 1992). I employed an iterative process, along the lines of the constant comparative method of Glaser and Strauss, and further elaborated in Strauss (1987), generally moving from open coding to thematic coding, to identify emerging patterns in the data. I incorporated in the analysis perspectives gained through interviews, analysis of documents, and survey responses, and included both support and counter-evidence for my emerging analyses (Hammersley & Atkinson, 1983). Finally, I selected organizing themes to report findings, focusing on higher-level categories that help explain the significant interactions going on in the context, with a particular focus on how the local setting (e.g., the individual in the classroom) relates to increasingly larger contexts (e.g., the university as academic institution).

---

[7]   The students appeared to be very relaxed and candid in these interviews. An example of this is a remark Alan made related to his desire to gain high-level ability in Chinese. He said, "I don't mean to sound like a dick...excuse me... but if Caucasians can do it why can't I do it?" He was referring to an experience he had while on an internship with a magazine in Beijing. Among the permanent staff were Caucasian Americans in their 30s or 40s who had begun studying Chinese as a foreign language in college. Alan's point was that, with his head start (his spoken Mandarin is *very* good), he should be competitive for positions such as theirs when he starts working.

Findings

Class comparison: Student ethnicity, first language, and dominant language

Demographic comparison of the two classes focused on ethnicity, home language background, and dominant language at the time of the survey (see Appendix B for detailed demographic information, Tables 5–7). A majority of the students in both classes self-identified as Chinese or Chinese-American (90% of the "bilingual" class; 62% of the "regular" class). The remaining students self-identified as being Asian-American, a specific Asian ethnicity (including Vietnamese, Japanese, Cambodian, and Filipino) or of mixed ethnic heritage, including half Japanese/half Chinese and half Asian/half Caucasian. There were no students without Asian heritage of some sort enrolled in either of the two classes.

Findings for "first language" revealed that a nearly-identical proportion of students in the two classes identified a variety of Chinese as their first language (55% Mandarin for the "bilingual" class and 54% Cantonese or a related dialect for the "regular" class). More students in the "regular" class (one-third), identified English alone as their L1 than did students in the "bilingual" class (one-quarter). Only one student in each class identified simultaneous development in English and another language (Mandarin and English for the "bilingual" class student; Cambodian and English for the "regular" class student); also, two students in the "regular" class identified Vietnamese as their L1. Finally, results for survey prompt "dominant language now" revealed (perhaps paradoxically) that a higher percentage of students in the "bilingual" class considered themselves to be English-dominant (95% of the "bilingual" class; 76% of the "regular" class). With the exception of one "regular" class student who said he was now dominant in Cantonese, those students who did not identify as being English-dominant reported being equally dominant in English and another language (varieties of Chinese in most cases).

The discrepancy between the stated placement policy (that students with background in any variety of Chinese be placed into the "bilingual" track) and actual class composition is apparent in these findings. A large number of students who identify Cantonese as their first language were enrolled in the "regular" track class. Further, at the time of the survey, more students in the "regular" class, Chinese 5R, identified themselves as being strongly bilingual in English and a form of Chinese than did those in the "bilingual" class, Chinese 2B (four students as opposed to one, as shown in Appendix B). It is also interesting to note that in the "regular" class, a majority of students who were not ethnically Chinese were bilingual to some degree in other Asian languages.

CHL learner comparison by class: Abilities in Mandarin and Cantonese

At this point in the analysis, an intentional separation is drawn between the theoretical constructs *heritage language learner* and *foreign language learner* for purposes of analysis. Detailed analysis will now be restricted to students who meet Valdés' definition of *heritage language learner*. This includes all 20 students in the "bilingual" class but only 14 of the 21 students in the "regular" class. Seven students in 5R can be classified as non-CHL learners (or foreign language learners), having had no regular exposure to any variety of Chinese in the home. However, many of these students are closely connected to Chinese culture. Of these seven students, four have a cultural connection to the language (that is, they identified themselves as having Chinese family members and said that they were interested in studying the language because of this connection) and could be considered heritage language learners by some definitions.[8]

The information presented in Table 3 summarizes students' spoken abilities in Mandarin and Cantonese, the two main varieties of Chinese mentioned in survey responses. Ratings are based on an analysis of students' survey responses regarding their self-reported Chinese ability, language use with family members, and prior study.

Table 3. **Mandarin and Cantonese abilities of CHL students in Chinese 5R and Chinese 2B upon entry into the CNU program**

		Chinese 5R, "regular" (Kelly's class)				Chinese 2B, "bilingual" (Alan's class)			
	3	4	2	2	0	1	1	2	0
spoken Cantonese ability	2	0	2	0	0	0	0	0	3
	1	3	0	0	0	0	1	1	3
	0	0	0	1	0	0	2	0	6
		0	1	2	3	0	1	2	3
		spoken Mandarin ability				spoken Mandarin ability			

Ability in Mandarin and Cantonese were rated separately for each student (in one case a student in 2B was rated for Mandarin and Taiwanese): 0, no stated ability; 1, some ability, mostly receptive; 2, productive ability, limited or infrequent use; 3, conversational or fluent. The numbers that appear in the boxes correspond to the number of students in the class who fit that profile; that is, in the Chinese 5R class there are four students who rated 0 for spoken Mandarin ability and 3 for spoken Cantonese ability (see top, left corner of table). Kelly is one of the two students in the "regular" class rated 2 on spoken Cantonese ability and 1 on spoken Mandarin. Alan is one of the six students in the "bilingual" class rated 0 for spoken Cantonese and 3 for spoken Mandarin."

On the left side, the shaded area of the table, weighted toward Cantonese proficiency, captures 92.9% of the CHL students in Chinese 5R. Shading the comparable area on the right, with an analogous weighting toward Mandarin proficiency, captures 75% of the students in the Chinese 2B class. The program does not state that separation between the tracks is based on the Chinese variety spoken in the home, but separation along dialect lines is apparent. To a noticeable degree, Mandarin-speaking students are found in the "bilingual" class and speakers of other varieties in the "regular" class.

The students in the Chinese 2B class all had some pre-existing ability in Mandarin, with one exception—a student whose ability before taking the class was in Cantonese only. However, fully two-thirds (14 out of 21 students) in the Chinese 5R class *also* had pre-existing abilities in some variety of Chinese before enrolling in classes at CNU. Seven of the students in the "regular" class may be as proficient in Mandarin as the lower third of the "bilingual" class.

Reading/writing ability

The other factor taken into consideration in the departments' placement policy is reading/writing ability, and the "bilingual" track description states that the classes are for

---

[8]   This is an important point that Hornberger and Wang (in press) raise, saying that learner agency to identify as a heritage language learner should be one portion of the definition of the term. Also, Carreira (2005) and Beaudrie and Ducar (2005) move to include such students as HLL by definition.

students with spoken ability in any dialect of Chinese who need to develop reading and writing skills. Table 4 compares the reading/writing abilities of the CHL students in the two classes.

Table 4.   Chinese 5R and Chinese 2B self-rated reading/writing ability upon entry into the CNU program

		Chinese 5R, "regular"		Chinese 2B, "bilingual"	
reading/	3	14.3%	(2)	15.0%	(3)
writing	2	50.0%	(7)	70.0%	(14)
ability	1	35.7%	(5)	15.0%	(3)

Each student was given a composite rating on a three-point scale based on survey responses to self-rating of reading/writing ability, prior study and context of study: *1*, none/minimal ability; *2*, prior study, mostly in U.S. community schools; *3*, good, including some study in a Chinese L1 context.

Results of this analysis indicate that a small but comparable percentage (approximately 15%) of CHL students with more advanced reading/writing ability (those rated a "3") were enrolled in the two classes. A difference appears between the two tracks at the middle and lowest levels. A total of 70% of the bilingual class was rated at the middle level compared to 50% of the regular class. The regular class had 20% more students rating a *1* in their reading/writing ability (35.7%) than did the bilingual class (15%).

Presented this way, the survey results give an overview of the kinds of CHL learners enrolled in each class. It appears that CHL distribution across the classes comes down primarily along dialect lines. At the low-intermediate level of the dual-track program, Cantonese-background students are primarily found in the regular classes and Mandarin-background students in the bilingual classes.

Placements and student voices

Turning now to the focal students, their comments help explain how this pattern emerged. The data presented here focus on Alan and Kelly's reasons for studying Mandarin at CNU and how they found potential in the program to meet their needs. Their comments show that they each needed to re-position themselves within the structure of the program, either actually or conceptually, to find ways to align their investment in Chinese with the language development possibilities offered by CNU's particular curriculum. Ultimately, the dialect boundary between the two tracks seems to be closely related to the students' re-positionings.

Alan: The desire to "know" Chinese
In some ways, Alan typifies a major portion of the students in the 2B class, coming into the program with strong conversational Mandarin skills, years of study in Chinese community school, but little ability to read or write in Chinese. In his classes at CNU, he characterized much of what he was studying as "re-learning" and "re-memorizing" characters. He expressed a high degree of confidence in his Mandarin speaking and listening skills, saying he could "even" understand speakers with a Beijing accent when he was in that city, but said of his reading ability, "…now in 'bilingual' I'm like I should know this word….I know I should know this from before [Chinese school when he was younger] but I need to re-learn it because I didn't take it seriously" (interview, 4/27/05). He expressed regret for not studying more, but as is true for many Chinese-American children, he found he lost interest in Chinese school as academic and extra-curricular activities associated with his mainstream school grew.

Alan expressed clearly a cross-situational tension about what it means to "know" Chinese saying, "…you know like most Asian parents will say, 'It's a shame that you didn't learn Chinese because you speak it so well'" (interview, 4/17/05). The clear implication is that speaking a language does not entail "knowing" the language. Alan has internalized this view to the point that he made this statement with no sense of irony. For him, his reasons for being in the classroom are clear. He doesn't know Chinese, meaning he can't read and write. He wants his Chinese to be as good as his English, and plans to use his bilingual ability to get a good job in China, and that means he needs to be literate.

He also expressed some of his beliefs about the ways it is necessary to progress to become literate; these are tied to program structure, on the one hand, where the class is following the "four skills" approach of the *Integrated Chinese* textbook, and to explicit knowledge of language on the other hand. He said, "[I] sometimes question why we're learning these stories, but [we] need to learn that before going on to upper division. [We're] learning important grammar not just wasting time on how to shop for blue jeans and a t-shirt."

Kelly: *There's no place for us (Cantonese speakers)*
Unlike Alan, Kelly, was not primarily focused on literacy development. Rather, she expressed a desire to improve her Chinese as a way of maintaining and improving connections with her family. She went to a Cantonese Saturday school for 8 years, beginning in pre-school, but lost interest as she grew older. She said that it was difficult to maintain her Cantonese growing up in the US, and that an increasing communication gap with her grandfather, and even her parents, was what prompted her to take Mandarin. She said, "…it's hard—I don't want to be one of those people who can't understand their family. I want to go back and visit and be OK" (interview, 4/19/05). As a double major in economics and Chinese, she saw that the language would be useful in the future with her career, but repeatedly stressed that it was her family connections that were her main motivation for studying the language. She was even trying to work on her Cantonese through her study of Mandarin, saying, "If I learn Mandarin, it's kind of like learning Cantonese too."

Kelly said that she was initially placed into the "bilingual" class, but the pace of the "regular" class gave her a much better opportunity to actually learn to *speak* Mandarin, something she felt she would not be able to do in the 2B course. She said,

> For [Chinese 1B] I actually tried to take that class, and I understood everything that the teacher was saying, but when he asked me to speak, I couldn't say anything… and they wouldn't spend time on the part I don't know [spoken Mandarin]. The only way to do that is to take the lower class [the "regular" classes] because that's how I learn how to say the words. (interview, 4/19/05)

She pointed out that her enrollment in the "regular" class is coming about because of a "gap" in the program—lack of Mandarin classes specifically for Cantonese speakers;[9] but she also pointed out that there are negative repercussions for non-CHL students enrolled in 5R.

When asked about how she viewed program effectiveness in terms of what she wanted to get out of her language study, she replied,

> I've gotten used to it…it doesn't address Cantonese speakers. [The program is] ignoring us. By pushing for more Bs, [they are] punishing people who are doing really well

---

[9]   CNU had offered such a class during the 1990s and it was still listed in the school's course catalogue. That class is once again being offered as of Fall Quarter, 2006.

> ...[students without background who] don't understand Cantonese but are doing good work and working really hard. [It would be] more effective to have a Cantonese program ...not teaching Cantonese as a language ..[I] don't expect that, but [I] would like it if there was a Cantonese transition course to Mandarin. That would be most effective.

Kelly's comment reflects her recognition that her choice, and the choice of other students like her, to move to 5R put pressure on the program to make the class more difficult.

Discussion

The mismatch between heritage learners and a foreign language curriculum

Kelly and Alan were both very clear about their reasons for studying Mandarin. Both expressed a gap in their lives in terms of what they are able to do with their Chinese and said they were taking classes at CNU to improve their abilities. A positive shift in investment in the heritage language as college students is typical of many young Chinese-Americans. Tse (1998) addresses these issues, common to CHL learners, from an identity development perspective, adapting general ethnic identity development models to the experiences of Americans of Asian descent. She links the affective factors involved in a four stage model, comprising unawareness, ethnic ambivalence/evasion, ethnic emergence, and ethnic identity incorporation to attitudes toward heritage language maintenance and language development. Both Alan and Kelly expressed sentiments that indicate they were moving out of the ethnic ambivalence/evasion stage, identified by Tse (2000) as being associated with a rejection of the heritage language. As college students, a convenient way to support this renewed interest in Chinese language is to enroll in Chinese classes.

However, convenience is a very small part of what makes a good match between a learner and a language program. Kelly and Alan each articulated their unique investment in studying Mandarin, emphasizing an interest in language development as a means to deepen their connections within certain Chinese social networks. To accomplish this, they expressed different orientations toward spoken and written modalities. This finding echoes a study by McKay and Wong (1996) where the authors applied the theoretical construct of investment to an ethnographic study of English language development in four junior high students who were recent immigrants from China. They found that the students showed different levels of investment across the modalities of language and that these differences were tied to social factors in the learning context. For Kelly and Alan, difficulties arise because the types of language teaching that would best meet their needs, as two very different types of CHL learners, have not traditionally been supported by universities (Kono & McGinnis, 2001). This situation may be changing, but nascent research on heritage language development has yet to make its way into college-level Chinese programs, to any great extent, in the form of materials and methods targeted to CHL learners. And this is certainly the case at CNU. Using a textbook that is explicitly designed for foreign language learners and based on an assumption that the "four skills" should be equally emphasized presents specific problems for Alan and Kelly.

Placement tensions

Alan was a strong student in the 2B class. His spoken Mandarin ability was on par with the top one-third of the class but he could not enroll in a higher level because he lacked the necessary literacy skills. But outside the classroom, within the context of his Chinese-speaking social networks, regardless of how well Alan could speak Mandarin, his ability was often discounted (by both himself and others) because he did not learn to read and write. For Alan, his "weakness" (lack of literacy) was much more salient than his strength (spoken Mandarin), and his motivation clearly reflected this. He found the class challenging because there were so many characters to "re-learn" and "re-memorize" yet in the university Mandarin program he is a type of learner often criticized for choosing to study the language precisely because his speaking skills are so strong (Kono & McGinnis, 2001). This is a judgment paradox brought upon Alan simply by choosing to study his heritage language in the university setting.

The program structure does not allow for separating students into different classes along all of the dimensions that vary, so the "bilingual" track of the CNU program enrolls students with vastly different speaking abilities in Mandarin, from highly productive to mostly receptive. Even the strongest speakers cannot progress much faster in their literacy development because of the extreme distance between the spoken language and the orthography. This problem is severe for Chinese, more so than for heritage languages that are written with a phonetic orthography.

In a way, Alan conceptually repositioned himself as a Chinese language learner to adapt to the materials and methods of the "bilingual" class—a class that is "designed" for learners like him in only the most superficial of ways. He found the content of the textbook familiar and boring, but rationalized why the program would take this approach, finding satisfaction in "learning important grammar." Such students often have command of structures presented at the beginning levels of a foreign language textbook even though they cannot explain the "rules." More advanced structures, those that students like Alan might need to expand their formal registers, are not presented until the higher levels. Meanwhile, a fundamental principle in SLA is that explicitly learning grammatical rules is not the same as acquiring a language, something Alan as a learner would not be expected to know but that language programs should take into consideration, particularly for students with strong spoken abilities. Further, Schleppegrell (2004) through a Systemic Functional Linguistics-based analysis of context-specific ESL literacy development argues that grammar cannot be separated from meanings, communicative purposes and contexts; it cannot be taught as an operating system, and then simply applied in new contexts. This understanding of literacy development would argue for the use of more authentic teaching materials, and a curriculum that emphasizes written communicative practice and inductive learning rather than the decontextualized, rule-focused, and explicit grammar teaching used at CNU.

Resisting department placement

The Cantonese-speaking students are also caught in a bind. Many already have basic literacy skills in Chinese, and they may understand spoken Mandarin to some extent, but most cannot speak it themselves, a point Kelly made repeatedly and that was also mentioned by Alan. In the "bilingual" class, Kelly saw that she was at a distinct disadvantage compared to students like Alan. Her investment in developing her Chinese ability, to maintain connection with her relatives and secondarily to improve her reading, would not be met by taking that class. The written materials were too easy for her and she found she did not have an opportunity to improve her ability to speak Mandarin. Re-positioning herself and moving to the "regular" track made sense for Kelly in terms of her primary focus on spoken communication.

At CNU, categorization seems to be flowing just as much from the bottom-up as it is coming from the top-down through policies and placement procedures. But policies create expectations and students' repositioning, the "bottom-up" shaping of the program, may be viewed as illegitimate because it is not a part of the official policy. Cantonese speaking students are enrolling in courses not "designed for them" but that may do a better job of meeting their needs.

Returning to the CNU program description of the "bilingual" track, the policy states that the one-year, accelerated track is for those students who have spoken ability in any variety of Chinese but who cannot read/write. This neutralizes an important distinction that is revealed in the findings; Chinese language variety, or "dialect," matters a great deal. Cantonese background speakers are not HLL learners of the same type as Mandarin background speakers. Cantonese speakers, who are clearly CHL students, were enrolling in the "regular" track for good reasons, but their presence in the "regular" classes put pressure on the department to make those classes more difficult. The few foreign language learners in the 5R class were then put at a disadvantage, a situation acknowledged by both the 5R teacher and Kelly, who expressed a high degree of admiration for the non-CHL learners in the class. But in the absence of additional resources—in particular the time, latitude, and resources to change the program to better meet the needs of the students—the situation for learners in the "regular" class was frustrating for everyone involved.

Mapping out the students' abilities and considering the focal students' differential investment in Chinese language development makes it clear that the make up of the classes was much more complex than the program descriptions of the two tracks could account for. A range of heritage language learners were enrolled in both tracks, and the program as it stood at the time of the study was clearly not reflective of the stated policy on tracking and placement. The graphing of class compositions illustrates a major challenge for creating CHL programs. How can programs be designed and placement procedures enacted that will do justice to the teaching of CHL (and non-CHL) students when CHL students' language backgrounds exhibit extreme degrees of heterogeneity along at least three dimensions—listening/speaking ability, reading/writing ability, and Chinese language variety?

Conclusion

Separating students along Mandarin versus non-Mandarin home exposure lines became a de facto categorization principle at CNU, one not expressed by the department, distinguishing the CHL students in the "bilingual" track from those in the "regular" track. This division was found to be closely related to the complex social circumstances surrounding the use and development of Chinese language ability for CHL learners. University CHL programs are grappling with ways of managing CHL learner heterogeneity, but learners are not passively sitting by, waiting to be managed. This study shows that some learners resist department placement decisions and enroll in the course they find best meets their needs. Also, the initial choice to engage in Mandarin study and then the decision to continue or drop out of the program from quarter to quarter has as much impact on the makeup of classrooms, in terms of students' backgrounds, as does initial placement. This study underscores the importance of the point McGinnis (1996) makes: a program that is truly responsive to the presence of CHL learners will continually monitor outcomes and adapt to changing circumstances. The point is expanded on here by showing that a constellation of factors may come together that result in unintended, but patterned divisions between students in different classes. When this is the case and an organic division emerges, as happened at CNU along "dialect" lines, a clear opportunity exists to improve the program.

A related point raised by this case study is that the fluidity of the placement process may not be well understood or appreciated. Unfortunately the only conception of student agency widely discussed as having an effect on placement is that some HL students try to "beat" the system (that is, they are trying to get placed so they can get an "easy A"). Kelly and Alan each exerted agency to be in the class that best met their needs, not as a way to get an easy grade. In fact, they both had to settle for a "second best" solution for their language development, enrolling in classes that were not constructed to accommodate their needs. In Kelly's case this is apparent to her classmates who feel it is not "fair" to be in class with students who already "know Chinese" (as one survey respondent put it) and in Alan's case it is apparent in the mismatch between his goals and those of the curriculum. The students are caught between making reasonable choices that best support their language development and the opportunities that are available in the context. Rather than a CHL or CFL program, the CNU classes are a hybrid, constructed by the interaction of curriculum, pedagogy, teachers and students. Resisting the "unequal grooves" concretized by institutions through policies and procedures that do not serve learners interests well is a huge challenge (Ramanathan, 2006). But the first step to making positive change is recognizing the social circumstances by which inequalities emerge and are inadvertently sustained.

References

Beaudrie, S., & Ducar, C. (2005). Beginning level university heritage programs: Creating a space for all heritage language learners. *Heritage Languages Journal, 3*(1). Retrieved August 22, 2006, from http://www.international.ucla.edu/lrc/hlj

Bloomaert, J., Collins, J., & Slembrouck, S. (2005). Spaces of multilingualism. *Language & Communication, 25*, 197–216.

Bourdieu, P. (1991). *Language and symbolic power* (G. Raymond & M. Adamson, Trans.). Cambridge, MA: Harvard University Press.

Brice-Heath, S. (1986). What no bedtime story means: Narrative skills at home and school. In B. B. Schieffelin & E. Ochs (Eds.), *Language socialization across cultures* (pp. 97–127). Cambridge, England: Cambridge University Press.

Carreira, M. (2005). Seeking explanatory adequacy: A dual approach to understanding the term "heritage language learner." *Heritage Language Journal, 2*(1). Retrieved August 1, 2006, from http://www.international.ucla.edu/lrc/hlj

Carspecken, P. F. (1996). *Critical ethnography in educational research: A theoretical and practical guide.* New York: Routledge.

Draper, J. B., & Hicks, J. H. (2000). Where we've been; what we've learned. In J. B. Miller & B. L. Webb (Eds.), *Teaching heritage language learners; voices from the classroom* (pp. 15–35). Yonkers, NY: American Council on the Teaching of Foreign Languages.

Dörnyei, Z. (2001). *Teaching and researching motivation.* Essex: Pearson Education Ltd.

Elder, C. (2000). Outing the native speaker: The problem of diverse learner background in "foreign" language classrooms: An Australian case study. *Language, Culture and Curriculum, 13*(1), 86–108.

Gardner, R. C., & Lambert, W. (1972). *Attitudes and motivation in second language learning.* Rowley, MA: Newbury House.

Gardner, R. C., & Tremblay, P. F. (1994). On motivation, research agendas, and theoretical frameworks. *The Modern Language Journal, 78*(iii), 359–368.

Gee, J. P. (1996). *Social linguistics and literacies: Ideology in discourses.* Bristol, PA: Taylor & Francis Ltd.

Glaser, B., & Strauss, A. L. (1967). *The discovery of grounded theory.* Chicago, IL: Aldine.

Hammersley, M., & Atkinson, P. (1983). *Ethnography: Principles in practice*. New York: Tavistock Publications.

Harklau, L. (1994). ESL versus mainstream classes: Contrasting L2 learning environments. *TESOL Quarterly, 28*(2), 241–272.

Hornberger, N. H., & Wang, S. (2008). Who are our heritage language learners? Identity and biliteracy in HL education in the United States. In D. M. Brinton & O. Kagan (Eds.), *Heritage language acquisition: A new field emerging*. New York: Routlege/Taylor & Francis.

Kagan, O. (2005). In support of a proficiency-based definition of heritage language learners: The case of Russian. *International Journal of Bilingual Education and Bilingualism, 8*(2&3), 213–221.

Kondo-Brown, K. (2003). Heritage language instruction for post-secondary students from immigrant backgrounds. *Heritage Language Journal, 1*(1). Retrieved June 29, 2006, from http://www.international.ucla.edu/lrc/hlj

Kono, N., & McGinnis, S. (2001). Heritage languages and higher education: Challenges, issues, and needs. In J. Peyton, J. Ranard, & S. McGinnis (Eds.), *Heritage languages in America: Preserving a national resource* (pp. 197–206). McHenry, IL: The Center for Applied Linguistics and Delta Systems.

Liu, Y., Yao, T., Shi, Y., & Bi, N. (1997). *Integrated Chinese: Level 2*. Boston: Cheng & Tsui Co.

Martin, J. R., & Rose, D. (2003). *Working with discourse*. New York: Continuum.

McGinnis, S. (1996). Teaching Chinese to the Chinese: The development of an assessment and instructional model. In J. Liskin-Gasparro (Ed.), *Patterns and policies: The changing demographics of foreign language instruction* (pp. 107–121). Boston: Heinle & Heinle.

McKay, S. L., & Wong, S. C. (1996). Multiple discourses, multiple identities: Investment and agency in second-language learning among Chinese adolescent immigrant students. *Harvard Educational Review, 66*(3), 577–608.

Norton, B. (2000). *Identity and language learning: Gender, ethnicity and educational change*. Harlow, England: Pearson Education.

Ochs, E. (1986). Introduction. In B. B. Schieffelin & E. Ochs (Eds.), *Language socialization across cultures* (pp 1–16). Cambridge, England: Cambridge University Press.

Peyton, J. K., Ranard, D. A., & McGinnis, S. (Eds.). (2001). *Heritage languages in America: Preserving a national resource*. McHenry, IL: The Center for Applied Linguistics and Delta Systems.

Ramanathan, V. (2005). *The English-vernacular divide: Postcolonial language politics and practice*. Tonawanda, NY: Multilingual Matters.

Ramanathan, V. (2006). *The English-vernacular divide: Postcolonial language policies and practice*. Clevedon: Multilingual Matters

Schieffelin, B. B., & Ochs, E. (1986). Language socialization. *Annual Review of Anthropology, 15*, 163–191.

Schleppegrell, M. J. (2004). *The language of schooling: A functional linguistics perspective*. Mahwah, NJ: Lawrence Erlbaum Associates, Inc.

Strauss, A. L. (1987). *Qualitative analysis for social scientists*. Cambridge, MA: Cambridge University Press.

Tollefson, J. W. (Ed.). (2002). Introduction: Critical issues in education language policy (pp. 3–16). In *Language policies in education: Critical issues*. Mahwah, NJ: Lawrence Erlbaum Associates, Inc.

Tse, L. (1998). Ethnic identity formation and its implications for heritage language development. In S. Krashen, L. Tse, & J. McQuillan (Eds.), *Heritage language development* (pp. 15–29). Culver City, CA: Language Education Associates.

Tse, L. (2000). The effects of ethnic identity formation on bilingual maintenance and development: An analysis of Asian American narratives. *International Journal of Bilingual Education and Bilingualism, 3*(3), 185–200.

Valdés, G. (2001). Heritage language students: Profiles and possibilities. In J. Peyton, J. Ranard, & S. McGinnis (Eds.), *Heritage languages in America: Preserving a national resource* (pp. 37–80). McHenry, IL: The Center for Applied Linguistics and Delta Systems.

Wang, S., & Green, N. (2001). Heritage language students in the K–12 education system. In J. Peyton, J. Ranard, & S. McGinnis (Eds.), *Heritage languages in America: Preserving a national resource* (pp. 167–196). McHenry, IL: The Center for Applied Linguistics and Delta Systems.

Watson-Gegeo, K. A. (1988). Ethnography in ESL: Defining the essentials. *TESOL Quarterly, 22*(4), 575–592.

Watson-Gegeo, K. A. (1992). Thick explanation in the ethnographic study of child socialization and development: A longitudinal study of the problem of schooling for Kwara'ae (Solomon Islands) children. In W. A. Carsaro & P. Miller (Eds.), *New directions for child development (Vol. 58): The production and reproduction of children's worlds: Interpretive methodologies for the study of childhood socialization* (pp. 51–66). San Francisco: Jossey-Bass.

Wiley, T. G. (2001). On defining heritage languages and their speakers. In J. Peyton, J. Ranard, & S. McGinnis (Eds.), *Heritage languages in America: Preserving a national resource* (pp. 29–36). McHenry, IL: The Center for Applied Linguistics and Delta Systems.

Appendix A: Language use survey

I am a (female / male) student in my (1st / 2nd / 3rd / 4th / 5th) year at UC Davis.

At the beginning of this quarter I had (freshman / sophomore / junior / senior / graduate) status.

I am majoring in _____ minor? _____

I identify my ethnicity as _____

Languages you learned growing up

I consider my first language (dialect) to be _____

I also speak _____

My dominant language now is _____

I have limited ability in (languages/dialects): _____

Growing up, if you didn't hear or speak Chinese on a regular basis, continue on the back.

Chinese language ability

Comment on your Chinese reading/writing ability prior to study at U.C. Davis _____
_____
_____

List the Chinese dialects you speak and/or understand and your level of ability (e.g., understand my parents' Taiwanese but not my grandmother's and I don't speak it, conversational ability in Cantonese) _____
_____
_____

Home language use

For each member of your family, list the relationship of the person to you and the language(s)/dialect(s) you speak with that person (e.g., mother—mostly Mandarin and a little English; older sister—nearly all English). For Chinese, please refer to specific dialects, not just "Chinese."

person	language(s)/dialect(s)
_____	_____
_____	_____
_____	_____

Where did you grow up?

In the US—I've never lived outside this country. I grew up in (city, state)
_____

Both outside and in the US—I lived _____ from (age) _____
until I was (age) _____ and then I moved to (city, state) _____

I've lived in a number of different places (please describe) _____

_____

_____

Chinese language study prior to U.C. Davis

Did you study Chinese before attending U.C. Davis? _____

If yes, what dialect(s) did you study? _____

What kind of classes did you take (weekend Chinese school, high school class etc.)? Please describe briefly (In the US or abroad? Where? How many hours per week? What material did you study? How long did you attend? Why did you take these classes?) _____

_____

_____

Mandarin study at U.C. Davis _____

_____

_____

Things I like about my Chinese classes: _____

_____

_____

Things I don't like about my Chinese classes: _____

_____

_____

Do you use Mandarin outside the classroom?

With classmates when studying	often	sometimes	seldom	never
With classmates talking about class	often	sometimes	seldom	never
With friends who also take Chinese classes at U.C. Davis			
	often	sometimes	seldom	never
With other friends	often	sometimes	seldom	never
With family members	often	sometimes	seldom	never
In restaurants/shops	often	sometimes	seldom	never

Other places/situations where I use Mandarin (i.e., student organization, church group, traveling etc.)?

_____   often   sometimes   seldom   never

_____   often   sometimes   seldom   never

Do you actively seek out opportunities to use Mandarin outside the classroom? If so, how_____

_____

_____

Appendix B: Class demographics

Table 5.   Distribution of students in Chinese 2B ("bilingual") and Chinese 5R ("regular") by ethnicity

	Chinese 2B	Chinese 5R
Chinese & Chinese American	90.0% (18)	61.9% (13)
Asian & Asian American	5.0% (1)	4.8% (1)
half Japanese/half Chinese	5.0% (1)	0
part Asian/part Caucasian	0	9.5% (2)
Vietnamese	0	9.5% (2)
Japanese	0	4.8% (1)
Cambodian American	0	4.8% (1)
Filipino	0	4.8% (1)

The category labels are taken from students' written survey responses. The number of students who self-identify with each category is expressed as a percentage of total survey responses for each class; the total number of responses (n) is shown in parentheses.

Table 6.   Distribution of students in Chinese 2B ("bilingual") and Chinese 5R ("regular") by response to the prompt, "first language"

	Chinese 2B	Chinese 5R
Mandarin	55.0% (11)	0
Cantonese	15.0% (3)	42.9% (9)
Taishan	0	4.8% (1)
Chaozhou	0	4.8% (1)
English & Mandarin	5.0% (1)	0
Vietnamese	0	9.5% (2)
Cambodian & English	0	4.8% (1)
English	25.0% (5)	33.3% (7)

Taishan (or "Toisan") and Chaozhou are both varieties of the Yue dialect, of which Cantonese is the regional standard. Taking these three first languages together, a total of 52.4% (n=11) of the students in 5R identify a variety of Cantonese as their first language.

Table 7.   Distribution of students in Chinese 2B ("bilingual") and Chinese 5R ("regular") by response to the prompt, "dominant language now"

	Chinese 2B	Chinese 5R
English	95.0% (19)	76.2% (16)
Cantonese	0	4.8% (1)
Chinese & English	5.0% (1)	4.8% (1)
Chaozhou & English	0	4.8% (1)
Taishan & English	0	4.8% (1)
Cambodian & English	0	4.8% (1)

16

Charting the CHL Developmental Path

Yun Xiao
Bryant University, Rhode Island

Based on data presented in this volume and elsewhere, this chapter describes the characteristics of the CHL learner language, examines its associated contextual and individual factors, and sketches the CHL developmental path. Linguistically, the CHL learner language is characterized by high variability, increasing attrition, and frequent use of code-switching. Several contextual factors are found to be associated with the development of CHL learner language, such as insufficient HL input, multi-level social contact, high pressure for social acceptance, and immigrant family background (i.e., learners' birth place, age of arrival, length of English immersion, family socio-economic status, and parental views). CHL learners' identities and motivations, which are found to be highly varied, also play an important role in HL investments and maintenance. Developmentally, the CHL learner language has a head start in the learner's home language but evolves along a path different from either L1A or L2A.

This volume found a moment to emerge when a national campaign was called for to tap heritage language (HL) proficiency, and, with sound empirical findings, it takes a first step toward constructing a multi-layered understanding of the HL phenomenon, with a focus on Chinese as a heritage language. To compete at the international level, the United States realized that it lacked adequate professional-level bilinguals, and that, for cost saving, HL prior skills should be tapped because such skills "would require non-native speakers of that language hundreds of hours of instruction to acquire" (Brecht & Ingold, 1998, p. 2). Although it appears to be vital and optimal, this campaign would be pragmatically driven at best if it is not theoretically warranted and empirically tested.

In this English-speaking culture, immigrant HLs have been traditionally underrepresented in the mainstream education system, and limited opportunities have been provided for HL learners to develop their skills. Researchers have reported that immigrant HL typically deteriorates, gets eroded, or lost (Li, 2003; Pease-Alvarez, Garcia, & Espinosa, 1991; Wong Fillmore, 1991) in the mainstreaming process, where foreign language education is increasingly eliminated from the core curriculum (Shin, 2006) and HL learners experience "an abrupt shift" from the HL to the dominant language (Bougie, Wright, & Taylor, 2003, p. 349). To gain acceptance, HL learners typically drop their home languages and make English their primary language (Li, 2003, 2006a; Pease-Alvarez, et al., 1991). As a result, they arrive at the foreign language classrooms not entirely as L1 speakers or L2 speakers of their HL (Lynch, 2003).

Unlike first and second language acquisition, which have been the focus of research for decades, research on HL learning or acquisition is still in its infancy and has not yet found a place in language acquisition theories (Lynch, 2003). We lack a coherent HL theory to guide research and pedagogical practice. So far, little is known about HL processing, such as how it is eroded, lost, maintained, or advanced. To spearhead the inquiry, HL researchers face fundamental theory-building questions, such as: What are the characteristics of HL learner language? What are the HL-associated contextual and individual factors? What is the effect of home background on HL learning or acquisition? And what is the developmental path of HL acquisition?

Studies with a focus on East Asian languages have examined various issues associated with HL development and found that first language background, age of immigration/arrival, HL language use, and socio-psychological constructs are significant contributing factors (Kondo-Brown, 2006). However, data with a focus on Chinese as a heritage language (CHL) are relatively sporadic. To fill this gap, contributors to this volume evaluated existing data and gathered new evidence based on the evaluation. We observed and documented findings from various perspectives (language socialization, language acquisition, acculturation, accommodation), theoretical frameworks (socio-educational, corpus linguistics, discourse analysis), research methods (ethnographic, longitudinal, cross-sectional, etc.), subject populations (college students, school-age children, first-generation immigrants, new arrivals, U.S.-born immigrant children, their parents, teachers), and instrumental apparatus (profiling, surveys, interviews, grammaticality judgment tests). These studies advanced the understanding of HL concepts and furnished empirical data to lay the foundation for a coherent HL theory. In this chapter, I will first describe the characteristics of CHL learning, review various CHL-related contextual and individual factors, and discuss the CHL developmental path, with evidence gathered in this volume and elsewhere.

The CHL learner language

In contrast to L1 learner language, which follows a universal learning time table and achieves uniform success when the learner reaches adulthood (Bley-Vroman, 1990), the CHL learner language exhibits skewed language skills accompanied by incomplete linguistic knowledge when the learner relearns his HL in his adult life. Linguistically, the CHL learner language is characterized by a high variability (Hendryx, this volume), an increasing attrition (Jia, this volume; Jia & Bayley, this volume), and a frequent use of code-switching (LI & Wu, this volume). Through several years of classroom observations, interviews, and a survey, Hendryx found that the CHL learner language can be roughly classified into four proficiency levels, which do not fit well into the ACTFL (American Council on the Teaching of Foreign Languages) proficiency framework, including (a) having very little command of Chinese with only a few rudimentary words or phrases, (b) having a smattering of speaking and listening skills but with marginal reading and writing abilities, (c) being fluent or nearly fluent in a dialect of Chinese but having little knowledge of spoken Mandarin, and (d) having a solid command of speaking, listening, reading, and writing skills.

In addition, CHL learner language shows, over time, a tendency of attrition or decline in language skills and morphosyntactic knowledge. Through a retrospective self-rating and a grammaticality judgment task, Jia (this volume) found that the CHL learners' proficiency declined in general, with reading and writing abilities being reduced even faster than speaking skills. Using multiple tasks such story retelling, multiple cloze test, and picture description, Jia and Bayley (this volume) found that the use of Mandarin perfective aspectual marker -*le*, a crucial perfective marker at both Chinese sentence and discourse level, by 36 CHL learners declined as their length of residence in the United States increased. Moreover, CHL learner language is found, like other immigrant HL languages, marked with frequent use of code-switching in real-life communication. In their extensive ethnographic observations with both audio and video recordings, LI and Wu (this volume) found that code-switching of various kinds, including the mixing of languages in the same utterance or alternation between languages in conversation, was often used by CHL learners to create a "safe" space in communications, and many of the teachers also code-switched, in contrary to school policies and their own beliefs.

Nonetheless, CHL learner language demonstrates exclusive L1 advantages in grammatical intuition and orthographic sensitivity. Ming and Tao (this volume) found that, compared to their non-heritage counterparts, CHL learners made many fewer mistakes in the use of morphosyntactic marker *le*, as evidenced in the data collected from a large-scale discourse production task. It is likely that CHL learners have the grammatical intuition that enables them to avoid such errors. Moreover, although Chinese script is logographic and notoriously difficult, Koda, Lü, & Zhang (this volume) found that CHL children were sensitized to certain formation regularities in Chinese characters and developed them rapidly, even though their print input and experience were very limited. This supports previous findings that college CHL learners did significantly better than their non-heritage counterparts in grammaticality judgment and translation tests, an indicator that CHL learners brought prior L1 grammar knowledge to the foreign language classroom (Xiao, 2004).

Contextual factors

Several contextual factors are found to be associated with the development of the CHL learner language, such as insufficient HL input, multi-level social contact, high pressure for social acceptance, and immigrant family background.

Insufficient HL input

Like L1 learners, the CHL learners have childhood exposure to their L1 at home, but unlike L1 learners, who extend their L1 experience to formal school learning, the CHL learners' L1 experience beyond childhood exposure typically comes to a halt when they start kindergarten or grade school. Accordingly, its maintenance and advancement solely depend on the availability of informal learning, such as literacy study in weekend community HL schools or activities at home, neither of which has however been fruitful. Xiao (this volume) examined the home literacy environment of 127 CHL college students in three American universities and found that, compared to the mainstream dominant language, the CHL home literacy environment is bleak, where HL reading materials and literacy activities are, in most of the cases, inadequately constructed for its stimulation or attainment. Specifically, a large number of Chinese immigrant homes possessed zero to minimal HL reading materials, and level-appropriate HL recreational literature reading, so abundant in English and the leading foreign languages households in this country, were barely existent in their homes. By examining CHL literacy development among school-age students, Koda et al. (this volume) found that these children typically use Chinese at home, receive primary literacy instruction in English at school, and only pursue HL literacy in weekend Chinese schools, where the input available to them is heavily restricted in quantity. Dai and Zhang (this volume) also found that Chinese community schools are characterized by out-of-date traditional teaching practices, which are resented by a large number of youngsters. Such observations confirm Wang's (2004) 4-year-long extensive study of Chinese community schools, in which she found that "there was no sense of progress or achievement. Students basically stay at the same level, unable to move forward in their HL proficiency or literacy" (p. 368).

Multi-level social contact

CHL learners' multi-level social contact is another contextual variable that factors into their HL maintenance and development. Unlike Chinese as a L1, which is, in most of the cases, developed in monolingual settings, CHL learner language evolves in a multilingual setting through many different types and periods of social contact (Hendryx, this volume), and experiences enormous linguistic/dialectal diversity within "Chinese" as well as diversity within "the Chinese speaker" (Wiley, Klerk, Li, Liu, Teng, & Yang, this volume). Many CHL learners have social contact with speakers of various Chinese languages, dialects, and sub-dialects, which are not always mutually intelligible. It is not uncommon that a CHL learner does not understand his "Chinese"-speaking counterparts or classroom instructors. And a large number of fluent "Chinese" speakers come to the Chinese language classroom to learn how to speak "Chinese." Furthermore, learners' personal experience with their HL is also tremendously varied, which in turn contributes to the large disparity in CHL proficiency, as reported by Man (2006). It is noted that some CHL learners spend more time in their native country, while others leave there at a young age. Some live in a region where Chinese is spoken on a regular basis, while others have only sporadic contact. And some spend considerable time and effort in community HL schools or after-school Chinese language programs, while others do not.

High pressure for social acceptance

Data in this volume show that, under the omnipresent driving force of assimilation and acculturation in the mainstream schools, CHL learners typically perceive their home language as having lower social status and being less prestigious, while English has a higher social status and is more prestigious (Dai & Zhang, this volume). To gain social acceptance, CHL learners tend to abandon their HL and switch to English even when they speak or write to their siblings or Chinese friends, with their HL use being limited only to parents and grandparents at home (Dai & Zhang). Such findings confirm previous findings that when linguistically and socially unprepared HL children are suddenly placed in mainstream schools, they are under tremendous pressure for social acceptance and for dominant language proficiency, which results in gradual abandonment of their home language (Valdés & Figueroa, 1994; Wong Fillmore, 1991).

Immigrant family background

A number of studies in this volume indicate that, situated in an immigrant setting, CHL learner language is influenced by various immigrant-contextualized variables, such as learners' birth place, age of arrival, length of English immersion, family socio-economic status, and parental views. Jia and Bayley (this volume) found that CHL learners' birth place is a significant variable in their CHL development in that, in all three tasks in their study, students born in China outperformed students born in the US; specifically, the China-born students produced longer and more elaborate narratives and were more likely to use the morphosyntactic marker -le in both obligatory and optional contexts. The likely reason is that China-born children may have prior exposure to input in larger quantity and better quality than their U.S.-born counterparts.

For first-generation immigrants, age of arrival in the US, that is, the starting point of systematic exposure to English, is also a significant predictor of CHL proficiency and maintenance (Jia, this volume). Specifically, those who are exposed to English at a younger age and immersed in it for a longer time achieve a lower level of CHL proficiency, while those who arrive in the US at an older age and have more HL use at home, achieve a higher level of CHL proficiency. Such findings are supported by Jia and Bayley (this volume), who found that the longer the learners' U.S. residence, the poorer their CHL performance.

Contrary to the mainstream concept that the higher the family socio-economic status, the better the pupils' performance, Jia (this volume) found that the lower HL family income predicts significantly higher CHL proficiency, and learners from higher income families constitute the most vulnerable population, with reading and writing abilities being the areas most subject to attrition. One likely reason is that lower family income is more closely associated with lower educational levels and poorer English abilities of parents and grandparents; thus, the use of home language is vital and indispensable. On the other hand, higher-income families are more likely to hold mainstream professional jobs and have better English skills, where HL use tends to become marginalized. Jia and Bayley (this volume) demonstrate that, in their narrative retelling task, learners who had frequent use of Chinese at home outperformed those who did not in the production of morphosyntactic marker -*le*.

Parental views

Parents' views of the role of HL in their children's lives are found to exert significant impact on their children's CHL maintenance and advancement. Parents were found more concerned about their children's English proficiency and school work than their HL development, in that they viewed their primary responsibility as preparing their children for the mainstream skills with which to compete for desirable social and economic roles in the dominant society. Consequently, their home HL literacy environment was inadequate for HL attainment, and their children's studies in Chinese HL schools typically ended when the children entered kindergarten or grade school (Xiao, this volume). This supports previous findings (Li, 2006b) that CHL parents believe that Chinese is a hindrance to their children's English development, especially accent acquisition and grammar learning. And they immediately stop their children's Chinese learning once their children no longer need Chinese-English translation to facilitate their school work. Such parental views or beliefs obviously warrant a wake-up call, that is, societally based RLS (reversing language shift) cannot be accomplished at all if it is not accomplished at the intimate family and local community levels (Fishman, 1991, p. 4).

Individual factors

Like L1 learners, HL learners are characterized by a unique set of individual attributes such as identity and motivation.

Identity

The present data show that learners' ethnic identity plays an important role in their HL maintenance and development. To HL learners, ethnic identity is a key factor, namely, one's attitudes toward one's own ethnic group influence his interest in developing and maintaining his HL abilities (He, this volume). In his growth, the CHL learner goes through a unique process of forming and transforming his CHL identity and re-creating his own identity (He, this volume). As predicted by Tse's (2001) four-step ethnic model (i.e., unawareness, ambivalence, emergence, and formation), CHL learners typically perceive their HL cultural identities very differently and show a high degree of variability in growth. Dai and Zhang (this volume) found that while a small number of CHL learners identify with Chinese culture, the rest of them identify either with both Chinese and American cultures, or with only American culture, or, worse, with neither culture. Moreover, most of them are found to feel marginalized: "Those in America see me as Chinese, while those in China see me as an American" (Dai & Zhang, this volume). While those learners who experience ethnic ambivalence have a negative attitude towards their HL maintenance, those who have a stronger Chinese cultural identity show positive attitudes toward their HL leaning and have significantly higher self-rated CHL proficiency (Jia, this volume).

Motivation

It is anticipated that learners' high variability of ethnic identity leads to high variability of motivation in their HL maintenance. Coincidentally, studies in this volume revealed conflicting results regarding CHL learners' motivations. While one study found that the primary motivation for all these learners was integrative but not instrumental motivation (Hendryx, this volume), the other found that CHL students were more influenced by instrumental and less by integrative motivation (Lu & Li, this volume). Moreover, Kelleher (this volume) demonstrates that learners' varied motivations lead to varied investments in their HL development. For instance, some learners with a motivation to maintain family bonding invest primarily in oral communication skills and secondarily in reading abilities.

Charting the HL developmental path

By examining various contextual and individual factors associated with the CHL learner language, this volume strives to address fundamental theory-building issues, one of which is charting the HL developmental path. Our data show that CHL learners acquire repertoires of language forms associated with contextual dimensions (He, this volume) and individual factors as well. CHL learner language has a head start in the learner's home language but evolves along a path different from either L1A or L2A, as illustrated in Figure 1.

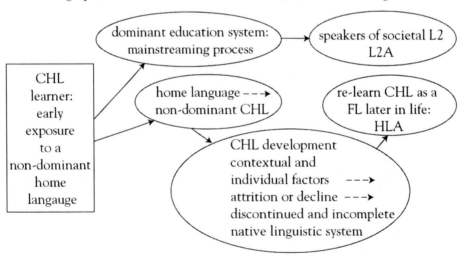

Figure 1.   The CHL developmental path

As shown in the figure, the HL learner has an early exposure to his L1, involuntarily switches to the dominant L2, goes through a mainstreaming process, becomes a speaker of the dominant L2, and comes to the language classroom to relearn his HL as a foreign language in his later life. Over the developmental time, the learner's L1 lives a short life and transforms into a HL linguistic system, marked with incomplete grammar knowledge and skewed language skills. Using this model, answers become evident to questions puzzling many HL researchers for a long time, such as: Is HL learning L1A or L2A? Is the HL speaker a L1/L2 speaker of his HL? And what is the effect of early exposure to one's HL on its subsequent learning?

The model indicates that HLA is neither L1A nor L2A, although it shares commonalities with both. As the literature reveals, L1 acquisition is about the ultimate uniform success of a native linguistic system, and L2 acquisition is about the restructuring of the learner's interlanguage system. Our data show that HL acquisition is about reconstructing a "discontinued" and incomplete native linguistic system, and that the learner's childhood exposure to his HL provides rudimentary HL linguistic abilities and native-speaker grammar intuition. Thus, the model predicts that, given the hurdles caused by the various social and linguistic constraints, learners' early exposure to his HL plays an important role in its subsequent learning and success, which sheds light on Valdés and Figueroa's supposition (1994) that HL learners will, over time, become stable bilinguals whose two languages play complimentary roles in their everyday lives (p. 14).

The model also confirms previous findings from both language acquisition and neurolinguistic perspectives that early exposure has a positive effect on its subsequent learning. Au and Romo (1997) compared first-time adult learners of college-level Korean/Spanish with re-learners of prior experience and found that childhood experience with a language—even if incomplete and/or discontinued—helped adults learn what was typically most challenging to first-time learners, such as phonology and morphosyntax. From a neurolinguistic perspective, Stowe and Sabourin (2005) showed that early exposure to one's L1 had indisputable effect on its later development in that the same brain areas, which were used for both L1 and L2 processing, were more efficiently employed in L1 than in L2.

By finding new data and confirming the previous data, this volume initiates a CHL research framework and suggests a model of HL acquisition, which paves the way for future HL research and education. The results will, on one hand, stimulate research on CHL and beyond and, on the other, provide teachers and administrators with well-grounded guidance for the advancement of HL proficiency. To illuminate language acquisition theories, future research should explore the state or shape of HL learner language after the learner involuntarily switches to the dominant L2, by asking questions such as, What is the shape of the later stage of HL? Is it dormant or lost? And what is the best way to bring it alive if it is dormant or lost?

References

Au, T. K., & Romo L. F. (1997). Does childhood language experience help adult leaners? In H. C. Chen (Ed.), *The cognitive processing of Chinese and related Asian languages* (pp. 417–441). Hong Kong: Chinese University Press.

Bley-Vroman, R. (1990). The logical problem of foreign language learning. *Linguistic Analysis, 20,* 3–49.

Bougie, E., Wright, S. C., & Taylor, D. M. (2003). Early heritage-language education and the abrupt shift to a dominant-language classroom: impact on the personal and collective esteem of Inuit children in Arctic Quebec. *International Journal of Bilingual Education and Bilingualism, 6*(5), 349–373.

Brecht, R. D., & Ingold, C. W. (1998). *Tapping a national resource: Heritage languages in the United States*. Eric Digest ED424791.

Fishman, J. A. (1991). *Reversing language shift: Theoretical and empirical foundations of assistance to threatened language*. Clevedon, England: Multilingual Matters LTD.

Kondo-Brown, K. (Ed.). (2006). *Heritage language development: Focus on East Asian immigrants*. Philadelphia: John Benjamins Publishing Company.

Li, G. (2003). Literacy, culture, and politics of schooling: Counternarratives of a Chinese Canadian family. *Anthropology & Education Quarterly, 34*(2), 182–204.

Li, G. (2006a). *Culturally contested pedagogy: Battles of literacy and schooling between mainstream teachers and Asian immigrant parents*. Albany: State University of New York Press.

Li, G. (2006b). The role of parents in heritage language maintenance and development. In K. Kondo-Brown (Ed.), *Heritage language development: Focus on East Asian immigrants* (pp. 15–32). Philadelphia: John Benjamins Publishing Company.

Lynch, A. (2003). The relationship between second and heritage language acquisition: Notes on research and theory building. *Heritage Language Journal 1*(1), 11–17.

Man, E. Y. (2006). First language use and language behavior of Chinese students in Toronto, Canada. In K. Kondo-Brown (Ed.), *Heritage language development: Focus on East Asian immigrants* (pp. 209–242). Philadelphia: John Benjamins Publishing Company.

Pease-Alvarez, L., Garcia, E. E., & Espinosa, P. (1991). Effective instruction for language-minority students: An early childhood case study. *Early Childhood Research Quarterly, 6*, 347–361.

Shin, S. J. (2006). High-stakes testing and heritage language maintenance. In K. Kondo-Brown (Ed.), *Heritage language development: Focus on East Asian immigrants* (pp. 127–144). Philadelphia: John Benjamins Publishing Company.

Stowe L. A., & Sabourin L. (2005). Imaging the processing of a second language: Effects of maturation and proficiency on the neural processes involved. *International Review of Applied Linguistics in Language Teaching, 43*(4), 329–353.

Tse, L. (2001). Heritage language literacy: A study of U.S. biliterates. *Language, Culture and Curriculum, 14*(3), 256–268.

Valdes, G., & Figueroa, R. A. (1994). *Bilingualism and testing: A special case of bias*. Norwood, NJ: Ablex Publishing Corporation.

Wang, S. (2004). Biliteracy resource eco-system of intergenerational language and culture transmission: An ethnographic study of a Chinese-American community. Unpublished doctoral dissertation, University of Pennsylvania, Philadelphia.

Wong F. L. (1991). When learning a second language means losing the first. *Early Childhood Research Quarterly, 6*, 323–346.

Xiao, Y, (2004). L2 acquisition of Chinese topic-prominent constructions. *Journal of the Chinese Language Teachers Association, 39*(3), 65–84.

About the Contributors

Editors

Agnes Weiyun He, primary editor, is an associate professor of applied linguistics and Asian studies at the State University of New York at Stony Brook. She applies linguistic anthropology, conversation analysis, and functional linguistics to the study of language development, with a focus on Chinese. She is the author of *Reconstructing Institutions: Language Use in Academic Counseling Encounters* (1998, Greenwood), co-editor (with R. Young) of *Talking and Testing: Discourse Approaches to the Assessment of Oral Proficiency* (1998, John Benjamins), as well as author of over twenty research articles. Her work has been funded by the Spencer Foundation, the National Academy of Education, and the U.S. Department of Education.

Yun Xiao, secondary editor, is an associate professor of Chinese and chair of the Modern Languages Department at Bryant University. Her research interests are second language acquisition and pedagogy, heritage language learning, and Chinese teacher education. Her recent publications include dozens of articles and book chapters. She is also the principal author of *Readings in Chinese Literature Series* (Cheng & Tsui, 2007) and co-author of book series of *Teaching Chinese as a Foreign Language* (Cheng & Tsui, in press).

Authors

Robert Bayley is a professor of linguistics at the University of California, Davis. His research interests center on language variation, minority language maintenance, and language socialization. His recent book-length publications include *Language as Cultural Practice* (2002, with S. R. Schecter), *Language Socialization in Bilingual and Multilingual Societies* (2003, Ed. with S. R. Schecter), *What's Your Sign for PIZZA? An Introduction to Variation in ASL* (2003, with C. Lucas & C. Valli), and *Sociolinguistic Variation: Theories, Methods, and Applications* (2007, Ed. with C. Lucas).

Jin-huei Enya Dai is an assistant professor in the graduate school of language and educational linguistics at Monterey Institute of International Studies, an affiliate of Middlebury College. She applies cognitive linguistics, linguistic anthropology, philosophy, and sociology to language study and heritage language acquisition. She is the author of "'Love You' Doesn't Mean 'I Love You': Just a Way to Say Goodbye. The Nature of Leave-Taking and Its Pragmatic Applications in Mandarin Chinese," to appear in *CJK Proceedings*, an online volume of NFLRC Networks (in press, University of Hawai'i).

Gerda de Klerk is a doctoral student in the college of education, Arizona State University. She has published in the areas of language policy, urban education, and education in Africa. Her research interests are in quantitative data analysis, particularly large dataset analysis to inform educational policies.

Patricia A. Duff is a Professor in the department of language and literacy education and past director of the UBC Centre for Intercultural Language Studies for which she coordinated symposia and funded projects for several years on heritage language education. Her publications include books, journal articles, and chapters in edited volumes in applied linguistics, dealing with qualitative research methods, generalizability, language socialization, second language acquisition, and task-based language teaching/learning. Her research has been funded by grants from the Social Sciences and Humanities Research Council of Canada and the Spencer Foundation/National Academy of Education.

Jason D. Hendryx holds a M.A. in Chinese language and literature and will receive a Ph.D. in curriculum and instruction from the college of education at the University of Washington, Seattle. His research interests include foreign language teaching methodologies, language play, heritage language instruction, teaching and learning metaphors, and professional development for language teachers. He is currently an instructional consultant with the Center for Instructional Development and Research (CIDR) at the University of Washington where he consults with foreign language instructors on teaching effectiveness.

Gisela Jia is an associate professor of psychology at Lehman College, The City University of New York. She received her B.A. in English language and literature, her M.A. in linguistics from Beijing University, and her Ph.D. in cognitive/developmental psychology from New York University. Her research interests are bilingual development and second language acquisition. Adopting a developmental perspective, she has studied how U.S. children (from infancy to adolescence) with Chinese as home language develop bilingual skills. She has published in peer-reviewed journals and books and has served as a consultant for state and local educational agencies regarding policies related to bilingual students.

Li Jia was an associate professor of English in China before coming to the United States in 1998 for her advanced degrees. She received her Ph.D. in culture, literacy, and language at the University of Texas, San Antonio in 2006 and is currently teaching ESL at the same university. Her research interests center on second language acquisition, TESOL, language variation, and language socialization.

Ann M. Kelleher is a Ph.D. student in linguistics at the University of California, Davis. Her research interests include the socio-political contexts of Chinese language development in the US, ideological and pedagogical perspectives on heritage language education, and second "dialect" development. Her research draws on ethnographic approaches, critical discourse analysis, and non-generative perspectives on grammar. She also works as a consultant for the Center for Applied Linguistics in Washington, DC, on the Alliance for the Advancement of Heritage Languages (www.cal.org/heritage).

Keiko Koda is a professor of second language acquisition and Japanese in the department of modern languages at Carnegie Mellon University. Her research on second language reading and biliteracy development is published widely in journals, books, and book chapters. Her recent publications include *Insights into Second Language Reading* (2005, Cambridge University Press), *Reading and Language Learning* (2007, Blackwell), and *Leaning to Read Across Languages* (2007, Lawrence Erlbaum).

Duanduan Li is an assistant professor of Chinese applied linguistics at the University of British Columbia where she directs the Chinese Language Program in the department of Asian studies and the Chinese Proficiency Test (HSK) Centre. Her research interests include sociolinguistics, pragmatics, language socialization, second language acquisition (both of Chinese and English), and heritage language teaching and learning. Her research has been published in the *Canadian Modern Language Review* and *System* as well as in edited books. She also has published three Chinese language textbooks and is currently working on another textbook, *Advanced Chinese for a Changing China*. Her current research is supported by a 3-year grant from the Social Sciences and Humanities Research Council of Canada.

Guofang Li is an associate professor of teacher education at Michigan State University. Li specializes in second and foreign language education, bilingual education, family literacy, and minority involvement. Li's major publications include four books, *"East is East, West is West?," Home Literacy, Culture, and Schooling* (2002, Peter Lang), *Culturally Contested Pedagogy: Battles of Literacy and Schooling Between Mainstream Teachers and Asian Immigrant Parents* (2006, SUNY Press, winner of 2006 Ed Fry Book Award, National Reading Conference), *"Strangers" of the Academy: Asian Women Scholars in Higher Education* (2006, Stylus,), and *Culturally Contested Literacies: America's "Rainbow Underclass" and Urban Schools* (in press, Routlege).

Mengying Li is a Ph.D. student in the Mary Lou Fulton College of Education, Arizona State University. She is interested in international higher education and Chinese heritage language education. She currently works at the office of the president.

Li Wei is a professor of applied linguistics at Birkbeck, University of London, UK. His main research interests are bilingualism, including bilingual education, and cross-cultural pragmatics. He is author of *Three Generations Two Languages One Family* (1994, Multiligual Matters,), and editor of *The Bilingualism Reader* (2007, 2nd edition, Routledge,), *Opportunities and Challenges of Bilingualism* (with A. Housen & J.-M. Dewaele, 2002, Mouton), *Bilingualism: Beyond Basic Principles* (with A. Housen & J.-M. Dewaele, 2003, Multilingual Matters), *Handbook of Multilingualism and Multilingual Communication* (with P. Auer, 2007, Mouton), and *The Blackwell Handbook of Research Methods in Bilingualism and Multilingualism* (with M. Moyer, 2007, Blackwell). He has served as principal editor of *International Journal of Bilingualism* (Kingston Press) since 1997.

Na Liu is a Ph.D. student in college of education, Arizona State University. Her research interests have been in second language acquisition and teaching, heritage language maintenance, language policy, Chinese language diversity, and global languages. Currently, she is doing research on Chinese heritage language maintenance and attitudes toward Chinese language diversity among Chinese immigrants and international students.

Chan Lü is a Ph.D. student of second language acquisition at Carnegie Mellon University. Her research interest is biliteracy acquisition. She is the recipient of the 2006 Jiede Empirical Research Grant for Chinese Pedagogy/Chinese Applied Linguistics from Chinese Language Teachers Association.

Xuehong Lu

Scott McGinnis is the academic advisor for the Defense Language Institute, Washington office. Between 1999 and 2003, he served as executive director of the National Council of Less Commonly Taught Languages at the National Foreign Language Center. His 22 years in the language teaching profession have included a decade as supervisor of the Chinese language programs at the University of Oregon and University of Maryland. Dr. McGinnis has authored or edited five books, and over 40 book chapters, journal articles, and reviews on language pedagogy and linguistics for the less commonly taught languages, Chinese and Japanese in particular.

Tao Ming is a Ph.D. candidate in the Asian languages & cultures department at the University of California at Los Angeles. His research focus is on syntax, discourse and grammar, second language acquisition, heritage language learning, and corpus linguistics. He has presented at more than 10 conferences and his papers have appeared at some proceedings of the conferences. His dissertation is on the acquisition of aspect. His current project includes Chinese relative clauses and the acquisition of aspect by Chinese heritage learners.

Hongyin Tao is an associate professor of Chinese language and linguistics in the department of Asian languages and cultures, with a joint appointment in applied linguistics and TESL at the University of California, Los Angeles. Prior to UCLA, he taught at the National University of Singapore and Cornell University. He is the Chinese language program director at UCLA. His areas of expertise include Mandarin discourse and grammar, applied linguistics, and English/corpus linguistics. He has recently edited a special issue for *The Heritage Language Journal* on Chinese as a heritage language. His recent work on discourse approaches to advanced language teaching has been supported by the U.S. Department of Education.

Yun Teng is a doctoral student at the division of educational leadership and policy studies, Mary Lou Fulton College of Education, Arizona State University. His research interests in the field of language policy include standardization of the Chinese languages and Chinese as a heritage language in the United States.

Terrence G. Wiley is a professor of language policy and applied linguistics at Arizona State University where he co-directs the language policy research unit of the ASU Southwest Center for Educational Equity and Language Diversity. He is author of *Literacy and Language Diversity in the United States* and numerous books and articles on language policy, politics, and language education. He co-edits the *Journal of Language, Identity, and Education* and the *International Multilingual Research Journal*.

Chao-Jung Wu is a research fellow at Birkbeck, University of London, UK. After completing her B.S. in pharmacy at National Taiwan University in 1993, she went on to earn an M.A. in educational studies at the University of York in 1995. She was awarded a Ph.D. in 2001 for her thesis "Learning Cultures: The example of learning Chinese as community language in Chinese schools in the UK." Her publications include "Look who's talking: Language choices and culture of learning in UK Chinese classrooms" *Language and Education* (2006), 20(1), 62–75.

Chin-Lung Yang is an assistant professor of the department of linguistics at the University of Hong Kong. He applies multi-disciplinary cognitive/neurocognitive paradigms to the study of higher-order language comprehension in reading and language learning across languages, with a focus on Chinese and English. He has written and co-written more than 10 research articles, including "Word-to-text Integration Processes: Neurocognitive Indicators and Reading Skill Differences" (*Applied Cognition*, in press), "ERP Indicators of Text Integration across Sentence Boundaries" (*JEP: LMC*, 2006), and "The Comprehension of Coreference in Chinese Discourse" (*Handbook of East Asian Psycholinguistics, Vol. I: Chinese Psycholinguistics*, 2006). His work has been funded by Chiang Ching-Kuo Foundation for International Scholarly Exchange (US), China Times Cultural Foundation, and the University of Hong Kong.

Ping Yang is a Ph.D. student in the Hugh Downs School of Human Communication at Arizona State University. Her research interests include language learning and maintenance, global education, and intercultural adaptation and communication. She has published and presented a number of articles on second language acquisition, heritage language education, and intercultural adaptation. She is currently engaged in the research in the Language Policy Research Unit and Chinese Language Research Project team at Arizona State University.

Lihua Zhang currently teaches Chinese as a heritage language and as a second language in the department of East Asian languages and cultures at the University of California at Berkeley. She has published one book on contrastive linguistics and several articles. She has been working on online instructional materials and has developed curriculum and instructional materials for teaching Chinese as a heritage language to Chinese dialect speakers. Her interests include bridging theory and practice in language acquisition and pedagogy, integrating culture into language instruction, and employing technology in language learning.

Yanhui Zhang is a Ph.D. student in second language acquisition at Carnegie Mellon University. Her research interests include Chinese literacy development, bilingual education, and computer assisted language learning. She is a co-author of *Chinese Link: Zhong Wen Tian Di: Elementary Chinese* (2006, Pearson Education), and *Zhong Wen Tian Di: Chinese Link–Intermediate Chinese* (2008, Pearson Education).

NFLRC Monographs

Monographs of the National Foreign Language Resource Center present the findings of recent work in applied linguistics that is of relevance to language teaching and learning (with a focus on the less commonly-taught languages of Asia and the Pacific) and are of particular interest to foreign language educators, applied linguists, and researchers.
Prior to 2006, these monographs were published as "SLTCC Technical Reports."

PERSPECTIVES ON TEACHING CONNECTED SPEECH TO SECOND LANGUAGE SPEAKERS

JAMES DEAN BROWN,
KIMI KONDO-BROWN
(Editors)

2006

This book is a collection of fourteen articles on connected speech of interest to teachers, researchers, and materials developers in both ESL/EFL (ten chapters focus on connected speech in English) and Japanese (four chapters focus on Japanese connected speech). The fourteen chapters are divided up into five sections:
- What do we know so far about teaching connected speech?
- Does connected speech instruction work?
- How should connected speech be taught in English?
- How should connected speech be taught in Japanese?
- How should connected speech be tested?

290 pp.

ISBN(10): 0–8248–3136–5
ISBN(13): 978–0–8248–3136–3 $38.

PRAGMATICS AND LANGUAGE LEARNING volume 11

KATHLEEN BARDOVI-HARLIG
CÉSAR FÉLIX-BRASDEFER
ALWIYA S. OMAR
(Editors)

2006

This volume features cutting-edge theoretical and empirical research on pragmatics and language learning among a wide-variety of learners in diverse learning contexts from a variety of language backgrounds (English, German, Japanese, Persian, and Spanish) and target languages (English, German, Japanese, Kiswahili, and Spanish). This collection of papers from researchers around the world includes critical appraisals on the role of formulas in interlanguage pragmatics and speech-act research from a conversation-analytic perspective. Empirical studies examine learner data using innovative methods of analysis and investigate issues in pragmatic development and the instruction of pragmatics. 430 pp.

ISBN(10): 0–8248–3137–3
ISBN(13): 978–0–8248–3137–0 $30.

CORPUS LINGUISTICS FOR KOREAN LANGUAGE LEARNING AND TEACHING

ROBERT BLEY-VROMAN
HYUNSOOK KO
(Editor)

2006

Dramatic advances in personal-computer technology have given language teachers access to vast quantities of machine-readable text, which can be analyzed with a view toward improving the basis of language instruction. Corpus linguistics provides analytic techniques and practical tools for studying language in use. This volume provides both an introductory framework for the use of corpus linguistics for language teaching and examples of its application for Korean teaching and learning. The collected papers cover topics in Korean syntax, lexicon, and discourse, and second language acquisition research, always with a focus on application in the classroom. An overview of Korean corpus linguistics tools and available Korean corpora are also included. 265 pp.

ISBN 0–8248–3062–8 $25.

NEW TECHNOLOGIES AND LANGUAGE LEARNING: CASES IN THE LESS COMMONLY TAUGHT LANGUAGES

CAROL ANNE SPREEN
(Editor)

2002

In recent years, the National Security Education Program (NSEP) has supported an increasing number of programs for teaching languages using different technological media. This compilation of case study initiatives funded through the NSEP Institutional Grants Program presents a range of technology-based options for language programming that will help universities make more informed decisions about teaching less commonly taught languages. The eight chapters describe how different types of technologies are used to support language programs (i.e., Web, ITV, and audio- or video-based materials), discuss identifiable trends in e-language learning, and explore how technology addresses issues of equity, diversity, and opportunity. This book offers many lessons learned and decisions made as technology changes and learning needs become more complex. 188 pp.

ISBN 0–8248–2634–5 $25.

AN INVESTIGATION OF SECOND LANGUAGE TASK-BASED PERFORMANCE ASSESSMENTS

JAMES DEAN BROWN
THOM HUDSON
JOHN M. NORRIS
WILLIAM BONK

2002

This volume describes the creation of performance assessment instruments and their validation (based on work started in a previous monograph). It begins by explaining the test and rating scale development processes and the administration of the resulting three seven-task tests to 90 university level EFL and ESL students. The results are examined in terms of (a) the effects of test revision; (b) comparisons among the task-dependent, task-independent, and self-rating scales; and (c) reliability and validity issues. 240 pp.

ISBN 0–8248–2633–7 $25.

MOTIVATION AND SECOND LANGUAGE ACQUISITION

ZOLTÁN DÖRNYEI
RICHARD SCHMIDT
(Editors)

2001

This volume—the second in this series concerned with motivation and foreign language learning—includes papers presented in a state-of-the-art colloquium on L2 motivation at the American Association for Applied Linguistics (Vancouver, 2000) and a number of specially commissioned studies. The 20 chapters, written by some of the best known researchers in the field, cover a wide range of theoretical and research methodological issues, and also offer empirical results (both qualitative and quantitative) concerning the learning of many different languages (Arabic, Chinese, English, Filipino, French, German, Hindi, Italian, Japanese, Russian, and Spanish) in a broad range of learning contexts (Bahrain, Brazil, Canada, Egypt, Finland, Hungary, Ireland, Israel, Japan, Spain, and the US). 520 pp.

ISBN 0–8248–2458–X $25.

STUDIES ON KOREAN IN COMMUNITY SCHOOLS

DONG-JAE LEE
SOOKEUN CHO
MISEON LEE
MINSUN SONG
WILLIAM O'GRADY
(Editors)

2000

The papers in this volume focus on language teaching and learning in Korean community schools. Drawing on innovative experimental work and research in linguistics, education, and psychology, the contributors address issues of importance to teachers, administrators, and parents. Topics covered include childhood bilingualism, Korean grammar, language acquisition, children's literature, and language teaching methodology. 256 pp.

[in Korean]

ISBN 0–8248–2352–4 $20.

A FOCUS ON LANGUAGE TEST DEVELOPMENT: EXPANDING THE LANGUAGE PROFICIENCY CONSTRUCT ACROSS A VARIETY OF TESTS

THOM HUDSON
JAMES DEAN BROWN
(Editors)

2001

This volume presents eight research studies that introduce a variety of novel, non-traditional forms of second and foreign language assessment. To the extent possible, the studies also show the entire test development process, warts and all. These language testing projects not only demonstrate many of the types of problems that test developers run into in the real world but also afford the reader unique insights into the language test development process. 230 pp.

ISBN 0–8248–2351–6 $20.

A COMMUNICATIVE FRAMEWORK FOR INTRODUCTORY JAPANESE LANGUAGE CURRICULA

WASHINGTON STATE
JAPANESE LANGUAGE
CURRICULUM GUIDELINES
COMMITTEE

2000

In recent years the number of schools offering Japanese nationwide has increased dramatically. Because of the tremendous popularity of the Japanese language and the shortage of teachers, quite a few untrained, non-native and native teachers are in the classrooms and are expected to teach several levels of Japanese. These guidelines are intended to assist individual teachers and professional associations throughout the United States in designing Japanese language curricula. They are meant to serve as a framework from which language teaching can be expanded and are intended to allow teachers to enhance and strengthen the quality of Japanese language instruction. 168 pp.

ISBN 0–8248–2350–8 $20.

FOREIGN LANGUAGE TEACHING & MINORITY LANGUAGE EDUCATION

KATHRYN A. DAVIS
(Editor)

1999

This volume seeks to examine the potential for building relationships among foreign language, bilingual, and ESL programs towards fostering bilingualism. Part I of the volume examines the sociopolitical contexts for language partnerships, including:

- obstacles to developing bilingualism
- implications of acculturation, identity, and language issues for linguistic minorities.
- the potential for developing partnerships across primary, secondary, and tertiary institutions

Part II of the volume provides research findings on the *Foreign language partnership project* designed to capitalize on the resources of immigrant students to enhance foreign language learning. 152 pp.

ISBN 0–8248–2067–3 $20.

DESIGNING SECOND LANGUAGE PERFORMANCE ASSESSMENTS

JOHN M. NORRIS
JAMES DEAN BROWN
THOM HUDSON
JIM YOSHIOKA

1998, 2000

This technical report focuses on the decision-making potential provided by second language performance assessments. The authors first situate performance assessment within a broader discussion of alternatives in language assessment and in educational assessment in general. They then discuss issues in performance assessment design, implementation, reliability, and validity. Finally, they present a prototype framework for second language performance assessment based on the integration of theoretical underpinnings and research findings from the task-based language teaching literature, the language testing literature, and the educational measurement literature. The authors outline test and item specifications, and they present numerous examples of prototypical language tasks. They also propose a research agenda focusing on the operationalization of second language performance assessments. 248 pp.

ISBN 0–8248–2109–2 $20.

SECOND LANGUAGE DEVELOPMENT IN WRITING: MEASURES OF FLUENCY, ACCURACY, & COMPLEXITY

KATE WOLFE-QUINTERO,
SHUNJI INAGAKI
HAE-YOUNG KIM

1998, 2002

In this book, the authors analyze and compare the ways that fluency, accuracy, grammatical complexity, and lexical complexity have been measured in studies of language development in second language writing. More than 100 developmental measures are examined, with detailed comparisons of the results across the studies that have used each measure. The authors discuss the theoretical foundations for each type of developmental measure, and they consider the relationship between developmental measures and various types of proficiency measures. They also examine criteria for determining which developmental measures are the most successful and suggest which measures are the most promising for continuing work on language development. 208 pp.
ISBN 0–8248–2069–X $20.

THE DEVELOPMENT OF A LEXICAL TONE PHONOLOGY IN AMERICAN ADULT LEARNERS OF STANDARD MANDARIN CHINESE

SYLVIA HENEL SUN

1998

The study reported is based on an assessment of three decades of research on the SLA of Mandarin tone. It investigates whether differences in learners' tone perception and production are related to differences in the effects of certain linguistic, task, and learner factors. The learners of focus are American students of Mandarin in Beijing, China. Their performances on two perception and three production tasks are analyzed through a host of variables and methods of quantification. 328 pp.

ISBN 0–8248–2068–1 $20.

NEW TRENDS & ISSUES IN TEACHING JAPANESE LANGUAGE & CULTURE

HARUKO M. COOK
KYOKO HIJIRIDA
MILDRED TAHARA *(Editors)*

1997

In recent years, Japanese has become the fourth most commonly taught foreign language at the college level in the United States. As the number of students who study Japanese has increased, the teaching of Japanese as a foreign language has been established as an important academic field of study. This technical report includes nine contributions to the advancement of this field, encompassing the following five important issues:

• Literature and literature teaching

• Technology in the language classroom

• Orthography

• Testing

• Grammatical versus pragmatic approaches to language teaching

164 pp.
ISBN 0–8248–2067–3 $20.

SIX MEASURES OF JSL PRAGMATICS

SAYOKO OKADA YAMASHITA

1996

This book investigates differences among tests that can be used to measure the cross-cultural pragmatic ability of English-speaking learners of Japanese. Building on the work of Hudson, Detmer, and Brown (Technical Reports #2 and #7 in this series), the author modified six test types that she used to gather data from North American learners of Japanese. She found numerous problems with the multiple-choice discourse completion test but reported that the other five tests all proved highly reliable and reasonably valid. Practical issues involved in creating and using such language tests are discussed from a variety of perspectives. 213 pp.
ISBN 0–8248–1914–4 $15.

LANGUAGE LEARNING STRATEGIES AROUND THE WORLD: CROSS-CULTURAL PERSPECTIVES

REBECCA L. OXFORD
(Editor)

1996, 1997, 2002

Language learning strategies are the specific steps students take to improve their progress in learning a second or foreign language. Optimizing learning strategies improves language performance. This groundbreaking book presents new information about cultural influences on the use of language learning strategies. It also shows innovative ways to assess students' strategy use and remarkable techniques for helping students improve their choice of strategies, with the goal of peak language learning. 166 pp.

ISBN 0–8248–1910–1　$20.

TELECOLLABORATION IN FOREIGN LANGUAGE LEARNING: PROCEEDINGS OF THE HAWAI'I SYMPOSIUM

MARK WARSCHAUER
(Editor)

1996

The Symposium on Local & Global Electronic Networking in Foreign Language Learning & Research, part of the National Foreign Language Resource Center's *1995 Summer Institute on Technology & the Human Factor in Foreign Language Education*, included presentations of papers and hands-on workshops conducted by Symposium participants to facilitate the sharing of resources, ideas, and information about all aspects of electronic networking for foreign language teaching and research, including electronic discussion and conferencing, international cultural exchanges, real-time communication and simulations, research and resource retrieval via the Internet, and research using networks. This collection presents a sampling of those presentations. 252 pp.

ISBN 0–8248–1867–9　$20.

LANGUAGE LEARNING MOTIVATION: PATHWAYS TO THE NEW CENTURY

REBECCA L. OXFORD
(Editor)

1996

This volume chronicles a revolution in our thinking about what makes students want to learn languages and what causes them to persist in that difficult and rewarding adventure. Topics in this book include the internal structures of and external connections with foreign language motivation; exploring adult language learning motivation, self-efficacy, and anxiety; comparing the motivations and learning strategies of students of Japanese and Spanish; and enhancing the theory of language learning motivation from many psychological and social perspectives. 218 pp.

ISBN 0–8248–1849–0　$20.

LINGUISTICS & LANGUAGE TEACHING: PROCEEDINGS OF THE SIXTH JOINT LSH-HATESL CONFERENCE

CYNTHIA REVES
CAROLINE STEELE
CATHY S. P. WONG
(Editors)

1996

Technical Report #10 contains 18 articles revolving around the following three topics:

- Linguistic issues—These six papers discuss various linguistic issues: ideophones, syllabic nasals, linguistic areas, computation, tonal melody classification, and *wh*-words.
- Sociolinguistics—Sociolinguistic phenomena in Swahili, signing, Hawaiian, and Japanese are discussed in four of the papers.
- Language teaching and learning—These eight papers cover prosodic modification, note taking, planning in oral production, oral testing, language policy, L2 essay organization, access to dative alternation rules, and child noun phrase structure development. 364 pp.

ISBN 0–8248–1851–2　$20.

ATTENTION & AWARENESS IN FOREIGN LANGUAGE LEARNING

RICHARD SCHMIDT
(Editor)

1996

Issues related to the role of attention and awareness in learning lie at the heart of many theoretical and practical controversies in the foreign language field. This collection of papers presents research into the learning of Spanish, Japanese, Finnish, Hawaiian, and English as a second language (with additional comments and examples from French, German, and miniature artificial languages) that bear on these crucial questions for foreign language pedagogy. 394 pp.

ISBN 0–8248–1794–X　$20.

VIRTUAL CONNECTIONS:
ONLINE ACTIVITIES & PROJECTS
FOR NETWORKING
LANGUAGE LEARNERS

MARK WARSCHAUER
(Editor)

1995, 1996

Computer networking has created dramatic new possibilities for connecting language learners in a single classroom or across the globe. This collection of activities and projects makes use of e-mail, the internet, computer conferencing, and other forms of computer-mediated communication for the foreign and second language classroom at any level of instruction. Teachers from around the world submitted the activities compiled in this volume—activities that they have used successfully in their own classrooms. 417 pp.

ISBN 0–8248–1793–1 $30.

DEVELOPING
PROTOTYPIC MEASURES
OF CROSS-CULTURAL
PRAGMATICS

THOM HUDSON
EMILY DETMER
J. D. BROWN

1995

Although the study of cross-cultural pragmatics has gained importance in applied linguistics, there are no standard forms of assessment that might make research comparable across studies and languages. The present volume describes the process through which six forms of cross-cultural assessment were developed for second language learners of English. The models may be used for second language learners of other languages. The six forms of assessment involve two forms each of indirect discourse completion tests, oral language production, and self-assessment. The procedures involve the assessment of requests, apologies, and refusals. 198 pp.

ISBN 0–8248–1763–X $15.

THE ROLE OF
PHONOLOGICAL CODING
IN READING *KANJI*

SACHIKO MATSUNAGA

1995

In this technical report, the author reports the results of a study that she conducted on phonological coding in reading *kanji* using an eye-movement monitor and draws some pedagogical implications. In addition, she reviews current literature on the different schools of thought regarding instruction in reading *kanji* and its role in the teaching of non-alphabetic written languages like Japanese. 64 pp.

ISBN 0–8248–1734–6 $10.

PRAGMATICS OF
CHINESE AS
NATIVE & TARGET
LANGUAGE

GABRIELE KASPER
(Editor)

1995

This technical report includes six contributions to the study of the pragmatics of Mandarin Chinese:

- A report of an interview study conducted with nonnative speakers of Chinese; and
- Five data-based studies on the performance of different speech acts by native speakers of Mandarin—requesting, refusing, complaining, giving bad news, disagreeing, and complimenting.

312 pp.

ISBN 0–8248–1733–8 $15.

A BIBLIOGRAPHY OF
PEDAGOGY &
RESEARCH IN
INTERPRETATION &
TRANSLATION

ETILVIA ARJONA

1993

This technical report includes four types of bibliographic information on translation and interpretation studies:

- Research efforts across disciplinary boundaries—cognitive psychology, neurolinguistics, psycholinguistics, sociolinguistics, computational linguistics, measurement, aptitude testing, language policy, decision-making, theses, dissertations;
- Training information covering program design, curriculum studies, instruction, school administration;
- Instruction information detailing course syllabi, methodology, models, available textbooks; and
- Testing information about aptitude, selection, diagnostic tests.

115 pp.

ISBN 0–8248–1572–6 $10.

PRAGMATICS OF JAPANESE AS NATIVE & TARGET LANGUAGE

GABRIELE KASPER
(Editor)

1992, 1996

This technical report includes three contributions to the study of the pragmatics of Japanese:

- A bibliography on speech act performance, discourse management, and other pragmatic and sociolinguistic features of Japanese;
- A study on introspective methods in examining Japanese learners' performance of refusals; and
- A longitudinal investigation of the acquisition of the particle *ne* by nonnative speakers of Japanese.

125 pp.

ISBN 0–8248–1462–2 $10.

A FRAMEWORK FOR TESTING CROSS-CULTURAL PRAGMATICS

THOM HUDSON
EMILY DETMER
J. D. BROWN

1992

This technical report presents a framework for developing methods that assess cross-cultural pragmatic ability. Although the framework has been designed for Japanese and American cross-cultural contrasts, it can serve as a generic approach that can be applied to other language contrasts. The focus is on the variables of social distance, relative power, and the degree of imposition within the speech acts of requests, refusals, and apologies. Evaluation of performance is based on recognition of the speech act, amount of speech, forms or formulæ used, directness, formality, and politeness. 51 pp.

ISBN 0–8248–1463–0 $10.

RESEARCH METHODS IN INTERLANGUAGE PRAGMATICS

GABRIELE KASPER
MERETE DAHL

1991

This technical report reviews the methods of data collection employed in 39 studies of interlanguage pragmatics, defined narrowly as the investigation of nonnative speakers' comprehension and production of speech acts, and the acquisition of L2-related speech act knowledge. Data collection instruments are distinguished according to the degree to which they constrain informants' responses, and whether they tap speech act perception/comprehension or production. A main focus of discussion is the validity of different types of data, in particular their adequacy to approximate authentic performance of linguistic action. 51 pp.

ISBN 0–8248–1419–3 $10.

Printed in the United States
116562LV00003B/63-78/P